Visual Culture in the Modern Middle East

VISUAL CULTURE IN THE MODERN MIDDLE EAST

RHETORIC OF THE IMAGE

EDITED BY CHRISTIANE GRUBER AND SUNE HAUGBOLLE

Indiana University Press
Bloomington and Indianapolis

This book is a publication of
Indiana University Press
Office of Scholarly Publishing
Herman B Wells Library 350
1320 East 10th Street
Bloomington, Indiana 47405 USA

iupress.indiana.edu

Telephone orders   800-842-6796
Fax orders   812-855-7931

Library of Congress Cataloging-in-Publication Data

Visual culture in the modern Middle East : rhetoric of the image / edited by
     Christiane Gruber and Sune Haugbolle.
          pages   cm.
     "The contributions were first presented at the April 2009 conference
"Rhetoric of the Image: Visual Culture in Political Islam," held in Magleaas,
Denmark"—Acknowledgements.
     Includes bibliographical references and index.
     ISBN 978-0-253-00884-8 (cloth : alk. paper) — ISBN 978-0-253-00888-6
(pbk. : alk. paper) — ISBN 978-0-253-00894-7 (ebook) 1. Art and society—
Middle East--Congresses. 2. Visual communication—Middle East—Congresses.
3. Arts, Modern—20th century—Middle East—Congresses. 4. Popular culture—
Middle East—Congresses. I. Gruber, Christiane J., [date] II. Haugbolle, Sune,
[date]
     NX180.S6V475   2013
     700.103—dc23

                                                      2013016444

          1   2   3   4   5   17   16   15   14   13

CONTENTS

ACKNOWLEDGMENTS

Above all, we would like to thank our contributors, all of whom have worked hard and patiently in the editorial process of this volume. The contributions were first presented at the April 2009 conference "Rhetoric of the Image: Visual Culture in Political Islam," held in Magleaas, Denmark, under the auspices of the New Islamic Public Sphere Programme at Copenhagen University. We are grateful for the financial and intellectual support of the program, in particular its director Jakob Skovgaard-Petersen, and Charlott Hoffmann Jensen, who was a brilliant organizer of the event. We wish to thank everyone present at the conference for playing their part in the rich discussions and debates that took place, including Ali Atassi, Zakir Hossein Raju, Layal Ftouni, and Vasiliki Neofotistos, whose contributions are regretfully not included here.

For their helpful comments and help, Christiane wishes to thank Peter Chelkowski, Ulrich Marzolph, and Ali Boozari. Many thanks also go to Sune, who led the way with the conference in Copenhagen, and whose sharp intellect, hard work, and patience saw this volume reach completion. Christiane is also indebted—for the fourth time—to Janet Rauscher, who agreed to copyedit the entire volume prior to its submission to Indiana University Press. At the press, our heartfelt thanks go to Robert Sloan for his unwavering and enthusiastic support of this and other projects in Islamic studies, art history, and visual culture. Last but certainly not least, we are grateful to the Freer Fund in the Department of the History of Art at the University of Michigan, which provided a generous publication subvention that made the inclusion of a color-plate insert possible.

For his part, Sune would like to thank Walter Armbrust, Daniella Kuzmanovic, Andreas Bandak, Lucie Ruzova, Samuli Schielke, Roschanack Shaery-Eisenlohr, and Sonja Hegasy for valuable help and theoretical pointers in the writing process. A great many more have influenced my thinking on visual culture, too many to mention here. In Palestine, Nathalie Khankan, Basil Ayish, Kefah Fanni, 'Adil Samara, Moslih Kanaaneh, Abdul Rahim al-Shaykh, and Vera Tammari all opened their doors to me and offered invaluable help. Thanks to Christiane, without whom this book would surely not have seen the light of day and whose lively wit, exceptional discipline, and good humor make any joint project a pleasure. Most of all, I am grateful to Lindsay Whitfield for her loving support throughout this project, for coping with my absences and frustrations, and for believing in my abilities to see my ideas through.

CHRISTIANE GRUBER & SUNE HAUGBOLLE

Visual Culture in the Modern Middle East

CHRISTIANE GRUBER AND SUNE HAUGBOLLE

Expanding the Borders of Visual Culture

From television and computer screens to billboards and magazines, images speak to modern human beings, shaping our social imaginaries and our visual cultures.[1] The term "visual culture" describes the mechanisms that produce and recycle visual material in various public cultures. Moreover, since the late 1980s it has come to designate a new interdisciplinary field of study, departing from the traditional methods of art historical inquiry to incorporate theoretical insights from literature, anthropology, sociology, cultural theory, gender studies, film, and media studies in order to examine a wider range of visual materials. Largely a disciplinary off-shoot of cultural studies, which gained prominence in England from the 1950s onward,[2] the more narrowly defined field of visual culture has not been without its problems and critics. Debates continue to unfold, calling into question, for instance, whether visual culture is indeed an academic discipline with specific methodologies and objects of study, or, conversely, an interdisciplinary movement whose course may be more short-lived than expected.[3]

Through the proliferation of visual culture readers, anthologies, studies, and journals, the very least that one can say is that a large scholarly apparatus has emerged, suggesting strongly that visual culture is a field that over the last three decades has engendered rich and textured discussions on the manifold roles of images in the public domain of everyday life.[4] Anchored within such discourses, this volume takes the position that visual culture indeed functions as a productive field of inquiry and is most useful as an interface between the many disciplines that treat visuality—predominantly, though not exclusively, in modern and contemporary cultures.

At the center of this multidisciplinary field of research—propagated largely, to date, by scholars of Euro-American popular materials—are questions about image production and reception, as well as the culturally contingent practices of looking. Without a doubt, the field's scholarship has revolved around television, the internet, and advertising.⁵ Additionally, visual phenomena as varied as cinema, painting, photography, cartoon and poster arts, graffiti and street art, videos, and online digital production have been of interest, as all share common traits in that they represent the world through images—still or moving—in turn contributing to the development of collective notions of shared cultural identity and values.

Today, as with the paradox of culture itself, visual culture is both globalizing and localizing—quite often simultaneously.⁶ Satellite and internet media especially allow for a complex interconnectedness of global systems in which images are produced and consumed on a wider scale and quicker pace than ever before. In such cases, visual spheres of interaction are determined less by geography than by technology. The prominence of new media within the field's scholarship does not indicate that visual culture is merely a function of new and faster means of communication since the internet revolution, or that the study of visual materials should be simply placed under the fold of media studies.⁷ Indeed, humans are not more visual today than they were in the past; they simply function in different scopic regimes, which include multiple modern systems of communication that often combine sound, text, and image in which the visual cannot be "hypostatized" as a wholly different substance or entity.⁸

Visual representations and constructions of the world are by no means particular to the modern era. Indeed, pictured narratives have illuminated humankind's secular life and religious experiences throughout the centuries in a wide range of cultural contexts. This said, the mass media have nevertheless changed the speed of production and circulation of images around the world, delocalizing them from their original cultural milieus for immediate reception and creative rearticulation in new geographical and social contexts. Because of the possibilities afforded by near-instantaneous televisual and digital communication, visual culture's disciplinary boundaries have become porous, and its borders have expanded to encompass various areas of the world. As a result, new geographical, temporal, and aesthetic domains must be established and explored within a discipline that to date has been largely characterized by its approach to popular materials in modern Euro-American contexts.⁹

The aim of this volume is to expand the field's object domains and methodological approaches by exploring the ways in which images and visuality function beyond Europe and North America—more specifically, within modern Middle Eastern contexts. These contexts include, primarily, countries in the Middle East, as well as zones, real or digital, in which an individual or a collective body—defining itself in the broadest possible terms as "Middle Eastern" and sometimes "Muslim"—presents and projects itself by visual means. Tackling visual materials and practices of image-making and spectatorship in Middle Eastern contexts is an important undertaking, particularly in light of the flawed notion that images do not exist or are prohibited in Islam, a misconception that became greatly entrenched in the public perception of Islam during and after the *Jyllands-Posten* cartoon controversy of 2005–2006.

Related to this misconception is the notion that Muslim-majority societies in the Middle East are largely dominated by sounds, recitation, and listening. A European modernist hierarchy of the senses—which emerged during the Age of Enlightenment and retained its relevance through the twentieth century—privileged visuality and the ostensibly measured (and masculine) gaze of the rational individual, who perceives and controls the world. The gaze occurs in viewers through a process of hailing or interpellation and, much like images, can be quite varied, ranging from naïve, assaultive, policing, to normalizing. It also can catalyze a kind of ocular pleasure (or "scopophila," per Freud) in its viewing audience, thereby engendering both voyeuristic and exhibitionist tendencies.[10]

Conversely, as Charles Hirschkind has demonstrated, Muslim societies have been depicted in Orientalist frameworks as displaying a preference for the reception of sound over the production and consumption of images.[11] To support such evidence, scholars have highlighted the ways in which knowledge in the Islamic world has been transmitted via oral learning (*sama'*), as well as through practices of oral prayers (*du'a'*) and qur'anic recitation.[12] Due to its relationship to textual literacy, orality within Islamic traditions has benefited from the attention of a number of scholars (including Michael Cook and Hugh Kennedy), who have elucidated aural practices, their links to textual systems, and the transmission of knowledge more broadly. While such discussions are fruitful in many ways, they nevertheless tend to gloss over visuality, viewership, and the image's many manifestations and roles within modern Muslim contexts, including those holistic systems of creative expression that, more often than not, encompass a panoply of sensory experiences.

We believe that it is necessary to move beyond such facile binaries, even if public debate seems only too happy to return to them. Practices of writing and reading, listening and watching, together form important expressive cultures in all societies, including those of the Muslim Middle East. The problem is that the surface of sensory cultures in the Middle East, and their links to other regimes of the senses, has barely been scratched. Visual culture can help us move in the direction of studies that take overlapping sensory registers seriously, and the studies that emerge can serve as important correctives to popular misconceptions, which patently fail to engage with the image and the discursive spaces that it generates. Just as importantly, visual culture helps to understand mass-mediated cultural production and its impact on modernity since the nineteenth century, in both secular and Islamic registers.

Images in Visual and Virtual Space

In the 1980s, the "cultural turn" had its most noticeable impact in Middle East studies through the work of Edward Said.[13] Since the 1990s, other theorists of culture and society—prime among them Talal Asad, Michel Foucault, Antonio Gramsci, and Timothy Mitchell—have influenced new work on varied topics concerning the Middle East. A number of significant monographs published since the 1990s have in common a theoretical preoccupation with how to situate and analyze culture, understood as a "whole way of life" made meaningful through systems of symbolic representation, in relation to social structures and the politics of identity.[14] All of this work proceeded apace despite the fact that culture as a bounded concept generates skepticism among scholars, which is to be expected given the dark shadow cast by the earlier, essentializing Orientalist discourses on Islamic and Middle Eastern cultures, against which Middle East Studies has had to reconstruct itself.

The concept of culture has been subject to general uneasiness in anthropology and area studies at least since Clifford Geertz published *The Interpretation of Cultures* in 1973.[15] Despite raising any number of methodological and theoretical problems concerning the relationship between material culture and culture as a bounded concept, cultural production (in its various iterations, including visual ones) has become increasingly important to the national, ethnic, religious, and political ethnographies of discursive communities in contemporary Middle Eastern societies. As a result, Middle East scholars have produced a series of interesting studies on cultural production,[16] nationalist cultures,[17] memory cultures,[18] and other forms of non-essentialist cultural formations, in turn placing visual materials at the center of their investigations.

Within the study of image-making after the "cultural turn," W. J. T. Mitchell has identified what he considers a distinctive "pictorial turn," which itself engendered visual culture as the disciplinary offspring of art history and cultural studies.[19] Although the notion of a "pictorial turn" can be debated, certainly the field of visual culture moves scholarship beyond the fine arts, expanding into the study of new imaging technologies, methods of reproduction, and the mass media. Representations of all kinds are understood as worthy of inquiry, since they form a significant mode of generating meaning among the many other signifying systems that make up the totality of culture.[20]

To date, visual culture has tended to address the mass media, especially photography and television. As Susan Sontag has eloquently pointed out, photographic images are powerful entities because they are fluid and thus interfere deeply with our perception of what is "real." She notes: "Notions of image and reality are complementary. When the notion of reality changes, so does that of the image, and vice versa."[21] In other words, image can become perceived reality, and reality may turn out to be nothing but projected image, conflating both viewing systems into a cyclical circuit of ontological repartees.

Likewise, televisual images reveal that the projection of reality can be constructed as sequenced movement so as to create moving representations, themselves even closer to perceived reality through the analog of motion. By creating cinematic myths of "truth" and "realism," subjective visual constructions nevertheless remain simulations that emerge from technical productions, audiovisual presentations, and audience readings. As in photographic practices, televisual images project a kind of reality through visual signs, whose meanings are formulated by those who produce them (i.e., the encoders) and those who receive them (i.e., the decoders). Inevitably, such signs partake in a kind of "period rhetoric"—which, as Stuart Hall has pointed out, actively engages in the semantic codes of a culture—and take on various ideological dimensions through the many contextual references in different discursive fields of meaning.[22]

A long line of critics, from the Frankfurt School to Foucault and Bourdieu, have warned against the false perceptions of freedom in scopic regimes dominated by market forces and/or the nation-state, which undergird power relations in modern societies and are, so the critics claim, a potential threat to democratic politics.[23] In such cases, the apparent fidelity of the representation to the object or concept represented (what one might call the illusion of reality)[24] results from discursive practices and various encodings that have been so naturalized by the viewer that they appear altogether absent.[25] This cultural criticism, which originated in Euro-American spheres, has gained currency in Muslim contexts,[26] as new private and semi-private audiovisual media in the Arab Middle East and beyond have generated a wealth of mass-consumed narratives on authenticity and reality in recent years. Several of the articles in this volume engage with these narratives and the ways in which they engender multiple public spheres stimulated by carefully constructed televisual discourses.[27]

Modern images of "reality" are tension inducing and subject to debate—not to mention productive of passive cognition that may lead to an uncritical adoption of the mass-mediated image of reality. However, none of the studies presented here suggests linear power relations between hegemonic producers and a receptive, duped audience. Rather, "reality TV" and "authentic" TV dramas have created new spaces for contesting the meanings of national culture, religion, and social norms. One of the most popular genres on satellite television is the Islamic talk show. Islamic talk shows, starring hugely popular television preachers, draw on a range of traditional Islamic cultural codes to create a mass-mediated discourse imbued with authenticity, even in the examples of self-styled modernizers like the Egyptian Amr Khaled. Their clever reinvention of Islamic images has created arguably the most powerful, if vastly differentiated, vehicle for the Islamic revival. In contrast, another genre of satellite television that attracts millions of viewers, the *musalsal* (drama series), has provided a space for more creative critiques of fundamentalism, as Christa Salamandra argues in her article about Syrian-produced *musalsals*. This space emerges because many Syrian producers hail from an enduring tradition of Arab secularism, which subtly coexists and overlaps with a liberal Islamic impulse, emerging through and despite economic support from the more culturally conservative Arab Gulf countries.

As media ownership and viewer demographics become increasingly regional, different national sensibilities inevitably collide. Contestations often revolve around Islamic norms, as in the case of music videos. The viewing of highly eroticized music "clips" impels practices of disciplined sight and image making, particularly in societies in which revivalist forms of Islamic morality have become dominant. In her contribution, Patricia Kubala discusses public debates about viewing within contemporary Islamist reform projects in Egypt that seek to cultivate the politico-ethical conditions for a virtuous Islamic polity and public. The question of public morality is even more pronounced in the case of Lebanon and Saudi Arabia, two Arab public spheres with very different sensibilities and media histories that now, due to their central position and symbiotic relationship in Arab television ownership and production, have become closely entangled. As Marwan Kraidy explains in his contribution, the intensely staged reality in shows like *Star Academy* have exhibited pan-Arab tensions between a Lebanese brand of liberalism seen as conspicuous, and Saudi Wahhabist Islamists bent on preserving cultural norms. Despite their opposition, as Kraidy demonstrates, the debate surrounding *Star Academy* has in fact forced Saudi Wahhabis to move from a discourse of censorship to a new critical engagement with television. Here, again, mass-mediated images engender discussions and cultural transformations that cannot be described in terms of hegemonic producers and a passive audience, but instead feed ongoing ideological transformations and televisual constructions of contemporary "reality" in the Muslim world.

Like television, the internet also includes visual representations that construct virtual public spheres. Because digital images are highly prone to circulation, adaptation, and even subversion, they function as polyvalent and polysemic tools of communication. Just as importantly, within image-making and -viewing practices digital images have altered concepts of space through their illocality, and have undermined the concept of authorship through the fact that they are simulations, rather than objects per se, or visual copies of objects.[28] As W. J. T. Mitchell notes, a modern society lives not just through spectacle and surveillance but, perhaps even more importantly, through its simulacra.[29] And today more than ever, visual simulations help to define and convey cultural identities due to the border-breaching possibilities of digital communication.

Digital images have been deployed in a variety of secular and Islamicizing contexts in the contemporary period. In particular, mass mediation has changed the use of visual materials, including those harnessed by Islamist groups, through the various overlaps and cross-references between religious and secular ontologies in cross-cultural contexts. For instance, digital symbols and pictures have been used, sometimes viciously, in European production so as to essentialize and vilify Islam, as in the case of the *Jyllands-Posten* cartoons discussed in Christiane Gruber's study. In her contribution, Gruber explores the speciation of one particular digital image of the Prophet Muhammad wearing a bomb-turban across various media outlets, including the worldwide web. This—and the other defamatory cartoons of Muhammad published in the Danish newspaper—in turn regenerated and altered Islamic artistic traditions, including in the capital city of Iran, which now includes a prominent mural painting of the Prophet Muhammad. Through attack and consequent riposte, images emanating in European spheres thus affect the reception and (re-)articulation of visual culture in Muslim societies today.

This give-and-take system of cultural differentiation via image production certainly has been quickened by digital imagining, but processes of image borrowing have occurred in other media outlets, even before the widespread use of the internet. In fact, as demonstrated in the contribution of Pamela Karimi, images, diagrams, and charts produced in Western magazines and home decoration books were co-opted and put to new use in illustrated copies of Ayatollah Khomeini's *Tawzih al-Masail* (Guide to Problems), a handbook of behavior governing home life that became popular shortly before, during, and after the 1979 Revolution in Iran. In these picture books, images are dislocated from their normal or expected contexts, thereby creating new maps of meanings in which media consumers can also act as media "tinkerers."[30] Just as importantly, images in such cases undergo oppositional visual readings through the technique of bricolage (a piecing together of forms), itself frequently used as a deliberate tactic to appropriate cultural forms and to construct new cultural norms.[31]

Despite the obvious importance of television and the internet to procedures of borrowing, changing, and subverting visual readings for cultural ends, the modern and postmodern image profusion cannot merely be related to an electronically wired public sphere. Much of the ideological transformation of image use and production in the twentieth century must be located in the public sphere, which is the subject of two articles in this volume. Inevitably, public space throws light on material culture and the localizing effects of images. Nationalist iconography is negotiated spatially both through architecture—often the natural stage for state-centered constructions—as well as through what Henri Lefebvre calls the "construction of space" in everyday life.[32] The national monument constructed to inscribe central power in urban space, on the one hand, and smaller, more transient modes of spatial production such as graffiti, gravesites, and banners, on the other hand, exemplify two approaches to spatial representation. Whereas nation-states often construct images of national histories that seek to collate divergent cultural expressions under the guise of one national discourse, public culture tends to reshape these images through the filter of local sensibilities that resist homogenization.

The schism between local and national space is particularly pronounced in the rhetoric of martyrdom and memory, especially in the Iranian case surrounding dead soldiers from the Iran–Iraq War (1980–88). Ulrich Marzolph, in his article, examines the "crystallized commemoration" that the Iranian state has sought to instill by painting large-scale murals in Tehran's cityscape. Over time, the meanings "fixed" by symbols change, as their original referents are forgotten and the public sphere is rewritten and overwritten by contending social actors. Despite the state's best attempts to fix history in eternalizing images, memory is transient and ever evolving. The same can be said about archetypes from Islamic history, which have been used and re-used through the centuries. As

Stefan Heidemann points out in his study of the political iconography of the premodern hero Saladdin, history has proven a changing terrain for political actors adopting the very same symbols for Orientalist, nationalist, and Islamist purposes. Whereas these ideologies, and the scopic regimes accompanying them, have certainly been opposed, today the discourses of nationalism and Islam intersect, as political Islam is increasingly used for the advancement of ethno-nationalist purposes.

In the Tandem of Islamic Art

Visual culture as a multidisciplinary field of inquiry provides one means to investigate the various televisual, digital, and spatial "image machines"[33] that are used to promote and persuade viewers through visual performance and perception. However, the discipline of visual culture should not, and could not, wholly displace the field of art history in the analysis of visual materials in tangible or digital zones of contention. To substitute one field for the other would mean simply replacing one method of inquiry for the next when both provide benefits—and display limitations, as well.

Despite the usefulness of visual culture, the field of art history continues to function as an effective and versatile discipline that retains and explores notions of artistic creativity, originality, and quality through its historically sensitive investigations, which pinpoint and examine moments of artistic excellence across the ages and in various cultures. Indeed, art history is much more than a simple "way of describing concrete artifacts and their provenance," as Mieke Bal would have it,[34] and is also much more than visual culture's disciplinary antagonist, as other scholars have tended to view it.[35] Rather, art history's key concern with aesthetics helps to complement inquiries into the more social dimensions of visual production, which have been of prime concern in recent years. This is not to say that art historians have not been interested in the myriad social practices linked to artistic production; rather, the exploration of aesthetics is largely overlooked within the newer disciplines of cultural studies and visual culture, and it is with the issues of aesthetics, taste, and value in particular that art history provides useful theoretical and methodological tools. It is thus important to place into conversation and contraposition visual culture and art history, with the hope that new dialogues and directions will emerge from their effervescent intersections.

The challenges in placing into dialogue the disciplines of visual culture and Islamic art history in particular should not be underestimated. First, visual culture as a discipline struggles with theoretical questions about the shape and meaning of the visual, especially the constructed nature of vision—that is, the ways in which forms of viewing become constitutive for subjectivities and social structures. Visual culture, therefore, refers to the systems through which ways of viewing are learned, passed on, and encoded in Althusserian systems of signs that contribute to the individual's ability to make sense of the social world. At the same time, and perhaps in a self-fulfilling prophecy, visual representations create and reinforce those same systems. To speak of hermetically sealed visual cultures, be they European, American, Muslim, or Middle Eastern, is obviously nonsensical in a world of interconnectedness and long-established global systems of mechanical reproduction of images. Nor does it make sense to discuss visual culture as sealed off from other sensory regimes, as pointed out earlier. Rather, the aim of studying visual culture must be to investigate the structure and process of ideology that creates subject positions through the production of visual artifacts that compel individuals to look, observe, and, at times, listen.

Islamic art history, likewise, has struggled with various hurdles, including its general position within the larger discipline of art history. As Robert Nelson famously noted in his 1997 article "The Map of Art History," Islamic art has faced two main problems, which are best evidenced by the manner in which it is included in art history survey books: first, it is the only category of art defined by a religion rather than a geographical sphere, temporal period, or artistic movement; second, it is consistently sandwiched between the sections on the ancient world and the Middle Ages.[36] As a result, art produced in Muslim spheres is not infrequently presented in books on world art as driven by religious impetus or aims alone, a premise that disregards its nonreligious expressions and contexts. Additionally, from a structural perspective, it appears as if ensconced in a perennial state of medievalism, regardless of its many artistic manifestations and trajectories through the centuries. Part of that medievalism is the expectation that Islamic art writ large has been preserved in a premodern cocoon state in which art is closely linked to religious, ritualistic functions that Walter Benjamin describes in his famous essay "The Work of Art in the Age of Mechanical Reproduction." Without taking into consideration the implications of mass reproduction of images, one is also blinded to the political effects of art. Curiously, then, the pristine preservation of Islamic art as a premodern category maintains it as a nonpolitical, or nonsocial, object of analysis. To state that Islamic art is far from being solely a medieval religious, nonsocial, or apolitical phenomenon would be to point out the gruelingly obvious.

Despite this truism, the modern period until very recently has been the focus of only limited attention. One has only to turn to major reference works on Islamic art—chief among these Sheila Blair and Jonathan Bloom's *The Art and Architecture of Islam, 1250-1800* (1996)—to notice that Islamic art after the colonial period and into the twentieth century was simply not represented (well or at all) within the field's primary reference works and teaching tools. The reasons for this silence are due to the supposed decline in artistic production in Muslim lands during and after the colonial period, the influence of Western aesthetics on Islamic artistic traditions, and the discarding of traditional handicrafts in favor of the European attitude of "art for art's sake."[37] These reasons certainly hold validity but do not justify the silence that loomed large until the 1990s, when new scholarly efforts began to pave the way for the study of Islamic art during the modern period.

A major turning point occurred with the publication of Wijdan Ali's *Modern Islamic Art* in 1997, which focused primarily on the developments, as well as continuities, of Islamic art over the course of the twentieth century. Ali's efforts gave great impetus to the study of modern Islamic art, carving out new domains of inquiry for students and scholars interested in modern art as a living practice inscribed within market forces and Islamic art as a long-lived tradition with its own history. Both domains—the "modern" and the "Islamic"—created new possibilities and frameworks of interpretation while simultaneously calling into question exactly where the field of modern Islamic art might best be situated as an emerging discipline.

The answer to such a question remains to be fully explored. What can be said at the moment is that, with a bustling art scene in America, Europe, and the greater Middle East, modern art produced in Muslim countries or by artists defining themselves as belonging to the Muslim diaspora has been on a sharp rise in the past few years. For example, the year 2006 witnessed significant print and exhibition activities all tackling, to one degree or another, the problem and predicament of modern Islamic art. Two shows in particular, *Word into Art* at the British Museum and *Without Boundary* at the Museum of Modern Art in New York, have set the stage for posing further questions.[38] Such inquiries include, for example, how "Islamic" modern Islamic art and visual culture really are, the ways in which global forms interact with local traditions, and whether there is anything inherently "Islamic" about the pictorial and calligraphic modes that are practiced today.

Secular and Islamist Image Contestations

The title of this book signals that we are not willing to confine visual culture in the Middle East to a fruitless search for some vaguely defined culturally "Muslim" mode of visual production and reception. Whether laudable or not, defining the term "Islamic" in Islamic art has been one of the aims of traditional Islamic art history, in the search for an overarching boundedness of artistic expression across the Muslim world—despite a wide array of regional, linguistic, and cultural variations. However, the search for unity cannot be the research agenda for studying modern visual culture. Rather, the writers in this volume are interested in how the variable image speaks in contexts where Islam is part of the life-worlds that imbue cultural spaces with meaning. Because viewing—the coding and decoding of images—is determined by cultural context, Islamic subjectivities naturally play a large role in Muslim-majority societies with ascendant Islamic movements and new media that generate new Islamic public spheres.[39] However, other frameworks, iconographies, and sensitivities are neither overridden nor marginalized by those of Muslim actors. Rather, we assert that the genealogies of religious and secular modernity, in Talal Asad's terms, must be traced to the same modern mass culture.[40] The challenge, as we see it, is to understand how the symbiotic—but also at times contested—relations between secular and religious subjectivities shape visual lexicons, be these deployed in artistic production of the highest caliber or within the mundane spheres of everyday life.[41]

Part of that challenge must be to properly historicize image contestations and, more broadly, the effect of "new media" from the earliest modern period to today. As Reinhard Schultze noted more than twenty years ago, a better understanding of the way in which Islamic culture became a commodity in the modern period could transform both Middle Eastern and Euro-American historiographies of the region.[42] Many new studies, following Timothy Mitchell's groundbreaking *Colonizing Egypt,* have since shed light on the interrelations between modernity and mass culture.[43] Because of Mitchell, we know how crucial the representational strategies of colonial powers were for establishing new political orders in the nineteenth century.[44] Techniques of mass mediation made new means available for state actors and elites to shape social norms by putting the world on visual display and thereby establishing a political order's axiomatic state. The International and Colonial Expositions, for example, served as a grand mechanism to represent the "Orient" in the modern period, constructing and exhibiting it through a power-laden mode of visual presentation and consumption.[45] Here, as in many other cases, it is clear that images are always produced within the dynamics of power as well as within arenas of conflicting ideologies.

Perhaps ironically, similar imaging techniques were employed for counter-hegemonic purposes, and for a wealth of different intellectual and political projects in the early modern public spheres of Middle Eastern states. Technological developments, new political formations, and urban cultures of media and the arts all fed the development of institutions, social formations, and, crucially, new conceptions of the individual and the social body that departed from the pre-colonial world.[46] In short, whether they supported or resisted European influence, actors in Muslim-majority countries did so in a language determined by modernity, which frequently included Western ocular-centrism supported by new technologies of image making.[47]

Colonial hegemonic power, modern technology, modernist discourse, and modern social organization all combined to produce nation-state formation and middle-class culture around the turn of the twentieth century. Modernity was the premise of new, ordered urban spaces, political print cultures (magazines, newspapers, banners, posters, etc.), and, from the 1920s onward, cinematic cultures. Mass media generated creative classes of cultural producers and new categories of mass consumers. While mass media undoubtedly nurtured a Westernized liberal elite, it also allowed the Islamic intellectuals of the *nahda* to blossom, with their distinctly modern magazines and organizations, not to mention the very modernist dichotomies of *taqlid* (blind imitation) versus *ijtihad* (independent interpretation) they in turn promoted.[48]

The most extreme laic position resulting from these modernist dichotomies, Atatürk's Turkey, also produced some of its most powerful imagery. Yasemin Gencer, in her study of Turkish cartoons from the 1920s, explores how satirical mass culture subverted the icons of *taqlid* while creating and emphasizing a new secular iconography. Through these striking cartoons, we see the early Turkish Republic not only negotiating its relation to the past, but also a young state creating itself through a new and carefully formulated iconography. Elsewhere too, not least in Egypt, promoting the icons of liberalism and secularism became one of the primary functions of public culture in the interwar period. The commoditization of culture created new creative classes whose position as producers of images, including at times anti-Islamic ones, afforded them powerful voices within the public sphere.

When the regional tides changed—and scopic regimes of the region's postcolonial states, which promoted Arab nationalism, socialism, and developmentalism, gradually replaced the liberal era from the 1940s on—many of these elites retained their privileged place in the hierarchies of national cultural production. While modernism remained the dominant cultural mode,[49] much of visual culture produced in the 1950s and 1960s referred more dogmatically to the collectivities of state, nation, and people. This change reflects increased state ownership of the cultural sector. But the icons of nationalism also became tied to the short-lived success in the 1960s, and consistent failure since the 1970s, of the post-colonial states. The perceived failures of secular nationalism after the 1967 defeat to Israel gave life to subversive popular culture. Haugbolle, in his article about the Palestinian cartoonist Naji al-Ali, examines the graphic nature of cultural critique. He argues that al-Ali's iconic images of Palestinian suffering—including his most famous creation, the ragged but stubborn boy Handhala—reflect growing criticism of the failed political projects of liberation, independence, and unity in the 1970s and 1980s. Like the Turkish satirical subversions of Islamic heritage in the 1920s, al-Ali's images attack the failings of a truth regime, namely that of the contemporary Arab states, by juxtaposing the symbols of Arab unity with a civilian experience of disillusion.

The lived experience of state failure gives impetus to Islamist groups as much as to secular oppositional culture and politics. Religious and secular ideologies have generally accommodated each other since the heyday of secular nationalism. Ibrahim Al-Marashi's article on the chaotic mesh of symbols to be found in the imagery of Islamist groups in post–2003 Iraq provides an analysis of the overlaps, but also tensions, between state iconography and the images of art, internet material, cartoons, cinema, television, and street signs that deride, satirize, negotiate, and in other ways express sensibilities at odds with nationalist icons. In today's Iraq, Islamist groups carefully construct systems of signs that refer to, and willfully omit, histories of the Shiite and Sunni communities, the Iraqi state, and Arab nationalism. However, as Al-Marashi's and other authors' contributions to this volume illustrate, even the most self-consciously "purified" and "Islamic" imagery often borrows from the more recent products of modern Euro-American visual culture.

The more carefully one looks at visual materials produced in the modern Middle East, the more difficult it becomes to pinpoint or uphold a putative divide between what some might wish to define as non-Islamic/secular and Islamic/religious imageries. Images circulate freely between cultural realms and are appropriated for many purposes. Such a case is highlighted by Özlem Savaş in her study of a European painting of a crying boy, which was co-opted and given new layers of meaning within Turkish Islamist spheres from the late 1970s onward. More recently, contemporary Turkish illustrated children's books also seem inspired by the Christian children's enrichment literature so prominent in America. As Umut Azak notes, the crossovers between secular and Islamic forms within printed books and other media created for a juvenile audience have played a critical role in a sustained process of "Islamization" in contemporary Turkey. These exchanges also have enabled Islamists to usurp optimistic, forward-looking narratives of national history and human development from the secular parties, resulting in a "happy," bourgeois Islam, content with its ascendant position in Turkish culture—in the process shedding images of revolutionary, even apocalyptic, change so prevalent in marginalized Islamist groups elsewhere in the region.

Toward a New Rhetoric

Visual culture as lived practice creates subject positions through image relations, in which the viewer exists in and contributes to a society marked by practices of looking and various visual industries that cater to an ever-expanding public. To better comprehend the study of visual production and reception, along with vision and visuality, visual cultures must be studied in localized contexts rather than through totalizing or universalizing discourses. For these reasons, this volume's aim consists in situating and studying the image, its multiple functionalities, and its socio-cultural dimensions within a variety of modern Middle Eastern contexts.

Pivoting from the center of visual culture is the omnipresent, centrifugal image, embedded in journals and books, projected onto television screens, painted onto canvases and cement walls, and implanted into the nooks and crannies of virtual space. In these many real and virtual zones the image does not merely exist qua image, however. Much more importantly, the image serves as a powerful carrier of meaning as well as a sign that hails viewers by "speaking" to them through the symbolic language of form, a kind of interpellation that in turn requires of them a number of active, interactive, and interpretative acts. In order to understand visual messages, the viewing audience thus must possess a particular kind of literacy acquired through a process of cultural training, itself a form of apprenticeship achieved by the learning and naturalizing of pictorial codes. Within expressive cultures, these processes of learning to see in culturally contingent ways are often entwined with culturally contingent ways of hearing and speaking.

The complementary notion that images speak and viewers retort, thereby engendering a colorful and sometimes volatile enmeshment of discursive dealings, is one that has been explored by Roland Barthes, to whom both the contents and the title of this volume pay tribute. In his "Rhetoric of the Image," Barthes informs us that all systems of ideology are formed through rhetorical tools, and that rhetoric itself is built through a set of connotators. The image—like other modes of expression and representation, linguistic or otherwise—includes a wide array of connotators that certainly can "speak" to us, but whose intelligibility is nonetheless always bound by culturally encoded practices of looking, not to mention spectatorial preparedness and consciousness as well.[50] Thus, in the rebounding to-and-fro between the image and its viewer, a visual manifestation frequently turns into a two-way conversation.

But dialogue can quickly turn to debate, as cultural orders are very rarely uncontested or monologic. Instead, cultural formation and differentiation occur through the coexistence of hegemonic and counter-hegemonic discourses—that Gramscian "moving equilibrium"[51]—to which images contribute but one of many grammatical and sensorial systems of signification that can be variously encoded and decoded. For these reasons, interpretative stances on visual signs exist in multiples, and, as Stuart Hall notes, the interpretation of such signs can either fall within the purview of dominant paradigms or be adaptive or even oppositional in character.[52] At times they can be both simultaneously, complicating simple binaries and stressing the fact that the practice of visual exegesis emerges from complex circuits of creating and receiving visual messages within modern systems of multidirectional communication.

Beyond these two dichotomizing categories, a third possibility can also be proposed: namely, as John VanderLippe and Pinar Batur suggest in their contribution to this volume, that images operate in a tertiary space that is carved out from the divide between the visual construction of a given order and its contestation through counter-images. This third space heralds a "nexus of contention," a term proposed by VanderLippe and Batur to describe an interstitial and tense zone existing between the myth of consensus and its questioning. Certainly, one concern that emerges again and again in the various studies in this volume is that of a split between dominant and subversive narratives, between secular and religious articulations, between Islamic and non-Islamic spheres. While admitting to such divides, and their enormous appeal across the world, this volume nevertheless aims to provide a constructive abrogation of simple dichotomies in order to generate a third space of discourse that engages with both sides of the debate.

In brief, we wish this volume to stress a series of negativities in order to prompt new discussions of visual materials within and beyond the Middle East. Such negativities include, for instance, the image's heterogeneity, illocality, impurity, and instability; that is, its lack of a fixed and single mode of operation both at an iconographic level and within practices of looking within various scopic regimes. Scholars of visual culture, including Mieke Bal, indeed have argued that the visual is impure and culture is shifting,[53] thereby creating fruitful tensions that are worthy of scholarly analysis. These interstices have been theorized by scholars of globalization,[54] and they also have been the focus of scholars of visual culture, itself a discipline whose object domains have largely been restricted to modern Euro-American realms of cultural production.

Image discourses and debates in cultural practices have emerged and matured in the Middle East during the modern period as well and so today are positively ripe for exploration. By delving into the varied rhetoric of the image within and beyond Muslim contexts, we hope that this volume will contribute to a new rhetoric *about* the image that moves past culturalistic and historicist frameworks. The studies in this volume initiate such a dialogue by adopting a localized and ethnographic approach and by placing the visual image at center stage. In doing so, they aim to shed new light on how visual systems function as discursive tools, how images serve as vehicles for meaningful exchange, and how practices of looking provide channels for cultural contestations within a complex system of communicative exchanges within and beyond the Middle East.

NOTES

1. For a further exploration of the concept of imaginaries, see Taylor, *Modern Social Imaginaries.*

2. More broadly, cultural studies and visual culture are related to the so-called cultural turn in social sciences, a process whereby culture, discourse, and narrative since the 1970s have moved from the humanities to become central to the understanding of the social world. See Hunt and Bonnell, "Introduction," 1–34.

3. For some of the debates on visual culture, see the "Visual Culture Questionnaire" published in *October* 77 (1996); and for a critical approach to visual culture as a "bundle" of disciplines that does not constitute true academic multidisciplinarity, see Bal, "Visual Essentialism and the Object of Visual Culture," 7; and Elkins, *Visual Studies,* 28. Critics of visual culture are quick to point out its "cobbling" or "magpie" effect, with "loose" or "hodge-podge" methodologies that suggest that it is more of a movement than an independent field of study. For them, visual culture thus represents an evanescent and anamorphic collage of existing practices that, brought together, are nothing but a disorganized, ineffectual, illegitimate, and

even misguided extension of art history and other disciplines in the humanities, whose net result is the leveling of all cultural values. See Dikovitskaya, *The Study of the Visual after the Cultural Turn,* 18; and Elkins, *Visual Studies,* 18–20.

4. For two recent historiographic reviews of the field and its integration into academic curricula, see Dikovitskaya, *The Study of the Visual after the Cultural Turn;* and Elkins, *Visual Studies.*

5. Mieke Bal criticizes this recurrent emphasis of visual culture, stating, "I am tired of the fetishistic fixation with internet and advertising as exemplary objects" (Bal, "Visual Essentialism and the Object of Visual Culture," 25).

6. On the paradox of culture as both localizing and globalizing, see Wallerstein, "The National and the Universal," 91–105; and Wolff, "The Global and the Specific," 161–73.

7. As suggested in 2002 by Mark Poster in his brief article "Visual Studies as Media Studies."

8. On scopic regimes, see Martin Jay, "Scopic Regimes of Modernity," 3–38; and on the dangers of isolating and treating independently the visual components of cultural production, see Bal, "Visual Essentialism and the Object of Visual Culture," 13.

9. Elkins, *Visual Studies,* 36, 41, 60.

10. On the range of gazes and scopophilia, see Sturken and Cartwright, *Practices of Looking,* 76, 87.

11. Hirschkind, *The Ethical Soundscape,* 13–18.

12. For qur'anic recitation, see K. Nelson, *The Art of Reciting the Qur'an;* and Graham, "Qur'an as Spoken Word," 23–40.

13. Orientalism added to the circulation of French poststructuralist thought in Middle East studies and spread its focus on linguistic, self-referential constructions of social reality beyond literary studies to politics and history in particular (Lockman, *Contending Visions of the Middle East,* 201–14).

14. On culture as a "whole way of life," see Hebdige, "From Culture to Hegemony," 359.

15. See Geertz, *The Interpretation of Cultures.* On the critique of culture as a bounded concept, see Abu-Lughod, "Writing against Culture"; and Fox and King, eds., *Anthropology beyond Culture.*

16. See, for example, Armbrust, *Mass Culture and Modernism in Egypt;* and Winegar, *Creative Reckonings.*

17. On which, see Abu-Lughod, *Dramas of Nationhood;* and Jankowski and Gershoni, *Redefining the Egyptian Nation, 1930–1945.*

18. For instance, see Khalili, *Heroes and Martyrs of Palestine;* and Swedenburg, *Memories of Revolt.*

19. W. Mitchell, "The Pictorial Turn," 89–94.

20. Dikovitskaya, *The Study of the Visual after the Cultural Turn,* 2.

21. Sontag, "The Image-World," 354.

22. Hall, "Encoding, Decoding," 96–97.

23. See Bourdieu, *On Television;* and Popper, "Against Television."

24. The more radical postmodern position holds that media have in fact become more real than reality itself. See Debord, *The Society of the Spectacle.*

25. Hall, "Encoding, Decoding," 95.

26. See Zayani, *The al-Jazeera Phenomenon.*

27. Sturken and Cartwright, *Practices of Looking,* 182. Talk and reality shows can provoke multiple audiences; these include in the studio, at home, and in the workplace (e.g., discussions in the lunch room or at a water cooler).

28. Sturken and Cartwright, *Practices of Looking,* 141–48.

29. W. Mitchell, *What Do Pictures Want?,* 32.

30. Sturken and Cartwright, *Practices of Looking,* 186.

31. Ibid., 64.

32. Lefebvre, *The Production of Space.*

33. Sturken and Cartwright, *Practices of Looking,* 130.

34. Bal, "Visual Essentialism and the Object of Visual Culture," 21.

35. On visual culture as a kind of anti-art history, see Dikovitskaya, *The Study of the Visual after the Cultural Turn,* 29; and Elkins, *Visual Studies,* 17.

36. See, for example, the table of contents from Janson's *History of Art,* reproduced in Nelson, "The Map of Art History," 34.

37. W. Ali, "The Status of Islamic Art in the Twentieth Century," 186–87.

38. See Porter, *Word into Art;* and Daftari, *Without Boundary.* Following on those, see most recently, Lowry, *Oil and Sugar.*

39. Eickelman and Anderson, "Redefining Muslim Publics," 1–18.

40. Asad, *Formations of the Secular.*

41. For the intertwined nature of secularism and Islamism, see Mahmoud, "Secularism, Hermeutics, and Empire," 323–47.

42. Schultze, "Mass Culture and Islamic Cultural Production in the 19th Century," 203–204.

43. For a historiographical discussion of visual culture in Middle East studies, see Armbrust, "Audiovisual Media and History of the Arab Middle East," 289–90.

44. Mitchell, *Colonizing Egypt.*

45. See Çelik, *Displaying the Orient.*

46. See Watenpaugh, *Being Modern in the Middle East;* Skovgaard-Petersen and Korsholm Nielsen, *Middle Eastern Cities 1900-1950.*

47. As Chalcroft and Noorani ("Introduction," 16) note, counterhegemony does not merely question dominant values, but rather rearticulates or reconfigures meanings actively constructed by diverse claimants. For a discussion of ocular centrism, see Jay, "Scopic Regimes of Modernity."

48. Schultze, *Mass Culture and Islamic Cultural Production in the 19th Century,* 203–204.

49. See Armbrust, *Mass Culture and Modernism in Egypt,* 94–115.

50. Barthes, "Rhetoric of the Image," 45, 49.

51. The notion of a "moving equilibrium" between political forces was originally developed in Gramsci's discussion of Fordism and the American worker. See Gramsci, *Selections from the Prison Notebooks,* 312.

52. On these various interpretative stances, see Hall, "Encoding, Decoding," 100–103.

53. Bal, "Visual Essentialism and the Object of Visual Culture," 19.

54. See for example Appadurai, *Modernity at Large.*

Visual Culture in the Modern Middle East

PART 1

"Moving" Images

FIGURE 1.1. Mural of Muhammad's ascension, located at the intersection of
Modarres and Motahhari Avenues, Tehran, Iran, 2008. *Author's photograph, 2010.*

CHAPTER 1

Images of the Prophet Muhammad *In and Out* of Modernity: The Curious Case of a 2008 Mural in Tehran

CHRISTIANE GRUBER

A colorful mural appeared at the busy junction between Modarres Highway and Motahhari Street in central Tehran in 2008, gracing the wall of an otherwise unremarkable five-story cement building (fig. 1.1 and plate 1). This mural does not depict what one would expect to see in Iran's post-revolutionary mural arts program: Ayatollahs Khomeini and Khamenei or the portrait of a martyr who died in the Iran–Iraq War (1980–88). These other mural subjects, which have graced and given meaning to the capital city's urban landscape over the past thirty years, represent a genre of public portraiture that stresses both the Islamic Republic's Shi'i-Persian identity and governance and the duty of all Muslims, both at home and abroad, to sacrifice themselves to a greater cause by fighting and dying in war.[1]

Casting aside such overt iconographies and messages, as is the case with many other large-scale paintings currently appearing on cement walls throughout Iran,[2] this mural instead depicts the Prophet Muhammad on the night of his heavenly ascension (*mi'raj*).[3] Depicted in an Islamic painterly style, Muhammad is shown wearing a green cloak with his arms folded at the waist, as he sits on his human-headed flying steed named Buraq. While Buraq bears delicate facial features, Muhammad's visage has been left blank but is nevertheless framed by his other prophetic attributes: his black tresses, white turban, and flaming gold nimbus. He ascends the skies, leaping through tiled archways that are decorated with epigraphic bands and guarded by disembodied angels who hover in midair.

The scene does not halt here. In the mural's lower right corner, a young and beautiful inhabitant of paradise, most likely a "bright-eyed" *huri,* climbs a tree that grows in a fertile valley of grass. From that tree, the *huri* picks a cluster of flower blossoms and hands it to a man who stretches his arms out to receive the offering. This man is perhaps a deceased soul being welcomed into the Garden of Eden, which Muhammad witnessed and visited on the night of his ascension. The young man wears modern and rather hip clothing; in fact, he could be any Iranian youth strolling through Tehran's streets and parks. Painted in repoussé with his back to the viewer and depicted in a photorealistic style, the figure has indiscernible facial features, suggesting that he represents a type rather than an identifiable individual. Judging from the traditional emphasis afforded to martyrs within Tehran's mural arts program since 1979, this type is most likely the martyr (or the martyr *in potentia*), that is, the corporate stand-in for individuals willing to perish for state-and-religion or in the "way of God" (*fi sabil Allah*), whose final reward is none other than paradise.

So what is one to make of this contemporary mural, its double *mi'raj*-martyrdom thematic, and its blending of old and new pictorial styles? What is its larger significance for understanding the diverse roles images play in the artistic traditions and visual culture of Iran today? And what does this mural tell us about figural representation and, more specifically, how a powerful icon such as the Prophet Muhammad can become a point of cultural contention or a symbolic pivot for the politics of identity on a global scale after the Danish cartoon controversy of 2005–2006?

This study aims to offer preliminary answers to these questions by focusing on this recent ascension mural in Iran, as well as on images of the Prophet in both Islamic spheres and European contexts. In particular, my aim is to determine how this particular mural engages with Iranian discourses that touch upon issues of tradition, identity, and belonging, while also advancing such claims within the complex cultural circuits and volatile religious entanglements of the post–9/11 world. In exploring the many issues raised by this one mural—the only of its kind to represent the Prophet Muhammad, openly and proudly, in a physical space in a Muslim-majority country—it is clear that contemporary images navigate the past and present tenses, local and global spheres, and real and virtual space. Much like sharp rhetoric, moreover, images like the ascension mural can act as powerful purveyors of ideologies and ontologies, because they likewise make arguments about knowledge and stake positions concerning truth and reality.

Indeed, besides manifestly discarding clichéd statements that Islam putatively prohibits figural imagery, especially representations of the Prophet Muhammad,[4] this ascension mural advances specific arguments while also staking several positions. Its arguments include promoting, first, the utmost rank and legitimacy of the Prophet Muhammad, who was invested by God with prophecy and knowledge of the otherworld on the night of his *mi'raj*; second, the transcendental beauty of Muhammad in the aftermath of the desecration of his image in the dozen satirical cartoons published in the Danish newspaper *Jyllands-Posten* in 2005; and third, the supreme value of fighting, and possibly dying, for a cause that is couched as being "in the way of God." In brief, the mural seeks to reclaim the Prophet Muhammad and his blessed beauty for the Islamic community by mounting a visual counterattack.

This "striking back" is ipso facto the mural's position, which is one that carefully harnesses an Islamic artistic past, editing its main features and rearticulating them to promote Iran's religio-national messages in today's global world. While navigating both the past and present, Islamic and non-Islamic discourses, this mural essentially stakes a Shiʻi-Persian stance of opposition and resistance, thereby offering an imaged repartee to what the Iranian regime perceives as demeaning hegemonic discourses on Muhammad and the Islamic faith in various media outlets, especially those stemming from the Euro-American, Christian "West."

In other words, this mural helps carve out a number of salient paths of critical inquiry in order to better understand visual culture as it takes shape within a specific modern Muslim context that willfully seeks to intersect with the politics of identity on a global scale. It also serves as a heuristic device for tracking public discourses on self and other, while at the same time functioning as a barometer for religio-cultural contestations within image-making traditions (and industries) in Iran and beyond. Perhaps more germane for the broader field of visual culture, moreover, this mural functions as a symbol that partakes in the deep semantic codes of a culture, thereby generating new discursive fields of meaning configured not through verbalized but rather visualized signs. As W. J. T. Mitchell would note, this mural indeed demands "equal rights with language,"[5] thereby inviting us to engage in interpretative acts of the visual via its various signifying systems and expressive cultures.

Tangled Skeins

The mural's artist, a female M.F.A student at Tehran University named Faezeh Rahmati, won the competition launched by Tehran's municipality (*shahrdari*) in 2008. The municipality's program on murals, fitted within its Bureau of Beautification (*sazman-i zibasazi*), selected her composition to adorn the blank side of the building, centrally located at the intersection of Modarres and Motahhari Avenues.[6] Before 2008, this building boasted a highly visible, large-scale banner of the Palestinian suicide bomber Rim Salah al-Riyashi (d. 2003), itself a duplication of a photograph taken immediately prior to her death. In the banner, this female martyr is shown holding her son and a rifle, exclaiming that she loves martyrdom more than motherhood.[7] For reasons that are unclear—to beautify the city? to remove an overtly martyrial message?—this worn-out banner was pulled down to make way for the ascension mural.

Once denuded of the banner, the building's empty wall was adorned with the more muted *mi'raj* scene, which the artist Rahmati entitled *A Bouquet of Flowers from the Ascent (Dast-i Gul az 'Uruj)*.[8] Thus, a contemporary black-and-white photograph of a female martyr ceded way to a vibrantly colored illustration of Muhammad's ascension, executed in a "classical" Islamic book arts style.

The mural's "classical" iconographic sources are easily identifiable. The artist admits that she drew upon and selected a series of scenes belonging to the famous Timurid illustrated manuscript of the *Mi'rajnama,* or Book of Muhammad's Ascension, that was produced in the city of Herat around 1436 CE (figs. 1.2–1.4). Boasting more than fifty paintings of Muhammad's ascension through the heavens, his encounter with prophets and God, and his visits to heaven and hell, this manuscript, held in the Bibliothèque nationale de France in Paris, is without a doubt a rare and stunning masterpiece of Islamic art. As such, it is frequently included in surveys of Islamic painting. Additionally, it also has been the subject of two studies, a handbook of illustrations prepared by Marie-Rose Séguy (in French, 1972; reissued in English, 1977) and a monographic study by the present author (2008).[9] Séguy's handbook was translated into Persian and published in 2006 under the title "Book of Ascension: The Miraculous Journey of His Majesty the Prophet" (*Mi'rajnama: Safar-i Mu'jiza-i Asa-yi Payghambar*). This Persian edition has since been displayed in the vitrines of academic bookstores lining Engelab Avenue, whence it served to inspire a number of publications, conferences, and art projects by scholars, students, and artists at Tehran University. Thus, Rahmati's mural is based on an Islamic fifteenth-century illustrated manuscript of Muhammad's ascension, made available via a handbook of its illustrations as published in a widely popular 2006 Persian edition.

This rather uncomplicated artistic and scholarly stemma notwithstanding, a few "technical" issues make this Book of Ascension manuscript more difficult to untangle. The manuscript's provenance, language, script, and pictorial language are, like the proverbial Gordion knot, almost intractably problematic, especially considering its reception and adaptation within a contemporary Iranian public milieu. Such problems are nonetheless illuminating in that they reveal what Iranian artists and other cultural entrepreneurs identify as their own "indigenous" tradition and heritage, put to tactical use in larger efforts, artistic or otherwise, toward self-identification both at home and on the world stage.

CHRISTIANE GRUBER

FIGURE 1.2. Muhammad ascends through the skies on his flying steed, Buraq, *Mi'rajnama* (Book of Ascension), Herat, modern-day Afghanistan, 1436–37. *Bibliothèque nationale de France, Paris, Suppl. Turc 190, folio 5r.*

FIGURE 1.3. Muhammad and the Angel Gabriel arrive at the gates of Paradise, *Mi'rajnama* (Book of Ascension), Herat, modern-day Afghanistan, 1436–37. *Bibliothèque nationale de France, Paris, Suppl. Turc 190, folio 45v.*

FIGURE 1.4. Muhammad and the *huris* in Paradise, *Mi'rajnama* (Book of Ascension), Herat, modern-day Afghanistan, 1436–37. *Bibliothèque nationale de France, Paris, Suppl. Turc 190, folio 49r.*

First is the issue of the manuscript's provenance, and thus its role within modern Iran's claims about territoriality and ethnicity. At the time that this Book of Ascension was produced in Herat for the Timurid ruler Shahrukh (r. 1405–47), Herat served as the capital of the Turco-Persian Timurid Empire. Although Herat does fall squarely within the larger orbit of the Persianate world, it is now located in Afghanistan, not Iran. This fact, which may seem rather straightforward and platitudinous, is certainly not free of complications. Here, Herat to a certain extent speaks to the larger Afghanistan "problem," especially in the aftermath of the U.S.-led Afghanistan war, which began in 2001 and remains ongoing. Since the beginning of the war, Iran has actively contributed to reconstruction, economic, and trade efforts with Afghanistan, not only to solidify its historical ties with its "Persian" neighbor, de facto expanding its sphere of influence, but also to curb the massive influx of Afghani refugees in Iran.[10] Although the mural does not promote Iranian claims to Afghanistan—be these cultural, political, or religious—it does nevertheless adopt and adapt an illustrated manuscript as a quintessential example of "Persian" art. Conveyed through such art forms, "Persian" territory and identity are in this instance expansive to say the least.

Second is the issue of language and script. Although perfecting Persian as the language of courtly and literary expression, Timurid rulers were particularly proud of their Central Asian Turkic roots and their Turco-Mongol lineage, stretching back to Genghis Khan (r. 1206–27). For these reasons, they placed great emphasis on Turkic customs, including language. The fifteenth century was marked by the use of Chaghatay Turkish for literary texts as well as the revival of Uighur script, itself having been used for the transcription of Buddhist texts during the Mongol period. One prominent case in point for the high status afforded to Chaghatay Turkish and Uighur script in the Timurid period is none other than the *Mi'rajnama* manuscript.[11] This Book of Ascension is composed in a Central Asian Turkic language and transcribed in a non-Arabic script. Today, both language and script would not be understandable or legible to a Persophone Iranian audience, which explains in part why the main text has been cropped out of the mural image. The other, perhaps deliberate, reason for the editing out of the Turkic-Uighur text may be that such a text would call into question the painting's homegrown "Persian-ness."

This leads to the third issue, namely the *Mi'rajnama*'s paintings. The manuscript bears an array of Sino-Central Asian Buddhist motifs, including polycephalous angels and angels sitting in yogic postures, which suggest, as the manuscript's language and script do, that its iconography should be considered a mélange of Islamic, Persian, Turkic, Central Asian, Buddhist, and Chinese elements—that is, a mix emerging in no small part thanks to an active pan-Asian exchange of goods and ideas during the fifteenth century. A palimpsestic artistic product par excellence, the illustrated *Mi'rajnama* resists simple categorization, bringing the urge to taxonomize Islamic book arts to a grinding halt. Put simply, the paintings included in the Book of Ascension manuscript are not simply "Islamic" and not only "Persian."

These tangled issues of territoriality, ethnicity, language, script, iconography, and form are muted, gleaned over, and turned into non-issues in the recently painted mural of Muhammad's ascension. And yet such silenced "non-issues" clamor for our attention because they force us to inquire—as Fereshteh Daftari and other scholars have in recent years—to what extent this mural and other contemporary artistic and pictorial forms should be called "Islamic" or not.[12] Related to and emerging from this question is to what extent the mural should be labeled an example of modern "Islamic" visual culture, a field that this volume aims to address. Here and elsewhere, the term "Islamic" should neither be used as a catch-term nor a given. To the contrary, it must be disentangled and unbundled, made untidy, even vexing.

Tenacious yet evasive, the term "Islamic" has held a steady place in art historical discourses inasmuch as it has successfully remained impervious to precise definition. Such scholars as Oleg Grabar have demonstrated that the term "Islamic" conveys a general sense of geographical, cultural, and religious unity despite the fact that regional pluralities and historical discontinuities are equally prominent factors.[13] Thus, the all-encompassing term "Islamic" is like a broad net cast to sea, catching many fish along the way. To give a few examples of this unstable predicament: If an artwork is produced in a Muslim country, it can be called "Islamic." If it is produced by a Muslim craftsman active anywhere in the world, likewise. If it somehow expresses or emerges from the Islamic faith, similarly. And if it includes Arabic script, a dead-giveaway ditto. In its semantic flexibility, the term "Islamic" thus comes to resemble a plastic art, molded by accretions and malleable at will and desire.

The flexibility of the term "Islamic" should make us ponder who is doing the bending and molding, and why. This exploration is particularly important in examining modern "Islamic" art and visual culture, both of which often aim to revive older pictorial and/or calligraphic forms. Resisting facile taxonomies along the way, heterogeneous forms of "Islamic" revivalism—what Daftari calls "post-Orientalism"[14]—should in essence be considered a (questionable and sometimes purist) discourse on tradition and authenticity. The resulting narrative aims to bypass inter-ruptions caused by colonialization as well as intrusions brought about by Westernization. Some scholars might argue that modern revivalist art forms—that is, visual cultures that harness and redeploy past expressive cultures within the Muslim world—are thus deserving of the appellation "Islamic."

Yet as Homi Bhabha notes, "such appeals to the 'past,' in the service of avant-garde art practices, are attempts at historical and aesthetic revi-sionism; they are ways of creating new cultural genealogies for nation-states."[15] Revivalist projects, be they political or artistic, certainly engage in a multiplicity of maneuvers, including, for example, selection, trans-lation, assimilation, imitation, appropriation, and adaptation. For visual culture in particular, canonic images and forms go through a process of declension, multiplying their forms across media, the latter generative of new places of meaning. Such revived but tinkered images act essentially as a means of reestablishing cultural bonds with a perceived artistic patri-mony in a greater "search-for-identity"[16] in a modern global world where cultural boundaries tend to blur and disappear.

This "search-for-identity" is certainly discernible in the *mi'raj* mural in Tehran. As one salient case in point, the mural highlights the fact that "Islamic" visual culture, both past and present, is made of tangled threads. These can intertwine and loosen, omit and simplify, combine and convo-lute. Like modern practices of bricolage, which reconfigure and dislocate art forms in order to create new products and meanings,[17] the ascension mural co-opts and boils down a rich pan-Asian artistic past to propel new messages about what is "Islamic" and what is "Persian" into the Iranian public sphere. In this instance, the modern delineation of Iran's "Islamic" and "Persian" artistic past is achieved by a selective purging of the lan-guage, script, and artistic forms aligned with Central Asian Buddhism—that is, of references that complicate a modern Persian-Islamic definition of self as fashioned in Iran and promoted to the rest of the contemporary world. The term "Islamic" is obviously not a passively inherited term or art form. Rather, it is an edited construct, pruned of perceived impurities that cannot be accounted for under the (at times) restrictive parameters of the rubric itself.

A "Custom Made" Tradition

How does the ascension mural discursively claim to be "Islamic" and "Persian," contributing to an Iranian "search-for-identity" through visual forms projected into the public domain? In basic terms, it does so by turning to the past and editing it, adding new linkages and enframements to "tradition." Thus, the mural serves as an inventive variation, a zone of activity, and a cultural recommitment in visual form.

Some scholars consider the process of turning to available materials and reconfiguring them a hallmark of modernity. According to George Kubler, for example, modernity is marked by originality and invention, but invention comprises not only a new position but, perhaps more importantly, an amalgamation of an existing body of knowledge.[18] It is thus a gradual and cumulative process marked by incrustations and transformations, if not full-fledged creative destruction. The mural thus should be considered an aggregate outcome, rather than a radical invention, that channels a new pathway for finding a place for tradition in the modern world.[19] Through a process of retention, addition, and disposal, the mural thus functions as an inventive variation on traditional art forms.

Similarly, as Nicholas Bourriaud notes in *PostProduction,* modern art is not so much about starting with a tabula rasa—for example, the blank slate of a building's cement wall—as about programming already available materials, tuning them in order to achieve a particular pitch. Indeed, Bourriaud notes that "artists today program forms more than they compose them: rather than transfigure a raw element, they remix available forms and make use of data."[20] An artwork like the *Mi'rajnama* manuscript or its later iterations (including the mural) is "no longer an end point but a simple moment in an infinite chain of contributions."[21] An original work is thus revisited and reproduced, even reconquered,[22] its collective equipment tooled for a range of new purposes. The ascension mural in Tehran is therefore not just a revisiting and editing of tradition; it is also a zone of activity within a long line of artistic engagements.

For modern Iranian art in particular, Hamid Keshmirshekan notes that modern interactions with the past lead to Neo-Traditional art, in which artists of the post-revolutionary period seek to balance the historical past with modernist ideals in order to create an identifiable "modern Iranian plastic language."[23] Iranian artists practicing in the Neo-Traditional mode, whether during the 1990s or today, are certainly interested in issues of Iranian identity as expressed through cultural recommitment. Through the promise of artistic commitment, certain visual forms tend to be emphasized, excluded, altered, or added in order to profess what is perceived as an "Islamic" and/or "Iranian" identity.

The Islamo-Iranian synthesis is clearly present in the pictorial language of the ascension mural in Tehran, which, through its omissions and additions, asserts a clear religious stance and moral ideal. We have already seen the ways in which the mural adapts the *Mi'rajnama*, simplifying its cultural-linguistic intricacies. Alongside this reduction of a complex pan-Asian past we cannot fail to notice three alterations of the Timurid manuscript's ascension paintings: (1) the epigraphic addendum above the Prophet Muhammad's head; (2) the insertion of a young man painted in a photorealistic style; and (3) the erasing of Muhammad's facial features. All three of these modifications are discussed in detail here in order to show how the modern *mi'raj* mural reinvents tradition, turning it into a zone of interactivity, with the aim to reassert and recommit to an Islamo-Iranian identity through the powerful vehicle that is visual culture.

Returning to the paintings in the *Mi'rajnama*, it is clear that the mural's artist Rahmati has drawn upon and conflated at least three different scenes from the original manuscript. The first represents Muhammad's night journey on Buraq as he leaves Mecca for Jerusalem (fig. 1.2 and plate 2); the second shows Muhammad's arrival at the gates of paradise, whose entryways are lavishly decorated with illuminated bands and topped with inscriptions (fig. 1.3); and the third depicts Muhammad's arrival in paradise and his observing of the *huris*, who amuse themselves as they chat and climb flowering trees (fig. 1.4).

The excerpting and collapsing of elements drawn from these three (or more) paintings found in the Timurid manuscript may seem at first glance a chance encounter of pictorial devices dislocated from their original contexts. However, as one begins to look more carefully at the various iconographic elements, it becomes quite clear that a coded operation is in play. In the case of this particular mural, I argue that a negotiated reading of Islamic artistic tradition is at work, adding a religio-national inflection, thereby changing the primary meaning of an original image, or even series of images, through an act of visual appropriation and cut-and-paste techniques.

Let us first examine the three-part inscription visible in the mural. In the original manuscript, the three illuminated gates the Prophet approaches also include a tripartite inscription, which reads the Shi'i creed or *wilaya*: "There is no god but God, Muhammad is the Messenger of God, and 'Ali is the Vicegerent of God" (fig. 1.3). The Shi'i *wilaya* adds a third and final clause to the traditional proclamation of faith, or *shahada*, which is uttered in Sunni spheres of the Islamic world and is one of the five pillars of Islam. Since the believer witnesses that there is only one God and that Muhammad is His messenger, the *shahada* serves as a basic article of faith that proclaims a strict monotheistic belief system, in which an omnipotent and singular God has sent a number of prophets to humankind, the last and most authoritative among whom is the Prophet Muhammad.

Over time and in Shi'i milieus, however, the *shahada* expanded to gain a third clause, one proclaiming that 'Ali is the vicegerent or intimate friend of God.[24] This added phrase effectively promotes the right to rule of the members of the Prophet's household, the *ahl al-bayt,* and their descendants, the imams. This branch of Islam is called Shi'ism: it was declared the state religion of Iran in the early sixteenth century, and today its largest branch (Twelver Shi'ism) remains the dominant form of Islam practiced in Iran. For both religious *and* political reasons, today Shi'i beliefs and practices are actively sponsored by the Islamic Republic's various governmental organizations and cultural institutions, including Tehran's municipality.

The original manuscript painting includes the statement in its correct sequence, as one would expect, over the course of the three gates, reading from right to left—but the mural does not. It has flipped the Shi'i creed, so that it now includes the last clause "'Ali is the Vicegerent of God" (*'Ali wali Allah*) first, inscribed directly above the Prophet's head, followed by the clauses "Muhammad is the Messenger of God" (*Muhammad rasul Allah*) and then "There is no god but God" (*La illa ila Allah*). This reversing of the Shi'i creed's three clauses should strike the acculturated viewer as very bizarre, even anathema.

I know of no other case in which the Shi'i *wilaya* has been reversed purposefully and in such an overt way. It thus cannot be considered a mistake or a haphazard flipping of phrases. To the contrary, it appears that the artist Rahmati may have wished to "Shi'ify" the Prophet's *mi'raj* by placing directly above his head the most important addendum of the Shi'i creed—that is, the proclamation of 'Ali's ascendancy—so that this apparently ecumenical image might gain an overtly sectarian patina. It is an epigraphic alteration that is certainly calibrated and whose stakes are high.

This kind of partisan positioning, whether covert or overt, has had a long tradition within both texts and images of Muhammad's ascension within the Islamic world. While some *mi'raj* narratives have aimed to assert the superiority of members of the Sunni community, typically described as inhabiting pavilions in paradise, other tales of a Shi'i bent, produced especially during and after the sixteenth century in Iran, sought to argue for Shi'i legitimacy. One common way authors effectuated a "Shi'ification" of their ascension texts was by describing Muhammad's arrival in the uppermost heaven, at which time God reveals to him not only his prophecy and his community's duties but also that 'Ali is his intimate friend and rightful successor (*wali*) on earth. In Shi'i *mi'raj* tales, the ultimate revelation to Muhammad of 'Ali's primordial status and highest authority serves to emphasize and strengthen the Shi'i community's own claims to power and legitimacy.[25]

These sectarian claims have been included in Persian Shi'i ascension texts and images since the Safavid period as well. This is particularly the case for illustrated manuscripts, in which images complement and/ or expand upon their accompanying texts. For instance, in a number of sixteenth- and seventeenth-century Safavid illustrated manuscripts, the Prophet is depicted ascending to the heavens as he extends his signet ring (the symbol of his rulership) to 'Ali, himself metaphorically represented as a leonine angel.[26] During the Qajar period, a number of illustrations included in lithographed books repeat *mi'raj*-lion scenes or depict 'Ali in a fully fleshed form as he awaits Muhammad's arrival in paradise.[27] The ascension mural in Tehran thus belongs to a corpus of Persian Shi'i ascension images stretching back five centuries. Such images included in manuscripts, lithographed books, or painted on a cement wall pursue an unbroken pro-Shi'i agenda through the techniques of sectarian argumentation afforded by visual language.

In sum, by overtly including the Shi'i *wilaya,* the mural defines itself as supportive of the Shi'i cause through its inscriptional program. Second, by writing the creed backward and placing 'Ali's name immediately above the Prophet's head, the mural insinuates, by hierarchical visual positioning, the superiority of 'Ali's vicegerency over Muhammad's prophecy. And finally, by being placed so prominently in the Iranian public sphere, the mural also functions, per Liyakat Takim's fitting expression, as a form of "inverse taqiyya"—that is, as an overt assertion, rather than a dissimulation, of Shi'i presence and identity.[28]

Once in full view, this mural that embraces "inverse taqiyya" in effect gains political tenor, which, although admittedly muted, is detectable in the image of the young man inserted in the lower right corner. Who is this man or what does he represent? Why is he standing in paradise? Why is a *huri* offering him flowers? Why is his back turned to us? And why is he depicted in a photorealistic style rather than in a Neo-Traditional Islamic book arts style?

In order to begin to answer these many questions, we must first locate the ascension mural within the broader context of Tehran's post-revolutionary mural arts program, in which the theme of martyrdom as inscribed within a Shi'i soteriological worldview has taken center stage since the time of the Iran–Iraq War in the 1980s. Scattered throughout the sprawling city that is Tehran are countless murals of known and anonymous martyrs, or *shahids,* who perished on the war front. Sometimes their faces appear as bust profiles on cement walls, accompanied by brief biographical notices. At others, as in the case of this mural, a martyr is left unnamed, thereby functioning as a stand-in for a generation of young men turned martyrs. In addition to serving as visualized vaults for the vanished, these murals turn Tehran's cityscape into a pilgrimage route that urban witnesses consciously or unconsciously undertake, as if they were navigating amid the personal hagiographies of saints inhumed within an urban necropolis.

In recent years, murals representing martyrs have come under increasing attack by many young Iranians, including the staff of Tehran Municipality's Bureau of Beautification.[29] They consider martyrial scenes particularly vulgar and distasteful, and also judge the theme of martyrdom as necrophilic, dépassé, and obstructive to the therapeutic act of moving onward to less sinister goals in life than seeking death. To many young Iranians, murals of martyrs scattered across Tehran turn the city into a "musée macabre" desperately in need of aesthetic and thematic revision.[30] It is therefore not surprising that murals with overtly martyrial messages have started to be removed and replaced with more abstract renditions, which nevertheless attempt to retain the basic message of the original mural. Examples of this attitudinal and artistic shift are borne out by ample visual evidence, a topic discussed by Ulrich Marzolph in his contribution to this volume. To this corpus of cosmetically enhanced martyrial murals we can add the *mi'raj* mural since it, too, essentially replaces a graphic rendition of a female martyr.

Both from a situational and contextual point of view, the ascension mural seems to maintain the message of martyrdom through the insertion of a young man standing in paradise and accepting flowers, perhaps as a reward for his self-sacrificial acts. For the acculturated viewer, literate in the post-revolutionary rhetoric on martyrdom in Iran and visually conversant in the mural arts program in Tehran, interpreting this figure is not an onerous task: the image's message, as Stuart Hall notes, contains its own modality, functioning as a distinct sign-vehicle through the operation of culturally contingent codes.[31] Thus, the viewer's ability to properly decipher this image determines the success of the communicative exchange between the encoder, the sign, and its recipient. More prosaically, the viewer is bound to "get it" since the means is also the message.

Much like signs and forms, style also operates as a visual system that is encoded and decoded.[32] The pictorial style selected by the artist Rahmati is thus worthy of exploration as well. The artist herself notes that she purposefully selected two styles for the mural: a "miniature painting" style, which symbolically represents paradise, and a photorealistic style, which denotes the "mortal" world.[33] The book arts style used in the mural is intended to represent a distant century, in which the Prophet lived and embarked on otherworldly miracles, as well as the trans-temporal, cosmic realms, which Muhammad visited on the night of his ascension. This style essentially functions as a mnemonic clue to both past-time and non-time. Conversely, the photorealistic style depicts the mortal and material world, itself tactile yet transient. Via this stylistic binary, Rahmati visually ensconces martyrdom in the present tense, claiming that it does not belong solely to past-time, post-time, or non-time. Through her bifurcated style, she instead argues that martyrdom—as a notion and perhaps a practice, too—is, or at least should be, the imperative of the here and now.

What we can detect in this mural is a dual espousal of abstraction and photorealism, styles that indeed must be selected, on the one hand, and then interpreted, on the other. Abstraction in this case is not simply about the modernist project to shed the burden of textuality or the embracing of pure form. On the contrary, abstraction is harnessed and tactically unleashed in the public sphere so as to accentuate certain discourses on authenticity and identity, along with their intersections in various temporal planes. Similarly, naturalism is not merely an automatic rendering of optical reality. Rather, it functions as an idiom of persuasion in favor of martyrdom, its currency and legitimacy, and its ultimate rewards. Through form and style, the ascension mural thus posits that both the Prophet Muhammad and martyrdom belong to a rich and long-lived "tradition"— one that can be excavated, reaffirmed, and tailor-made to suit certain religio-political ideologies as these are artfully crafted within the scopic regime of modern Iran.

The Years of Muhammad

Besides promoting the superiority of Shi'i Islam and the salvific recompense for martyrdom by means of iconographic insertions, the mural's third and last manipulation is of the depiction of the Prophet Muhammad. As is clearly noticeable in the mural, the artist Rahmati has represented Muhammad with a blank face, despite basing her composition on the *Mi'rajnama*'s paintings, which in no way shy away from showing the Prophet's facial features (see figs. 1.2–1.4). The decision to remove Muhammad's features, however, was not of her own making. The original sketch that she submitted to the municipality included his features; only after its acceptance as the winning design for the building's wall did the staff in the municipality's mural arts program request their removal (along with the erasure of the bodies of the angels, which now appear as floating disembodied heads).

In interviews, the staff's reasons for the removal of Muhammad's facial features remain largely unarticulated. Instead, it seems that a general consensus, however loosely or unconsciously formed, concerning the impermissibility of representing the Prophet in the public sphere led the way to the mural's final edit. This consensus abrogated an original Islamic pictorial source and altered its course in the modern period, showing how discourses on Islamic art are perennially formed and reformed depending on need, circumstance, and anxieties linked to image-making more broadly. In the process, this unspoken consensus also gained the status of "common knowledge"—one that seems to have emerged from the overarching rhetoric found in both Muslim and non-Muslim countries, stipulating that Islam forbids figural imagery, most especially representations of the Prophet.[34] This form of knowledge, which is often overly simplified or purged of its complexities, has achieved the powerful status of "given," a largely unquestioned status quo capable of sidestepping or even trumping historical data.

The erasure of Muhammad's features in the ascension mural consequently must be examined in a twofold manner: first, in light of the history of representations of the Prophet, and second, within discourses on Muhammad as these emerged in Iran immediately after the Danish cartoon controversy. These lines of inquiry overlap, as visual culture and cultural politics similarly intersect in the mural in order to advance an argument about the Prophet. Indeed, through its visual disquisition on authenticity and identity, the image reclaims Muhammad as a prophetic exemplum, whose ability to perform miracles is manifest and whose splendor is unfathomable. The mural thus closely echoes counter-arguments to the Danish cartoons prevalent in the Islamic world, which claim that Muhammad is not merely a boorish instrument for distortion, derision, and fear-mongering, but rather the paradigmatically beautiful, miracle-working Messenger of God, whose diminished authority must be reasserted and whose vilified legacy must be redressed. The mural thus attempts to give visual form to a new contraposition, itself couched as a tradition, canon, or even a "given" that is nonetheless constructed and reconstructed through multiple modes, including the pictorial.

First, the ascension mural's position on Muhammad can be determined via its place in Islamic pictorial traditions, especially within the history of depictions of the Prophet in Persian book arts. A number of representations of Muhammad were included in illustrated manuscripts produced under the aegis of Ilkhanid, Timurid, and Safavid elite patrons from ca. 1300 to 1700.[35] During these four centuries in particular, there is a noticeable development in prophetic iconography.

During the Ilkhanid and Timurid periods, representations of the Prophet were included primarily in illustrated biographies and histories. In such manuscripts, including the Timurid *Mi'rajnama*, Muhammad is represented with his facial features on full display, as well as with other prophetic attributes, such as his turban, black tresses, and a flaming gold nimbus (see figs. 1.2–1.4). He is depicted as a mortal leader and prophet, touched by divine irradiation, whose facial features and bodily form remain materially real and fully visible to their beholders.

A shift occurred over the course of the sixteenth century, when Muhammad's facial features were frequently covered with a white facial veil (fig. 1.5). Although anxieties about depicting humans certainly did play a role, the reasons for camouflaging the Prophet's face in paintings produced during the Safavid period are not due solely to a reactionary impulse to prohibit graven images. Rather, as pictorial compositions they are conceptually sophisticated, linked to metaphorical thinking and poetic visualizations of the prophetic corpus and its fluctuation between the realms of the earthly and sacred, the seen and unseen. Safavid painters, perhaps influenced by Sufi ideas at the time, thus began to shed the veristic mode in favor of pictorial abstractions. These in turn reveal creative attempts to show Muhammad in both his human and superhuman dimensions, as both invisible divine flux and visible bodily matter. In such paintings, Muhammad is rendered as a mortal being—corporeal, tangible, and visible in his physical casing—and also as a consecrated prophet whose prime identity markers—that is, his facial features—remain "veiled" from human perception and cognition.[36]

From around 1700 onward, the picture is more fractured, as illustrations of the Prophet Muhammad diminish in number and their conventions vary between veristic and abstract modes. For example, Qajar manuscripts, lithographed books, paintings, and verbal icons (*shama'ilnamas*) produced in Iran during the nineteenth century show the Prophet both with his facial features visible and provided with a facial veil.[37] Although the facial veil appears to be the preferred idiom, it does not altogether displace pre-Safavid illustrative practices of representing the Prophet unveiled. In other words, from about 1700 until the last quarter of the twentieth century, prophetic portraiture is only standard insomuch as it systematically oscillates between two iconographic conventions.

FIGURE 1.5. The Prophet Muhammad's ascension, Jami, *Yusuf va Zulaykha* (Joseph and Potiphar's Wife), Shiraz, 975/1567–8. *Topkapı Palace Library, Istanbul, H. 812, folio 10v.*

In the last decades of the twentieth century and to the present day, other representations of the Prophet can be found, including in mass-produced materials. Although contemporary popular ephemera continue to show the Prophet both as a veiled and unveiled adult,[38] one of the most popular Iranian images prior to the cartoon controversy depicts the Prophet as an adolescent boy, with his head slightly tilted and sporting an open smile (fig. 1.6 and plate 3). Widely available as a poster, postcard, and even as a wall-hanging from the 1990s until 2006, this image of a young Muhammad, which was produced in many different versions with various colors and details, is said to have been copied from a painting of a young Muhammad, recognized in his youth as a prophet by the Christian monk Bahira, now held in an unidentified museum in Europe. However, as Pierre Centlivres and Micheline Centlivres-Demont have demonstrated, the modern Iranian image of the Prophet is not at all based on a European painting of Muhammad. Instead, it is a copy of a photograph, entitled either "Young Arab Boy" or "Muhammad," that was shot by the Orientalist photographers Lehnert and Landrock while they were stationed in North Africa during the first decade of the twentieth century. In other words, the image of a young Prophet Muhammad that was so popular in Iran at the turn of the twenty-first century was based on a (possibly misinterpreted) Orientalist photograph of around 1905–1906 showing a young Arab boy named Muhammad.[39]

At the same time as this image circulated, other Muhammad-centered products appeared on the market, including Persian translations of Euro-American scholarly works on the Prophet's life. One such translation, mentioned previously, is the 2006 Persian edition of Séguy's handbook on the Timurid Book of Ascension, whose illustrations served as the basis for Rahmati's ascension mural. This edition was in preparation before the Danish cartoon controversy, which, along with its non-mural scale, may explain why the Prophet's facial features were not Photoshopped out of the tome. Moreover, this publication appeared on the market at the same time as four other noteworthy events unfolded: (1) the Danish debacle of 2005–2006; (2) the declaration of 2006 as the "Year of the Noble Prophet" in Iran; (3) the publication of a series of illustrated children's book on the life of the Prophet; and (4) the prohibition of images of the young Muhammad (as in Figure 1.6), which indeed are no longer available for purchase in Iranian stores and markets today.

These four events effectively take us out of the realm of the history of art and into the domain of cultural politics. In our media-saturated global world, the use and abuse of images, including those of the Prophet Muhammad, is not simply about illustrating a written message and thus

FIGURE 1.6.
Muhammad as
a young boy
among the
stars and plan-
ets, postcard
purchased in a
supermarket,
Tehran, Iran.
*Author's photo-
graph, 2004.*

making a point rhetorically. The image per se is a method of argumentation and a tool for persuasion, at times more vociferous than verbal disputation. This is particularly the case for satirical images and political cartoons and caricatures, which are often belligerent in tone, thereby revealing a particular individual's masked feelings of hatred, oppositional mindsets, and latent urges toward aggressive acts.[40] Without a doubt, the 2005–2006 Danish satirical cartoons of Muhammad were explosive and, above all, revelatory of anti-Muslim sentiments and prejudices circulating among a number of European Christian communities at the time.[41]

　　Much like other exercises in ridicule and invective, the Muhammad cartoons did not emerge in isolation and without able interlocutors. To the contrary, the Danish satirists had a number of built-in audiences capable of deciphering and responding to the cartoons' messages. After all, as Arthur Clark analogizes, the satirist is like "a conversationalist who cannot shine in soliloquy."[42] It is indeed through such image colloquies and contentions that a larger picture of European post-9/11 preconceptions and biases about Islam, along with their global repercussions, can be traced—and graphically so.

Take, for example, the most infamous of the dozen Danish cartoons, drawn by Kurt Westergaard. This cartoon—not illustrated here but widely available on the internet—depicts the disembodied and bearded face of the Prophet, topped by a turban that turns into a bomb with a lit wick. The Prophet is represented as staring aggressively out toward the viewer, hailing and, Medusa-like, paralyzing his audience into a rather discomforting exchange of gazes.[43] When asked about his cartoon, Westergaard defended his position, saying: "I wanted to show that terrorists get their spiritual ammunition from Islam . . . [but] that does not mean that all Muslims are responsible for terror."[44] Although Westergaard attempted to provide nuance to his message in subsequent explanations of his cartoon, what remains obvious at the visual level is that Muhammad, the Messenger of Islam and the Prophet of Muslims, is equated to nothing more than a suicide bomber. Thus, the cartoon functions as a kind of political invective in pictorial form, or, per Ernst Gombrich's fitting expression, a weapon of sorts that condenses formal devices and thus "telescopes a whole chain of ideas into one single pregnant image."[45] It thus is both transgressive and synoptic, as well as visually revealing of an antagonistic mentality to, and fear of, Muslims as embodied by a martyrial image of Muhammad. In short, here Islam is depicted as nothing more than the compound term "Islamikaze."[46]

Westergaard's cartoon shows Muhammad turned ticking bomb. The pictorial shortcut mythologizes the world of politics and religion by physiognomizing it,[47] while also providing a gloss on an appallingly reduced, yet salient and topical, form of knowledge about Islam: namely, suicide bombings and attacks. Beyond this condensed syllogism, as Jytte Klausen notes, in this and the other Danish cartoons, Muhammad is (at best) rendered grotesque, cartoonish, vulgar, and ugly. He is not transcendent and beautiful, as he is depicted in Islamic literary and artistic traditions throughout the centuries.[48]

Opposites thus attract. In Islamic thought, Muhammad's eyes are radiant—but here they are menacing, seemingly fixing a target. Moreover, Muhammad's beard is described as sweet smelling and a marker for his prophetic maturity in Islamic texts; in the cartoons, his beard is a marker of an unkempt and unhygienic individual. In Islamic texts Muhammad's turban also is described as a mark of distinction bearing the aura of his power and authority.[49] Likewise, Islamic images include the flaming prophetic aureole, emerging as a golden blaze from his turban. Conversely, the cartoon takes the Prophet's headgear well beyond the racial slur "rag-head" and transforms it into an instrument for death and destruction. And finally, Muhammad's prophetic nimbus—sacred, irradiating, and generative—has been expunged, leaving nothing but a wick flaming in its stead.

An inversion of tidal proportions has occurred, and it is this inversion that rippled across the Islamic world after the publication (and multiple republications) of the Danish cartoons. Unsurprisingly, Muhammad had to be reclaimed rhetorically in Islamic spheres and, in Iran most especially, reinverted and reinvented at an iconographical level. In Iran, responses to the Danish cartoons surpassed the occasional government-sponsored demonstrations and the Satirical Book of the Year competition mocking the Holocaust. More muted but indubitably more significant within the perdurable realms of Iranian public life and culture was Ayatollah Khamenei's declaration of the year 1385 (2006) as "The Year of the Noble Prophet." In his *Noruz* (New Year's) declaration, Khamenei mentioned the Danish cartoons, along with the February 2006 bombing of the 'Askiri Mosque in Samarra, one of the most important Shi'i mosques in the world. In the face of such adversities, the Ayatollah further noted that Iran had hoisted the banner of Islam and had tolerated hardships with pride by following the Prophet Muhammad's character traits, including his steadfastness, dignity, mercy, and moral righteousness.[50]

The declaration of 2006 as the "Year of the Noble Prophet" in Iran served as a retort intended to reclaim Muhammad as a prophetic model for the Islamic faith. It also should be seen as a direct reaction to what was perceived as an affront to Islam within Europe and an attack specifically on Shi'i Islam within Iraq. Rather risibly, that same year witnessed in Iran the renaming of Danish pastries as the "flowers of Muhammad" (*gul-i Muhammadi*), an idle shuffling of food monikers reminiscent of French fries' christening as "Freedom fries" by American conservatives irritated at France's opposition to the 2003 U.S.-led invasion of Iraq.

On a more serious note, the year 2006 also launched endeavors in multiple domains of Iranian creative expression, including painting and publishing. To name just one example here, in 2006 a series of fourteen illustrated children's books on the life of the Prophet Muhammad was published by the Institute for the Intellectual Development of Children and Young Adults (*Kanun-i Parvarash-i Fikri-i Kudakan va Nujavanan*). These books targeting a juvenile audience included many depictions of the Prophet, in which Muhammad is typically represented with a blank, glistening white face or with a radiant head shaped like the full moon (fig. 1.7 and plate 4). Despite culling from premodern Persian book art traditions, which include veristic depictions of the Prophet Muhammad, the illustrations included in the children's books entirely and without exception omit Muhammad's facial features. This erasure must not be understood as solely speaking to a gradual abstraction of prophetic iconography within Islamic artistic traditions, which, as we have seen, was fluid in Iran well into the modern period. Instead, what is certainly at play is a reaction to the Danish cartoons—a reinversion of prophetic iconography in which the ugly, menacing features of the Prophet are literally "defaced" and rendered too brilliant to behold.

In contemporary Iranian visual culture, Muhammad's face thus could function as a platform for public speech to voice counter-arguments about Islam and its revered Messenger. That this message would not be lost to Iranian readers and viewers—not to mention art historians—is attested to by the popularity of images of Muhammad and their entanglements with regime-sponsored projects, publications, and proclamations in Iran during and after 2006.

In thinking more broadly about the ascension mural of 2008, it becomes clear that it is deeply enmeshed in an eclectic array of visual materials, ranging from "Classical" Islamic painting, the Danish cartoons, Persian translations of Euro-American scholarly works, and children's books on the life of the Prophet. The sources are premodern and contemporary, Islamic and non-Islamic, de facto challenging facile art historical binaries. Just as significantly, they reveal that cultural icons, including most recently the Prophet Muhammad, are often used, reused, parodied, inverted, and redeployed for a variety of ideological purposes. As a discursive tool within various visual landscapes, Muhammad indeed operates as a powerful signifying system for cultural construction and contestation in the volatile arena of today's global politics. In one European context (the Danish cartoons) he is made to look unsightly and hostile, while in a modern Iranian milieu he is visually reclaimed and depicted as quintessentially beautiful, having been touched by the flux of divine selection, in which his unseen facial features are so radiant that they are restorative of his prophetic status and transcendental splendor.

The Loaded Image

Perhaps the ascension mural in Tehran is not such a curious case after all. Indeed, it is just one empirical datum in a complex circuit of images

FIGURE 1.7. The Prophet Muhammad, depicted with a moon-shaped face, ascends
to the skies on Buraq's back. Painting by Muhammad 'Ali Baniasadi included in
the children's book *Aftab-i Afrinash (Sun of Creation)* written by Babak Niktalab
and Afsaneh Sha'bannejad (Tehran: Kanun-i Parvarash-i Fikri-i Kudakan va
Nujavanan, 1386/2006), 46.

produced within the dynamics of power and ideology in our modern world. Within global image machines, Muhammad plays a centripetal role because he is always constructed in the eyes of his beholders, who themselves engage in the retrieval and revision of a perceived cultural heritage or engage in resistant practices of seeing. These deliberative encounters between images today reveal a number of hidden transcripts, one of which attempts to define Islam.

Various cultural and artistic strands percolate and coalesce into that which is defined as "Islamic" today. Discursively claimed, "Islamic" subjectivities, art, and visual culture are not—and arguably never have been—formed in a vacuum, without a dialogic system of call-and-response. In the case of modern Islamic visual culture, it is clear that images today tend to be rooted within complex entanglements, located as it were within global scopic circuits and regimes that they both embrace and reject simultaneously. Additionally, modern Islamic visual culture is also processual in that it builds upon a self-defined heritage that is sought, revived, parsed (even pruned), and angled through new ideological positions and framings. As is the case for the 2008 *mi'raj* mural in Tehran, images in the Islamic world, including those of the Prophet Muhammad, are not just based on internal Islamic traditions—however loosely, narrowly, or erroneously these might be defined—but also are ignited by outside factors, including European satirical cartoons that are external to and derisive of Islam.

Images are thus both loaded and locutionary: they are saturated with many forms and communicate multiple messages. They also carve out complex maps of meanings that must not be simplified into crude dichotomies such as "Islamic" vs. "non-Islamic" or the flawed Huntingtonian divide of "West" vs. the "Rest." Rather, these modern images must be explored across time and in synchronicity, as well as within their local environments and through cross-cultural frameworks. And most importantly, they must be carefully "read" so as to unravel the *ins* and *outs* of the many discourses that attempt to give shape to a particular vision of Islamic modernity.

NOTES

1. For a discussion of Iranian murals from the time of the Islamic Revolution to ca. 2008, see Gruber, "The Message is on the Wall," 15–46; and Marzolph, "The Martyr's Way to Paradise," 87–98.

2. For the most recent murals in Iran, which embrace abstract expressionism and tend to discard overtly martyrial messages, see Ulrich Marzolph's contribution to this volume and Karimi, "Imagining Warfare, Imaging Welfare," 47–63.

3. On Islamic *mi'raj* texts and images, see most especially the following two volumes of collected articles: Gruber and Colby, *The Prophet's Ascension;* and Amir-Moezzi, *Le voyage initiatique en terre d'islam.*

4. There exist numerous studies of Islamic attitudes toward images and image-making practices. These are most succinctly summarized in Grabar, "Islam and Iconoclasm," 45–52. On representations of the Prophet Muhammad in Islamic artistic traditions more specifically, see Gruber, "Between Logos (*Kalima*) and Light (*Nur*)," 1–34.

5. W. Mitchell, *What Do Pictures Want?*, 47.

6. For a detailed discussion of the Tehran municipality's Bureau of Beautification, see Karimi, "Imagining Warfare, Imaging Welfare." The "beautification" endeavors are discussed briefly in comparison to the City Beautiful Movement in Gruber, "The Message Is on the Wall," 44.

7. For a description and image of the worn-out banner of Rim Salah al-Riyashi as photographed in 2007 on this building, see Gruber, "The Message Is on the Wall," 34–37, fig. 10. The inscription on the banner reads (in English, with translations in Arabic and Persian included as well): "My children, I do love; but martyrdom I love more."

8. I thank Ali Boozari, who interviewed staff at the Tehran municipality and Faezeh Rahmati on my behalf in April 2010.

9. See Séguy, *The Miraculous Journey of Mahomet;* and Gruber, *The Timurid Book of Ascension* (*Mi'rajnama*).

10. For an overview of Iran's economic and governmental ties with Afghanistan after 2001, see "Country Profile: Afghanistan, August 2008."

11. For a discussion of Chaghatay Turkish and Uighur script, along with their use in the Book of Ascension manuscript and other fifteenth-century Timurid texts, see Gruber, *The Timurid Book of Ascension,* 267–69.

12. See Daftari, "Islamic or Not," 10–27.

13. Grabar, "What Makes Islamic Art Islamic?," 247–51. Grabar warns against seeking a single definition of Islamic art. However, he does suggest three criteria: that Islamic art (1) has social dimensions and applications, (2) is marked by ornamental abstractions and geometric forms, and (3) balances unity with plurality.

14. Daftari, "Islamic or Not," 25.

15. Bhabha, "Another Country," 34.

16. This expression is borrowed from W. Ali, *Modern Islamic Art,* 138.

17. On bricolage as a tactic of appropriation and deliberate commodification of long-lived artistic traditions, see Sturken and Cartwright, *Practices of Looking,* 59, 223.

18. Kubler, *The Shape of Time,* 64.

19. On aggregates and inventions, see ibid., 70.

20. Bourriaud, *PostProduction,* 17.

21. Bourriaud, *PostProduction,* 20.

22. Naef, "Reexploring Islamic Art," 167. As Siliva Naef notes, for Arab art, modernity was from the beginning a way of not only *reviving* but also *reconquering* the past.

23. Keshmirshekan, "Discourses on Postrevolutionary Iranian Art," 143. For a further discussion of Neo-Traditionalism in Iran, also see Keshmirshekan, "Modern and Contemporary Iranian Art," 10–37.

24. On the Shi'i *wilaya*, also known as the "third *shahada*" (*al-shahada al-thalitha*), see Takim, "From *Bid'a* to *Sunna*," 166–77. On the expression "third *shadada*" in particular, see ibid., 177.

25. For Shi'i ascension tales, which sometimes also describe the ascension of the imams, see most especially Colby, "The Early Imami Shi'i Narratives and the Contestation over Intimate Colloquy Scenes in Muhammad's *Mi'raj*," 141–56; and Amir-Moezzi, "L'Imam dans le ciel," 99–116.

26. On Safavid *mi'raj*-lion compositions, see Gruber, "When *Nubuvvat* Encounters *Valayat*"; and "Me'raj ii. Illustrations," fig. 3.

27. On Qajar ascension images, see Boozari, "Persian Illustrated Lithographed Books on the *Mi'raj*."

28. Takim, "From *Bid'a* to *Sunna*," 170.

29. Karimi, "Imagining Warfare, Imagining Welfare."

30. For an example of a university student's aversion to such murals, see the personal interview cited in Gruber, "The Message Is on the Wall," 45.

31. Hall, "Encoding, Decoding," 91.

32. On realism and naturalism serving as codes, see ibid., 95.

33. Communication between Ali Boozari and Faezeh Rahmati, April 2010, provided to author by Ali Boozari.

34. See "Q&A: Depicting the Prophet Muhammad." In this Q&A piece, poorly argued and unsupported statements that are typically found in other media sources include, for example, "Of course, there is the prohibition on images of Muhammad." Another example of this anxiety can be found in Moustafa Akkad's 1976 movie *al-Risala* (The Message), also produced in English as *The Message* starring Anthony Quinn (1977). In *The Message*, the Prophet Muhammad does not appear on screen; rather, the camera itself functions as the Prophet's viewpoint.

35. For a detailed analysis of these materials, see Gruber, "Between Logos (*Kalima*) and Light (*Nur*)."

36. For a discussion of the Prophet's facial veil in Safavid paintings, see Gruber, "When *Nubuvvat* Encounters *Valayat*."

37. For representations of Muhammad in Qajar art, see Ekhtiar, "Infused with Shi'ism."

38. For a 2001 postcard of the Prophet Muhammad represented as an unveiled adult, see Gruber, "Between Logos (*Kalima*) and Light (*Nur*)," 253, Figure 15.

39. For a discussion of this image of a young Muhammad, see Centlivres and Centlivres-Demont, "Une étrange rencontre"; and Grabar and Natif, "The Story of Portraits of the Prophet Muhammad," 36–37, and fig. 4.

40. For a discussion of satirical images as expressive of latent, deep-seated hatred, see Gombrich, "The Cartoonist's Armoury," 139; and for their use as "invitations" into aggressive acts, see Kris, "The Psychology of Caricature," 174, 180.

41. There are many articles on the Danish cartoon controversy that focus on the issues of freedom of expression, racism, xenophobia, arrogance, and violence. However, the most in-depth analysis of the controversy can be found in Jytte

Klausen's book-length study, *The Cartoons That Shook the World*. On cartoons as revelatory of cultural prejudices, see in particular Cavanagh and Kirk, "Introduction," 5.

42. Clark, "The Art of Satire and the Satiric Spectrum," 45.

43. On the engaging and transfixing "Medusa Effect" of images of persons who gaze frontally toward their viewers (including Uncle Sam), see Mitchell, *What Do Pictures Want?*, 36–38.

44. Cited in Freedman, *The Offensive Art*, 152.

45. Gombrich, "The Cartoonist's Armoury," 130.

46. This term is borrowed from Israeli, *Islamikaze*.

47. On this process, see Gombrich, "The Cartoonist's Armoury," 139.

48. Klausen, *The Cartoons That Shook the World*, 142–43.

49. On the Prophet's turban, see the bilingual Arabic–English edition of al-Tirmidhi's (d. 880) *Shama'il al-Nabi* (The Characteristics of the Prophet) published as *Shamaa-il Tirmidhi*, 108–11.

50. For Ayatollah Khamenei's *Noruz* 1385 speech, see: http://farsi.khamenei .ir/message-content?id=208.

CHAPTER 2

Secular Domesticities, Shiite Modernities: Khomeini's Illustrated *Tawzih al-Masail*

PAMELA KARIMI

The extensive use of propagandist imagery by the Islamic Republic and the subsequent scholarly attention paid to this phenomenon has somehow eclipsed the use of visual imagery published by religious scholars and activists prior to Iran's 1979 Revolution. Of the hundreds of publications disseminated by religious groups before the revolution, *Nabard-i Millat*—the widely distributed weekly newspaper of the religious fundamentalist organization Fadaian Islam published in the first half of the 1950s—is particularly striking. This periodical is filled with political cartoons that portray the cleric-founder of Fadaian Islam, Navvab Safavi (1924–55), juxtaposed with "demonized" images of political figures from the West and the East.[1]

An image from a 1951 issue of *Nabard-i Millat* shows Navvab Safavi's portrait rising above the horizon in larger-than-life guise (fig. 2.1); light pours into the dark space of the picture from below Navvab's chin. The light emanating from Navvab overcomes the darkness of the world, leaving no space for "imperialist" powers. England, Russia, and the United States are personified, accompanied by other, less identifiable, world leaders, escaping the watchful gaze of the ascending Navvab. The caption reads: "Fadaian Islam: These sturdy and powerful eyes will follow the criminals' journey to hell."

The views of religious groups were not always conveyed through such negative renderings; some used visual vocabulary to communicate their (nonpolitical) religious thoughts in modern ways. This approach is apparent in books published in the 1960s and 1970s by Ayatollah Abdol Karim Biazar Shirazi (hereafter called Shirazi). Shirazi spent five years in the West (United Kingdom and Canada) in the 1970s, but even before his departure from Iran he sought to bridge the gap between Western knowledge and traditional Shiite Islam. His books, which were designed for youngsters, include: *Qur'an va tabia't* (The Qur'an and Nature, 1960), *Khoda va ekhteraat az didgah elm va qur'an* (God's Creation and Manmade Inventions from the Point of View of Science and the Qur'an, 1975), and *Din va danesh* (Religion and Knowledge, 1982).

FIGURE 2.1. An image from the front page of the weekly *Nabard-i Millat* vol. 30, no. 9 (1951). The caption reads: "Fadaian Islam: These sturdy and powerful eyes will follow the criminals' journey to hell."

Shirazi employed illustrations in a religious text that might otherwise have seemed passé to his intended audience, who were exposed to Western-style publications and illustrated books.[2] Consider two pages from *Religion and Knowledge,* meant to educate readers about the content and meaning of two verses from the *Sura* (chapter) *Al-An'am* and *Al-Nahl* of the Qur'an (fig. 2.2). While Arabic verses appear on top of each page, the word-for-word Persian translations, as well as the "scientific" interpretations of the verses, serve as captions for images taken from encyclopedias read by children in the West.[3]

This juxtaposition of old and new, Western and traditional, scientific and Qur'anic, was implemented in another publication by Shirazi: *Imam Khomeini's New Risaleh,* or *Tawzih al-Masail*[4]—literally, "guide to problems," a handbook of behavior governing home life, among other issues, written by the *mujtahids,* or highest-ranking authorities of Shiite Islam. The book was first published in Najaf, Iraq, in 1947, and was available only in Arabic, as *Tahrir al-Valsilah.* In the late 1970s Shirazi edited, designed, illustrated, and translated *Tahrir al-Valsilah* into Persian. Khomeini approved the publication of this new edition himself, and the work was released between September 1980 and the summer of 1982 in four volumes: *Worship and the Development of Self, Commerce and Economic Issues, Family Matters,* and *Political Responsibilities and Government Roles.*

Each volume also carried the title of *Imam Khomeini's New Risaleh* and featured portraits of Ayatollah Khomeini, diagrams and scientific tables, and illustrations that—by Shirazi's own account—were intended for a modern Iranian audience.[5] Because of its focus on matters of hygiene and home life, the book was primarily read by young, educated housewives who—perhaps unlike their mothers, who lacked formal education and sought answers from local imams—could resolve their daily religious quests by referring to written sources. Although developed before and during the revolutionary years (1977–79), the illustrated *Tawzih* was first published in September 1980. It embodies Shiite scholars' modernization of daily religious practices in the last years of the Pahlavi era.

This chapter explores the *Tawzih* teachings about everyday consumer practices and household spaces as well as the ways in which the work blended "modern" household organization and behavior with traditional Islamic teachings, classifying certain behaviors and appliances introduced from the West as acceptable or not according to the traditional dichotomy of purity and filth. Further, the chapter demonstrates that the *Tawzih*'s illustrations are similar to those used in publications of the Pahlavi era but with a significant alteration: annotated with Islamic captions and quotes

FIGURE 2.2. Two facing pages from Abdol Karim Biazar Shirazi's *Religion and Knowledge*. While the text aims to educate readers about the meanings of two verses from the Qur'anic chapters *Al-An'am* and *Al-Nahl*, the images portray human adventures in space and on the moon.

from the Qur'an in an attempt to advocate for religious conservatism. Before delving into the content of the *Tawzih*, however, let us briefly examine the ways in which ethics of domestic life were presented in traditional Shiite texts.

Home Etiquette in Classical Books of Ethics and Shiite Literature

Twentieth-century Shiite literature on ethics can be described as an extension of and response to writings from the late 1600s, when the Safavid dynasty established a state-approved Shi'ism, and earlier.[6] While a full account of these sources is beyond the scope of this chapter, it is appropriate to classify the two types of literature that expounded on the ethics of home life. One contained religious themes derived predominantly from the *hadith* literature (the sayings of the prophet, imams, and the saints)[7] and was written by religious scholars. The second included both religious and secular subjects in books written by educated people who held respected positions in society but who often lacked religious authority. A sampling of books of ethics from the medieval and early modern periods allows a clearer picture of their significance in the twentieth century.

In the tenth century, the Baghdadi author Abu'l-Tayyib Muhammad al-Washasha (d. 936), in his book *Kitab al-Muashasha,* wrote about proper habits concerning eating, dressing, and general behavior within the home. Henceforth, social etiquette became the focus of many medieval books in the Arabic and Persian languages, including the *Qabusnama,* written in 1082 by a member of the Persian Zyarid dynasty, Keikavus ibn Wushmgir (d. 1012). In a chapter on the etiquette of eating, the author states that the "rule of Islam" (*shart-i Islam*) dictates that while eating with others one must take time from consuming food to converse with one's fellow diners.[8] This point is reiterated in a later medieval Persian book, *Kimiya-ye Sa'adat* (The Alchemy of Happiness), written by the eleventh-century theologian Abu Hamid Muhammad Ghazali (d. 1111). The book also addresses proper hygiene, such as washing one's hands before and after dining and making use of toothpicks. Similarly, in his *Ihya 'Ulum al-Din* (Revival of Religious Sciences), Ghazali again reminds his readers that the Prophet was a stern advocate of hygiene, referring to a saying by Muhammad, in which he inquires: "Why do you come before me with yellow teeth? . . . Use the toothpick. It is a purifier for the mouth and well pleasing unto God."[9]

In subsequent centuries, texts on the ethics of everyday life addressed similar topics.[10] Although written in different eras, each of these works considered behavior within the home. The philosopher Nasir al-Din Tusi (d. 1274), in his book *Akhlaq-i Nasiri* (in which he dedicates a whole chapter to household management), confirms this point: "What I mean by home is not the [physical] house built of sun-dried bricks, dirt, wood and stone, but rather the relationships among husband and wife, child and the person who nurtures him . . . be it all in a house built of wood or stone, a simple tent, or even a mere shelter in nature."[11]

The commentaries in these books are often of a religious nature and, hence, discuss ethics. Although women's actions are the dominant topic, it is the male authors who formulate both questions and solutions in these texts. Finally, many commentaries were derived from the *hadith* and the Qur'an, the two main texts that had already acquired normative status in Islam and were used as sources for Islamic law or *Shari'a.* Indeed, although various past writings and traditions influenced books of ethics, themes from the Qur'an and the *hadith* had the strongest influence.

In the seventeenth century, Shiite Safavid rulers sponsored a collection of new scholarly work on the ethics and etiquette of everyday life. Most of these works were written in the Persian language. Economist and author Afshin Molavi argues that—like the reformation pastors of Europe who used vernacular languages, as opposed to Latin, in their preaching and writing—many religious figures of the Safavid era, including Sheykh Bahayi and Mulla Muhammad Taqi Majlesi, chose Persian so that their works' reach would extend beyond the limited audience of religious scholars who were well versed in Arabic.[12] Such scholars included Muhammad Baghir Majlesi or Majlesi II (d. 1698), who was extraordinarily influential in his own time and well into the twentieth century. The historian Moojan Momen asserts,

> Up to [Majlesi's] time . . . Shi'ism had sat lightly on the population of Iran, consisting mostly of mere expressions of love for Ali and hatred of the first three caliphs. Majlesi sought to establish Shi'ism firmly in the minds and hearts of people. Majlesi was the first to write extensively in Persian on such a wide range of subjects and in a manner that could be understood by the ordinary people.[13]

While Majlesi's Arabic encyclopedic collection *Bahar al-Anvar* (Oceans of Light) became a respected classic reference for contemporary seminaries in Iran, his Persian *Hilyat al-Muttaghin* (Countenance of the Pure) was meant to be read by average people. The latter included an astonishing array of topics, from complex theological matters to the proper way for the believer to enter or leave a house. He wrote about sexual intercourse; clipping fingernails, plucking nasal hairs, and playing with one's beard; proper ways of sneezing, belching, and spitting; entering and leaving the house; and curing diseases and internal ailments, including colic, gas, stomachache, and coughing. Many of Majlesi's remedies for illnesses, solutions for hygiene, and suggestions for improving personal conduct are irrational by modern standards. For example, when he refers to the sayings of Imam Jafar Sadeq (d. 765),[14] Majlesi writes that when putting on shoes, one must first put on the right shoe and then the left. He adds that, "if one walks in public with only one shoe on, Satan will haunt one."[15] He also suggests that reciting certain verses from the Qur'an shall cure one's eye infection.[16]

Literary critic Shahrokh Maskoob asserts, "[W]ith great efforts and diligence, [Majlesi] introduced to Shi'ism, amongst other things, a mass of superstitions."[17] The reprinting of Majlesi's *Countenance of the Pure* well into the twentieth century in some ways established the work as a hallmark of religious backwardness and a subject of humor (especially concerning its commentaries on sexual conduct) in the popular imagination. The sense of the *Tawzih* as humorous was propagated in contemporary Shiite books on ethics of life and personal conduct, especially the various versions of the *Tawzih*.[18] As literary historian Ahmad Karimi-Hakkak writes, "By addressing all of the hypothetical situations a true believer could or might face, leaving little to individual common sense, they opened themselves to harsh ridicule from their opponents, especially secular ... intellectuals of the twentieth century."[19] In response to such reactions, Shirazi discerned the need for a new *Tawzih,* one "that would appeal to a large audience."[20]

The Twentieth-Century Iranian Home: Between Modernity and Tradition

Missionaries, Western architects, and other foreign parties first initiated the "reform" of the Iranian home in the early twentieth century.[21] Soon the Iranian domestic market was flooded with a plethora of new, imported home goods. Iranian newspapers designate that as late as the mid-twentieth century many Iranians rejected imported commodities, viewing the new products as responsible for interrupting their daily routines and challenging traditional beliefs about the physical world. For example, an article in a 1944 issue of the popular magazine *Khandaniha* indicates that many Iranians preferred certain alkaline soil to commercial laundry soaps because the great medieval poet of Iran, Sa'di, had admired the aroma of this soil; traditionalists also rejected laundry detergents on the grounds that "its disgusting odor would remain with their clothes." In addition to the use of alkaline soil, the power of repeating aloud the *salavat* (expressing praise and greeting to God, Mohammad, and his descendants) while scrubbing the clothes was believed to be a major cleansing factor.[22]

Such practices might give the impression that religiously minded Iranians had no interest in the Western commodities embraced by secular Iranians. However, many religious figures welcomed certain imported commodities that they deemed useful and adapted them to local conditions. As average people became better informed about cleanliness and hygiene, and as the new house and its novel additions (including washing machines, refrigerators, and indoor plumbing) challenged traditional Shiite conceptions of purity and filth, religious thinkers sought to reconfigure traditional domestic rules. They divided household contents into two categories; natural elements (e.g., water) and artificial commodities (e.g., washing machines). Such works as *Imam Khomeini's New Risaleh* used this dichotomy to interpret Western transformation of spatial settings within the home.

Regulating the Body

An important theme in all four volumes of *Imam Khomeini's New Risaleh* (especially *Worship and the Development of Self* and *Family Matters*) is the dichotomy of *taharat* and *nijasat* (purity and filth), which regulates bodily functions and habits. Religious activities such as praying and reading the Qur'an are prominent features of traditional Iranian domestic life; to prepare for such rituals, one must be pure. Cleanliness as defined by the Qur'an and the *hadith,* however, is different from cleanliness according to modern science and medicine. In the updated *Tawzih,* traditional ideas are applied to modern products, settings, and activities. Foreign toilets, washing machines, and even a home's large plate-glass windows were subject to classification based on the old system of opposites.

Shiite regulations governing water (*ahkam-i ab*) fill a lengthy chapter, as water is considered to have the power to purify objects that are not inherently filthy. This cleansing water must, however, have certain qualities to be considered "clean" itself: rain water (*ab-i khalis*), spring water (*ab-i jari*), fresh well water (*ab-i qalil*), or water from a drain pipe with a capacity of three square feet (*ab-i kor*) may be used to wash filthy materials.[23] In the nineteenth century, classifications of water changed when Western medicine drew attention to waterborne epidemics that came predominantly from public baths; nevertheless, Shiite scholars continued to consider rules governing water applicable to daily life. *Imam Khomeini's New Risaleh* applied these rules to such modern appliances such as washing machines. According to *Imam Khomeini's New Risaleh,* the purity of clothes washed in the washing machine was determined by the amount and source of water used in the machine—detergents have no place in this process of cleansing.[24] Likewise, the use of foreign toilets is legitimate if one brings a bottle of water to use for washing after visiting the toilets (fig. 2.3).

Despite notions of cleanliness as defined by medicine and science, religious leaders demand that the faithful follow rules of cleanliness as written in the Qur'an and the *hadith.* Ideas proposed by Mary Douglas in her seminal book *Purity and Danger* provide insight into this logic: "In chasing dirt, in preparing, decorating, tidying, we are not governed by anxiety to escape disease, but are positively re-ordering our environment, making it conform to an idea."[25] Shiite regulations concerning dirt and cleanliness are likewise

قلیل به روی آن در صورتیکه در مرتبه اول آب از آن خارج گردد پاک می‌شود و باید بعد از هر دفعه با فشار آب آن خارج شود.

در مورد پیشاب کودک شیرخوار یک بار کافی است.

توالتهای خارجی

کسانی که در کشورهای خارجی اقامت دارند و یا به خارج سفر می‌کنند و مجبورند در راه، در هواپیما و در شهرهای اروپایی از توالتهای فرنگی استفاده کنند. تکلیفشان چیست ؟

در چنین توالتها می‌توان از بیده، یا شلنگ یا ظرف لوله‌داری مانند ظرفی که برای آب دادن گلدان مصرف می‌شود، استفاده کرد و خود را با آب شست و یا با کاغذ توالت خود را پاک کرد همچنانکه می‌توان حتی با سنگ، کلوخ، پارچه پاک خود را تمیز کرد. و میزان برطرف شدن آلودگی و پاک شدن است و همانطورکه در رسالهٔ تحریر الوسیله آمده:

FIGURE 2.3. A page from Khomeini's *Tawzih al-Masail* showing how to use washing machines and foreign toilets. Khomeini, *Imam Khomeini's New Risaleh*, 1:54.

resplendent with symbolic meanings. According to Shiite belief, natural settings (e.g., vegetation and earth)[26] are often considered clean unless manipulated by humans or affected by "inherently filthy"[27] animals (e.g., carnivores, dogs, and pigs).[28] When Shiites come in contact with unclean substances or animals, they must observe the rules governing impure (*najis*) and pure (*taher*), especially before they prepare to say their daily prayers. In the past, these rules were taken even more seriously. For example, a toilet, even if cleaned, was considered dirty and could not be inside the house. Jews, Christians, Zoroastrians, and those who had had contact with "inherently filthy" animals were not allowed to drink from water fountains used by Muslims, nor were they accepted in the same bathhouses as observant Muslims. But as the historian Kevin Reinhart reminds us, "impure persons are not necessarily dangerous or contagious to the community because impurities are transient and can be transformed or concealed through the performance of ritual acts."[29] Indeed, the rites of purification are often symbolic.[30] For example, the ritual of ablution includes only washing the distinctive features of a person: face, hands, and feet. Furthermore, when water is scarce, fine sand and dust can be used as substitutions.[31] Thus, the symbolic demonstration of the act of cleansing—rather than actual cleanliness—is what is of paramount importance in Islam.[32]

The embedded metaphorical meanings in religious rituals and performances lead us to yet another aspect of modern Shiite approaches to cleanliness and filth—those that surpass toilets and washing machines to encompass broader subjects.

Indeed, the commentaries in all four volumes of *Imam Khomeini's New Risaleh* define not only the home, but the entire world, from an Islamic perspective. Prayer, pilgrimage, and the ethics of commerce acquire new meanings in the larger geographical setting. The whole world is simplified in an image that at first glance might seem appropriately childlike: one's place on the planet is defined by one's orientation toward the K'aba (fig. 2.4). In addition to supplementing the text, this illustration suggests the ways in which *Imam Khomeini's New Risaleh* attempts to bridge the gap between a Muslim's daily life and global realities—a theme that is strengthened through the choice of images selected for the volume on family life.

Sanctifying Consumption: Modern Homes and Shiite Housewives

Shirazi's illustrated *Tawzih* immediately became a bestseller and influenced the youth in exactly the same way that colorful magazines of the

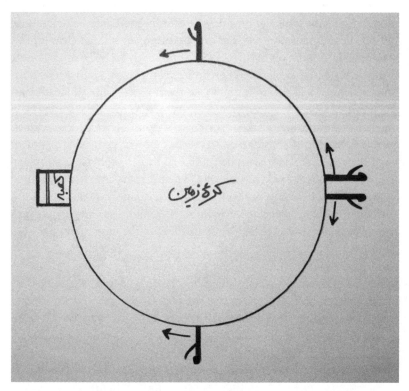

FIGURE 2.4. A guide to the direction of the qibla. Khomeini, *Imam Khomeini's New Risaleh,* 1:101.

shah's period had captivated them.[33] Still, the bland layout of his *Tawzih* makes one wonder how it could have competed with dozens of attractive alternatives, such as *Zan-e Ruz,* an Iranian women's magazine that delighted its readers with colorful commercial advertisements and iconic figures of Western pop culture. Whether the work would have held any interest for those not already "committed to the faith" would be difficult to determine, but those with religious backgrounds found the *Tawzih* captivating.[34] The most intriguing aspect of the book to the present study is that it invites the reader on a visual journey very similar to that presented in the commercial representations that filled popular magazines of the 1970s.

Pahlavi periodicals were extraordinarily rich in colorful advertisements. Like popular illustrated advertisements, most of the images in Shirazi's volumes are, by his own account, cut from North American (mostly Canadian) publications and pasted onto the pages of the *New*

Risaleh—creating a montage that depicts Western objects and lifestyles. In addition, the objects that Shirazi displays are named, as are the subjects of the advertisements. In the *Family Matters* volume, for example, the section that prohibits alcohol opens with a labeled bottle of wine. Like two illustrated advertisements, featuring labeled bottles of Smirnoff vodka and Canada Dry, from the mid-1960s and 1970s, respectively, the image of the wine bottle in Shirazi's book is labeled by a passage from the *Sura Ma'idah* that associates alcohol consumption with satanic deeds (figs. 2.5–2.7).

The techniques for making the product look more desirable (such as juxtaposing the Canada Dry bottle with a pretty woman and multiplying the Smirnoff bottle in the backdrop) are not in use on Shirazi's pages. Neither is the composite nature of the advertisements—to accommodate simultaneous readings (e.g., associating sexual pleasure with overcoming thirst)—a matter of concern on Shirazi's pages. By manipulating the original images (taken from Western publications), Shirazi reverses the meanings associated with them in their original context. In this way, he gives new meanings to the functions of certain objects through both textual descriptions and pictures.

That Western advertisements acquire contradictory meanings when incorporated into Shirazi's work is also apparent in his description of the importance of curtains and the enhancement of visual privacy at home. Typical curtain advertisements in the late-Pahlavi popular press often gave an aura of fantasy to the home. A good example of such an approach is a Trevira curtains advertisement from a 1966 issue of the popular women's magazine *Zan-i Ruz* (Woman of Today). The advertisement focuses on the curtains' appearance from the exterior of the house: translucent, placing the interior and its contents—specifically, the woman of the house—on display (fig.2.8). This focus on the home's exterior appearance is strengthened by a long caption: "The curtain is where the first impression from your house and workplace is given to the visitor." Thus, the primary function of the curtain in this advertisement is neither to create privacy nor to block the harsh sunshine; the curtain is used to give a more desirable and inviting image of the interior to outsiders.

This function of the curtain is reversed in the *Tawzih,* where the author draws a link between women's bodies, the home, and visual barriers. In the volume that considers family life, two facing pages feature an image of women's jewelry (as well as a shell and pearl) on one side and a master bedroom on the other. The master bedroom resembles one found in a Western suburban home, while the jewelry seems to demonize the materialism of the shah's regime. The caption of the first page reads: "Which one is more

FIGURE 2.5. An advertisement featuring labeled bottles of Smirnoff vodka from the weekly *Zan-i Ruz* (Women of Today), issue 67 (June 1966).

valuable? A pearl in a shell or what is deemed an ideal woman as described by the Qur'an? Or cheap jewelry that can be found everywhere?" The image on the opposite page comes with this caption: "Which one is more decent and appealing? A house with covered [curtained] windows? Or a veil-less and curtain-less home?" (fig. 2.9 and plates 5–6). The two illustrations recall Juan Eduardo Campo's interpretation of *Sura Nur* of the Qur'an:

> [R]ules governing access to domestic space are regarded as similar to rules governing exposure and access to the human body. The very presence of these rules in the Qur'an, together in one place, lends itself to the creation of a perduring linkage between the house, the human—especially female—body, and sexual relations. Following the rules entails purity, goodness, and blessing in the

کانادادرای
نوشابه گوارا
و نشاط آور

FIGURE 2.6. An advertisement featuring Canada Dry from *Tehran Musavvar* (Tehran in Images), issue 1586 (April 1974).

eyes of God. To violate them is as good as following in "the footsteps of Satan."[35]

Following this Qur'anic tradition, while the pearl in the shell could symbolize a woman's virginity and a protective enclosure, the curtain would substitute the veil for her body (fig. 2.6). As Campo states, "confinement within domestic space thereby becomes a substitute for a woman's control of her body."[36]

In the popular press, interior schemes are presented from the point of view of outsiders, while Shirazi displays an interior from an insider's point of view. By displaying familiar, colorful images, he delivers the religious information in a way that reflects trendy advertisements and magazines. In this sense, the reader is encouraged to "buy" the religious information

فصل چهارم

نوشیدنیهای
حلال و حرام
اشربه:

FIGURE 2.7. An image showing a wine bottle labeled with a passage from the Qur'anic chapter *al-Ma'idah* that associates alcohol consumption with satanic deeds. From Khomeini, *Imam Khomeini's New Risaleh,* 3:215.

as if it were a commodity. The strong emphasis on the "visual" also demonstrates the extent to which Shirazi attempted to marry the traditional with a new paradigm of sensory experience. Customarily, Muslims obtained religious information orally: they brought their questions to the mosques, where the imams offered solutions. Imams also provided regular sermons that, in the words of the anthropologist Charles Hirschkind, "demand[ed] a particular affective-volitional responsiveness from the listener."[37] The listeners to the sermons, Hirschkind continues, "hear with the heart" and so are able to live more piously and avoid moral transgression."[38] With the introduction of cassettes, listening to tape-recorded recitations of the Qur'an and sermons became a routine activity among all dedicated Muslims (i.e., not only in Egypt, where Hirschkind conducted his research, but also

FIGURE 2.8. An advertisement featuring Trevira curtains from the weekly *Zan-i Ruz* (Women of Today), issue 11 (April 1965).

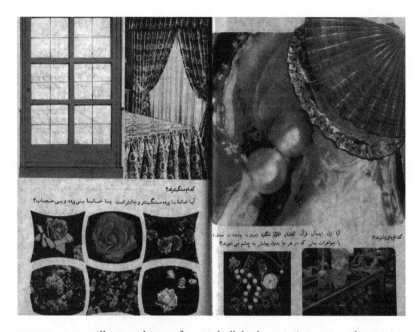

FIGURE 2.9. Two illustrated pages from Ruhollah Khomeini's treatise. The caption on the right page reads: "Which one is more valuable? A pearl in a shell or what is deemed an ideal woman as described by the Qur'an? Or cheap jewelry that can be found everywhere?" The image on the left page is provided with another caption posing further rhetorical questions: "Which one is more decent and appealing? A house with covered [curtained] windows? Or a veil-less and curtain-less home?" Khomeini, *Imam Khomeini's New Risaleh,* 2:46–47.

in Iran).[39] The mechanically reproduced sermons might have satisfied those whose more traditional upbringing allowed finding an instantaneous affinity between the sound of the sacred word and devoutness. However, the act of listening arguably became less appealing among the majority of young Iranian TV-watchers and popular magazine readers who, by the 1970s, had already developed a keen interest in the visual illustration of various subjects. By shifting from the traditional discipline of listening to that of viewing, Shirazi used an innovative approach to the dissemination of religious knowledge—an approach that seems appropriate for the age of mechanical reproduction of images and a time of high rates of literacy among young Iranians. After all, Shirazi's design was an attempt to attract a literate young audience sharing an affinity for visual learning.

Above all, the book seems to have been designed for a female readership. Multiple interviews conducted during 2006–2007 reveal that young,

PAMELA KARIMI

educated Iranian women who believed in Islam and the fundamentals of the revolution read the book more than their male counterparts did. Shirazi's choice and arrangement of images reveals a specific attempt to modify Shi'ism for the modern Muslim homemaker. Most of them portray domestic settings, homes, natural environments, and food. In the manner of scrapbooking, they were cut from popular publications and pasted onto the pages of the *Tawzih*. The making of scrapbooks—cutting images from newspaper ads and pasting them into diaries and journals—was extremely popular among the young women of the 1960s and the 1970s (fig. 2.10). In comparing the book to examples of Iranian women's scrapbooks during the shah's era, it becomes clear that the *Tawzih* was assembled in this manner in order to appeal to the tastes of the young women of that time.

Further, the diagrams and flow charts are reminiscent of the nutritional charts that had been used by American and European home economists who had attempted to reform the Iranian home in the first half of the twentieth century. These educators had come from a generation that utilized charts and graphs, and these were the rather dated materials that Shirazi also incorporated into his work.

Envisioning Orderliness:
Medieval and Modern Encounters in Everyday Life

Shirazi's maps and charts can be categorized in the "scheme of sacred geography,"[40] to borrow a term from the historian David A. King. Shirazi's map of the direction of the qibla reminds us of the medieval qibla maps that exaggerated the ka'ba and frequently depicted Mecca larger in scale compared to other cities in the region on display. One can sense a similar quality in both abstract medieval Islamic maps and the diagrams and maps presented by Shirazi in the *Tawzih*. Both are intended to give a sense of discipline to Muslims' daily lives. Just as in some simplified, diagram-like medieval Islamic maps, the over-simplification of the diagrams of the *Tawzih* (figs. 2.11 and 2.12) is purposeful and not due to ineptness.[41] After all, as King reminds us, medieval Islamic maps "showed a sophisticated grid of a kind not known on any other map prior to the twentieth century."[42] Like medieval Islamic maps, the diagrams presented in the *Tawzih* are in fact more useful for organizing one's everyday life according to Islamic beliefs than for representing any physical reality. Above all, these diagrams call for inhabiting and enacting an Islamic everyday life.[43]

The diagrams and charts of the *Tawzih* attempted to bring the time and space of classical Islam into the everyday life of contemporary Iranians;

FIGURE 2.10. Scrapbook made by a nineteen-year-old Iranian woman, 1969.
Courtesy of Khadijeh Talattof.

they were an effort to standardize and rationalize religious information. In a sense, they embodied the Western orderliness and discipline that had long been encouraged by the Pahlavi state. At the same time, the *Tawzih* can be perceived as competing with the thoughts of Western-educated Shiite intellectuals such as the sociologist Ali Shariati and the essayist Jalal al-i Ahmad. Shariati and al-i Ahmad both came from Shiite clerical backgrounds. Al-i Ahmad was more critical of secularism and Westernization than was Shariati, locating the cultural roots of Iranians in Islam. After al-i Ahmad's death, Shariati aimed to construct a popular and modernist Shiite society.[44] Shariati advocated a "return to one's roots," and his efforts were directed toward reconciling modernity not only with "Iranian-ness" (as often encouraged by more secular intellectuals) but also with "Shiite-ness."[45] Both Shariati and al-i Ahmad espoused appreciation for Islamic values, but they were ultimately seen as Western individuals in the eyes of the clerics who came to power after the revolution.[46] Indeed, the commentaries in the *Tawzih* would have seemed trivial to Shariati, who argued against people blindly obeying clerics (which the *Tawzih* encourages). Shariati believed that this blind submission had begun during the Safavid period (he termed "Safavid Shi'ism") and contrasted with the pure "Alid Shi'ism" (from Ali, the first Imam of Shiites).[47]

Nonetheless, just as Shariati had called for a popularization of Shiite Islam,[48] the diagrams and charts of the *Tawzih* helped translate the language of Shiite rituals into a popular form. Generally speaking, it is safe to suggest that the *Tawzih* borrowed selected ideas from more intellectual Shiite discourses and secular Western ideas, casting aside the rest.

Conclusion

The ideas concerning domesticity and daily life explored in this chapter demonstrate the interplay that existed between Western initiatives and Iranian religious figures who rebuffed or refashioned these influences to fit their needs. *Imam Khomeini's New Risaleh* has often been portrayed as a reactionary rejection of Western transformations—but in fact, it was a key factor in the creation of Shiite modernity. At the end of the Pahlavi era a hybrid of Shi'ism and modernity was imaged and imagined in many sites, particularly in the notion of a Westernized Iranian home. Eventually this hybrid was ardently opposed by conservative revolutionaries, who drew a sharp distinction between local and imported goods, specifying the appropriateness of household objects according to traditional views. Oppositions such as *halal* vs. *haram* (accepted vs. forbidden by God) and *taharat* and *nijasat* (purity and filth)—terms once applied primarily to the human body and its environment—were more strongly applied to imported commodities by conservatives.

Joint Iranian–Western enterprise (so-called "montage") was considered *haram,* as described in early post-revolutionary books, such as Hasan Tavaniyanfard's *Karkhanejat-i Montage: Iqtisad-i Shirk* (Montage Factories: The Sinful Economy). Tavaniyanfard claims that montage products give rise to a montage culture that affects the society and, most importantly, religion itself. Thus, it is no surprise that later editions of Khomeini's "montage" *Tawzih*—including those during his lifetime and after the revolution—excluded all "collaged" images of Western household furniture. In the following decades, the Iranian state media frequently showcased

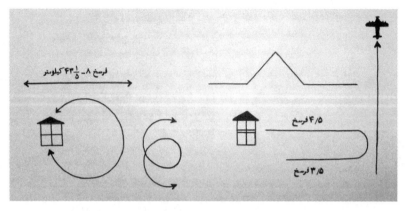

FIGURE 2.11. Diagram showing rules of prayer while away from one's home.
Khomeini, *Imam Khomeini's New Risaleh,* 2:101.

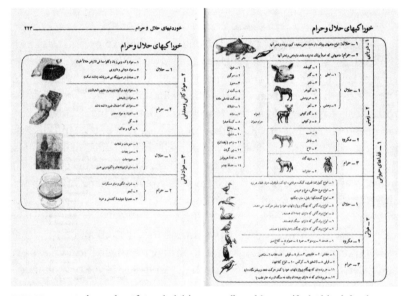

FIGURE 2.12. A chart classifying *halal* (accepted) and *haram* (forbidden) food.
Khomeini, *Imam Khomeini's New Risaleh,* 3:222–23.

the "humble" home life of Khomeini, where everything looked bland and
simple. Even the chairs were covered with white sheets (perhaps to conceal the "foreignness" of their form). Since Khomeini's death in June 1989,
students are taken every year to his house to witness the simplicity of his
home life, as well as, on occasion, to participate in a painting competition
called "illustrating Khomeini's chair" (fig. 2.13).

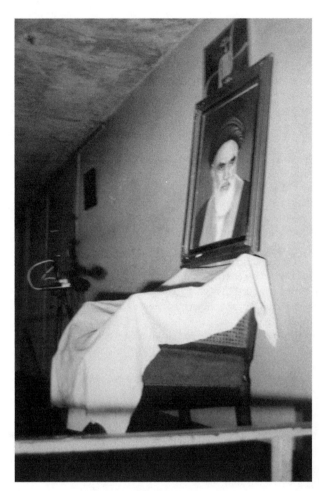

FIGURE 2.13.
Khomeini's
chair. Jamaran,
Tehran. *Image
courtesy of the
Organization
for Cultural
Heritage (Miras-e
Farhangi), Tehran,
Iran. Fol. 1854.*

Imam Khomeini's New Risaleh has been reprinted several times since Shirazi's first edition in 1980, but the subsequent editions never incorporated images. On the other hand, the model established by Shirazi has lived in on other publications. Unlike the early post-revolutionary period, today one finds an abundance of illustrated religious volumes on ethics of daily life in bookstores across Iran. By using images, Shirazi empowered religious messages and reached greater numbers of people. Before the ability to disseminate visuals was readily available, printed lessons or arguments were one-dimensional and limited in scope. The *Tawzih* transformed, albeit perhaps moderately, the conventional forms of religious cultural production in Iran. In a broader sense, the case of the illustrated *Tawzih* confirms that

Islam and modernity have in many ways been attuned to one another.[49] Thus, the focus of the *Tawzih* on religious practices and the myriad forms of religious cultural production should not be regarded simply as a reactionary rejection of modern ways of life, but rather as a key factor in the creation of a different form of modernity in twentieth-century Iran.

NOTES

1. On Fadaian Islam, see Abrahamian, *Iran between Two Revolutions,* 258–59; and Behdad, "Islamic Utopia in Pre-Revolutionary Iran," 40–65.

2. Thanks to the Institute for the Intellectual Development of Children and Young Adults (*Kanoon-e parvareshi fekri koodakan va nojavanan,* also known as Kanoon), which was initiated in the late 1960s by the empress Farah Pahlavi, Western children's illustrated books were increasingly translated and published in Iran in the 1960s and 1970s. These books were available both through both bookstores and the libraries of the Kanoon, which could be found in all major cities. For more information regarding the activities of the Kanoon and children's illustrated books, see Sadeghi, "Infrastructure," 34–39.

3. Ayatollah Abdol Karim Biazar Shirazi, interview by author, March 12, 2007, Tehran, Iran.

4. Among Iranians, these texts, published by all Shiite *mujtahids,* are known as *Tawzih al-Masa'ils* or *Tawzih* and hence inspire the title for this article.

5. Shirazi, interview.

6. For more information regarding Shi'ism under the Safavids, see, for example, Abisaab, *Converting Persia.*

7. This is unlike Sunni Islam, according to which *hadith* refers only to the sayings of the Prophet. Shiite Muslims find justification for their practices in the Qur'an and in the lives of the Prophet, his companions, and family. A characteristic of this belief is an emotional devotion to the *ahl al-bayt* (the household of the prophet). See Schubel, *Religious Performance in Contemporary Islam,* 15.

8. Pancaroglu, "Serving Wisdom," 64–65.

9. Faris, *The Mysteries of Purity,* 37.

10. Pancaroglu, "Serving Wisdom," 59–68.

11. Tusi, *Akhlaq-i Naseri,* 207.

12. Molavi, *Persian Pilgrimages,* 179.

13. Momen, *An Introduction to Shi'i Islam,* 116.

14. The sayings and orders of the Imam Jafar Sadiq (the eighth Shiite Imam), especially in the field of medicine and the treatment of the sick, had already been used by Shiite scholars for centuries.

15. Majlesi, *Hilyat al-Muttaqin,* 25.

16. Ibid, 194.

17. Maskoob, *Iranian National Identity and the Persian Language,* 141.

18. *The Countenance of the Pure* set the model for the future *Tawzih al-Masails* produced by various *mujtahids.* Its content, however, was later contested and revised. The *Tawzih al-Masail* produced (circa 1902) by Sheykh Morteza Ansari became a more legitimate model for numerous successive *mujtahids.* Other resources include

the *hadith* and the Qur'an as well as Arabic books of law accepted by twelver Shiites, such as Jafer ibn Ali Yahya's *Sharay-ih al-Islam fi Masail al-halal val haram.*

19. Ahmad Karimi-Hakkak, interview with Afshin Molavi (cited in Molavi, *Persian Pilgrimages,* 180).

20. Shirazi, interview.

21. For more on the foreign contribution to improvement of Iranian domesticity, see, for example, Kashani-Sabet, "The Politics of Reproduction," 1–29; Kashani-Sabet, "Hallmarks of Humanism"; and Zirinski, "A Presbyterian Vocation to Reform Gender Relations in Iran," 51–56.

22. These activities were noted by missionary Bess Allen Donaldson in her book *The Wild Rue,* which was first published in London in 1938. Ten years after its publication in English, passages from the book were translated into Farsi and presented to Iranians through the popular magazine *Khandaniha.* See Ali Javahir Kalam, "*Rakhtshui* Iranian," *Khandaniha* 4, no. 36 (Shanbeh, 9 Urdibihisht, 1323/ Saturday, May 1944): 9–10. The tone of the article's author (who was perhaps also the translator of Donaldson's passages) is condescending, and by selecting critical excerpts from Donaldson's book the author highlights the backwards nature of Iranians who lacked such appliances as irons and washing machines.

23. Vahidi, "*Ahkam-i Abha,* [Classification of Water Types]," in *Ahkam-i Abha,* 24–25. In *The Wild Rue,* Bess Allen Donaldson writes extensively about her observations of Iranian's ideas concerning the purity of water; see Donaldson, *The Wild Rue,* 138–37.

24. Khomeini, *Imam Khomeni's New Risaleh,* 1:52–54.

25. Douglas, *Purity and Danger,* 12.

26. A dish licked by a dog (an "inherently filthy" being) would be clean if one first covers it with soil and then washes it with water. See Khomeini, *Imam Khomeni's New Risaleh,* 1:52.

27. Vahidi, "*Nijasat-i batini* [Inherent Filth]," in *Ahkam-i Abha,* 37–63.

28. Ibid., 60.

29. Reinhart, "Impurity/No Danger," 1–24. This content appears in Bauer, "Corrupted Alterities," 237.

30. Reinhart, "Impurity/No Danger," 4.

31. Ibid., 6.

32. Bauer, "Corrupted Alterities," 237.

33. Shirazi, interview.

34. This information is derived from interviews with two schoolteachers, three housewives, two engineers, and a university professor. Interviews by author, February–April 2007, Tehran, Iran.

35. V. 21, *Nur.* See Campo, *The Other Side of Paradise,* 21.

36. Ibid., 22.

37. Hirschkind, "The Ethics of Listening," 624.

38. Ibid., 627.

39. Ibid., 624.

40. King, "Two Iranian World Maps," 63.

41. See Savage-Smith, "Memory and Maps," 109–27. Savage-Smith's argument is limited to a particular school of cartography known as the Balkhi School, which is characterized by very stylized line-work and extreme abstraction.

42. King, "Two Iranian World Maps," 66.

43. The content of this chapter on *halal* and *haram* are mostly taken from Jafer ibn Ali Yahya's *Sharay-ih al-Islam fi Masail al-halal val haram,* whose interpretation of Islamic law is widely accepted among the twelver Shiites.

44. Keddie, *Roots of Revolution,* 165. On the topic of Shiite modernity in Iran, see also Chehabi, *Iranian Politics and Religious Modernism.*

45. As Keddie asserts, Shariati's efforts were not something new or particular to Iran during his era. Reconciliation of multiple identities was espoused by many Arab ideologists, for example Anouar Abd al-Malek, who saw Islam as the basis of anti-imperialist action. A. Abdel-Malek, "Political Islam—Positions," unpublished text from the Round Table on Socialism in the World, 1978, Cavtat, September 1978, cited in Keddie, *Roots of Revolution,* 188.

46. Mirsepasi, *Intellectual Discourse and the Politics of Modernization,* 78. See also Keddie, *Roots of Revolution,* 188–90.

47. Keddie, *Roots of Revolution,* 202–204.

48. Ali Shariati, "What Should We Lean On?," in *Nashriye Sazman-i Danishjuyan* [The Publication of the Students' Organization] 2 (1962), quoted in de Groot, *Religion, Culture, and Politics in Iran,* 165.

49. This topic has been studied extensively in the context of Shiite Lebanon and Egypt. See, for example, Deeb, *An Enchanted Modern;* and Starret, "The Margins of Print," 117–39.

PAMELA KARIMI

CHAPTER 3

Memory and Ideology:
Images of Saladin in Syria and in Iraq

STEFAN HEIDEMANN

Through its cultural heritage a society becomes visible to itself and to others. Which past becomes evident in that heritage and which values emerge in its identificatory appropriation tells us much about the constitution and tendencies of a society.

—JAN ASSMANN, "Collective Memory and
Cultural Identity," 133.

Since the Middle Ages, Saladin has been one of the most influential figures of historical memory in Eurasia. He was used as a symbol of the noble enemy, of war with the West and Israel, and of peace.[1] In various incarnations he was also a national hero. During the Lebanon War of 2006, even Nasrallah, the Shi'i leader of the Hizbullah in Lebanon, was eulogized by Syrians as the "Saladin of the modern age."[2] Moreover, after the fall of Saddam Hussein, the Sunni *Kata'ib Salah al-Din* in Iraq chose Saladin as the eponym for their guerrilla war against the Shi'i government and American troops.

Bernard Lewis, in his 1975 Princeton lecture series *History: Remembered, Recovered, Invented,* was one of the first to study the political use of the past in the Middle East.[3] Eric Hobsbawm's studies further advanced the analysis of the *Invention of Tradition* (1983) as an attempt to establish continuity with a suitable historic past, focusing on the deliberate "political mass-producing of traditions."[4] Jan Assmann's *Das kulturelle Gedächtnis* (1992) allowed for a more refined comprehensive approach. According to Assmann, any collective memory of a symbol or figure creates orientation within a group and identity for the individual. Cultural memory is reconstructive, as knowledge of the past is aligned anew with contemporary needs.[5]

In the post-colonial states in the Middle East, invented pasts enforce social, "national" coherence where it has not existed before. Historical rhetoric legitimizes current ideologies and identities across religiously and ethnically diverse populations. Symbols and figures of collective memory must be emotionally meaningful and resonant for the audience; they presuppose knowledge and memory among the targeted groups and require, as Hobsbawm states, "broadcasting on the wavelength to which the public is already tuned in."[6] In modern states the resonance of such historical rhetoric is established largely by compulsory school attendance.[7] Political resonance, political orientation, and national identity are fabricated by means of the public presence of these memory figures—represented on monuments, statues, or murals, or transmitted via endlessly reproduced carriers of images and meaning, such as posters, banknotes, stamps, coins, political slogans, popular movies, and television programs.

This essay explores the memory figure "Saladin" and his application across different media, emphasizing the use of his image in contemporary Syria. The first part of this study summarizes the Western origin of the memory figure to explain its emergence in the Middle East, which did not have a visual memorial culture before the late nineteenth century. The second part considers the Iraqi case to contrast it with its Syrian counterpart in the third part. Both states have or had a Baathist government and used the figure of Saladin nearly simultaneously but to different ends.

Similar to other modern memory figures in the Middle East, such as Hammurabi,[8] Nebuchadnezzar,[9] and Cyrus,[10] Saladin's memory owes much to Western scholarship and popular culture beginning in the eighteenth century. The reconstructed Saladin figure was appropriated in the Middle East in the age of imperialism and nationalism.[11] From the late nineteenth century on, his memory was continually rearranged. Visual political culture emerged in the late Ottoman period slowly, and Saladin was one of the first historical figures to be adopted. The memory figure of Saladin and its role in the construction of collective identities is paradigmatic because its appropriation was different according to predominant state ideology and ethnicity. Its use in different nation-states at the same time allows comparisons that are not possible with more territorially confined memory figures. Other significant strands of appropriation and use of "Saladin" can be seen in Egypt in the 1960s, in the contemporary Kurdish national movement, and in other states and regions.[12] These are largely excluded from the present study because the Egyptian memory reached its apex in the 1960s and the Kurdish memory communicates different issues.

Remembering the Historical Saladin

As a ruler Saladin towered high above his contemporaries. He was born in 1138 to a Kurdish family of Saljuq–Zangid military nobility in

STEFAN HEIDEMANN

Tikrit, a city in the north of modern-day Iraq. In 1164 he arrived in Egypt as a member of a Syrian Zangid relief force for the Shiite Fatimid caliphate, which he brought to an end in 1169, restoring the sway of the Sunni 'Abbasid caliphate. In subsequent years, Saladin captured Syria and northern Mesopotamia from his fellow Muslim rulers. After Reynald de Chatillon (ca. 1125–87) broke a truce, Saladin defeated the entire Crusader army in the battle at the Horns of Hattin in Palestine in 1187, and took Jerusalem after about ninety years of Crusader rule.[13] He died in 1193. One of several contemporary panegyric chroniclers and close associate of Saladin, the military judge Baha' al-Din ibn Shaddad (d. 632/1234), eulogized his piety, his respect for Islamic law, his sense of justice, his charity, and his generosity. His work formed the base for subsequent images of Saladin.

Opinions differ about the continuation of Saladin's memory after the fall of Acre in 1291 and the end of Crusader rule in Syria.[14] In pre-colonial times within the Arab-Islamic world at large, Saladin played almost no role as a memory figure. More than Saladin, the Mamluk sultan Baybars (r. 1260–77) was remembered as the pious champion of Islam and jihad. In cultural memory Baybars was the hero who fought Crusaders, Mongols, and infidels.[15] His achievements and adventures, and thus his memory, were orally transmitted in the famous epic collection *Sirat Baybars* (The Life of Baybars). Baybars was certainly more popular than Saladin in Egypt and parts of Syria, but Saladin never fell completely into oblivion: Mamluk chronicles always include the story of the Crusades and his deeds.[16] In Palestine, Saladin remained revered: at the end of the Mamluk period the chief *qadi* of Jerusalem, Mujir al-Din (d. 867/1462–63), wrote a history of Jerusalem and Hebron, *al-Uns al-jalil bi-tarikh al-Quds wal-Khalil* (The Exalted Friendliness in the History of Jerusalem and Hebron). A substantial part of the two volumes chronicles the Crusades and the rise of Saladin, the battle of Hattin, and the taking of Jerusalem. Anecdotes illustrate that the fear of a return of the Crusaders was still alive in Mujir al-Din's lifetime.[17]

European Rediscovery and Romantic Invention

Werner Ende, Hannes Möhring, Carole Hillenbrand, Magaret Jubb, Jean Richard, Stefan Conermann, and, more recently, Anne-Marie Eddé have studied the discovery and reception of Saladin in western European and the Arab world.[18] The modern Western discovery of Saladin began in 1732, when Albert Schultens (1686–1750), a scholar from Leiden, Netherlands, published his Latin translation of the Arabic panegyric account of Saladin's deeds written by the military judge Ibn Shaddad. At the beginning of the rise of Oriental studies and philology, Saladin was the first Muslim ruler of the Middle Ages with whom the European educated classes were familiar. In the nineteenth century, numerous novels about the Crusades and Saladin helped to create his popular European image. In 1825 Sir Walter Scott (1771–1842) turned the enlightened Saladin into a literary monument in his novel *The Talisman*.[19] Between 1870 and 1881 the first statue of Saladin was subsequently integrated into the Scott Monument built in the city of Edinburgh.[20]

The Hamidian Saladin

Between the 1870s and 1914 Europe saw a wave of invention of political traditions to accommodate the new and transforming European states and societies. These traditions found their expression in a proliferation of public monuments.[21] The first memorial connected with Saladin in the Middle East was created in 1878. At the end of the political liberalization and modernization of the Tanzimat period (1839–76), Sultan 'Abd al-Hamid II (r. 1876–1909) chose an authoritarian path of modernization. More traditional strategies of reaffirming and legitimizing power were replaced by or supplemented with new ideologies such as pan-Islamism,[22] which was deemed more suitable to the modern world.[23] As in Europe, a repository for a new, elaborate ideological language was found in memory figures of the past.[24] 'Abd al-Hamid repeatedly accused Europe of leading a "Crusade" against the Ottoman Empire. The Crusades became once again a metaphor in the political consciousness of the Middle East.[25] The region's population was unfamiliar with historical monuments such as those erected in Europe since the Renaissance. The general Ottoman Islamic avoidance of public images prevented a similar cult;[26] in fact, not even the Russian–Turkish War of 1877–78 resulted in the creation of large-scale war memorials.[27]

Early Ottoman monuments took a different shape: 'Abd al-Hamid erected clock towers throughout his empire and commissioned the restoration and repair of politically and religiously meaningful monuments and tombs, such as those of the founders of the Ottoman dynasty.[28] According to Şükrü Hanioğlu, 'Abd al-Hamid attempted to establish a form of Ottomanism with a Muslim tinge in order to promote domestically a pan-Islamic ideology that would curb nascent proto-nationalist activities.[29]

Within Syria, the period between the 1870s and 1908 saw the transition to architectural modernity in Damascus.[30] The Wali Diya Pasha had begun with the excavation and reconstruction of the tomb *(turba)* of Saladin in Damascus in 1876, as is recorded by an inscription. Two years later, in 1878,

STEFAN HEIDEMANN

'Abd al-Hamid commissioned a new marble cenotaph for Saladin's tomb, which today stands adjacent to the medieval wooden sarcophagus (fig. 3.1).[31] This cenotaph counts among the first historical monuments in the Ottoman Empire, as well as the first memorial honoring Saladin in the Middle East. To emphasize its political meaning, the cenotaph was executed in the Ottoman Baroque style. Much like western European historicism, it was considered a marker of modernity at the time. The memorial dates to the same year as the Ottoman defeat in the Russian–Turkish war and the Congress of Berlin. With this cenotaph, 'Abd al-Hamid wished to proclaim his imperial presence in the Syrian province and connect himself with al-sultan al-ghazi[32] Saladin, the defender of the faith against the Crusaders. Saladin thus was visually and rhetorically appropriated by the Ottoman sultan during a moment of political confrontation.[33]

Like contemporaneous European national monuments erected in honor of historical heroes, the cenotaph displays a conflation of religious and patriotic elements. A golden framed portrait of Saladin still hangs above the entrance within the tomb; it probably dates to the same period and became important for subsequent visual representations of the Muslim hero (fig. 3.2 and plate 7). This portrait of a turbaned Saladin is signed by the otherwise unknown artist 'Abd al-Wahhab. The text below the image praises Saladin as the ruler of Egypt and Syria (al-Sham) but does not mention the Crusades. From the time of its restoration onward, the turba of Saladin in Damascus received markedly more attention than that of Baybars, which in 1296/1878 was transformed into a library—open to the public in 1297/1880—with bookcases standing over his cenotaph.[34]

In 1898 the journey of the German kaiser Wilhelm II (r. 1888–1918) to the Middle East attracted greater attention to the figure of Saladin among Ottoman political circles. The kaiser linked himself with several historical figures, including the Crusader emperor Frederick Barbarossa (r. 1155–90),[35] who was a contemporary of Saladin and an equally noble and legendary ruler-hero who died on his way to the battlefields of Syria. Wilhelm delivered a famous speech on the Ottoman sultan as well as a eulogy of Saladin that was soon translated into Arabic. While in Damascus, Wilhelm also dedicated a brass laurel wreath to Saladin's tomb.[36] The Egyptian poet Ahmad Shawqi (1868–1932) composed an ode (qasida) on Wilhelm's praise of Saladin, celebrating the fact that the Kaiser had made the Middle East more aware of the glorious sultan Saladin.[37] Henceforth, Saladin became a major memory figure in the Middle East, paving the way for further uses.

In early March 1914, two Ottoman airplanes flew from Istanbul to Damascus with several stopovers on their way to Cairo in demonstration of

FIGURE 3.1. Cenotaph of Saladin, Damascus, commissioned by 'Abd al-Hamid II in 1878. *Photograph by the author, November 2006.*

modern Ottoman air power after the lost Balkan Wars (1912–13).[38] Coming from Beirut, the first plane and its pilots enjoyed a splendid reception in Damascus. After taking off from Damascus, however, the plane crashed east of Lake Tiberias. The young Turkish dictator Enver Pasha (1881–1922) ordered the bodies of the two pilots to be transferred by train to Damascus, where they were buried beside Saladin's tomb to connect their memory as martyrs (*shahid*) with that of the *ghazi* sultan of Islam. About a week later the second airplane arrived in Damascus. On its way to Cairo it, too, crashed—into the sea just off the coast of Jaffa. One pilot died, and he was also buried beside Saladin's tomb.[39] An obelisk memorial was erected at the crash site in the Golan,[40] while a column monument was made in Istanbul.[41] The 1920 visit of the French high commissioner Henri Gourand (1867–1946) to the tomb of Saladin—and his often repeated sentence, *"Saladin, nous voilà"* (Saladin, here we are)—became a trope in memories of Saladin in Syria, where they came to represent anti-imperialist resistance.[42] In 1940 the Syrian national leader and resistance fighter against the French mandate, 'Abd al-Rahman Shahbandar (1880–1940), was also honored with burial beside Saladin's tomb.[43]

❦

STEFAN HEIDEMANN

FIGURE 3.2. Portrait of Saladin in the tomb of Saladin, Damascus, presumably ca. 1878. *Photograph by the author, November 2007.*

Saladin's rising popularity also can be measured by the increasing number of theatrical plays and novels in Oriental languages that explore his deeds.[44] The first scholarly biography of Saladin was written in Arabic by Ahmad al-Biyali and published in Cairo in 1920.[45] After World War I— and more so during the French Mandate in Syria and Lebanon, as well as the British Mandate in Palestine—the figure of Saladin was employed as a political metaphor in the rhetoric of Arab resistance against imperialism and Zionist expansion. The most memorable occasion for this usage of the Saladin metaphor was during the Hattin Day rally that was organized by the Istiqlal Party in Haifa on August 28, 1932. Several thousand people attended, coming from the Damascus province, Lebanon, Palestine, and Transjordan. At the rally, Rashid Rida (1865–1935) delivered a historic speech, "Dhikra Salah al-Din wa-ma'rakat Hattin," condemning the Zionists' expansionist policy.[46]

After Israel's foundation in 1948, the victory at Hattin and the retaking of Jerusalem became the dominant themes in the political rhetoric on Saladin. After the unification of Egypt and Syria in 1959, President Jamal 'Abd al-Nasir (1918–70) became for a short period linked to Saladin. The apex of this rhetoric can be seen in the Egyptian film director Youssef Chahine's (1926–2008) *al-Nasir Salah al-Din* (1963). The movie projected Nasserist secular ideology and the struggle for Palestine through the lens of the Crusades and the heroic exploits of Saladin. The film remains a resonant classic in the Middle East. In Egyptian propaganda and media, however, the Saladin allusion was not further exploited or repeated due to the socialist nature of the Nasserist ideology.[47]

Saddam Hussein as Saladin Reincarnated

Beyond Egypt, Saladin also played a role within the visual rhetoric of Iraqi nationalism, which—beginning around 1968—mainly drew on the heritage (*turath*) of the ancient Orient to connect the Baath revolution to the millennia-old history of the country.[48] After a final transition of power in 1979, Saddam Hussein instigated a monumental personality cult, identifying himself with various political rulers of Iraq's past who were meaningful either to all Iraqis or to certain religious and ethnic groups. Saddam Hussein embodied all of them—not only Hammurabi, the wise lawgiver, and Nebuchadnezzar, the enslaver of the Jewish people, but also various early Islamic caliphs, such as 'Ali ibn Abi Talib, or al-Mansur. He even allowed allusions linking himself to the Prophet Muhammad.[49] The emphasis on ancient Mesopotamia as "Semitic" allowed integrating Iraqi nationalism and superiority into a pan-Arab political discourse.[50] The depiction of Saddam Hussein as the incarnation of all historic Iraqi rulers was staged as a highly crafted ideological monologue directed at the Iraqi people or groups in order to unite them under one nation, which he himself aimed to embody. In the process, archaeology and the display of largely reconstructed historic sites served to bolster his propaganda.

It is not clear when Saddam first began to incarnate Saladin. However, the former Iraqi president was born in Tikrit, as was Saladin. Saddam's adopted birth year of 1937 (instead of his actual birth year of 1939) may have been altered in order to prove that he was born exactly eight hundred years after Saladin.[51] Moreover, the governorate north of Baghdad, created in 1976, was named after the hero.[52] Nevertheless, until the late 1980s Saladin played only a minor role in Saddam's visual rhetoric. After all, Saladin had never been ruler of Iraq, and other figures were deemed far more suitable for political embodiment.[53] For confrontation with the Jewish state, Nebuchadnezzar served as a sufficiently strong national metaphor.[54] Between 1980 and 1988, the political and military confrontation with Iran was paramount, and accompanied by several other appropriate memory figures, but not Saladin. In 1987, the year of the eight-hundredth anniversary of the taking of Jerusalem, Iraqi propaganda slowly put Saladin into focus and came to equate Saddam Hussein with the hero of the Crusader period.[55]

The Iraqi invasion of Kuwait (1990–91), along with territorial retaking by American and allied troops, changed the political outlook of the entire region. After 1991, adjustments of state ideology to the new political realities tended to lack a defined focus. Resources remained sparse as well.[56] A new stress on medieval Arab heritage emerged during the war, at which time Saddam tried to raise pan-Arab sympathies by firing Scud missiles toward Israel, thereby connecting his war with the Palestinian cause.[57] For the American-led invasion, the term "Crusade" became current on both sides, with different meanings. Saddam viewed Iraqi resistance against international control as part of the greater Arab struggle of liberation from the Christian "Crusaders." As a result, he instantly identified himself with Saladin.[58] The anti-Israeli theme of the victory of Hattin and the liberation of Jerusalem pictured Iraqi resistance as part of the same "Mother of all Battles" (umm al-ma'arik), the Gulf War, which he claimed to have won.[59] The Hattin theme also supported Saddam-as-Saladin as claiming leadership of the Arab world. The Iraqi stress on Saladin and Jerusalem thus functioned as an answer to similar propaganda systems instigated by Iran.[60]

The visual arts formed part of Saddam's propaganda machine. He commissioned the so-called Qasr al-Salam (The Palace of Peace) between 1995 and 1999. Four gigantic bronze busts of himself, each four meters high and mounted on low octagonal plinths, complemented the splendor of a courtyard (Fig. 3.3 and plate 9).[61] Although Saddam wears the uniform of a contemporary military commander in chief, his strange headgear seemingly contradicts modern attire. It recalls a medieval helmet, evoking the age of Saladin, but it alludes in fact to an architectural monument: the Dome of the Rock in Jerusalem.[62]

FIGURE 3.3. Three of four busts depicting Saddam Hussein with the Dome of the Rock as a helmet, Baghdad, October 20, 2005. *Photograph courtesy of the U.S. Department of Defense, Jim Gordon no. DA-SD-06-07153.*

FIGURE 3.4. Statue of Saddam Hussein as Saladin in Tikrit, July 18, 2003. *Anonymous photograph.*

In February 2001, Saddam announced the formation of "al-Quds Army," one of his many private armies, with the propagandistic aim of liberating Palestine from Israeli rule.[63] In 2001 a mural in Baghdad depicted him leading tanks into battle against the new "Crusaders," side by side with Saladin.[64] In Tikrit two identical equestrian statues were created for the top of a medieval-style domed presidential palace. The statues depicted Saddam with a drawn sword and pennants, guiding four missiles into battle—his accoutrements blurring the distinction between the medieval hero-ruler and the twenty-first-century one.[65] In an interview in March 2003, the Iraqi sculptor Abdul Jabar stated: "Saddam and Saladin are the same. Saladin fought the European invaders who came to steal Iraq's treasures. And now the U.S. is coming to steal our oil."[66]

Immediately after Saddam's fall, statues of Saladin as well as those of Saddam Hussein were pulled down and destroyed (fig. 3.4).[67] A new Saladin rhetoric emerged in Iraq with the formation of the Shiite government. On the one hand, the new regime erased names of sites and places in Baghdad. For example, a Saladin statue was renamed to commemorate a companion of 'Ali ibn Abi Talib.[68] On the other hand, the Sunni guerilla group of the Kata'ib Salah al-Din, the military wing of the Islamic Front for the Iraqi Resistance (al-Jabha al-Islamiyya lil-Muqawwima al-'Iraqiyya)—operating at least since 2004—combined sectarian violence with a modern publicity campaign against Shiites and Americans in the name of their almost pan-Islamic eponym. A new use of the Iraqi memory figure Saladin had evolved, this time put to sectarian use.[69]

Saladin and Syrian Nationalism

In Syria, the figure of Saladin draws on a different set of memories in the visual cult of rulership.[70] However, as Carole Hillenbrand has proposed, the simple equation—Saladin, conqueror of Jerusalem, congruent with Hafiz al-Asad (r. 1970–2000) in his war efforts against Israel—is not applicable.[71]

The personality cult of Hafiz al-Asad, the first president of Syria to instigate such a rhetorical apparatus, evolved slowly during the mid-1970s. By the mid-1980s, it inflated enormously due to Soviet advisers who were consulted for the public staging of al-Asad's image, which came to resemble a Soviet-style personality cult.[72] In endless permutations the image of Hafiz al-Asad—praised as "our leader for eternity [qa'iduna ila l-abad]"—occupied every public space.

State propaganda promoted al-Asad's extraordinary abilities as a pharmacist, teacher, doctor, lawyer, and so forth; the ruler more than represented the people, he was "the people."[73] In 1984 the first statue of Hafiz al-Asad was inaugurated in front of the new national library in Damascus. There, he is depicted with an open book—the embodiment of learning and erudition.[74] From 1982 on, visual and political discourses became increasingly a staged dialogue.[75] City councils, trade unions, and other groups and organizations had to display images of al-Asad while swearing a "binding covenant ['ahd]" or an "oath of allegiance [bay'a]." These monuments are found all over Syria. The neutral foil of al-Asad images—as officer, statesman, and father of the country—thereby allowed for their widespread use in oaths of allegiance by Christians, Jews, Muslims, socialists, nationalists, and others.

In posters and statues, al-Asad remained always himself and so is never dressed as a historical hero. The conflict with Israel is embodied in the images of the Tishrin War. Having several Palestinian refugee camps and Palestinian militia leaders and fighters within the country, the Asad regime refrained from committing itself too much to the Palestinian cause—by far and large avoiding, for example, a visual "Dome of the Rock" theme. In contrast to the Iraqi personality cult, moreover, al-Asad abstained from monumentality.[76] But his image was everywhere, and his secret services made him a perpetually vigilant president. Consequently, the historical theme is almost entirely absent from Syrian visual political rhetoric.[77] However, there exist exceptions to this rule, some of which contain overt references to Saladin.[78]

One of the first publically available images of Saladin in Syria was printed on a banknote series first issued in 1977 (fig. 3.5 and plate 8).[79] The image of Saladin, quite obviously copied from the late Ottoman depiction in Saladin's tomb (see fig. 3.2), was conflated with a view of Krak de Chevalier, the citadel of the Knights Hospitaller that Saladin besieged in vain in 1188. The Muslim hero is here juxtaposed with one of the famous historical landmarks in Syria without necessarily implying any specific political message.[80]

By the end of the 1980s a new Saladin rhetoric emerged, in large part inspired by the regime's effort to rewrite national history. The Baath party had pursued similar projects in 1965, between 1975 and 1977, and in 1985. In July 1987 a scholarly symposium was held in Damascus to celebrate the eight-hundredth anniversary of Saladin's victory at Hattin. Ulrike Freitag, who attended all of the sessions, concluded that the symposium was clearly intended to legitimize the regime by constructing a historical

STEFAN HEIDEMANN

FIGURE 3.5. Twenty-five-pound Syrian banknote, 1978, first issued 1977.

line between Saladin, Jamal 'Abd al-Nasir, and Hafiz al-Asad.[81] Already in the 1980s al-Asad had complemented his office with a painting of Saladin and a reference to the Battle of Hattin. In 1991 a referendum confirmed al-Asad as president; a slogan on a widely distributed poster advertised al-Asad's historical achievement: "*Min Hattin ila Tishrin.*" The slogan refers to the decisive victory of Saladin and draws a parallel to the October War of 1973, when Egypt and Syria had attacked Israel on Yom Kippur. After some initial military successes, the October war ended with the total defeat of the Arab armies and a disastrous continuing loss of the Golan Heights for Syria. Nevertheless, in the emphatic political self-praise of Egypt and Syria, the war was declared a historical victory, similar to Saladin's successes at Hattin.[82] As a result, the slogan was frequently used in Syrian propaganda until the late 1990s.[83]

The Saladin monument by the Syrian sculptor 'Abdallah al-Sayyid that stands in front of the citadel of Damascus is most likely the best-known modern monument in Syria (fig. 3.6 and plate 10).[84] The restoration of the citadel of Damascus as a national monument was begun in the middle of the 1980s, and by the end of that decade the last remaining military and police installations had been removed, the curtain walls and towers had been rebuilt, and archaeologists had begun to explore the citadel. In 1992 an equestrian statue of Saladin, made of greenish painted fiberglass,

FIGURE 3.6. Statue of Saladin in Damascus, made by 'Abdallah al-Sayyid, 1992. *Photograph by the author, August 2003.*

was installed as a complement to the citadel's gate, one hundred meters north of the entrance of the Suq al-Hamidiyya.[85] The equestrian figure is surrounded by three armed warriors.[86] Their shields depict the "eagle [al-'aqab] of Saladin," a heraldic device that is used in Syria, Egypt, Iraq, Palestine, and Yemen. The "eagle of Saladin" itself is a modern invention, as Saladin never made use of a specific blazon.[87] The horseman type is similar to Western equestrian monuments of knights, though the dramatic posture inches closer to modern plastic toys.

The Damascene monument depicts Saladin as a national hero, corresponding to the citadel behind him. The extra figures at the croup of the horse are two enchained Crusaders (fig. 3.7), representing the battle of Hattin and the loss of the Kingdom of Jerusalem. The one on the right side, with the crown at his feet, is King Guy de Lusignan (c. 1150–94), and the other figure is Reynald de Chatillon, who caused the fatal battle. Only at the base of the monument can an inscription be found, gilded since 2008, praising *"Jerusalem's Liberation"* in several languages (fig. 3.8).

STEFAN HEIDEMANN

FIGURE 3.7.
Statue of Saladin
in Damascus,
1992, with the
figures of Reynald
de Chatillon and
Guy de Lusignan.
*Photograph by the
author, November
2005.*

FIGURE 3.8.
Statue of Saladin
in Damascus,
1992, with a
detailed view of
the inscription
praising the libera-
tion of Jerusalem.
*Photograph by the
author, November
1995.*

Despite the references to Hattin and Jerusalem, this monument lacks the typical markers of the personality cult of al-Asad and of the Arab-Muslim conflict with Israel—namely the emotionally resonant standard attribute, the Dome of the Rock[88]—most likely because defeated Christian Crusaders are unsuitable as a symbol for the Zionist state. There is also no allusion to the Syrian attributes of the conflict, namely the Tishrin War or the Golan occupation. The aspect of Jerusalem—the conflict with Israel—recedes behind another useful meaning and memory: Saladin as national hero. This meaning becomes clear in the use of the monument in visual culture. The image of the Saladin monument was introduced on two-hundred-pound banknotes in 1997.[89] Its reading is specified by its adjacent image, namely the national Tomb of the Unknown Soldier (darih al-jundi al-majhul), which occupies the central register (fig. 3.9). The design of the banknote connects the memory of the national hero with the memory of recently fallen national heroes, thereby emphasizing the historical dimension of their sacrifice. Since the early 1990s Saladin has served in public rhetoric as a symbol of national unity with only a moderate religious undercurrent. Within the socialist, secular Syrian state—where conservative Islam attracts increasing attention among the populace—Saladin functions as an Islamic national symbol, without representing modern Islamist discourse per se.

Since his election in 2000, President Bashar al-Asad has receded from the excessive personality cult of his father, although his propaganda, designed by Lebanese advertising agencies, remains ubiquitous. The visual political rhetoric turned increasingly toward national and only cautiously toward Islamic themes starting in about 2005.[90] Even in the case of the Golan Heights, campaign posters follow more the aesthetics of commercial advertisements, and thus are devoid of images of military confrontation.[91] Despite this more muted rhetoric, Bashar al-Asad's firm stance in the dormant war with Israel remains a cornerstone of his political legitimization.

In Syria, Saladin rhetoric bloomed with several television series.[92] In 2005 the Australian film director Ridley Scott released a Saladin epic entitled *Kingdom of Heaven*.[93] It conveyed exactly the kind of rhetoric that would resonate in Syria. The depiction of Saladin by the popular Syrian actor Ghassan Massoud (born 1958) contributed much to the movie's extraordinary success in the Middle East, especially in Syria.[94]

On May 6, 2005, the film debuted at the same time in the United States and in Syria—a novelty in film history. At the Damascus premiere the audience celebrated the film enthusiastically.[95] 'Abd al-Nasir Hasu, a columnist for the Syrian daily *al-Thawra*, praised the film for bringing justice to the Arabs, to Islam, and to Salah al-Din (Saladin). He was surprised by the posi-

STEFAN HEIDEMANN

FIGURE 3.9. Two-hundred-pound Syrian banknote, 1997.

tive portrayal of Saladin, because he was unaware of how the Saladin figure had been romanticized in the West.[96] Ghassan Massoud explained in an interview that he found inspiration for his depiction of Saladin besides his recent reading largely in his school education and probably his consumption of the recently broadcast television series.[97] For him, Saladin "has been a role model for us since our youth."[98] The politically correct, albeit romantic, Saladin of Ridley Scott thus collided with the resonant national Saladin of Syrian political rhetoric.[99] This surprising congruence is remarkable because Saladin as memory figure was transferred to and revived in the Middle East more than 120 years earlier.

Conclusion

The current memory figure of Saladin is a product of Western and Middle Eastern imagination. In the eighteenth century, European philology had recovered the historical Saladin but also novelized and romanticized him. He became the archetype of the noble and sage Muslim enemy-hero. In the Middle East, especially in Palestine, Saladin was never completely forgotten, although in the memory of the Middle East he was superseded by Sultan Baybars, a hero who fought Crusaders and infidels. Parallel to the invention of political traditions with historical references in Europe between 1870 and 1914, the memory figure of Saladin was deemed useful in the Middle East. In the 1870s, with the modernization efforts of 'Abd al-Hamid, the Crusades and Saladin were recalled into political rhetoric. In 1878 the sultan commissioned a cenotaph for Saladin in Damascus, symbolizing Ottoman modernity and the sultan as defender of the faith. In 1898 the visit of the German kaiser Wilhelm II to the tomb of Saladin finally made the political public of the Ottoman Empire aware of the Western image of Saladin while also bolstering the political rhetoric of 'Abd al-Hamid himself. During the Mandate period Saladin was remembered in the political rhetoric against Western military imperialism in general and against Zionist expansion in particular.

At the end of the 1980s, Saladin rhetoric resurfaced in Iraq and Syria. After the Gulf War the figure of Saladin in Iraq was conflated—in a grotesque manner—with the monumental and excessive personality cult of Saddam Hussein. In a staged monologue, Saddam declared himself the incarnation of Saladin, who had resisted and emerged triumphant against "Crusaders." The combination of references to the Dome of the Rock, which marks Saladin, and the conquest of Jerusalem, attempted to represent Saddam as a hero for the Palestinian, pan-Islamic, and pan-Arab cause.

The political rhetoric in Syria was different. Starting in the mid-1970s, Syria boasted a pronounced Soviet-style personality cult centered on president Hafiz al-Asad. The cult was staged as a dialogue, with responsive oaths of allegiance. At the end of the 1980s, with the attempt of the Baath party to rewrite national history, the figure of Saladin moved into the center of national propaganda for a short time. The military achievements of al-Asad were compared with those of Saladin, "from Hattin to Tishrin," but he and Saladin were not equated in a blunt manner. The Palestinian and Islamic cause, which was always symbolized by the Dome of the Rock, was carefully avoided in Saladin images sponsored by the Syrian government. Saladin rhetoric in Syria took a distinct national turn, independent from the ubiquitous personality cult. This reading found its most visible expression in the Saladin monument of 1992 in front of the citadel in Damascus, in which Saladin is depicted as a national hero. Although today's political rhetoric of Bashar al-Asad refrains from historical allusions, Saladin has remained a resonant memory figure: the 2005 movie *Kingdom of Heaven*—with the popular Syrian actor Ghassan Massoud as its chief protagonist—transmitted exactly that image of Saladin as a national symbol. History learned through compulsory school attendance had made Saladin a resonant national memory figure, and the film promoted him as such. At the same time, Massoud's Syrian Saladin corresponds to the

STEFAN HEIDEMANN

Saladin emerging from the Western interpretation and its turn toward "political correctness."

NOTES

1. See, for example, the wooden statue of Saladin in combination with Bernard of Clairvaux (1090–1153) and the Jewish sage Rashi (1040–1105) located in Latroun Monastery, Israel, inaugurated in 2006. I am grateful to Yisca Harani for this information.

2. Mohjak, "al-Suriyyuna yarawna fi Nasri llahi Salaha l-Dini l-'asra l-haditha," posted July 2006 at Andareen.com. He reports on the Nasrallah hype in Damascus during the Lebanon War of 2006. The rhetoric ironically blanks out that Saladin fiercely suppressed Shiites.

3. The lectures are compiled in B. Lewis, *History*. For a similar approach see Silberman, *Between Past and Present*.

4. Hobsbawm, "Inventing Tradition," 1–14; and Hobsbawm, "Mass-Producing Traditions," 263–307.

5. J. Assmann, *Das kulturelle Gedächtnis,* and "Collective Memory and Cultural Identity."

6. Hobsbawm, "Mass-Producing Traditions," 263; and Wedeen, *Ambiguities of Domination,* 9–10, 14–15.

7. Hobsbawm, "Mass-Producing Traditions," 263–64; and Wedeen, *Ambiguities of Domination,* 15. For the case of Iraq see Baram, "A Case of Imported Identity," 289–290, 293.

8. In 1901 the stele with Hammurabi's code of law was discovered in Susa, Iran, by the French archaeologist Jacques Jean-Marie de Morgan (1857–1924) and the Assyriologist Jean-Vincent Scheil (1858–1940). It is now on display in the Musée du Louvre, Paris.

9. Before World War I, the Ishtar Gate of Babylon built by Nebuchadnezzar (r. ca. 605–ca. 561 BCE) was discovered by Robert Koldewey (1855–1925) and the German Oriental Society. It is now on display in the Pergamon Museum in Berlin.

10. B. Lewis, *History;* and Ende, "Kollektive Identität und Geschichte in der islamischen Welt der Gegenwart," 161.

11. Ende, "Wer ist ein Glaubensheld und wer ist ein Ketzer?" 70–94.

12. Other countries that make specific use of the memory figure Saladin are France, Egypt, Jordan, Palestine, and Israel.

13. Saladin built a memorial known as Qubbat al-Nasr (The Dome of Victory) at the site of Hattin, which soon fell into oblivion. See Kedar, "The Battle of Hattin Revisited," 190–207.

14. Riley-Smith, "Islam and the Crusades in History and Imagination, 8 November 1898–11 September 2001," 151–52, 160, supposes the almost complete oblivion of the Crusades in the Middle East after the end of the Crusades.

15. Ende, "Wer ist ein Glaubensheld und wer ist ein Ketzer?"

16. Works that devote almost twice as much space to Baybars as to Saladin include Mamluk chronicles of the fifteenth century, such as al-Maqrizi's and Ibn

Taghribirdi's histories, and Egyptian chronicles of the nineteenth century, such as al-Jabarti's (d. 1825–26) 'Aja'ib al-athar, and 'Ali Mubarak's (d. 1893) Al-Khitat al-jadida al-tawfiqiyya. Early Syrian chronicles of the thirteenth and fourteenth centuries, such as works by Ibn Wasil, al-Yunini, and Abu l-Fida', are more in the Ayyubid tradition and thus place greater emphasis on Saladin.

17. Mujir al-Din al-'Ulaymi (d. 867/1462–63), Kitab al-Uns al-jalil bi- tarikh al-Quds wal-Khalil (Cairo, 1866). Gerber, Remembering and Imagining Palestine, 61–68.

18. Ende, "Wer ist ein Glaubensheld und wer ist ein Ketzer?" and "Kollektive Identität und Geschichte in der islamischen Welt der Gegenwart"; Möhring, "Der andere Islam," 131–56, "'Saladin, der edle Heide' Mythisierung und Realität," 160–75, and Saladin, 91–104; Hillenbrand, The Crusades, 589–616, and "The Evolution of the Saladin Legend in the West," 497–510; Jubb, The Legend of Saladin in Western Literature and Historiography; Richard, "Les transformations de l'image de Saladin dans les sources occidentales," 177–87 ; Conermann, "Muslimische Ritter," 221–72; Eddé. Saladin, 570–82.

19. On the reception of The Talisman, see Lincoln, Walter Scott and Modernity, 105–108, 116–17.

20. The Scott Monument was built between 1840 and 1846. The Saladin statue was probably produced after 1870, in the second effort to fill the niches, but before 1881, when its description was published; see Colston, History of the Scott Monument, Edinburgh, 96, 102. The sculptor was Clark Stanton (1832–94). Saladin is represented with a scimitar in an effort to behead Reynald de Chatillon, who is not represented.

21. Hobsbawm, "Inventing Tradition," 1–14; see also A. Assmann, "Zur Mediengeschichte des kulturellen Gedächtnisses," 54.

22. Karpat, The Politicization of Islam.

23. Hanioğlu, A Brief History of the Late Ottoman Empire, 125–27.

24. Hobsbawm, "Inventing Tradition," 6.

25. Karpat, The Politicization of Islam, 144, 173; and Hanioğlu, A Brief History of the Late Ottoman Empire, 129. In 1899 the first comprehensive account of the Crusades in Arabic was published in Egypt; this work refers to 'Abd al-Hamid's complaint about the European Crusade (al-harb al-salibi) against the Ottoman Empire in the form of politics. See Sayyid 'Ali al-Hariri, Al-Akhbar al-saniya fi l-hurub al-salibiyya (Cairo: 1899), 2; Ende, "Wer ist ein Glaubensheld und wer ist ein Ketzer?," 81–82; and Hillenbrand, The Crusades, 592.

26. Kreiser, "Ein Freiheitsdenkmal für Istanbul," 296–314.

27. Syria's first monument in European fashion was the column constructed in Marja Square in Damascus in 1904/1905, commemorating the first telegraph line between Istanbul and Mecca; see S. Weber, "Zeugnisse kulturellen Wandels," 680, no. 419, and Damascus, 2:255–56, no. 406. For the culture of monuments in the Ottoman Empire, see also Kreiser, "War Memorials and Cemeteries in Turkey," 184.

28. Karpat, The Politicization of Islam, 229–30; and Deringil, The Well-Protected Domains, 26–35.

29. Hanioğlu, A Brief History of the Late Ottoman Empire, 142.

30. Hudson, Transforming Damascus, 17.

31. S. Weber, "Zeugnisse kulturellen Wandels," 666, no. 396, and Damascus, 1:242, 420, 2:241–42, no. 388. For the change in style in Damascus in the late nineteenth century, see S. Weber, "Ottoman Damascus of the 19th Century," 731–40.

STEFAN HEIDEMANN

32. Saladin's title *al-sultan al-ghazi* appears within the inscription on the cenotaph.

33. The first modern biography of Saladin in Turkish, written by the young Ottoman historian Namik Kemal (1844–88), was published in 1872; see Ende, "Wer ist ein Glaubensheld und wer ist ein Ketzer?" 80.

34. As late as 1326/1908 the cenotaphs of Baybars and his son were restored; see S. Weber, "Zeugnisse kulturellen Wandels," 495, no. 57, and *Damascus. Ottoman Modernity and Urban Transformation,* 2:137–38, no. 196.

35. The mythology of the Hohenstaufen was linked to the rebirth of the Holy Roman Empire of the German nation, which the Hohenzollern believed they would fulfill. Only in the second instance, this mythology was connected with the Crusades. For example, the Kyffhäuser monument in Thuringia, Germany, was built between 1890 and 1896 in the spot at which, according to folklore, the emperor Frederick would appear again to rejuvenate the empire.

36. Jaschinski, "Des Kaisers Reise in den Vorderen Orient 1898," 30–31; Hudson, *Transforming Damascus,* 107–108; and S. Weber, *Damascus,* 2:241–42, no. 388.

37. The *qasida* is reprinted in F. Ali, "Šauqi, der Fürst der Dichter," 146. Ahmad Shawqi wrote in the pan-Islamic journal *al-Mu'ayyad* about the effect of the speech: "What concerns us, the entirety of the Muslims, nine-tenths of us were without knowledge [about Saladin] until Wilhelm introduced us to him"; see Ende, "Wer ist ein Glaubensheld und wer ist ein Ketzer?" 84.

38. In August 1914 the Ottoman military owned eight airplanes, while the flight schools had another four. See Erickson, *Ordered to Die,* 228.

39. In Damascus the tombstone of the third Jaffa pilot gives the date as March 8, 1330 (1914). For the Damascus receptions of all three pilots, see al-'Azm, *Mudhakkirat Khalid al-'Azm,* 1:16–18. For the Jaffa crash see also Heikal, "Jaffa . . . As It Was," 20. An Ottoman mural in a Damascus mansion commemorated the arrival of the airplane; see S. Weber, *Damascus,* 2:451–53.

40. A monument was built at the site, east of Lake Tiberias, today eight hundred meters east of Kibbutz HaOn on the Israeli side of the Golan. It is a central obelisk with inscriptions, flanked by two eagles positioned on a globe. The tombstones provide conflicting dates for the crash. Those on the HaOn monument state that the crash occurred on 3 Rabi' II, 1332 AH (March 1, 1914) or 14 Shubat 1329 Maliyya (February 27, 1914). The monument was inaugurated in May 1914. The two tombstones in Damascus, however, give March 3, 1330 Maliyya (1914) as the date of the crash (*tarikh al-suqut*). The tombs in Damascus were first restored in 1340 (1921–22). Schools were named after the leading pilot, Fethi Beg, as was, in 1934, a town in the southern Turkish province of Muğla.

41. Kreiser, "War Memorials and Cemeteries in Turkey," 184–85.

42. Ende, "Wer ist ein Glaubensheld und wer ist ein Ketzer?" 87. Also see Najdad Azour's film *A Vision for Saladin* (2005); and 'Abd al-Nasir Hasu, "Salah al-Din al-Ayyubi shakhsiyyat al-marhala bayna shashatay al-sinima wal-tilifiziyun," *al-Thawra,* August 9, 2005, http://thawra.alwehda.gov.sy/.

43. The fifth person buried in the courtyard was Yasin al-Hashimi (1894–1937), prime minister of Iraq, who in 1936 was deposed in a coup d'état. He escaped to Syria, where he died two months later. His tombstone appears to have been made in the Asad period.

44. Among them is a play by Jurji Zaydan (1861–1914): *Salah al-Din Ayyubi.*

45. See Ende, "Wer ist ein Glaubensheld und wer ist ein Ketzer?" 80.

46. Rida, "Dhikra Salah al-Din wa-ma'rakat Hattin," 593–606; Ende, "Wer ist ein Glaubensheld und wer ist ein Ketzer?" 86; Gerber, *Remembering and Imagining Palestine,* 124–25; Matthews, *Confronting an Empire, Constructing a Nation,* 153; and Peled, "Annals of Doom," 167–68.

47. Halim, "The Signs of Saladin," 78–94; Shafik, *Arab Cinema,* 169–70, and *Popular Egyptian Cinema,* 43–44, esp. 104–107. The famous authors Naguib Mahfouz, 'Abd al-Rahman al-Sharqawi, and Yusuf al-Siba'i contributed to the screenplay.

48. Baram, "Territorial Nationalism in the Middle East," 425–29.

49. See Baram "A Case of Imported Identity"; Bengio, *Saddam's World,* 80–85; and Long, *Saddam's War of Words,* 73–80.

50. Bengio, *Saddam's World,* 165–66, 168; Davis, *Memories of State,* 151, 152, 164–69, 273.

51. Bengio, *Saddam's World,* 82.

52. On the introduction of ancient Mesopotamian and medieval Islamic names into the administrative map of Iraq, see Baram, "Territorial Nationalism in the Middle East," 425.

53. Reid, "The Postage Stamp," 86.

54. For an early reference, see Baram, "A Case of Imported Identity," 297, 305. For Saddam Hussein's pre-1991 fixation on Nebuchadnezzar, see al-Khalil, *The Monument,* 68–77.

55. Bengio, *Saddam's World,* 82–83; and Long, *Saddam's War of Words,* 76, 106–10.

56. Davis, *Memories of State,* 221–69.

57. See also Davis, "The Museum and the Politics of Social Control in Iraq," 95–96, which does not list medieval Iraq as a central focus of the Iraqi museums.

58. Bengio, *Saddam's World,* 83. The ideological context of the word "Crusade" for the Americans was the phrase "morale crusade" as an emphatic expression of the war's purpose. See Atkinson, *Crusade,* 4.

59. Davis, *Memories of the State,* 228.

60. Gruber, "Jerusalem in the Visual Propaganda of Iran," 168–97.

61. At the end of 2003 these busts were removed for smelting; see Atwood, "Looters in the Temple."

62. For an analysis of earlier, almost "vulgar" monuments, see al-Khalil, *The Monument.* Moreover, in 1998 a postage stamp series was issued on "Jerusalem Day" showing—from the right to the left, in Arabic reading order—Saddam, Saladin, and the Dome of the Rock placed above the Iraqi flag. In stamps issued in 2002 for Jerusalem Day, Saddam appeared in front of the Dome of the Rock with a suit, hat, and gun.

63. Cline, "Does Saddam Think He's a Modern-Day Saladin?"; and Woods, *The Iraqi Perspectives Report,* 48–51.

64. Appleby, "Jihad Is Not Just a Word for War." Compare a similar or identical picture in Hillenbrand, *The Crusades,* 595, plate 9.1.

65. "Shadows of Tikrit: Inside the Presidential Palace with the US Army 4th Infantry Division, Photography by PA McKee III" (site discontinued), http://www.shadowsoftikrit.com. Another unfinished bronze equestrian statue of Saddam, also referring to Saladin in its iconography, was discovered in the famous foundry on

the 'Umar Shaykh Street in Baghdad. The reason for the incomplete state of the statue, however, was the death of sculptor some years earlier. See Holmes, "Did Saddam Mimic Saladin."; and McGeough, "A Visit to a Street of Thousand Saddams."

66. McGeough, "A Visit to a Street of a Thousand Saddams." See also Issa, "Despite Oil and Greenery, Iraq Was Still Very Impoverished."

67. The statue in Tikrit was destroyed by explosives on July 18, 2003. Its metal was reused to cast the U.S. 4th Infantry Division memorial in Fort Hood, Texas (http://www.shadowsoftikrit.com).

68. A statue of Saladin, erected after the 1990–91 Gulf War, near the site of Baghdad's ancient northern gate, was renamed after the Shiite saint al-Malik al-Ashtar, a companion of 'Ali ibn Abi Talib; see Dagher, "Rewriting History in Bronze."

69. On this subject, see Ibrahim al-Marashi's contribution to this volume.

70. For the general differences between the personality cults in Iraq and Syria, see Wedeen, *Ambiguities of Domination*, esp. 28–29.

71. See Hillenbrand, *The Crusades*, 600.

72. On the origin of al-Asad's personality cult, see Wedeen, *Ambiguities of Domination*, 34–35.

73. Al-Asad came from an underprivileged religious minority of suppressed peasants, the Alawites, and transcended the boundaries of ethnic and religious loyalties in Syrian society with the help of this cult. Ibid., 39–40.

74. Ibid., 35.

75. Ibid., 20–21.

76. The oversized golden statue of al-Asad with a Bedouin *abaya* in al-Raqqa (built between 1985 and 1992, ca. 10 meters high) is a provincial exception to the national rule.

77. Exceptions are found in numerous local monuments that combine historical and touristic monuments with images of Hafiz al-Asad and his family. Most date to the 2000s. For example, at the main entrance to al-Raqqa, a monumental mural made of underglaze painted tiles shows Bashar al-Asad with a turban, referring to Harun al-Rashid, and sitting in front of the famous medieval Baghdad Gate of al-Raqqa. An identification of both rulers does bear little political significance. It is designed by local artists at the entrance of the city to express urban pride in local archaeological monuments and to praise the nation's leader.

78. The medieval fortress Saone, east of Lattakia, with the Arabic name *Qal'at Sahyun* (Citadel of Zion), was renamed *Qal'at Salah al-Din* (Citadel of Saladin) in 1957, after the Suez War and in commemoration of Saladin's seizure of the fortress in 1188. See Grandin, "Introduction to the Citadel of Salah al-Din," 142.

79. See Djaroueh, *Mawsu'at al-'umlat al-waraqiyya al-suriyya*, 474, no. SY 167, for a Syrian twenty-five-pound note.

80. The program of illustration of this series of banknotes comprises historical landmarks and, on the backs of the bills, the achievements of socialism and the state: workers, peasants, ports, dams, and the issuing national bank.

81. Freitag, "In Search of 'Political Correctness,'" 1–16, esp. 10. See also Baram, "Territorial Nationalism in the Middle East," 433–39.

82. This meaning of Saladin was conveyed in the October War Memorial. It lies on the highway Sitta Tishrin to the north, and is difficult to reach and rarely visited except by school classes, army cadets, and military detachments. The panorama

painted in the main rotunda depicts the battles of the October War. Before entering the panorama one encounters a circular hall in which Syrian victories throughout history are depicted in several paintings; one shows Saladin taking of Jerusalem. The panorama was a gift from the North Korean government. It clearly follows the visual aesthetics of Chinese/North Korean propaganda. The People's Democratic Republic of Korea also presented a matching panorama to the Egyptian government, which was inaugurated in Cairo on October 6, 1989. Most of the commemorative activities of the October War are depicted here; see Meital, "Deliberately Not Empty."

83. In 1997 these posters still were seen in Aleppo. Personal communication by Peter Wien, University of Maryland, March 15, 2006.

84. Carole Hillenbrand's supposition that Syria has no tradition of historical statues (Hillenbrand, *The Crusades,* 596) is not substantiated inasmuch as the statue of 'Adnan al-Malki (1913–55) in Muhajirin, Damascus, is historical. Also, in Aleppo's Christian quarter, numerous bronze busts from the middle decades of the twentieth century commemorate various historical personalities. Other statues or bronze busts in Damascus honor such poets as Abu'l-Ma'arri (973–1057), whose depiction is located close to the statue of al-Malki.

85. In the first decade of its existence, the material of the statue decayed considerably, with several cracks, fading paint, and rusted and bent iron swords. In 2007 the statue underwent a superficial restoration by the Governorate of Damascus. It received new, although unfitting, bright olive green paint, new swords, and gilded inscriptions. The paravent screen was sponsored by DHL Company.

86. Carole Hillenbrand interprets one of the attending figures as a Sufi, an Islamic mystic, an idea the sculptor conveyed to her; see Hillenbrand, *The Crusades,* 596–97, 600. This idea, however, was not realized. All of the figures wear armor and weaponry and are apparently Muslim warriors. In 2003 a life-size plaster model of the statue still stood in the courtyard of the citadel.

87. An article in the newspaper *al-Thawra* declared him *al-'aqab afdal anwa' al-suqur* (hawk), and distinguished the bird from the Egyptian *nisr* (eagle), which was used during the United Arab Republic, but concedes that Saladin had an *'aqab* on his banner. In the classical language, *'aqab* and *nisr* are synonymous for "eagle." On the subject, see "al-'aqab shi'ar suriya," *al-Thawra* (August 6, 2007), http://thawra .alwehda.gov.sy.

88. Occasionally Bashar al-Asad, Saladin, and the Dome of the Rock can be found together, such as in the courtyard of the handicrafts market in the Tekkiya, Damascus, above a shop entrance; information (fall 2005) courtesy of Joseph A. Green, Harvard Semitic Museum. This kind of images does not belong to the government's propaganda but to private devotion to the Palestinian cause and al-Asad.

89. Djaroueh, *Mawsu'at al-'umlat al-waraqiyya al-suriyya,* 532–533, no. SY 196. On July 24, 2010, a new series of banknotes (50, 100, 200 SP) were issued, dated 2009. These are almost devoid of any party or national propaganda, depicting famous Syrian archaeological artifacts, historical monuments, the Asad library, and the building of the issuing authority, the Central Bank. Only the statue in front of the library, showing al-Asad as a scholar, on the back of the fifty-pound note, is a reference to the civilian side of the regime. The banknotes were designed by Robert Kalina, designer of the Euro-banknotes, and printed by the Österreichische

Banknoten- und Sicherheitsdruck GmbH. (http://banknotesworld.net/News/?x= entry:entry100812-125920). I am grateful to Essam Abou Fakher, Oldenburg, for this reference.

90. Slogans such as "*Suriya Allah hamiha*" (Syria, may God protect her) could be seen in November 2007 at the entrance of the Suq al-Hamidiyya.

91. Posters depicting a marathon as a mass rally for the prisoners of war of Golan were seen August 25, 2005, in Damascus. Moreover, a dove on a Syrian flag as illuminated symbol of hope for the peaceful regaining of the mountain ridge was observed at the headquarters of the Syrian weekly *al-Jawlan* in Damascus on November 6, 2007.

92. In the early 2000s, Saladin was very present in Syrian television. Beginning in 2001, thirty episodes of the series *al-Nasir Salah al-Din al-Ayyubi*, by the Syrian director Hatim 'Ali (b. 1962) and the writer Walid Sayf, were broadcast, illustrating Saladin's life based on Arabic sources. More experimental and provocative was the series by the Syrian producer and director Najdat Ismail Anzour, broadcast also in 2001: *al-Bahth 'an Salah al-Din* (thirty episodes). It searched for the "Saladin of our time," exploring the concepts of tolerance, and of dialogue between religions and cultures before the background of contemporary Middle Eastern conflicts. In 2005 Anzour, together with the writer Hassan M. Yousef, produced an art house version of it called *Ru'ya li-Salah al-Din / A Vision for Saladin*, in which the Syrian writer and the American writer Peter Joseph are engaged in an e-mail chat about the possible role of Saladin in the contemporary problem-ridden Middle East. See Hasu, "Salah al-Din al-Ayyubi shakhsiyyat al-marhala bayna shashatay al-sinima wal-tilifiziyun."

93. For previous Arab film adaptations of the Saladin topic see Shafik, *Arab Cinema*, 169–70. On the pre-release controversy on the film see Robb, *Ridley Scott*, 144–51, esp. 149.

94. Ghassan Massoud is a renowned Syrian actor and the author of several theater plays: (http://ghassanmasoud.com). He also portrayed al-Qadi al-Fadil in the television series *al-Nasir Salah al-Din* in 2001.

95. I am grateful to Joshua Landis, who attended the premiere in Damascus, for this information. Personal communication, April 13, 2006.

96. Hasu, "Salah al-Din al-Ayyubi shakhsiyyat al-marhala bayna shashatay al-sinima wal-tilifiziyun." Although he admitted that the "West" discovered first the importance of Saladin, he considered the West's image of Saladin basically nega-tive, in light of the confrontation between Muslims and Christians, and the lost Crusades.

97. On the role of Saladin in Syrian and Arab textbooks, and the emphasis on the "Arabs" as opponents of the Crusaders instead of the "Muslims" in Syrian textbooks, see Determann, "The Crusades in Arab School Textbooks," 208, 211.

98. Interview by Roumani, "A Modern Saladin Speaks His Mind." Additional interviews with Ghassan Masoud on his role as Saladin can be found in "A Dream Role: Ghassan Massoud on Salah al-Din, Syrian Actor and Making It Big," and "Shakhsiyyat Salah al-Din," http://ghassanmasoud.com/ar/.

99. Lincoln, *Walter Scott and Modernity*, 106, asserts a "clear influence" of *The Talisman* on Ridley Scott's movie.

CHAPTER 4

"You Will (Not) Be Able to Take Your Eyes Off It!": Mass-Mediated Images and Politico-Ethical Reform in the Egyptian Islamic Revival

PATRICIA KUBALA

At the beginning of 2005, Rotana—a major album production company and multi-channel satellite television network in the Middle East owned by Saudi Prince al-Walid bin Talal—added a new channel, Rotana Cinema, to its bevy of channels for music videos, entertainment programs, concerts, and religious programming (added in 2006). The Rotana channels began to run advertisements for the new cinema channel featuring one of the company's most famous and controversial music video stars, the voluptuous Lebanese pop singer Hayfa Wahbi. Set to the music of one of Hayfa's latest hits, "Hayat Qalbi" (Life of My Heart), the ad juxtaposed scenes of such sultry film icons as Nadia Lutfi and Hind Rustum, from Egyptian cinema's golden age, with shots of Hayfa batting her eyes seductively and proclaiming, "Rotana Cinema: Mish Hati'dar Tighammid 'Aynayk!" (you will not be able to take your eyes off it!). The ad was clearly designed both to capture viewers' attention as well as to compare Hayfa's sultry performances, which many Egyptian critics and audiences find scandalous, to those of some of the most famous and beloved stars of the national cinema industry. Many Cairenes instantly began to imitate Hayfa's eye batting and to incorporate the slogan into their repertoire of pop-culture references, used to poke fun at any number of daily situations, and for months after, it still provoked laughs.

In March 2005 the news site Albawaba.com reported that students at Alexandria University had staged a protest against the spread of risqué music videos and the satellite channels that broadcast them. One sign in particular caught the reporter's eye (fig. 4.1): Rotana's name and famous green trademark drawn next to the familiar slogan, "You will not be able to take your eyes off it!" The creators of the sign had drawn large x-marks over the name "Rotana" and the word "not" (mish), thereby cleverly changing the slogan to "You will be able to take your eyes off it!" Beneath this

FIGURE 4.1. Student protestors at Alexandria University, March 2005. The sign subverts the Rotana satellite channel's well-known slogan, "You will not be able to take your eyes off it!" altering it to instead read, "You will be able to take your eyes off it!"

aptly impertinent new slogan, at the bottom of the sign, its authors identified themselves as "The Youth of the Islamic Trend" (*shabab al-tayyar al-islami*).[1]

Student protesters demonstrating against Rotana's entertainment channels were following a long line of Egyptian reformers in their public stance against the immorality of mass-mediated images. At least since the time of the prominent Al-Azhar reformer Muhammad Abduh (1849–1905), the position of the Islamic tradition toward the visual arts, and the importance of fostering such arts for the project of Islamic revival, has been the subject of much debate among Muslim reformers in Egypt. These debates have revolved not only around the issue of the morality of images and the conditions of their licit production and reception (long the subject of discussion within Islamic legal and literary discourse), but also around a whole host of distinctively modern concerns, including the role that new visual art and entertainment genres might play in cultivating cultured publics, preserving cultural identity, and advancing civilization's progress. The flourishing of new aesthetic genres and the re-configuration of old ones gave rise to new arenas for the critique of prevailing social, ethical, political, and economic conditions, as well as to questions concerning the ethics of producing and consuming such genres in new public venues, engaging with them as a form of worshipping God, and putting them to use for the work of *da'wa* (exhorting fellow Muslims to the proper practice of their religion) and religious reform.

An adequate appreciation of the importance of this question to the project of Islamic reform in Egypt would require one to address the full range of issues and arguments in these debates, their complex historical instantiations, and the salient differences among and similarities between Islamist positions and those of other nationalist reformers, as well as their resonances with discourses on the arts and mass media in both other post-colonial contexts and in the modern West. Since it is beyond the scope of this chapter to attempt such a comprehensive survey and historical analysis, here I want to focus attention on one problematic of relevance to these debates.

In a recent article, Talal Asad urges scholars of secularism, religion, and politics to inquire into "how the bodily senses are cultivated or how they take shape in a world that cannot be humanly controlled, and hence into what politics these formations make possible or difficult."[2] Taking up Asad's suggestion, this paper asks how we might think about the sensorial politics involved in demonstrations such as those against the Rotana satellite networks. This paper explores this question through an examination of Islamist critiques of and interventions into the production and circulation of music videos in Egypt over the past few years and the power attributed to the images in these videos to either foster or threaten the development of sound Muslim subjectivities and societies. Through this discussion I attempt to elucidate the centrality of practices of disciplined sight and image-making within contemporary Islamist reform projects in Egypt that seek to cultivate the politico-ethical conditions for a virtuous Islamic polity and public.

The proliferation of music television in pan-Arab satellite broadcasting in the past decade has spawned a flurry of (mostly negative) commentary on the content of music videos (known as video clips in the Arab world) among Egyptian audiences, critics, artists, and producers across a broad spectrum of intellectual positions and religious and political commitments.[3] An intriguing element of this commentary is that although the music videos and artists that are criticized are rarely political in any conventional sense, critiques of these performers and their work are not limited to their perceived aesthetic shortcomings, but frequently take on

PATRICIA KUBALA

moral and political overtones.[4] Islamist-affiliated critics in particular tend to focus their attacks on the most risqué music videos—labeled *burnu klibhat* (porno clips) or *aghani al-'ura* (songs of nakedness) by their detractors—to the extent that the genre of music videos as a whole has now become associated with these examples. While the banal lyrics, hackneyed tunes, and apolitical nature of these videos also draw criticism, pious audiences and critics tend to object most vehemently to the revealing clothes and overtly seductive dancing of the female models and singers. These sexualized representations of female entertainers, as well as the considerable outcry against them, echo the centuries-old debate in the Islamic tradition over the moral character of artists and the potentially dangerous effect of dance, music, and entertainment upon the subjectivity of the audience and the political strength and stability of the *umma* (Muslim community).[5]

The disciplining of sight as essential to sexual morality and the maintenance of social order has been, of course, a subject of recurring concern within the Islamic discursive tradition. In a series of verses on modesty and proper interactions between men and women not related through kinship or marriage, the Qur'an (*Surat al-nur,* 30–31) admonishes both male and female believers to "lower their gaze" (*yaghuddu min absarihim* and *yaghdudna min absarihinna*) when they come into contact with one another.[6] The traditions of the Prophet and the writings of medieval scholars such as Abu Hamid al-Ghazali (1058–1111) warn against the "fornication of the eye" (*zina al-ayn*) and the social-sexual discord (*fitna*) that the undisciplined gaze engenders by arousing illicit desires.[7] The proliferation of film, photography, theater, and other visual arts and media in the colonial period led to an expansion of discussions of sight and sexual morality to address the permissibility of these new images, performance venues, and aesthetic forms.[8] The pages of Muslim Brotherhood magazines, newspapers, and other publications from the 1930s and 1940s are filled with editorials warning of the detrimental effects of the immoral spectacles on display in foreign-owned cinema houses, Parisian magazines, dance halls, and theatrical performances on the *umma* (especially its youth).[9] These warnings were accompanied by calls for government officials and Al-Azhar scholars to exercise their duty as Muslims (*al-amr bil-ma'ruf wan-nahy 'an al-munkar*) and proscribe the circulation of such images in the interest of safeguarding the moral health and well being of Egyptian society. In the post-1967 era of Islamic Revival in Egypt, stars of the national media and entertainment industry were frequent targets of popular cassette sermon preachers. In the 1980s, Shaykh 'Abd al-Hamid Kishk became famous for his sermons criticizing beloved national icons of the Egyptian art and entertainment industry, including Umm Kulthum and Muhammad 'Abd al-Wahhab. Shaykh Muhammad Mitwalli al-Sha'rawi and Dr. 'Umar 'Abd al-Kafi are remembered for their role in a wave of "conversions" and retirement of film, television, dance, and music starlets in the early 1990s. 'Abd al-Kafi, for example, would advise female performers:

> I wouldn't want my sister—and you are a sister to me—or my daughter or my wife, to embrace a man in the name of art . . . or to sleep with him in the same bed, surrounded by cameras and to call this art!!, or to strip to a swimsuit on the beach with him and we say this is art!! This is not the art that God wants.[10]

To further explore the politico-ethical importance of Islamist criticisms directed against satellite music television, and their grounding in a specific ethical-sensorial regime, I turn to an analysis of a debate about music videos from the program *Qabl an Tuhasabu* (Before You Are Judged), broadcast in 2005 on Iqra', a popular pan-Arab Islamic satellite channel that is part of the Arab Radio and Television (ART) network owned by the Saudi businessman Shaykh Salih Kamil.[11] This weekly show was devoted to exploring current social issues—such as drug addiction and terminal illnesses—in a way that emphasized how they threaten the Arab-Islamic *umma* as well as the role of Islam in speaking to the problems at hand. The program and other talk shows like it can be seen as a kind of televised form of *da'wa* that complements other forms of mass media put to use by Islamist reformers, such as cassette sermons and internet sites, all of which aim to improve the moral condition of the Muslim community.[12]

In the episodes devoted to the controversy over the video clips, which were referred to on the show as *aghani al-'ura* (songs of nakedness), the show's Egyptian host, Basma Wahbi, herself a repentant former model and actress, conducted a series of taped interviews with female singers and directors, intellectuals, young people, and children in Egypt and other Arab countries.[13] The program took the position that the video clip posed a moral threat to the Islamic and Arab *umma* as a whole, and not to one particular country. However, the program also taped a debate about the issue in which a group of public figures, all of them Egyptian, discussed the controversy over the video clip in the presence of a small group of Egyptian audience members. Hence, although the debate was broadcast on a transnational satellite channel, it nevertheless reflected the specifically national tensions and concerns of its Egyptian participants.

The debate occurred on the grounds of a villa outside of Cairo, in front of the garden's swimming pool. On one side of the pool, four participants were seated—a director of video clips, a female video clip singer, and two journalists with secular-nationalist outlooks toward the video clip. On the other side—literally—of the venue sat the Islamist-identified participants—a lawyer raising a court case against the Egyptian government for broadcasting video clips on its channels, a journalist, a composer, and a sociologist. The program host Basma Wahbi sat in the middle, and beside her, on the side of the Islamist participants, sat Dr. 'Abd Allah Barakat, an Azhari-trained shaykh. Although a significant part of this debate was devoted to attempts by Wahbi and Dr. Barakat to urge the singer and director to repent and retire from making video clips, more revealing and less predictable were the points of agreement and difference between the two journalists placed on the side of "supporters" of the video clip and the "detractors" on the other side.

These secular-nationalist journalists on the side of the "supporters" were also critical of many aspects of the video clip genre, but for reasons that most of the Islamist-identified participants, as well as the members of the audience, found insufficient; in turn, these two journalists objected to certain aspects of the program's framing of the issue and the debate. The debate on the talk show *Qabl an Tuhasabu* turned into a dispute over the nature of the agreed-upon limits necessary to engage in public discussion about the video clip, with the eventual result that the two secular-nationalist journalists silently withdrew from the debate in implied protest.

Throughout the debate, numerous points of disagreement arose between the journalist Maha Matbuli and the Islamist-affiliated participants. One of the most salient concerned the perceived source of the video clip threat, with host Basma Wahbi and most of the Islamist participants and audience members regarding it as the West's latest tactic in its "clash of civilizations" campaign to destroy Muslim society, this time through the corruption of its moral foundation. Indeed, the program sometimes referred to the video clip as a "weapon of mass destruction." In contrast, Matbuli regarded the spread of the video clip as due in part to a (implied Gulf-Lebanese) conspiracy against Egyptian art. This particular point of disagreement reflected a more fundamental difference between the two journalists and the video clip artists on the one hand, and Wahbi, 'Abd Allah Barakat, and other Islamist participants and audience members on the other, over whether discussion of the video clip should revolve around the subject of art and its pedagogical role in developing society, or around the threat that the video clip and other forms of popular entertainment pose to the ability of the Arab Muslim *umma* to cultivate virtuous communities and selves. Video clip singer Hanan 'Atiyya defended her work by comparing it to the films of beloved national singer/actress icons, such as Shadya, whom she admired as a child. Barakat seized upon her comments to illustrate that the wrongdoings of previous generations of artists negatively impacted the moral character of young people such as Hanan, and he warned that artists bear an enormous responsibility (*wizr*) before God for what they present, because millions of viewers imitate them and regard them as role models.[14]

But the greatest opposition was directed at Matbuli, who throughout the debate repeatedly insisted that she had not come to the show to talk about the video clip in terms of *halal* (permissible) or *haram* (illicit), but rather in terms of good or bad art. Objections to this position came both from audience members, who responded by saying that at the end of the day, the youth need to know whether watching video clips is right or wrong, and from Islamist-affiliated participants in the debate, such as the sociologist Ahmad al-Magdub and Wahbi herself, both of whom insisted that knowledge (*al-'ilm*) cannot be separated from religion (*al-din*).

This issue of the "secularization" of knowledge revealed itself most clearly in discussions of the threat posed to the moral well-being of video clip viewers. Matbuli suggested that parents take advantage of the presence of the video clip to educate (*yurabbi*) their children as to proper sexual mores and explain why certain video clips are inappropriate from a moral point of view as well as of poor artistic quality; the proper domain of this education (*tarbiyya*), in her view, lies in the privatized realm of the home. A person raised in this proper way, under the tutelage of the family, would only be affected by the negative aspects of the video clip, especially its sexually explicit images, if he or she were in some way mentally unbalanced, and would learn not to even want to watch such clips because of their low artistic standards. For Matbuli, then, watching or not watching certain kinds of video clips was a private matter of individual choice that in large part depended on the cultural awareness and moral upbringing that one might have.

Audience participants, as well as Barakat, strongly disagreed with Matbuli's position. Throughout the program, the shaykh reminded viewers and participants in the debate that it is the duty of every Muslim to attempt to prevent any kind of wrongdoing within the community before it takes place; anyone who shirks this duty also shares in the sin and will be punished for it. Because the video clip incites people to engage in illicit activities, it cannot be considered a matter of personal choice, as Matbuli would have it, but poses a threat to the well-being of the community as a whole. To illustrate this position, the shaykh told a long story about the prophet Moses nearly losing a battle due to the fornication of one soldier in his army; the wrongdoing of one member of the community almost resulted in the corruption of the whole. During this sermon, Matbuli left the debate without explanation and did not return, which the host Wahbi interpreted as an objection to the shaykh's, and the program's, insistence that any discussion of the video clip must be grounded in the authority of the Qur'an and the Prophet's *sunna* (sayings and doings).

After Matbuli's departure, the participants continued to debate her position. Audience members objected to Matbuli's presumption of the effectiveness of the family in inculcating proper sexual mores if public spaces were not simultaneously realized as a moral domain conducive to the upholding of the values taught within the private realm of the family. One might be able to avoid exposing one's child to the video clip channels in one's own home, an audience member conceded, but what happens when a child goes to school and meets less well-brought-up peers?

Another young man in the audience pointed out that the nature of television makes it extremely difficult to resist the temptation of watching video clip channels. He might be viewing a religious program, then flip the channel once the program ended, only to find inappropriate images that might lead his mind astray. This youth objected to Matbuli's formulation of a sound (*salim*) person as one who is able to regulate his or her sexual desires through a proper education and upbringing and hence be able to ignore the video clip channels or watch without being affected. By contrast, for this young man, as well as for Barakat, the healthy (male) Muslim subject is one whose natural and normal desires would be ignited by the lurid images of the video clip; anyone who watches the videos and remains unmoved must suffer from *al-burud al-jinsi* (sexual frigidity). Although morally strong persons, the young man continued, would be able, as the Rotana protesters mentioned at the beginning of this paper insist, to close their eyes to these temptations, it is not right to subject young people to these inner conflicts. Thus, in the view shared by Islamist participants and audience members on the program, it is the duty of every Muslim to practice and propagate morality not only in the home, but also to actively engage with political and social institutions to insist that they exercise the legal authority necessary to create a social domain that upholds Islamic values. One cannot merely, as Matbuli claimed, demand of well-brought-up viewers that they change the channel or turn off the television if they are personally offended or tempted. The broadcasting of sexually explicit images on the airwaves incites normal, healthy people to look at them and encourages them to act on these temptations; hence, they pose a threat to the moral well-being of the community as a whole and must be removed from public view.

Thus, what is at stake in this debate for the Islamist participants is not merely the question of good or bad art, a subject on which the program also takes a position by promoting an example of desirable artistic expression for the Muslim community to produce and consume—a song performed by school children and Wahbi about the plight of the Palestinians. In his seminal work on the practices of cassette sermon listening, ethical self-fashioning, and deliberative public debate that grounds the practice of da'wa in contemporary Egypt, Charles Hirschkind argues that Islamist criticism of mainstream Egyptian, Arab, and Western entertainment "is not simply a case of political criticisms being reflected onto the safer realm of culture."[15] Rather, pious preachers and audiences argue that most popular music, television, and film productions "engage and direct the senses toward moral dispositions—states of the soul—incompatible with the virtues on which an Islamic society rests."[16] The points of disagreement between the Islamist and secular-nationalist participants in the program revolved around the role of Islam in determining public morality and the kind of ethical and political subject that needed to be cultivated in order to protect against the perceived dangers of the video clip. These issues were debated by both Maha Matbuli and her Islamist opponents on the program in terms of the kind of scopic discipline—training the eye (one's own or those of others) to turn away from certain images, to perceive some images as "art" and others as a corruption of it, and to neutralize the potential harm of an image through a particular kind of ethical estrangement—necessary to sustain certain kinds of persons, politics, and publics. As Talal Asad observes, "whether deliberately cultivated or unintended, the senses are central to the public life in which people participate, to the ways they promote, resist, submit, or remain indifferent to the forces of political life, not because of what they mean, but because of what they do."[17] And as the above discussion makes clear, secular-nationalist as well as Islamist moral and political commitments are grounded in particular kinds of sensory regimes.[18]

This example of the debate over a video clip from the program *Qabl an Tuhasabu* also illustrates that the spread of private transnational Arab satellite television in the past decade is enabling the emergence of new spaces for the practice of Islamic *da'wa* in the mass media and generating renewed reflections on the role of media and entertainment in fostering social reform. Many of the new generation of satellite television preachers are actively encouraging young Muslims to create Islamic-appropriate alternatives to mainstream secular popular media culture and entertainment.[19]

PATRICIA KUBALA

The best-known of these is the Egyptian *da'iya* (preacher) 'Amr Khalid, who devoted an entire episode to the subject of culture and the arts on his popular show *Sunna' al-haya* (Lifemakers). Each week on this program, Khalid discussed a different aspect of social reform and encouraged viewers to participate in development projects to help bring about a *nahda* (revival or renaissance) in their local communities, countries, and ultimately, the Islamic *umma* as a whole. In an episode entitled "Culture, Art, Media . . . and Making Life," Khalid called upon "gifted young artists to participate with us in the project of *Sunna' al-haya,* and in the project of progress. There is no rise or progress without you and your addition; your role, help and support is very important for the implementation of this progress."[20] In the course of the program, Khalid urged talented young Muslims not to retire from or avoid participating in the arts, but instead to put their God-given talents to use in the service of their communities. The following extended excerpt from the program is quite significant, for it explicitly draws upon the Islamic discursive tradition in order to assign the image a privileged role in the transmission of the Prophet's teachings:

> I will tell you an important Hadith in which you will see a very unusual scene. It was narrated, "One day while we were sitting with the Messenger of Allah there appeared before us a man whose clothes were exceedingly white and whose hair was exceedingly black; no signs of journeying were to be seen on him and none of us knew him (everybody was looking, the picture is very important. At present, media is the equivalent of picture). He walked up and sat down by the Prophet, he didn't greet any of the companions. Resting his knees against his and placing the palms of his hands on his thighs (on the Prophet's thighs! What a strange posture), he said, 'O Muhammad (he did not say Messenger of Allah), tell me about Islam.' The Messenger of Allah said, 'Islam is to testify that there is no god but Allah (until the end of the phrase).' He said, 'You have spoken rightly,' and we were amazed at him asking him and saying that he had spoken rightly. He said, 'Then tell me about *Iman*' [faith]. He said, 'It is to believe in Allah . . .' He said, 'You have spoken rightly.' He said, 'Then tell me about *Ihsan*' [good works]. The Prophet replied. Then He said, 'You have spoken rightly.' Then he took himself off and did not greet us." What would you do if you were with them? You would have been surprised by what you had just witnessed. The Prophet could have ascended the *minbar* [an elevated platform used for preaching] and simply told the companions what Islam and faith signify. The

man left and all the companions were astonished. The Prophet asked the companions, "Do you know who the questioner was?" They said, "Allah and His Messenger know best." He said, "He was Jibril [the angel Gabriel], who came to you to teach you your religion." Jibril came in human form. Why do you think all this happened? It was to engrave the meaning in their hearts. Did you see how Islam believed that a picture is more effective than speech? This is one of the most fundamental Hadiths in our religion. Is there any stronger evidence than that?[21]

What is so striking about this excerpt from Khalid's program is his claim that "Islam believed that a picture is more effective than speech." Western scholarship on religion and media tends to treat Christianity as a "visual" religion and Islam as an "auditory" one.[22] Likewise, studies of the Islamic *da'wa* movement in twentieth-century Egypt have for the most part focused on its deployment of ethical speech as a means to engender in listeners ("to engrave in their hearts") the affective dispositions (such as fear of God, modesty, humility, etc.) that ground virtuous conduct and guide them toward correct modes of being and acting.[23]

Yet we cannot regard Khalid's claim as entirely new. Indeed, since the late nineteenth century, in addition to their attacks on the perceived immorality of secular-national media and entertainment, Muslim reformers in Egypt have also deliberated on the usefulness of ocular-centric Western-imported media technologies and aesthetic forms for the *umma* and debated the question of what kind of art and entertainment it is that God wants. While some reformers have regarded these media technologies and aesthetic forms as morally suspect in and of themselves, others called for their appropriation in ways that would benefit the development of Muslim society.[24]

Following a trip to Italy at the turn of the century, Muhammad Abduh praised Europe's image-based methods (museum collections, illustrated dictionaries and encyclopedias) for transmitting and preserving knowledge, and called upon Muslims to emulate these practices in order to strengthen and preserve the language, literature, and sciences of the *umma*.[25] Rashid Rida (1865–1935), Abduh's student and editor of the journal *al-Manar*, responded to transnational readers' concerns over such issues as listening to the radio, the capture and display of photographic images, and the participation of Muslim women in theatrical performances. On this latter point, Rida accepted in theory that a Muslim woman may act so long as she appears without make-up, properly dressed, and in socially uplifting roles that do not violate Islamic prohibitions or encourage any kind of indecency; in practice, however, the reigning immoral conditions of the theater effectively ban her from participation.[26]

An attitude similar to Rida's toward European-introduced arts seems to have informed major figures of the Muslim Brotherhood. As cited earlier in this paper, Hasan al-Banna', the movement's founder, called for the banning of gambling clubs, establishments that served alcohol, dance halls, and other aspects of European life in flagrant violation of Islamic norms that flourished under British colonial rule, and he called for the strict regulation of films and plays. He recognized, however, the central role that modern mass media could play in disseminating the Brothers' message of social reform:

> [T]he methods of propaganda [al-da'wa] today are not those of yesterday. The propaganda of yesterday consisted of a verbal message given out in a speech or at a meeting, or one written in a tract or letter. Today, it consists of publications, magazines, newspapers, articles, plays, films, and radio broadcasting. All these have made it easy to influence the minds of all mankind, women as well as men, in their homes, places of business, factories, and fields. Therefore it has become necessary that propagandists [du'ah] perfect all these means so that their efforts may yield the desired results.[27]

In this vein, the Brotherhood's magazines and newspapers published poems, short stories, and plays, and featured columns on cinema and art in their pages, and during al-Banna'''s lifetime the organization created a traveling theater troupe devoted to the production of Islamic drama.[28] In his manifesto on Islamic art (Manhaj al-fann al-islami [Program for Islamic Art]) in the early 1960s, Muhammad Qutb (brother of Sayyid Qutb) held up the Irish playwright John Synge's Riders to the Sea as paradigmatic of the pious aesthetic principles outlined in the book, but he expressed his view of contemporary Egyptian cinema in terms reminiscent of Rida's judgment of the theater in his day:

> As for cinema, in my estimation it is the last art that might enter into the purview of Islamic art, not because cinema in itself is forbidden, but because it is, in its present vulgar, pornographic, and dissolute state, very far from an Islamic atmosphere. However, it, like all other art, can become Islamic if it follows the principles of Islamic art that we have clarified in previous chapters of the book.[29]

From the 1970s through the 1990s in Egypt, small-scale experiments in Islamic literature and drama of the kind called for by Qutb took place, most notably by the prominent Egyptian writer and television personality Mustafa Mahmoud.[30] Other tracts outlining an Islamic vision for the arts followed Qutb's, including Muhammad 'Imara's *al-Islam wal-Funun al-Jamila* (Islam and the Beaux-Arts) and Yusuf al-Qaradawi's *al-Islam wal-Fann* (Islam and Art).[31]

But as was discussed earlier in the paper, the post-1967 era of Islamic Revival in Egypt was marked by calls in the 1980s and 1990s from prominent preachers for entertainers, particularly female stars, to repent and retire. Although most of these "repentant" artists left the entertainment industry, a few, such as Huda Sultan, donned the veil but continued to work under conditions acceptable to their new sense of religiosity. These artists overwhelmingly attributed their retirement to their newfound piety, but an additional reason might perhaps have been the unavailability of suitable work. The Egyptian Radio-Television Union for many years refused to allow veiled female broadcasters to appear on its channels, and Egyptian films and serials shown on state television channels tend to marginalize or satirize Islamist characters.[32] But since the late 1990s, many "repentant" performers and media personalities have followed the path of Huda Sultan.

The advent of transnational satellite television broadcasting in the Arab world in the late 1990s has been accompanied by an explosion in private, commercial television productions with Islamic themes, and the growth of religious satellite television programming in the last decade has provided numerous opportunities for formally retired male and female media personalities to utilize their talents, this time appearing in Islamic-appropriate dress as preachers, hosts of talk show programs, or actors in television serials with suitably pious roles.

In the Egyptian cinematic industry, a growing number of filmmakers, actors, and actresses, veiled and unveiled, refuse to visually portray sexually explicit scenes, appear in immodest clothing, or depict immoral characters. The new regime of morally disciplined representations in the "clean cinema" trend, as Egyptian critics have dubbed it, marks a shift in the post-1967 Islamic Revival toward regarding the entertainment industry as an arena for refashioning religio-ethical norms, particularly ones surrounding the female body and sexuality. In this extremely politicized site of social reform, as Karim Tartoussieh notes in a perceptive analysis of clean cinema, "[t]he sinfulness of art—a discourse that was prevalent in the 1980s and resulted in many female actors renouncing their artistic careers and veiling—is replaced by a different discourse that is amicable to popular culture as an arena of social purity and morality."[33] This alternative discourse of *al-fann al-hadif* (purposeful art) stresses the responsibility of the artist to serve as a model of moral decency and to convey socially constructive messages in his or her work.

In the genre of music television, the phenomenal success in the Arab world of British singer-composer Sami Yusuf's first album and video, *al-Mu'allim* (The Teacher, referring to the Prophet Muhammad), started a trend among Egyptian and Arab pop singers, as if once it were proven that a market did indeed exist for Islamic pop music, others were inspired by (or more cynically, perhaps, decided to capitalize on) his success. More and more "family-values" style music videos appeared on music satellite channels in 2005, as well as music videos with explicitly Islamic themes; these are broadcast not only during the month of Ramadan and around the time of other major religious holidays, but also throughout the year. In late December of 2008, the first pan-Arab satellite channel devoted entirely to Islamic-appropriate music videos and entertainment programs began transmission on satellites in Europe and the Middle East. Called 4Shbab (For Youth) and created by Ahmad Abu Hayba, an Egyptian producer who has worked closely with the preacher 'Amr Khalid, the channel advertises itself as "Islam's Own MTV." Speaking at an English-language press conference in Cairo in March 2009, Abu Hayba explained that the channel sought to present an image of a proper Islamic lifestyle and that with the launch of the channel, "for the first time, Islam is speaking with pictures, not with big words." The slogan (rendered in Egyptian dialect) for the channel is "4shbab hanitghayyar [for youth we will change]," and an English-language press release for the channel's launch outlined its mission:

> Mainstream pop videos are bombarded with lewd imagery that blatantly contradicts the values of most people in the Middle East. It is precisely this phenomenon that led to the launch of 4Shbab, competing for the hearts and minds of young Muslims all over the world and proving once and for all that it [Islam] can embrace the technologies of the 21st century.[34]

The rhetoric of this press release suggests that we cannot understand the *da'wa* movement's investment in mass-mediated visual aesthetics as a crucial site of social and ethical reform in recent years without considering the current geopolitical moment in which "competing for the hearts and minds of young Muslims all over the world" is hardly on the agenda of Islamist groups alone. For it is not only in the rhetoric of such preachers as 'Amr Khalid and producers as Ahmad Abu Hayba that we encounter the notion that a picture may be more effective than speech, and the Islamist participants on the 2005 program *Qabl an Tuhasabu* were fully aware of the political-rhetorical force reaped by naming the music video a "weapon of mass destruction."

To return to the example of Rotana with which I began, to appreciate the full irony of the student protesters' subversive reversal of the Rotana slogan, it is necessary to take into account that the channel's financer, Prince al-Walid bin Talal, has acknowledged that his involvement in pan-Arab media production is not merely a financial enterprise, but also a means to counteract the dominance of religious conservatives in the region and protect its youth from dangerous interpretations of Islam that lead to religious extremism.[35] The prince is not alone in the view that mass-mediated entertainment programming counters the effects of religiosity gone astray, for promoting leisure practices for youth such as sports, cinema, and theater as alternatives to mosque-based activities,[36] and supporting television serials and films that warn the public of the dangers of Islamist groups[37] have been central to the post-Sadat Egyptian state's campaign to curb the influence of Islamist reformers. Additionally, of course, the Western media has long equated Islamic "extremism" with iconoclasm (the Taliban destruction of the Bamiyan Buddhas, for example), artistic censorship (the Rushdie affair), and a general phobia of modern media technologies. Hence it must follow, as the *New York Times* reported in a recent article entitled "A New Role for Iraqi Militants: Patrons of the Arts," that a turn toward the arts among Islamist groups is a turn away from extremism and toward moderation.[38] The rhetorical effect of terms such as "moderation" and "extremism" consists precisely in their ambiguity and obscures the relationships between sensory practices, politico-ethical subjectivity, and public political commitments that this paper has tried to elucidate.

As Jessica Winegar has recently argued, we ought to be wary of discourses that celebrate Middle Eastern and Islamic art as transcending cultural and political differences and "building bridges among humanity" because such suggestions tend to reproduce the same orientalist, clash-of-civilizations arguments that underpin and are used to justify the war on terror as well as more "diplomatic" U.S. government interventions (such as the Muslim World Outreach program) in the politics of the Middle East. In her analysis of the ways "art" and "humanity" are invested with emotional energy in post–9/11 Middle Eastern and Islamic exhibitions in the United States, Winegar asks: "Can the emphasis on art as evidence of humanity really erase stereotypes of Middle Eastern Muslims as un-human destructive terrorists, or does this framing depend on these stereotypes for its own definition and execution?"[39] She notes an "overriding emphasis" in the manner in which these exhibitions are curated and marketed "on art as a means for Middle Easterners to critique their contemporary gender relations and religion (seen as related), and to liberate themselves from certain, presumably oppressive, aspects of both. Moreover, there is an unprecedented concentration on religion (Islam) as a problematic site in need of either erasure or significant civilizing."[40]

Winegar's article reminds us of the geopolitical implications of the kinds of questions that this paper (and the volume as a whole) seeks to pose. An inquiry into the sensorial politics that structure Islamist critiques of and interventions into the production of mass-mediated images in contemporary Egypt must ask not only how particular modes of disciplining and educating the senses enable a certain ethics of public responsibility and political engagement, but also what kinds of political conditions sustain, make intelligible, or close off the possibility of the cultivation of such practices and their consequent relevance to public life. For such are the stakes involved in asserting that "you will (not) being able to take your eyes off it."

NOTES

1. *Al Bawaba,* "Protests against Seductive Music Videos Erupt in Egypt."

2. Asad, "Thinking about Religion, Belief, and Politics," 54.

3. The number of channels devoted to broadcasting music videos has increased steadily over the past decade and exceeded fifty by 2006. See Sakr, *Arab Television Today,* 122. Access to the free-to-air channels depends on the size of one's satellite dish; additionally, subscription-only packages include additional music video channels and many more variety channels, both private and government run, broadcast music videos some of the time. For further discussion of the satellite music television industry, refer to Sakr, *Arab Television Today;* and Kraidy and Khalil, *Arab Television Industries.*

4. See Frishkopf, *Music and Media in the Arab World,* for a range of critical and historical perspectives on the music video clip and the controversy surrounding it in Egypt and the Arab world.

5. See van Nieuwkerk, *"A Trade Like Any Other";* Shehadi, *Philosophies of Music in Medieval Islam;* K. Nelson, *The Art of Reciting the Qur'an;* and al-Faruqi, "Music, Musicians, and Muslim Law," 3–36.

6. It is beyond the scope of this chapter to adequately address the question of gender and the gaze as it has been treated within the Islamic discursive tradition as well as by contemporary Western theorists of the image. Both traditions emphasize the sexual pleasure often evoked by the gaze and wrestle with the mesmerizing power that images may exercise over their beholders—what W. J. T. Mitchell terms "the Medusa effect" (*What Do Pictures Want?* 36). The classical texts of the medieval Islamic literary canon are replete with tales of the beguiling and socially disruptive effect of the sight of beautiful females on male onlookers—and beautiful males on

female onlookers. (For an interesting treatment of this point in connection with the illustrated manuscript tradition and the work of the twelfth-century poet Nizami, see Soucek, "Nizami on Painters and Painting," 9–21.)

In the materials produced by modern Islamist reformers in Egypt on the dangers of mass-mediated visual culture, the detrimental effects of seductive female images on male viewers' piety and well-being are an issue of pervasive concern. Female viewers are also described as negatively influenced by these images of seductive females, and female performers frequently are chastised for corrupting their young and impressionable Muslim sisters (see the analysis of the televised debate over music videos later in this essay for further discussion of this point).

The susceptibility of female viewers to tempting images of male performers is also a matter of controversy and concern, as witnessed recently by condemnations of Arabic satellite television broadcasts of the Turkish television series *Nur,* whose handsome and romantic male lead was blamed for disrupting marriages across the Arab world. See Buccianti, "Turkish Soap Operas in the Arab World."

7. Al-Ghazali, *Ihya' 'Ulum al-Din,* vol. 3, 128.

8. Cook, *Commanding Right and Forbidding Wrong in Islamic Thought,* contains a useful summary of late-nineteenth- and early-twentieth-century deliberations on these new media and aesthetic forms. See the collected *fatwas* of Rashid Rida for specific examples of rulings on photography and motion pictures (volume 2 *fatwas* 249 and 280; volume 3 *fatwas* 396 and 439; volume 4 *fatwa* 547); theater (volume 2 *fatwa* 210; volume 3 *fatwa* 418; volume 4 *fatwa* 504 and 548); and the burgeoning magazine and advertising industries (volume 3 *fatwa* 314). Rida, *Fatawa al-imam Muhammad Rashid Rida.*

9. Hasan al-Banna"s tract "Toward the Light" (in Wendell's *Five Tracts of Hasan al-Banna')* lists a number of leisure and entertainment sites in need of pious supervision and censorial reform. For a representative critique of the immoral state of prevailing notions of "art" and its attendant aesthetic forms in 1940s Cairo, see the editorial entitled "Art" in the November 20, 1943, edition of the magazine *al-Ikhwan al-Muslimun* (Abd al-Badi', "Al-Fann," 6). An anonymous editorial published in the same magazine a few years later targets a particular company—Jawzy Film—à la the Rotana protesters with whom I began this paper ("Sharikat Jawzy Film," 11).

10. Cited in Abu-Lughod, *Dramas of Nationhood,* 243. For a further discussion of the conversions of performers, see Abu-Lughod, "Movie Stars and Islamic Moralism in Egypt," 53–67; Shafik, "Prostitute for a Good Reason," 711–25; Tartoussieh, "Pious Stardom," 30–43; van Nieuwkerk, "From Repentance to Pious Performance," 54–55; and van Nieuwkerk, "'Repentant' Artists in Egypt," 169–96.

11. One of the first Arab satellite television channels devoted to religious programming, Iqra' promotes itself as a family-values oriented channel with a variety of program formats (religious lessons, talk shows, Islamic dramas) and an extensive range of content that seeks to address all aspects of being a Muslim in the modern world. The channel features an impressive array of programs hosted by celebrated personalities, including formally trained religious scholars, popular charismatic preachers, and "repentant" former singers and actresses. See Sakr, *Arab Television Today;* Kraidy and Khalil, *Arab Television Industries;* and Moll, "Islamic Televangelism," for further discussions of Iqra' and the emergence of religious channels as a niche market within the Arab satellite television industry.

PATRICIA KUBALA

12. See Moll, "Islamic Televangelism," for an excellent discussion of new modes of tele-visual Islamic preaching and new forms of Islamic media production as technologies of pious self-cultivation.

13. The Egyptian press in 2008 reported that Basma Wahbi had taken off the veil and "retired" from religious television production.

14. Shadya in fact was among the performers who retired and donned the veil in the early 1990s.

15. Hirschkind, *The Ethical Soundscape,* 127.

16. Ibid.

17. Asad, "Thinking about Religion, Belief, and Politics," 53.

18. While I have hoped to explicate in the above example the relevance of particular configurations of scopic discipline for understanding the debates over music video clips in contemporary Egypt, it is not my intention to argue that "Islamist" and "secular" ethical-sensory regimes, forms of reasoning, aesthetic practices, and moral ends are completely distinct. While I cannot adequately address this question here, I point the reader to fruitful discussions of the issue in Moll, "Islamic Televangelism"; Winegar, "Purposeful Art between Television Preachers and the State," 28–29; and Hirschkind, *The Ethical Soundscape,* esp. chaps. 2 and 5. These authors point to a variety of ways in which the terms "secular-nationalist" and "Islamist" are inadequate to describe the complicated network of sensory histories, civilizational discourses, aesthetic conventions, modes of public debate, and flows of capital that undergird religious media production practices and discourses about the arts and entertainment in modern Egypt.

19. For further discussion of this point, see Winegar, "Purposeful Art"; and Moll, "Islamic Televangelism."

20. Khalid, "Culture, Art, Media . . . and Making Life." The Arabic recordings of these lectures are posted on 'Amr Khalid's website, http://www.amrkhaled.net, along with translations into English and several other languages.

21. Ibid.

22. See Moll, "Islamic Televangelism," on this point.

23. Hirschkind, *The Ethical Soundscape;* and Mahmood, *The Politics of Piety.* To date there is a dearth of studies that foreground the ways in which different sensory regimes—particularly the visual and the auditory—correspond with one another in the *da'wa* movement. One site of productive departure for thinking about this question is Hirschkind's study of homiletics and ethical listening practices in modern Egypt, in which he argues that as cinema, theater, television, and other mass-mediated images come to dominate the sensory and aesthetic experience of audiences, preachers increasingly deploy rhetorical techniques that evoke the visuals and performance conventions of these aesthetic forms in their sermons (Hirschkind, *The Ethical Soundscape,* chap. 5). See also Moll, "Islamic Televangelism," for a discussion of the visual and the auditory in Islamic televangelism in Egypt.

24. For an interesting example of debates over aesthetic form, see the discussion of nineteenth- and early-twentieth-century deliberations over theater in Talima, *Hasan al-Banna' wa-tajribat al-fann.*

25. Abduh, *Al-A'mal al-kamila lil-Imam Muhammad 'Abduh,* 2:202–203.

26. Rida, *Fatawa al-imam Muhammad Rashid Rida,* 4:1420.

27. Al-Banna', *Five Tracts of Hasan al-Banna'*, 46. In this passage, translator Charles Wendell chooses the word "propaganda" as the translation of the Arabic *al-da'wa* and "propagandists" for *du'ah*. The terms "preaching" and "preachers" perhaps more accurately reflect al-Banna''s intent. For further discussion of the importance of *da'wa* to modern Islamic reform projects in Egypt see Hirschkind, *The Ethical Soundscape;* and Mahmood, *The Politics of Piety.*

28. R. Mitchell, *The Society of the Muslim Brothers,* 292–93. See Talima, *Hasan al-Banna' wa-tajribat al-fann,* for an extended discussion of the Muslim Brotherhood's artistic projects under the leadership of Hasan al-Banna'.

29. Qutb, *Manhaj al-Fann al-Islami,* 203.

30. For further discussion of Mahmoud's literary projects see Malti-Douglas, *Medicines of the Soul.*

31. Al-Qaradawi, *Al-Islam wal-Fann;* and 'Imara, *Al-Islam wal-Funun al-Jamila.*

32. See Abu-Lughod, "Finding a Place for Islam," 493–513; Abu-Lughod, *Dramas of Nationhood;* Armbrust, "Islamists in Egyptian Cinema," 922–31; and Khatib, "Nationalism and Otherness," 63–80.

33. Tartoussieh, "Pious Stardom," 41.

34. I thank Lillie Gordon for providing me with a copy of the press release and her field notes from the channel's press conference held at the Sofitel Gezira Hotel, Cairo, on March 5, 2009.

35. Sakr, *Arab Television Today,* 123, 155.

36. Hirschkind, *The Ethical Soundscape.*

37. See Abu-Lughod, "Finding a Place for Islam"; Abu-Lughod, *Dramas of Nationhood;* Armbrust, "Islamists in Egyptian Cinema"; and Khatib, "Nationalism and Otherness."

38. Myers, "A New Role for Iraqi Militants."

39. Winegar, "The Humanity Game," 677.

40. Ibid., 660–61.

PART 2

Islamist Iconographies

The Muslim "Crying Boy" in Turkey: Aestheticization and Politicization of Suffering in Islamic Imagination

ÖZLEM SAVAŞ

A group of paintings known as Crying Boys—attributed to Italian painter Bruno Amadio (1911–81), also known as Bragolin—gained widespread popularity in many parts of the world in the 1980s. Portraying the tearful faces of children, these works have inspired various popular cultural practices, including the establishment of fan clubs and the telling of urban legends devoted to the subjects' "curse."[1] In the 1970s and 1980s one of these paintings became especially popular in Turkey (fig. 5.1 and plate 11). Initially, Crying Boy was in vogue in the private realm, displayed in many working- and middle-class homes—reproductions even served as a salient wedding gift. The face of Crying Boy later appeared in public spaces, including shops and coffeehouses, as well as in rear windows of long-distance buses and trucks; the striking image also was reproduced on postcards, paintings, and posters sold by street vendors. With tears in his eyes, Crying Boy used to gaze at people everywhere, from homes to cafés to highways.

At the same time, Crying Boy emerged in a specifically Islamic context with his appearance on the cover of the first issue of the magazine *Sızıntı*, in 1979. The editorial text, written by one of the leading figures of political Islam in Turkey, opened with a proclamation to the child: "we took this road for you." Since that time, this picture has become part of the Islamic visual vocabulary in Turkey. This article explores the place and power of Crying Boy in Islamic political imagination and visual culture in Turkey, from the 1980s to the present day.

An image's meaning is not inherent but emerges from a complex social relationship that involves its producers and viewers. Images acquire multiple meanings when they are viewed, interpreted, and appropriated into various social, cultural, and historical contexts.[2] As noted by W. J. T. Mitchell, they attain social lives when they are viewed in diverse ages and places.[3] Christopher Pinney proposes thinking of images as containing their own contexts, which precede any specific temporal or geographic context.[4] He criticizes the scholarly view of objects and images that considers them

FIGURE 5.1. Crying Boy picture popular in Turkey during the 1970s and 1980s.

empty spaces to be invested with meanings by other forces—culture and history, for example. He argues that their qualities are merely reduced to "biographies" and "social lives." Therefore, Pinney suggests, "it may be more appropriate to envisage images and objects as densely compressed performances unfolding in unpredictable ways and characterized by what (from the perspective of an aspirant context) look like disjunctions."[5]

The manner in which Christopher Pinney regards images—as having a complex identity that unfolds in various ways as they pass through the paths of different narratives and imaginations—offers a useful theoretical framework for addressing the circulation of Crying Boy in Turkey. This article explores Crying Boy's path through a particular Islamic imagination in Turkey and demonstrates the ways in which a visual image originating in Europe unfolds its identity in an Islamic context. It is important to note, however, that Crying Boy can never be considered solely an Islamic image in Turkey. In other words, the Islamic imagination can never fully "possess" this image. Indeed, the appropriation of Crying Boy into an Islamic

ÖZLEM SAVAŞ

context has remained widely unknown by many. Neither can the secular and the religious appropriations of Crying Boy be regarded as incompatible or opposed to each other. Rather, the tearful face of an innocent child unfolded itself in a variety of cultural contexts simultaneously, as viewers strove to explain the reason for the subject's tears.

Exploring the dialogue between a picture and its beholder, W. J. T. Mitchell suggests that pictures "speak to" us, as "they present, not just a surface, but a *face* that faces the beholder."[6] As it is almost impossible to pay no attention to the face of a tearful child who directs his gaze at the viewer, Crying Boy transfixes its viewers and invites them into a dialogue by requiring them to discover the reason for boy's tears. The lack of any clue in the picture about why the child is crying opens a wide range of possibilities of who or what provoked the tears. As the subject's pain can be explained by a variety of reasons, the Crying Boy picture can be interpreted in various ways.

This article seeks to explain the tears of the Crying Boy as reproduced on the cover of the first issue of *Sızıntı* and to explore the dialogue between Islamic imaginations in Turkey and the tearful face of an innocent child. First, I will address the position of the Crying Boy picture in popular culture and national imaginations in Turkey. Next, I will explore the meaning and value of the Crying Boy who appears on the cover of *Sızıntı*, analyzing the conjunction of this image and the caption directed to him and locating this image within a particular Islamic imagination that relies on tears and childhood innocence. Finally, I will discuss the power of Crying Boy in today's political Islam in Turkey, where the image's narrative is based on the discourse and ideology of undeserved suffering.

Crying Children in Turkish Popular Culture

During the 1970s and 1980s, Crying Boy pictures were viewed, possessed, and valued in Turkey for many reasons. Some valued the Crying Boy picture only for its popularity; some displayed it on the wall of the living room because it was a wedding gift. Others cherished it for the beautiful face of the child: with his Western appearance—his blond hair and blue eyes—Crying Boy was a candidate for the most beautiful child in Turkey. Pregnant women would contemplate this image while hoping for a beautiful child—who, however, would not cry much. Some mothers used Crying Boy as a means of disciplining their children, warning them that he cries because he misbehaved and was punished. Long-distance bus drivers pinned the picture to the rear window of their buses in order to warn other drivers: "Do not drive fast; you may leave behind orphans." Today, Crying Boy is no longer fashionable (except in Islamic contexts); instead, it is often satirized. In one cartoon, for example, Crying Boy is weeping because of cutting onions during long hours of work in a restaurant. Fenerbahçe soccer fans created a version of the Crying Boy picture, in which the child wears a Galatasaray uniform as he cries in defeat. In a television sitcom, a Crying Boy picture completes the kitschy decoration of the living room of a character who is of rural origins and struggling for upward social mobility in a ritzy Istanbul neighborhood.[7]

All of these individual uses of Crying Boy seek to explain his tears. Yet, as several critics who examine the life of Crying Boy in Turkey observe, viewers' reactions to his tears are complex and varied. For Murat Belge, Crying Boy evokes the deep feeling of guilt in Turkish society toward its children.[8] Other scholars note that Crying Boy stirs in Turkish society a collective unconscious tinted with feelings of misery, repression, isolation, and resentment at having been treated unjustly. For Necmi Erdoğan, Crying Boy provokes distress, suffering, and oppression deep inside and serves as a "surface on which memory of past defeats, speechlessness and oppressions were registered."[9] Likewise, for Nurdan Gürbilek, Crying Boy is crying for the maltreatment with which he copes despite his innocence, just as an "innocent" Turkish society cries for the same reason. She sees in the tearful face of Crying Boy a reflection that society perceives itself not as a guilty adult but as a devastated and heartbroken child. Rather than positioning themselves as cruel antagonists of the child, viewers identify with him by feeling downtrodden and victimized. In other words, the image's beholders contemplate their own sorrows in the innocent face of Crying Boy.[10]

It is important to note that Crying Boy is only one of many images of innocent-yet-suffering children that dominated Turkish popular culture in the 1970s. The value of the Crying Boy image can only be grasped by considering its inherent references to other images and texts on childhood suffering. For example, a familiar character of popular films in the 1960s and early 1970s is a lonely, suffering child, usually an orphan, who struggles to survive in a big city but bears the affliction with great dignity.[11] The child character—often named Ömercik, Sezercik, or Ayşecik[12]—has to struggle with pain and evil, which he or she does not deserve to experience at such an early age. Similarly, the main character of popular novels by Kemalettin Tuğcu, which were widely read in the 1970s, is a miserable, poor, often orphaned child whose happy childhood was interrupted by trauma or disaster.[13] However, these well-behaved and brave children, often boys, withstand all of the harm and ultimately rescue not only themselves but also their families from a world of brutality. Sometimes they even save those who mistreated them.[14]

Gürbilek argues that through these multiplied images of the innocent and suffering child who emerges triumphant, Turkish society can objectify its pain and achieve national honor out of deprivation. Yet, she notes, Crying Boy could become a metaphor of a collective social suffering as long as the pain could be divorced from its accompanying negative emotions; that is, as long as pain could be depicted in the image of a child who is suffering yet dignified. Despite misery and orphanhood, these children—with their blond, well-combed hair, blue eyes, clean clothes, and sunny faces—appear purified from moral contamination and devoid of the feelings of revenge and violence that tend to be outcomes of pain.[15] Gürbilek characterizes Crying Boy as follows:

> Indeed, this face tells us not the suffering, but being exposed to suffering though not deserving it. This child stands for being persecuted despite being innocent, being punished despite being guiltless, being victimized by an unjust act. . . . The suffering child also symbolizes resistance for those who behold him. More than an irrecoverable feeling of terror experienced at an early age, an intense desperation, or a frightening revenge, which emerges sooner or later, he points to a dignity saved despite everything. He is hurt deep inside, scarred at an early age, but despite this (or perhaps because of this) he does not break down; he resists the world that treats him badly. . . . Suffering experienced at an early age in a brutal world now appears in front of us as the source of dignity, virtue, and goodness.[16]

In sum, Crying Boy has usually been perceived as an innocent child who is suffering because of some guilty others and has generated powerful national discourses in a society that perceives itself as sinless yet suffering. Fethi Açıkel regards such pain-centered psychologies and political discourses as the most significant ideological articulation of the Turkish Right.[17] As mentioned previously, Crying Boy pictures were not merely put to religious use; rather, they were popular images in nonreligious social narratives about undeserved suffering. Moreover, in Islamic imagination, the tears of Crying Boy can unfold in another context of interpretation, which is based on the merit of crying in the manner of God in order to seek and establish a better world order.

Crying Boy in Islamic Imagination

The Crying Boy picture first appeared in an Islamic context with its inclusion on the cover of the inaugural issue of *Sızıntı* in 1979 (fig. 5.2 and plate 12).[18] *Sızıntı* is described as "the monthly magazine of *ilim* [science] and culture,"[19] published by the "community of Fethullah Gülen," which is the most influential among the many Nurcu movements that are based on the writings of Said Nursi (1878–1960).[20] The Gülen movement, as M. Hakan Yavuz notes, has been the most significant Islamic social and political movement in Turkey, because it reframes nation, state, and identity within an Islamic framework. The movement promotes a religious-national vision of Turkey and a Turkish-Islamic identity in order to build a country that can retrieve its historical power and leadership in the Turkish and wider Islamic world by appropriating its Ottoman past. It aims to "bring 'God' back into life, institutions and the intellect."[21] The movement has tried to achieve legitimacy from the Turkish state by presenting itself as a "soft" and "moderate" form of Islam; it also seeks to attain worldwide influence through its emphasis on brotherhood, tolerance, reconciliation, and peace.[22]

Although the group initially avoided political activity, the Gülen movement assumed a conservative-nationalist position in the 1970s as a response to the polarization of Turkey into competing left and right ideologies, and particularly to the rise of the left. During this period, rather than engaging actively in politics, the movement focused on the market, educational institutions, and media, through its groups of followers and by establishing its own institutions.[23] The Gülen community attributes a particular significance to media and owns various publishing houses and broadcasting companies.[24] Fethullah Gülen himself disseminates his ideas through a wide range of media, including videotapes, television, the internet, books, and essays in magazines. He is a columnist in *Sızıntı,* and his essays are often republished in the newspaper *Zaman,* itself owned by the Gülen community.

Yavuz considers the publication of *Sızıntı* in 1979 as "the major leap of Gülen's movement," the goal of which is "to give a Muslim orientation to a new generation of Turks to help them to cope with, benefit from, and if necessary resist the process of modernity."[25] The Crying Boy that appeared on the cover of the first issue of *Sızıntı* has become a pervasive symbol of the magazine and of the Gülen movement, whose visual imagery rests first and foremost on the iconography of weeping. The Crying Boy on the cover of *Sızıntı* is accompanied by two texts. The first is a line of poetry, entitled

ŞUBAT 1979
SAYI: 1
YIL : 1

FIGURE 5.2. Crying Boy on the cover of *Sızıntı*, February 1979.

"Uyan" (Wake Up) and written by Mehmet Akif Ersoy, one of the acclaimed poets of the Islamic movement in Turkey.[26] The poem reads: "Say, you do not have compassion for your *nefs* [soul]; have you no compassion for your child?" The second text reflects the editorial for the first issue, written by Gülen under a pseudonym. Titled "To Stop This Pain, Child," his essay addresses Crying Boy directly:

> We took this road for you. In order to share your pains, to stop your suffering, to gratify your heart and soul. Do not be offended; we could not come on time to help you. Although I wanted to give voice to your song, by adding a melody from your song to my own cry, your mourning devastated me; your grief magnified in my eyes; I felt a deep sadness. . . . Who did deem you worthy of this? You were living in a safe country. You had a warm heart and

home. . . . Then, you arrived at this brutal garden. However, this was beyond your power. You could not find anyone who knows you. You were wretched. You were alone. You were deserted. Yesterday gave birth to today and today is laying uncertain, cloudy tomorrows. You are at the parting of the ways. Now let me be your hero within this disaster. I will use my plectrum for you, make your soul hear my cry. I will put my guilty head under your feet like a pavement stone, since I could not come to help you when necessary in this storm and fire. Let me apologize to you in the name of all guilty people: Forgive those who . . . caused your misery by contaminating your soul with brutality.[27]

The juxtaposition of the Crying Boy picture and the editorial text that addresses him epitomizes the conventional division of labor in image–text relations, which is described by W. J. T. Mitchell as "the straightforward discursive or narrative suturing of the verbal and visual."[28] That is, the speech directed at Crying Boy narrates, designates, and explains the meaning of and reason for his tears, and the Crying Boy image illustrates, exemplifies, and reinforces Gülen's words. Such a combination of image and words, Mitchell suggests, forms a "visible language," which is intended "to make us see."[29] What is it, then, that this image/text in the first issue of Sızıntı wants to make us see? How is the tearful and innocent face of Crying Boy anchored by Gülen's speech in the particular Islamic discourse of Sızıntı?

The current editor-in-chief of Sızıntı, Sedat Şentarhanacı, explains the first use of the picture in an Islamic context as linked to the historically specific circumstances in which the magazine was launched:

> This picture was used on the cover to further the aims of founding Sızıntı in 1979. Back then, the youth were in dreadful circumstances due to the political situation in the country. The youth were crying. They were crying because of the loss of moral and religious values. Sızıntı was founded with the aim of regaining these values. It was founded with saying the motto "To stop this pain, child." Sızıntı was against both the left and the right movements of that period. The former was glorifying communism and the latter was glorifying nationalism. Sızıntı was founded in order to vive the decaying belief in God. For example, the theory of evolution was gaining enormous popularity. Sızıntı is against it. It wanted to highlight the miracle of creation, based on science, in order to give the youth the values they need. Crying Boy stands for the crying youth of that time. Since then, this picture has become

sort of nostalgic for us. It has become the symbol of *Sızıntı*. We still employ this picture in our meetings, booklets, advertisements, and so on. Besides, Crying Boy is still valid for today's youth. The decay in the belief in God is always a threat for the youth.[30]

The original essay addressed to Crying Boy can be read in relation to the objectives of *Sızıntı* expressed by its current editor. Those words—directed at the youth of Turkey in the late 1970s, and accompanied by the image of Crying Boy—refer to the battle between left-wing and right-wing youth groups in Turkey, which led to the military coup on September 12, 1980. Just as Crying Boy is innocent but suffering, the Turkish youth is presented as innocent yet lured into committing violent acts: they were deprived of moral and religious values because of outside factors. However, unlike so many tearful children of Turkish popular culture, who survived without any moral degeneration and rescued themselves and others through virtue and dignity, the crying youth of the late 1970s had been contaminated by evil and needed a savior. In this case, salvation is no doubt Islam, or a return to Islam—a return promised by the Gülen movement and its monthly publication, *Sızıntı*.

Yet, the place and power of the Crying Boy picture in the Islamic imagination in Turkey extends beyond such a historically specific message. It is necessary to consider both the tearful face of a child gazing at viewers from the cover of *Sızıntı* and the speech directed at him in the editorial text within the larger context of Islam and contemporary Islamic political discourse in Turkey. Since its first appearance in an Islamic framework in 1979, the Crying Boy picture has been employed in many Islamic contexts. For example, in 2001 the Fazilet (Virtue) party, an Islamic political party, used Crying Boy on posters for its conference on corruption and poverty. Today, the Crying Boy picture is distributed free of charge as postcards by Islamic bookshops during the month of Ramadan.

However, Crying Boy cannot be isolated as a single picture and phenomenon. Its meaning and power arise from the persistent flow of images of crying that dominate today's Islamic visual culture in Turkey. Various photographs, illustrations, and drawings of pain and tears, mostly of children, circulate through a wide range of Islamic media, from television to print media to the internet. For example, a recurrent category in Islamic websites devoted to religious information and Islamic way of life is "crying child pictures" or "crying children."[31] Visitors to Islamic websites exchange photographs and drawings of the tearful faces of children, including the Crying Boy picture. These pictures are sometimes listed alongside categories such as "prayer," "life of the Prophet," "hajj," and "*tesettür*" (Islamic dress codes); sometimes they appear as a subcategory of "religious pictures," alongside others such as "Ka'ba pictures" and "mosque pictures." Certainly, current international politics play a significant role in the multitude of images of crying children in an Islamic context: some of the pictures of crying children exchanged on Islamic websites are images of destitute children in Iraq and Afghanistan, and on the cover of its March 2009 issue *Sızıntı* depicted a child's tearful face looming above a war scene in the foreground (fig. 5.3). Empathy with the pain of these children implies an Islamic solidarity against external oppression, particularly against the United States. For example, on an Islamic website, a child's tearful face is accompanied by the following words (fig. 5.4):

> He is a child who keeps the heaven in his closed eyes, whose forehead is caressed by the Prophet at tired nights. . . . His black eyes look at our eyes at every moment during his painful life. Constructing a mirror, he starts crying inside us. And, we carry a crying child in our heart. His name is: Palestine; his name is: Iraq, his name is: Afghanistan, his name is: . . . [32]

In short, the iconography of tears and childhood suffering forms a persistent and powerful visual language within an Islamic framework. The Gülen movement especially is characterized by the imagery of weeping; *Sızıntı* contains many photographs, drawings, and illustrations of tears and crying, mostly of children, which present, clarify, and reinforce its Islamic discourses. As Mitchell argues, a verbal representation "may refer to an object, describe it, invoke it, but it can never bring its visual presence before us in the way pictures do."[33] The Crying Boy picture, as well as other images of crying that illustrate articles in *Sızıntı,* endow this particular Islamic imagination with a lively and vital presence.

Tears and Childhood in Islamic Imagination

In order to understand Islamic discourses on the crying child, it is necessary to locate concepts of childhood and suffering within an Islamic context in general, and the Gülen movement in particular. The Gülen movement attributes a particular significance to the meaning and value of tears. Gülen is indeed known as the "crying hodja," because he cries while delivering sermons and speeches; his listeners accompany him in tears and voices of mourning. Tears, suffering, anguish, sorrow, grief, mourning, groaning, and crying seem to form the most significant themes addressed

FIGURE 5.3. Cover of *Sızıntı*, March 2009.

FIGURE 5.4. The image of a crying child, placed in the context of war on an Islamic website. The caption states: "I grew my hopes in tearful eyes and in prickly nightmares." From http://islam.seviyorum.gen.tr (accessed September 7, 2009; site discontinued).

in Gülen's essays published in *Sızıntı* and elsewhere, as well as by other *Sızıntı* columnists.

Gülen's essay "Bence Tam Ağlama Mevsimi" (I think, It Is Just the Time for Crying), first published in *Yağmur* in 2002 and republished in *Sızıntı* in 2005 and 2009, explores the prominent position attributed to tears in an Islamic context. For Gülen, tears are the expression of sorrow, joy, and compassion felt in the manner of God.[34] He differentiates crying for God from "ordinary crying," which is simply the result of the sensual and spiritual nature of humans. As crying for God is the "groans of love felt towards Him," other forms of crying that do not come from the heart are disrespectful to these tears.[35] Tears coming from the heart are equated with keeping one's self in the way of God because "grief and crying are the usual disposition of the friends of God, and weeping for God day and night is the most direct way of approaching God." In this essay, Gülen gives examples of tears shed by such prophets as Adam, Noah, Jacob, and Muhammad, and cites the Qur'an on the value of crying and its warnings to those who spend their lives solely in joy and laughter.[36]

In this religious context, crying is not only a way of approaching God, but also a means of achieving a better world. Gülen considers the *mü'min* (Muslim believer) as one who "weeps to prevent the world from groaning

ÖZLEM SAVAŞ

PLATE 1. Mural of Muhammad's ascension, located at the intersection of Modarres and Motahhari Avenues, Tehran, Iran, 2008. *Author's photograph, 2010.*

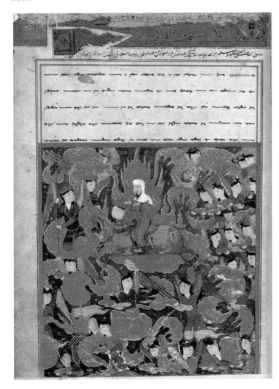

PLATE 2. Muhammad ascends through the skies on his flying steed, Buraq, *Mi'rajnama* (Book of Ascension), Herat, modern-day Afghanistan, 1436–37. *Bibliothèque nationale de France, Paris, Suppl. Turc 190, folio 5r.*

PLATE 3. Muhammad as a young boy among the stars and planets, postcard purchased in a supermarket, Tehran, Iran. *Author's photograph, 2004.*

PLATE 4. The Prophet Muhammad, depicted with a moon-shaped face, ascends to the skies on Buraq's back. Painting by Muhammad ʿAli Baniasadi included in the children's book *Aftab-i Afrinash (Sun of Creation)* written by Babak Niktalab and Afsaneh Shaʿbannejad (Tehran: Kanun-i Parvarash-i Fikri-i Kudakan va Nujavanan, 1386/2006), 46.

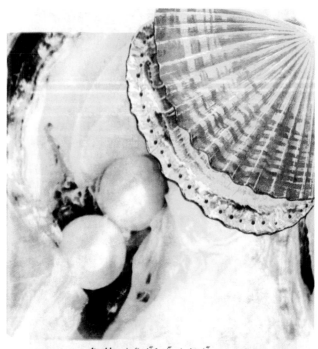

آیا زن ایده‌آل قرآن کَمَثَلِ اللُّؤْلُؤ مَکْنُون (مروارید پوشیده در صدف |
یا جواهرات بدلی که در هر جا بدون پوشش به چشم می‌خورند؟

کدام‌یک باارزشترند؟

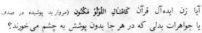

ABOVE AND FACING:
PLATES 5–6. Two illustrated pages from Ruhollah Khomeini's
treatise. The caption on the right page reads: "Which one is
more valuable? A pearl in a shell or what is deemed an ideal
woman as described by the Qur'an? Or cheap jewelry that can
be found everywhere?" The image on the left page is provided
with another caption posing further rhetorical questions:
"Which one is more decent and appealing? A house with
covered [curtained] windows? Or a veil-less and curtain-less
home?" Khomeini, *Imam Khomeini's New Risaleh*, 2:46–47.

کدام سنگینترند؟

آیا خانۀ با پرده سنگینتر و جالبتر است یا خانۀ بی پرده و بی حجاب؟

PLATE 7. Portrait of Saladin in the tomb of Saladin, Damascus, presumably ca. 1878. *Photograph by the author, November 2007.*

PLATE 8. Twenty-five-pound Syrian banknote, 1978, first issued 1977.

PLATE 9. Three of four busts depicting Saddam Hussein with the Dome of the Rock as a helmet, Baghdad, October 20, 2005. *Photograph courtesy of the U.S. Department of Defense, Jim Gordon no. DA-SD-06-07153.*

PLATE 10. Statue of Saladin in Damascus, made by 'Abdallah al-Sayyid, 1992. *Photograph by the author, August 2003.*

PLATE 11. Crying Boy picture popular in Turkey during the 1970s and 1980s.

PLATE 12. Crying Boy on the cover of *Sızıntı*, February 1979.

PLATE 13. *Ramazan Sevinci,* written by Betül Ertekin, illustrated by Gülan Gürkan Çizim Atölyesi, 2005, 19.

PLATE 14. *Dua Etmeyi Biliyorum,* written by Çiğdem Özmen, illustrated by Ahmet Keskin, 2008, 10, 11.

PLATE 15. Small poster of Muqtada al-Sadr. *Purchased by author, Basra, 2004.*

PLATE 16. Key chain. *Purchased by the author, Basra, 2004.*

PLATE 17. Surrealistic Mural. Tehran, Jomhuri Avenue, Courtyard of the Najmiye Hospital. ©Ulrich Marzolph, 2008.

PLATE 18. Mural of a green countryside with doves. Tehran, Meidan-e Fatemi. ©Ulrich Marzolph, 2009.

PLATE 19. Mural of Hosein
Fahmide. Tehran, Enqelab
Avenue, old version.
©*Ulrich Marzolph, 2004.*

PLATE 20. Mural of Hosein Fahmide. Tehran, Enqelab Avenue,
new version. ©*Ulrich Marzolph, 2009.*

ABOVE:
PLATE 21. Ramiz Gökçe (1900–1953), The Turkish Alphabet leaves the Arabic Alphabet in the dust, *Cumhuriyet,* November 30, 1928, Atatürk Kitaplığı, Istanbul.

LEFT:
PLATE 22. İbrahim Özdabak (b. 1957), *Untitled,* www.ibrahimozdabak.com, February 19, 2009.

and makes his tears turn into a river flowing into the heaven to prevent others from crying."[37] For Gülen, a lack of tears indicates the unawareness, heartlessness, conscienceless, and absence of compassion that make today's world a harsh and ungodly place. Therefore, his call for crying argues for the value of tears to the well-being of the world:

> It has been so long that our prayer rugs have been dry; for years, our ears have been longing for cries of the heart. . . . With this heedlessness, it must be very difficult to walk towards the future, to survive. . . . In these circumstances, the only thing we need is sorrow tears that will purify our soil across several centuries.[38]

As crying implies one's effort toward, or wish for, making the world more livable, people who cry from the heart are considered to be committing themselves to the well-being of others. In Gülen's essays, as well as in other contributions in Sızıntı, a person who cries—whether for God, for the world, or for others—often is symbolized by a candle, illuminating the world as it diminishes. Gülen presents himself as, and is perceived as, one who cries for the wellbeing of others and of the world. The value of Gülen's tears is also discussed in other contributions to Sızıntı. For example, Arvasi relates his experience of listening to a tape recording by Gülen:

> It is as if tears of hatip [preacher] are coming down to my heart and I am being touched as they come down to my heart. It is as if life is flowing into my heart that is at the threshold of death. While he is crying, I say, "the one whose eyes from which life flows, cry, cry because your tears are the lively water of dead hearts!," and I cry.[39]

Crying Boy is the preeminent visual symbol of the Gülen movement, which mythologizes crying and promotes imagery underpinned, first and foremost, by tears. The movement's identification with, or sympathy toward, Crying Boy implies a belief in crying in the manner of God and for the well-being of the world. It also serves as a proof of one's consciousness, love, compassion, innocence, purity, and longing for a better world. As the preoccupation of Islamic visual cultures with children—and particularly with crying children—reveals, the suffering child symbolizes the suffering of the innocent in a brutal world.

As Sander suggests, religious traditions express a child's innocence through the image of a relationship between God and humans, in which God is the father and humans are children. Therefore, in almost all religious mythologies, "the image of the child is used to represent innocence, humility, purity, wonder, receptivity, freshness, non-calculation, simplicity,

the absence of narrow ambitions and purpose, and other similar characteristics that are normally considered more or less indispensable for a
close relation to the transcendent."[40] Furthermore, unlike the prevailing
Christian view of children as born already contaminated with sin, Islam
considers the child to be "born as a good Muslim, free of sin, pure at heart
and with an innate disposition to follow . . . the 'straight path' according
to God."[41] Indeed, in Islam a child who dies before the age of a religious
education is saved.[42]

In the Islamic context of *Sızıntı*, as well, the child is represented as
innocent, pure, uncontaminated with evil and hate, and often as suffering due to the cruelty of a world that used to be a heavenly place but has
become merciless. Indeed, a child is born as a heavenly creature, with a
heart and soul that naturally follow the way of God, but the brutal world
and humans contaminate him or her with evil. For example, Dikmen's
poem "Masum Çocuk" (Innocent Child), published in *Sızıntı* in 1996, states:

> With tears in your eyes, "hold my hands," you were saying:
> "Tell me, can you understand my sorrow?
> Men are cruel. . . .
> My small world has collapsed in this brutality.
>
> . . .
>
> On the one hand, they gave me many playthings.
> On the other, they caused me to forget the Creator. . . ."
> Innocent child, why did they contaminate your stainless world?
>
> . . .
>
> Those who blindly burned you are aware of nothing.
> We are desperate; our hands are tied.
> If God says "God never dashes the hopes,"
> The new sun will rise as promised.[43]

To this particular Islamic imagination, an individual's identification
with a weeping child serves as proof of innocence before God and of pain
and suffering in a world brutalized by others. For the value attributed to
tears, good Muslims, innocent but suffering, cry not only because of their
pain but also for that of others, even for those who are guilty. These believers are aware of the suffering that takes place in a brutal and harsh world,
and they silently cry for the well-being of the entire world, with consciousness and compassion in their hearts. To put it simply, just as Crying Boy
is innocent but made to weep by others, those who see themselves in his
tearful face imagine and present themselves as crying because of the bru-

ÖZLEM SAVAŞ

tality of the world, bearing no responsibility for its causes. The guilty is the other. And, in such a context, regardless of the artist's intention, the Crying Boy picture occupies a powerful position in political Islam. The image of the tearful boy represents the innocent and blameless, the downtrodden, tyrannized, repressed, suffering subject at the center of discourses found in political Islam. By metonymy, Crying Boy refers to all imagery of suffering and its aestheticization in the political Islamic imagination in Turkey.

The Aestheticization of Suffering in Political Islam

Max Weber argues that common to all "religions of salvation" is a tendency to envisage the world as the locus of undeserved suffering, regardless of "whether the suffering actually existed or was a constant threat, whether it was external or internal."[44] Prophets of all three Abrahamic traditions are indeed seen as wretched, oppressed, victimized, and suffering subjects themselves. The Qur'an often refers to the cruelty, injustice, and oppression that Muhammad and other prophets faced. Their childhood years are narrated in the contexts of orphanhood, innocence, and repression. Moses was abandoned to the river in a basket; Jesus was born without a biological father; Muhammad's father died before he was born, and his mother died when he was a child. The description of prophets in orphanhood, desolation, misery, and innocence plays a significant role in their mythologies.[45]

The narrative of undeserved suffering is central not only to the religious mythology of Islam, but also to the Turkish-Islamic political imagination. Fethi Açıkel describes the psychology and discourse of the celebrated suffering, downtrodden, and wronged subject as "holy *mazlumluk.*"[46] He considers this character central to Turkish Islam and its political claims. The holy *mazlumluk* is not an anticapitalist or antimodern discourse, but rather a political project that is articulated in the context of modern economic and social structures. Constructed as a response to the harshness of the belated capitalization and fast-paced modernization of Turkish society, this ideology of suffering involves a variety of discursive formations, from the glorification of pre-capitalist values to anti-cosmopolitanism, from nostalgic historical narratives to individual feelings of suffering, and from nationalism to political Islam.[47]

For Açıkel, the discourse of holy *mazlumluk* is the desire and search for power. In the ideology of *mazlumluk,* individual feelings and expressions of suffering are transferred to an ambivalent political discourse—expressing a need and demand for limitless compassion and affection on the one hand, and a desire for power and revenge on the other. Indeed, the Prophet Muhammad's emigration from Mecca to Medina in 622 CE should be considered the beginning of political Islam, as it is the first moment of transformation from a discourse of *mazlumluk* to a discourse of power. The ideology of *mazlumluk* has great potential to be elevated to a revenge-seeking political project, as it involves a need for avenging the unjust treatment of "guilty others."[48]

The value attributed to tears in the Gülen movement stretches beyond one's inner crying for God and demonstrates the ways in which this Islamic political imagination operates within the ideology of *mazlumluk*. The aestheticization and politicization of suffering, which are best objectified in the tearful face of Crying Boy, seem to be the primary power of this movement. The Muslim Crying Boy "speaks to" those who cry because of the brutality of the world and for its well-being, withstanding the pain with great dignity in the way of God, though being mistreated, wronged, and downtrodden. In his essay entitled "Garipler" (Wretched Ones), Gülen defines *garip* (most likely referring to himself) as the one who commits himself to the well-being of others but is nevertheless dismissed, imprisoned, and exiled by those to whom he devotes himself. *Garip* is always suffering because of the decaying values of his society, but resists the brutality and threat he faces. He also never fears or gives up; most importantly, he never feels offended, especially "when he sees that the sparks that he disseminated to the soul of his nation are spreading all over the country"[49] (fig. 5.5). Thus, the celebration of suffering as such calls not only for resisting pain with dignity in the way of God but also for action to achieve an ideal world. On the emotional and tearful preaching style of Gülen, Yavuz states:

> His emotional preaching stirs up the inner feelings of Muslims and imbues his messages with feelings of love and pain. He targets people's hearts more than their reason, and this appeal to feelings helps him to mobilize and transform Muslims. Gülen's style is effective and forms a powerful emotional bond between him and his followers. He not only stirs up the emotions of the faithful but also exhorts them to self-sacrifice and activism. Thus he arms his followers with an emotional map of action to translate their heart-guided conclusions into action.[50]

The celebration and politicization of tears in the political Islamic imagination, embodied in the face of Crying Boy, serves to attract *mazlum* subjects, not simply by appealing to their hearts and emotions, but also, more powerfully, by articulating all forms of suffering with the pain felt in

FIGURE 5.5. Cover of *Sızıntı*, April 2001.

the way of God. As Açıkel argues, holy *mazlumluk* is an ideology that reorganizes relationships of collective subjects with reality. It leads the suffering subject to collaborate with others whom he or she believes share the same destiny against brutality and to identify with other examples of *mazlumluk*. In such an ideological framework, the suffering of Muhammad and the first Muslims in Mecca, the hardship experienced during the downfall of the Ottoman Empire, and cultural alienation during the modernization period can be associated with one another and articulated into the same political discourse.[51] Or, the childhood pains of the Prophet and the poverty of children whose fathers are unemployed can be projected onto the tearful face of Crying Boy at one and the same time. All forms of suffering, regardless of their reasons and contexts, can be translated into a discourse of suffering in the way of God.

Islamic popular culture in Turkey often addresses and reworks socioeconomic problems, such as suffering from poverty, migration from a village to a large city, transformations in the family, and so on, by associating them with Islamic ideas of suffering. For example, pain aestheticized through a discourse of *mazlumluk* is central to the themes of Islamic films such as *Bize Nasıl Kıydınız?* (How Did You Harm Us?), by Emine Şenlikoğlu, and Islamic-arabesque novels that have become widespread since the 1980s, such as *Minyeli Abdullah* (Abdullah from Minye) and *Derdimi Seviyorum* (I Appreciate My Grief). Based on a romanticized vision of the past, these texts attempt to bridge the problems of modernization and capitalism with the aestheticized pains of the *mazlum* subject of Islam.[52]

Articulating various forms of suffering in and through a political Islamic discourse is characteristic to most Turkish Islamic movements. For example, according to Fulya Atacan's study, Kaplan Grubu, a radical Turkish Islamic organization that was established in Germany and predominantly targets Turkish emigrants in Western Europe, exemplifies the ways in which diverse forms of suffering can be addressed and reworked by political Islamic discourses. Atacan argues that the organization imposes a sacred meaning on the difficulties of migration and displacement, of which the most significant is social exclusion, by convincing its followers that they were chosen as "Islam *mücahidi*" (fighter for Islam) in a non-Muslim setting. Thus, not only is their pain converted into a positive goal; their real social position, "the second-class Turkish worker," is transformed into a highly honorable social position.[53]

The success of employing politicized, Islamicized pain to attract masses can be observed within the current politics in Turkey. It is widely argued that Islam has been reconstructed by those who are at the margins, who mostly inhabit rural towns or the peripheries of large cities and seek an alternative to secular Westernization.[54] For example, the dramatic increase in votes for the Islamic Refah (Welfare) Party in the 1991 elections is explained by the group's success in appealing to the urban poor,[55] who have mostly migrated from rural areas and struggle to survive in a large city, and to small business owners, who have recently migrated from rural towns and attempt upward social mobility in the city.[56] The Refah Party managed to attract a large group of people who suffer from socio-economic problems and cultural alienation and to unite them under a shared Islamic identity, addressing misery, poverty, and pain. In its political campaign for the 1991 elections, the Refah Party employed the slogan "justice order" and used in its posters the pained faces of suffering people: a man who is facing bankruptcy due to high interest rates, a suffering prostitute, a little girl crying because her father has been fired from his job. Those images of suffering point to a new strategy employed by the Refah Party to attract not only its supporters, but also those suffering in the peripheries of large cities.[57]

It is important to note, however, that political Islam in Turkey can no longer be described as a peripheral identity supported solely by people at the margins. The Islamic way of life has witnessed the arrival of an Islamic middle class and even of "Islamist Yuppies,"[58] and the subsequent emergence of Islamic public sites of consumption and leisure, such as Islamic cafes, hotels, fashion shows, entertainment industries, and so on.[59] These new experiences seem to create a new Islamic understanding of the worldly life that can no longer privilege the ideology of *mazlumluk*.[60] Yet, far from vanishing, the ideology of *mazlumluk* continues to be attractive to the urban poor and maintains its power in constituting one of the core Islamic subjectivities in Turkey. For example, AKP (Justice and Development Party), the current government party in Turkey, seems to use a similar strategy of politicizing suffering, especially in its repeated image of "taking the side of the wretched." Indeed, its electoral success is partially explained by its ability to attract different classes, from business elites to the urban poor.[61]

The politicization of suffering in the Gülen movement is also apparent in the direct link constructed between suffering and the well-being of the nation. In his essay "Çile" (Suffering), Gülen suggests that nations and civilizations established by a suffering leader have a brilliant future, whereas those established by one who has never cried or suffered are prone to disappear. Indeed all "ideal periods" were raised by suffering people and later destroyed by their successors, who did not know the value of crying.[62] The ideal period to which Gülen refers is surely the lost imperial

Ottoman past, guided by a liberal Islam.[63] Indeed, Açıkel argues, the ideology of *mazlumluk* is historical in the sense that it is based on imagining a glorious, triumphant, and happy past that has been lost due to injustice. The Turkish-Islamic *mazlum* subjects see in the imperial past their tragic loss, caused by some guilty others, by whom they were wronged and mistreated. Simultaneously, this subject imagines a "just" future, when the power will be retrieved.[64]

Crying Boy complements this historical narrative of a glorious imperial past and its links to contemporary Turkey: the image refers to the Islamic *mazlum* subject whose happy past was disrupted by cruelty, and the imagery of childhood invokes a powerful nostalgia for a lost, peaceful world. As Patricia Holland argues in her analysis of the imagery of childhood in contemporary visual cultures, "in the constant renewal of childhood, this lost harmonious past remains forever present and promises a future in which innocence may be regained; in a world dominated by commercial imagery, a child claims to be outside commerce; in a world of rapid change, a child can be shown as unchanging; in a world of social and political conflict, a child may be damaged but remains untainted."[65] In the particular political Islamic imagination of the Gülen movement, the Crying Boy represents not only the suffering of the innocent in a brutal world but also the one who used to be happy in a lost past and who will achieve power and well-being in an ideal future. In such a historical narrative and political Islamic imagination, Crying Boy wins in the end.

In sum, Crying Boy is the embodiment of the historically constructed suffering subject of Islam and Islamic political imagination in Turkey. As the reason for his tears is explained in such a religious and political context, the image unfolds its identity in a particular political Islamic imagination in Turkey. Crying Boy is a political Islamic image, and can be appropriated in the Islamic ideology of *mazlumluk*. Hence, an Islamic visual culture cannot be said to draw necessarily on a distinct inventory of images. As the Islamic life of Crying Boy in Turkey demonstrates, a visual image that originated in a different context and space can be appropriated into an Islamic imagination. Indeed, Crying Boy derives its power in political Islam—though this may seem paradoxical—from the fact that it is not an inherently Islamic image.

Images have the capacity to speak to viewers who are susceptible to the issues that they raise and to "hail" them as the subjects they imagine.[66] Crying Boy gazing at people from the cover of *Sızıntı* speaks to the innocent-yet-suffering Muslim, who forms the core subject of political Islam. An image with inherent Islamic associations, such as the artistically calligraphed name of God or a replica of Ka'ba in Mecca, would not have the same ability to articulate various forms of suffering within the Islamic ideology of suffering in the manner of God. Crying Boy, as part of a larger visual culture—that is, as an image that is not merely claimed by the Islamic imagination—speaks to a broader society. It speaks not only those to those who have Islamically oriented worldviews, but also to those who feel pain and suffering for any reason whatsoever.

NOTES

I would like to thank the editor of *Sızıntı*, Sedat Şentarhanacı, for his explanations of the place of the Crying Boy image in the magazine's biography. I am also indebted to Engin Öncüoğlu for his explanations of the Arabic and Persian words as well as the Islamic contexts in the editorial text of the first issue of *Sızıntı*. Thanks are also due to the editors of this volume, Christiane Gruber and Sune Haugbolle, for their insightful comments on this chapter.

1. The urban legend of the curse of Crying Boy emerged in Great Britain in 1985, when the tabloid newspaper *The Sun* published the article "Blazing Curse of the Crying Boy," which reported that Crying Boy pictures were found undamaged among the ruins of burned houses. *The Sun* later asked its readers to send their Crying Boy prints to the newspaper in order to defeat the curse, and the tabloid tale expanded into a campaign of destroying the prints that the readers had sent in (Clarke, "The Curse of the Crying Boy").

The Crying Boy image has aroused feelings not only of fear but also of love and admiration, as demonstrated by its fan club established in the Netherlands (www.cryingboyfanclub.nl).

2. On the ways in which meanings and contexts change, see Sturken and Cartwright, *Practices of Looking*, 45–71.

3. W. Mitchell, *What Do Pictures Want?* 93.

4. Pinney, "Things Happen," 268. Pinney follows the idea of Mount Hageners that an image "contains its own prior context." This work is cited in Marilyn Srathern, "Artefacts of History."

5. Pinney, "Things Happen," 269.

6. W. Mitchell, *What Do Pictures Want?* 30.

7. The sitcom is titled *Avrupa Yakası* (The European Side).

8. Belge, *Tarihten Güncelliğe*, 265–69.

9. Erdoğan, "Ağlayan Çocuk," 40.

10. Gürbilek, *Kötü Çocuk Türk*, 37–51.

11. Ibid., 41.

12. The diminutive suffix -*cik* added to these names implies youth, which in turn cues cuteness, innocence, and vulnerability.

13. Among the novels by Kemalettin Tuğcu are *Satılan Çocuk* (Child Who Is Sold), *Yetim Ali* (Orphan Ali), *Yetimler Güzeli* (Beautiful of the Orphans), *Babasızlar* (Fatherless Ones), and *Büyüklerin Günahı* (Sin of Adults).

14. Gürbilek, *Kötü Çocuk Türk*, 40.

15. Ibid., 37–51.

16. Ibid., 39.

17. Açıkel, "Kutsal Mazlumluğun Psikopatolojisi."

18. *Sızıntı* means "leak." The magazine is also published in English, German, Russian, Arabic, and Albanian. It is found in forty-two countries and reaches 850,000 readers. See "Sızıntı Celebrates 30th Year."

19. *Sızıntı*'s emphasis on science seems to have resulted from its radical attack on Darwin's theory of evolution and its aim to present creation by God "scientifically."

20. On the Gülen community and movement, see, for example, Yavuz and Esposito, *Turkish Islam and the Secular State;* Yavuz, *Islamic Political Identity in Turkey,* 179–206; and Kömecoğlu, "Kutsal ile Kamusal."

21. Yavuz, *Islamic Political Identity in Turkey,* 182.

22. Ibid., 179–206.

23. Ibid.

24. Among the media institutions owned by the Gülen community are the magazines *Sızıntı, Ekoloji, Yeni Ümit, Yağmur, Aksiyon,* and *The Fountain,* the newspaper *Zaman,* TV channel Samanyolu, and the radio stations Dünya and BURÇ.

25. Yavuz, *Islamic Political Identity in Turkey,* 183.

26. Mehmet Akif Ersoy (1873–1936) and Necip Fazıl Kısakürek (1904–83), the two most celebrated Turkish poets by Islamic movements, wrote on such themes as the loss of Ottoman Empire, the destructiveness of modernity, effects of the West on family values, and so on. Their narratives are based on romantic visions of the past, historical injustice, and repressed, suffering subjects who are called for recuperation. For Açıkel, these two poets can be considered the founders of the political discourse of suffering in Turkish-Islam. See his "Kutsal Mazlumluğun Psikopatolojisi."

27. Gülen, "Bu Ağlamayı Dindirmek İçin Yavru."

28. W. Mitchell, *Picture Theory,* 94.

29. Ibid., 114.

30. Sedat Şentarhanacı, in discussion with the author, February 20, 2009.

31. See for example, Mumsema islam Arsivi, http://www.mumsema.com; and islamiyet.gen.tr: Huzur dolu islami bilgi portalı, http://www.islamiyet.gen.tr (site discontinued).

32. See http://islam.seviyorum.gen.tr (site discontinued).

33. W. Mitchell, *Picture Theory,* 152.

34. The following are excerpts from a poem written by Gülen entitled "Tears":

> Tears are poetry whose words are written in drops,
> expressing joy and grief, hope and despair.
> When consumed with pangs of separation, melting like candle,
> man breathes in tears and speaks in tears.
>
> . . .
>
> Tears are water of life putting out fires,
> a membrane protective against the fire of Hell.
> By tears ideals find their realization in the outer world;
> by tears the arid world changes into Gardens.

An eye sincerely tearful is like an eye vigilant at the front.
Eyes shedding tears for God's sake do not see Hellfire.
The shedding of tears sounds the depths of desire.
Only they perceive this who sense God inwardly.

. . .

Weep so that the mountain said to surround the world may sunder
And water of life gush therefrom, and the dead be revived:
Weep so that the chains around the will may be broken,
And the cavalry of dawn come galloping one after the other!

Gülen, "Tears."

35. In his essay in *Sızıntı* entitled "Erkek Adam Ağlar" (Man Cries), Dağlı solves the problem with the common sentiment "men don't cry" in an Islamic context. For him, weeping over everyday problems that he must solve is unacceptable for a man, whereas crying in the way of Allah, with tears from the heart, is the expression of a delicate soul, rather than the loss of manhood.

36. Gülen, "Bence Tam Ağlama Mevsimi."

37. Gülen, "Allah Karsisindaki Durusuyla Mü'min."

38. Gülen, "Bence Tam Ağlama Mevsimi."

39. Arvasi, "Gözlerinden Hayat Akan," *Sızıntı*.

40. Sander, "Images of the Child and Childhood in Religion," 19.

41. Ibid.,18.

42. On children's rights according to Islamic law, see M'Daghri, "The Code of Children's Rights in Islam"; and Elahi, "The Rights of the Child under Islamic Law." On the Medieval Islamic concern for other issues related to children, such as physical development, childhood diseases, education, and psychology, see Giladi, "Concepts of Childhood and Attitudes towards Children in Medieval Islam."

43. Dikmen, "Masum Çocuk."

44. M. Weber, *From Max Weber*, 330.

45. Açıkel, "Kutsal Mazlumluğun Psikopatolojisi."

46. *Mazlumluk* is the state of feeling one's self as innocent but suffering, repressed, and downtrodden.

47. Açıkel, "Kutsal Mazlumluğun Psikopatolojisi."

48. Ibid.

49. Gülen, "Garipler."

50. Yavuz, *Islamic Political Identity in Turkey*, 183–84.

51. Açıkel, "Kutsal Mazlumluğun Psikopatolojisi."

52. Ibid.

53. Atacan, *Kutsal Göç*.

54. Yet, the rise of political Islam in Turkey should be regarded as not a rural but rather an urban phenomenon. See, for example, Gülalp, *Kimlikler Siyaseti*, 41–72; and Ocak, *Türkler, Türkiye ve İslam*, 115–16.

55. The share of votes for the Refah Party rose from 7.2 percent in the 1987 elections to 16.9 percent in the 1991 elections.

56. Gülalp, *Kimlikler Siyaseti*, 53.

57. Çankaya, *İktidar Bu Kapağın Altındadır*, 221–24.

58. White, *Islamist Mobilization in Turkey.*

59. See, for example, Kılıçbay and Binark, "Consumer Culture, Islam and the Politics of Lifestyle"; Göle, *İslamın Yeni Kamusal Yüzleri;* and Navaro-Yashin, "The Market for Identities."

60. See Umut Azak (in this volume) for an analysis of the recent transformation in illustrations of Islamic children's books within the context of today's market economy.

61. Önis, "The Political Economy of Turkey's Justice and Development Party."

62. Gülen, "Çile."

63. Yavuz, *Islamic Political Identity in Turkey,* 182.

64. Açıkel, "Kutsal Mazlumluğun Psikopatolojisi."

65. Holland, *Picturing Childhood,* 16.

66. Sturken and Cartwright, *Practices of Looking,* 45.

CHAPTER 6

The New Happy Child in Islamic Picture Books in Turkey

UMUT AZAK

As elsewhere, Islamism in Turkey has been a political and cultural project that challenges the dominant dichotomies of traditional/modern, public/private, and Islamic/non-Islamic.[1] Studies of the cultural transformation and the emergence of new subjectivities brought by Islamism demonstrate the high significance of "visibility" to the Islamist project,[2] which has altered the public sphere to emphasize the "Islamic" difference—often through dress codes for women. According to Nilüfer Göle, since 1990 Islamism has experienced a second phase, in which its cultural program has become more apparent. The movement's first phase was characterized by militant and revolutionary politics. In this second phase of Islamism, she suggests, "it is new social groups such as Muslim intellectuals, cultural elites, entrepreneurs, and middle classes that more greatly define the public face of Islam, thinking and acting in more reformist terms. Their social profiles are an outcome of the Islamist movement and modern secular education, market values, and political idioms. They are hybrid and embody to the extreme the ambivalence between Islam and modernity; they make a claim for Islamic difference, and yet accept certain imperatives of modern life."[3] As the vehicle through which a modern Islamic social imaginary and new Muslim subjectivities have been constructed and mediated to masses, the publishing sector has been the locus of this hybridity.[4] Çayır's study of Islamic novels that were widely read during the 1980s and 1990s demonstrates the ways in which these publications reflected the transformation of Muslim subjectivities from a communitarian self toward a more pluralistic and individual self in the context of increasing urbanization and globalization.[5] The most intriguing dimension of these publications is their representation of gender relations, providing idealized sex-role stereotypes that are promoted by the Islamist cultural project. The Islamic intellectual and literary field was also enriched by the growing influence of female Islamist intellectuals who could also contest the conventional gender roles adopted by Islamists.[6]

Children's literature has been another field in which the interaction between modernization and Islamization can be observed. Since the 1990s the market for Islamic children's books has grown rapidly. As a publisher of Islamic books for children states, the increased demand for the genre was largely due to parents who studied in the 1980s and 1990s under the influence of the rising Islamist movement, and who now wanted their children to read books that would prepare them for a pious life.[7] These young parents wished to raise their children in an Islamic way, albeit within the context of a secular market for children dominated by Western consumption patterns. They sought alternative, Islamic—but also attractive and colorful—picture books that would appeal to children. Hence, an increasing number of publishers have responded to this new market demand by employing teams of editors, authors, and illustrators who create a new language of Islam, accessible to young children. This study is an exploration of the new genre of Islamic picture books that compete with their secular counterparts, featuring high-quality paper decorated with colorful illustrations.

The term "picture book" refers to books for young children, communicating information and telling stories via the combination of text and illustration. These differ from illustrated stories, in which the narrative can be understood without the aid of pictures. Unlike the texts of illustrated stories, picture-book illustrations and text are interdependent.[8] Images explain, clarify, and complement words; the story is completed or extended by the illustrations.

The Islamic picture books that are the focus of this study do not match the state of the art in Europe, where the tradition of picture books dates to the seventeenth century.[9] These picture books are published at very low prices, despite their expensive materials, by Istanbul-based Islamic publishing companies that are subsidized by their respective communities and benefit from increasing demand in both national and international markets. The two Istanbul-based companies to which I will refer are TİMAŞ and Muştu, both of which have been publishing children's books in recent years for distribution in Turkey as well as in Germany. The annual number of printed copies of Islamic picture books varies between thirty thousand and a hundred thousand per title, depending on the book's popularity.

Saktanber, in her 1991 study of Islamic children's books, drew attention to these books' importance as "basic socializing agents which transmit social values, norms and behavior, and Islamic values."[10] Saktanber argues that, via visual images that are attractive to children, these books played an important role in an intergenerational transfer of specific cultural and Islamic values. I contend that the same holds true of recent Islamic picture books. I argue further, however, that the new styles of visual imagery used in these books in recent decades reflect the transformation of religiosity experienced by Islamist actors, as well as the latter's changing understanding of children and religious education.

Contemporary visual imagery of children in Islamic picture books can be understood within the framework of "childhood" as a historical and cultural category formulated by Ariès,[11] and the evolution of this concept in the context of Ottoman/Turkish modernization.[12] The social meaning of childhood and family life among the Ottoman elite began to be transformed alongside urbanization, expansion, and the secularization of education in the nineteenth century.[13] Publications about modern child-rearing practices, the expansion of educational institutions for young children, and a new interest in the health of children as future citizens contributed to the sentimentalization and idealization of childhood in the late nineteenth century.[14] The emergence of children's literature as a genre in the same period expanded with the publication of periodicals for children, which were the first examples of illustrated children's literature;[15] from the 1940s on, illustrated children's books were published as well.[16] Children's literature was considered an instrument for cultivating the ethical and national values of modern citizens until the 1960s. The development of a leftist children's literature in the 1960s and 1970s reproduced the old didactic style. It was in the 1980s that a new genre of Islamic children's books began to be published.[17] From the 1990s on, these new Islamic children's books— extracurricular sources for teaching Islamic tenets and values, developed alongside mainstream children's literature (traditional tales and modern children's books)—began to replace didactic language with a more friendly vocabulary, aiming to communicate with, rather than teach, children.

Islamic children's books relate religious stories of important historical events in the spread of Islam; of rules, obligations, and practices of worship; or of the duties of a Turkish Muslim child.[18] Some of these books— published by the Directorate of Religious Affairs or by private publishing houses—were also illustrated books, whose narrative contents were analyzed by Saktanber. Saktanber notes the striking "absence of an image of 'happy childhood' with its implications of free time reserved for visiting parks with playmates and a relaxed and pleasurable home life. Nor is there any concern to encourage the development in the child of an inquisitive, independent, creative mind, able to acquire the skills needed to function in society."[19] The picture books that are the subject of this study are strikingly different from the books analyzed by Saktanber.

The new Islamic children's books respond to a growing demand among middle-class pious parents who are eager to raise their children as conscious Muslims from an early age; this rising demand is accompanied by a recently increased interest in child psychology and a new pedagogical approach to the field of children's literature.[20] Since the 1990s, the field of children's literature has flourished, as is reflected in the special place given to these books during the 1993 TÜYAP Book Fair in Istanbul.[21] Recent academic research focused on picture books and their relation to children's psychological development has demonstrated the need to prioritize the child's self-development and to increase the entertainment factor at the expense of a didactic approach.[22]

This interest in child psychology led to a reevaluation of Islamic publications for children, completed by theologians under the auspices of the Directorate of Religious Affairs.[23] In 2005 the latter organized a congress specifically for children's publications. The report published subsequently includes a clause that emphasizes the need "to abandon the method of picturing children as passive and unable to ask questions, and to appropriate a new pluralistic and tolerant understanding and discourse respectful of their innate differences and individual differences." Additionally, the report encourages psychologists and literary writers to "[translate] religious concepts into children's language for a healthy development of religious feeling in children."[24] Indeed, the Directorate of Religious Affairs has recently been quite active in the sector of children's books. The directorate published picture books for children, with such titles as *I Learn My Religion, I Learn My Prophet, I Learn My Book, I Learn my Prayers, I Learn My God, I Learn My Worship,* and *I Learn My Morals;* more than eleven million copies were dispatched to Koran schools, prisons, libraries, and mosques throughout the country as well as in Europe.[25]

Publishing companies also were influenced by this new pedagogical approach to children's literature. The publication of colorful and alluring picture books—with titles such as *Stories of the Prophet, I Learn My Religion,* and *Everything Tells about God*—created a boom in the demand for religious children's books in both national and European markets. Emine Eroğlu, editor of TİMAŞ publishing house, interpreted this new situation in these words: "We have just discovered making books for children."[26] Publishers also created new magazines for children, with the aim of teaching the principles of Islam with a new language.[27] The goal of these new publications is to entertain children while conveying essential principles of Islam. In the words of the editor-in-chief of the magazine *Birdirbir,* Alpaslan Durmuş, their publication represents an attempt to construct a new "religious language" that can be easily understood and appropriated by young children.[28]

Visual Imagery in Islamic Picture Books

Contemporary Islamic picture books introduce the basic teachings of Islam to pre-school-aged and newly literate children between the ages of five and nine. Colorful illustrations are crucial for making the teaching of the basic tenets of Islam and Islamic values attractive to children. The books have a specific visual narrative, through which they reflect and reproduce a social reality influenced by the recent transformation of religiosity among the new middle classes in Turkey, which have adopted an Islamic way of life within the context of a market economy.[29]

The Islamist intention to construct an Islamic alternative to mainstream Western and secular publications for children remains vital. However, this political claim, based on opposition, has diminished as a more self-confident Islamist discourse has emerged. The editor of the Muştu publishing house states that the firm avoids representing a conflictual Islamic position.[30] Additionally, it also shuns "Western style depictions" and other forms of expression that imply Western superiority.[31]

TİMAŞ publishing house advertises that their aim in publishing Islamic children's books is "to explain the abstract concepts of religion to children at an early age in order to cultivate strongly religious generations."[32] The advertisement for the series *I'm Learning My Religion* states that the books, which are intended for five- to seven-year-old children, should be read aloud by parents; even if not understood by the children, the books "will create a positive effect at the level sentiments." First- and second-graders, the text asserts, will be able to read and understand the series on their own, and "they will have eventually a sound point of view and worldview in the rest of their lives."[33]

The very titles of the books suggest a novel approach: emphasis not on duties, principles, or concepts, but on the personal and active affection of children toward Islamic values and tenets. These titles—for example, *I Thank Allah, I Like Fasting, I Know How to Pray, I Know Who My Prophet Is, I Am Curious about Heaven, The Joy of Ramadan*[34]—reflect the books' pedagogical approach, which places the child and his or her needs, desires, and curiosity in the center (as recommended in several scientific congresses and research reports on the issue).

These new picture books are glittery, making them more visually attractive to children. Still, the illustrations are generally crude computer drawings, often commissioned from graphic designers working freelance for the publication companies. The lack of artists specializing in illustrating picture books is not specific to Islamic publications, but a general trait of this sector in Turkey.[35] Additionally, most of these books can be considered mere illustrated storybooks, the text of which can be understood without the pictures.[36] Nevertheless, the illustrations shape the reader's mental image and the understanding of the narrative, thus complementing, as well as decorating, the text.[37]

First, the way in which the concept of "family" is depicted is crucial in defining an "Islamic" identity in visual imagery: as opposed to illustrations in the official textbooks of religion,[38] which depict only old women wearing headscarves, in Islamic picture books young women who are part of pious and happy families are pictured in headscarves (figs. 6.1a–b and plate 13). Or, for instance, in a book titled *I Thank Allah,* the text narrates the story of Ayşe, who fell ill and was visited by her teacher.[39] The illustration complements the text by depicting the teacher in a specific way (fig. 6.2). Ayşe's teacher, who explains in later pages why one should thank Allah in every possible occasion, is a woman who wears the Islamic headscarf.[40]

The illustrations of these picture books reveal that the titles are published with specific assumptions about their readership. The child hero or heroine of the stories is a primary school student, often the only child in a family, who has his or her own bedroom in an urban flat[41]—in contrast to the poor, who are depicted as neighbors or children in need of benevolence (fig. 6.3).

> [*Oruç tutmak üzerine:*] *Açların, susuzların, kimsesizlerin neler hissettiğini anlamamız için bizim de benzer duyguları yaşamamız gerekiyor. O zaman fakirlere yardım etmek için can atıyor, bol bol sadaka veriyoruz.* ([About fasting:] In order to understand the poor, lonely people, we have to experience the same feelings as them. Then we will look forward to help and give them alms.)[42]

In these books, the poor are outsiders, in the margins of the stories, in need of the empathy and benevolence of the hero or the heroine. The story is never about a poor child who learns about Islam; the poor child is the beneficiary of the good Muslim child. As Navaro-Yashin emphasizes, "A certain popular and mainstream branch of Turkish Islamism . . . is interested not in overturning class distinctions per se, but in expending the domain of

FIGURE 6.1a.
*İlköğretim Din
Kültürü ve
Ahlak Bilgisi 4.
Sınıf,* written
by M. Akgül et
al., 2008, 111.

FIGURE 6.1b.
*Ramazan
Sevinci,*
written by
Betül Ertekin,
illustrated by
Gülan Gürkan
Çizim Atölyesi,
2005, 19.

FIGURE 6.2. *Allah'a Teşekkür Ediyorum,* written by Çiğdem Özmen, illustrated by Ahmet Keskin, 2008, 6–7.

middle-class taste and lifestyle to include norms expected of the believing Muslim."[43] Islamic circles composed of urban middle classes want "to render Islam a living social practice" by "actualizing a moral transformation" and disseminating what they see as "authentic," "real" Muslim culture.[44] But they want to do this within the existing social system. As asserted earlier by Kıvanç, "Islamic" companies active in several sectors hide their capitalism by transforming their activity into a mission.[45] This "Islamic capitalism" produces and reproduces inequalities, as argued by Tuğal.[46]

Another reason for the peripheral appearance of poverty in new Islamic picture books is merely commercial. Indeed, the ideal image of the child in contemporary Islamism is no longer the "crying boy" who had an iconic status among Islamists in the 1980s, as explored by Savaş in this volume. The "crying boy," who symbolized the injured and suffering Islamic self, is now replaced by the image of the smiling, happy child; the contemporary figure reflects the pride and self-confidence of the new

FIGURE 6.3. *Oruç Tutmayı Seviyorum,* written by Çiğdem Özmen, illustrated by Ahmet Keskin, 2008, 6, 20.

Muslim, who grew richer and replaced his radicalism with conservatism in the footsteps of the AKP (Justice and Development Party).[47]

Recent ethnographic studies have demonstrated that Islamists in Turkey integrated into the secular system and free market via their activism in civil, cultural, and economic spheres.[48] For instance, Tuğal's ethnographic study explores Islamists' incorporation into the capitalist system in the 2000s by tracing the "transition from Islamic radicalism to free market conservatism" in Sultanbeyli, a district of Istanbul known as a major Islamist locality.[49] The political success of the AKP, which was established by a young generation of leaders who split from the Islamist Welfare Party and defends secular, statist, pro-EU, and economic liberal policies, provide the background of this transition. The creation of an Islamic civil society in the form of foundations, cultural centers, and the like became the foundation of what Tuğal called an "alternative capitalism," which was marked by its entrepreneurs' differentiation of their lifestyles from the dominant secular business elite. "Separation of sexes" was again, as explained by Tuğal, "the key to this endeavor."[50]

Tuğal, in his observations of Sultanbeyli's transition from a model radical Islamic district to the support base of the AKP by 2006, describes this transformation as the "de-Islamization of everyday life." This de-Islamization, or secularization, was reflected, he observes, in the decreased use of Islamic language and speech patterns (such as the use of the Islamic greeting "selam-un aleyküm"—"peace be upon you"—or the phrase "inşallah"—"God willing") as well as in an individual's outward appearance (men beginning to shave off their beards or dying their hair).[51] Tuğal observed a parallel transformation in gender relations: gender segregation disappeared from the public sphere, including workplaces and even "at the very heart of the main Islamizing agent (or former agent), the political party."[52] The dress code for women had also changed in 2006, as the previous sober Islamic clothing (long coats) was replaced by more colorful clothes and veils. This more liberal religiosity, accompanied by the AKP's successful ideological shift from Islamic radicalism to conservatism, also influenced children's books and the visual imagery aimed at teaching Islam to children in an entertaining way.

This new concern for entertainment resulted in the publication of colorful and joyful picture books depicting the daughter or son of a very happy family—often with a name derived from Islamic history, such as Rabia, Sare, or Talha[53]—who appreciates the beauties of the world and learns about Islam from his or her parents, grandparents, uncle, or teacher.[54]

In an article analyzing the representation of childhood, different adult role models, gender relationships, and family environments in the illustrated religious children's books published before 1990, Saktanber argues that "females are neither non-existent or described in vague terms; when they do appear they are usually passive and dependent mothers. Girls are almost completely absent."[55] One cannot claim the same for the new Islamic picture books. Women in these illustrations also dress in accordance with Islamic codes, which require a headscarf covering the shoulders, long-sleeved blouses, and long skirts. They are depicted often as mothers, with headscarves if they are outside or without if they are at home,[56] and they are often busy with housework,[57] following the traditional sexist stereotyping not necessarily specific to Islamic children's books.[58] Nevertheless, these women are as active as their husbands in teaching the principles of Islam to their children (fig. 6.4).[59] Unlike in the picture books analyzed by Saktanber, girls appear in the pictures, alongside boys, learning about Islam without headscarves unless they perform the ritual prayer.[60] This relative decrease in sexism is due not only to the influence of feminism but also to the rising awareness of the simple market rule, as explained by the editor of Muştu publishing house: "Books should be also attractive for and inclusive of girls, who constitute half of the reader profile."[61] No statistics about the percentage of girls among the readers of these books are available; nevertheless, the thousands of girls, boys, and their parents— potential customers—who visit the annual Islamic Book Fair organized by the Turkish Religious Foundation in Istanbul confirm this editor's desire to publish books that are appealing to both boys and girls.

A main concern of Islamic picture books is belief. Illustrators have developed interesting solutions for depicting, for instance, the act of praying. Heart-shaped symbols or colorful flowers are appropriated and used for this purpose (fig. 6.5 and plate 14).[62] These visual symbols are used to portray religious contemplation as a cheerful practice, bringing joy and peace. Colorful pictures of nature provide settings for contemplating Allah and his creation. If the external environment is depicted, it is usually nature or the countryside, although silhouettes of a city with a mosque,[63] or the front of a mosque set in a city,[64] as well as an idyllic atmosphere also appear.[65]

Conclusion

There exist noteworthy differences between contemporary Islamic picture books and those analyzed by Saktanber two decades ago. Her finding of an "absence of 'happy childhood'" as the dominant characteristic of Islamic picture books for children no longer characterizes contemporary Islamic literature for young children. The degree of sexism has been also reduced, as evidenced by the increased visibility of girls and women in these illustrations. Furthermore, children are given a striking centrality in these illustrations, as individuals with needs, fears, or curiosity about nature and the universe.

Do these changes result from the increasing modernization and secularization of the Islamic middle classes? My answer is positive, as I contend that Islamization—in the sense of formation of new Islamic subjectivities and practices, albeit often under the guise of "tradition"—and modernization coexist and reinforce one another in the context of a market economy that prioritizes consumers' needs. The new Islamic picture books address the increasing desire among the educated, urban, and Islam-oriented middle classes to teach and transfer their Islamic worldview to their children in the most attractive, accessible, joyful, and rational form. These books serve the Islamist project of Islamizing society—and not the state,

FIGURE 6.4. Melek Çe, *Kalbimin Çiçeği Cennetin Müjdesi-Çocuk ve Dua-*, 2008, 10.

FIGURE 6.5. *Dua Etmeyi Biliyorum,* written by Çiğdem Özmen, illustrated by Ahmet Keskin, 2008, 10, 11.

as argued by Roy in his analysis of "post-Islamism"[66]—and also serve as signs of modernization, as they borrow visual imagery and modern pedagogical techniques from their secular and Euro-American counterparts. In sum, these picture books provide one example among many of the ways in which new Islamic modernities are envisioned in Turkey at the dawn of the twenty-first century.

NOTES

1. For a comprehensive account of Islamism in Turkey, see Aktay, *Modern Türkiye'de Siyasi Düşünce.*

2. Among the scholars who have explored the emergence of new Islamic subjectivities are Binnaz Toprak, Michael Meeker, Nilüfer Göle, Ayşe Saktanber, Jenny White, and, recently, Yael Navaro-Yahin, Ayşe Çınar, Kenan Çayır, Uğur Kömeçoğlu, Buket Türkmen, and Cihan Tuğal.

3. Göle, "Islamic Visibilities and Public Sphere," 4.

4. Toprak, "Islamist Intellectuals of the 1980s in Turkey," 2–19; and Meeker, "The Muslim Intellectual and His Audience," 153–88.

5. Çayır, *Islamic Literature in Contemporary Turkey*. Ali Bulaç refers to this transformation as the emergence of a "third generation of Islamists" from 2000 on. Bulaç, "İslâm'ın Üç Siyaset Tarzı veya İslâmcıların Üç Nesli," 49.

6. See the chapters by Yıldız Ramazanoğlu, Ayşe Saktanber, Sibel Eraslan,and Cihan Aktaş in Aktay, *İslâmcılık*, 804–36.

7. The editor in chief of Uğurböceği Publications, Ergün Gür, interviewed by Yılmaz and Dolmacı, "Ve yayıncılar çocuğu keşfetti."

8. Nodelman, *Words about Pictures*, 1.

9. The first book referred to as a picture book was *Orbis Pictus* (Visible World) by John Comenius in 1658. See Shulevitz, *Writing with Pictures*.

10. Saktanber, "Muslim Identity in Children's Picture-Books," 173.

11. Ariès, *History of Childhood*.

12. Onur, *Çocuk, Tarih ve Toplum*; and Okay, *Osmanlı Çocuk Hayatında Yenileşmeler 1850–1900*.

13. Duben and Behar, *Istanbul Households*.

14. Libal, "Childhood," 86–87.

15. Okay, *Eski Harfli Çocuk Dergileri*.

16. Sarı, "Çocuk Kitapları İllüstrasyonları," 58.

17. Neydim, "Çocuk Edebiyatının Ölüm Fermanı."

18. Saktanber, "Muslim Identity in Children's Picture-Books," 174–76.

19. Ibid., 185.

20. See the proceedings of the First National Symposium on Children's Culture, which was held at Ankara University in 1996: Onur, *Çocuk Kültürü*; and proceedings of the second National Symposium on Children's Literature held in 2006: Sever, *II. Ulusal Çocuk ve Gençlik Edebiyatı Sempozyumu*.

21. Alpöge, "Günümüz Çocuk Kitaplarında Çocuk İmgesi," 291.

22. Işıtan, "Resimli Çocuk Kitaplarının Benlik Kavramıyla İlgili Konuları İçermesi Yönünden İncelenmesi"; and Tuğrul and Feyman, "Okul Öncesi Çocukları için Hazırlanmış Resimli Öykü Kitaplarında kullanılan Temalar," 387–92.

23. Since 2003 the annual Congress of Religious Publications, organized by the Directorate of Religious Affairs, has included sessions on children's religious literature, emphasizing the need to improve the quality of children's publications in a way that would suit children's psychology and satisfy pedagogical concerns ("Türkiye I. Dini Yayınlar Kongresi Sonuç Bildirgesi"). In 2005 the congress was entirely dedicated to the theme of children's publications ("III. Dini Yayınlar Kongresi Sonuç Bildirgesi").

24. "III. Dini Yayınlar Kongresi Sonuç Bildirgesi."

25. "Diyanet 11 milyon kitap dağıttı."

26. Yılmaz and Dolmacı, "Ve yayıncılar çocuğu keşfetti."

27. The didactic style of previous Islamic magazines for children, and the lack of illustrations facilitating children's access to the texts, began to be criticized. See, for example, Yıldız, "Diyanet Çocuk Dergisi'nin Din Eğitimi Açısından Değerlendirmesi."

28. Olgun, "Birdirdir oynayalım dinimizi kavrayalım."

29. Yavuz, *Islamic Political Identity in Turkey*.

30. Eyüp Özdemir (editor of Muştu publishing house), in discussion with the author, Istanbul, February 2009.

31. The editorial regulations of Muştu express this last concern in these words: "the principle of avoiding using expressions that reflect a powerful West in a disappointing manner" (*"Batılı tasvir nevinden unsurlardan uzak kalmalı, ümit kırıcı şekilde batılı güçlü gösterecek ifadeler içermemelidir"*). See Muştu Yayınları, at http://www.mustu.com/kriterlerimiz.php.

32. Excerpt from Mehmet Emin Ay, "Çocuklarımıza Allah'ı Nasıl Anlatalım?" (Istanbul: TİMAŞ), http://www.timas.com.tr/index.php?key=tkg&id=237 (site discontinued).

33. Blurb for the series I'm Learning My Religion published by TİMAŞ publication company (http://www.timas.com.tr/index.php?key=tkg&id=631 [site discontinued]).

34. A series that aims to teach children ten different names of Allah using anthropomorphized animals as the main characters of the story also represents a novel method intending to address young children. A spider, for example, can thank Allah for teaching him how to spin his web. See *Serçe Kuşu Benekli Allah'ın Alîm İsmini Öğreniyor* by Nur Kutlu, Allah'ın İsimlerini Öğreniyorum—Set (Istanbul: TİMAŞ, 2007), 28. Other titles in this series include: *Denizatı Dıgıdık Allah'ın Rezzak İsmini Öğreniyor; Su aygırı Hipos Allah'ın Rezzak İsmini Öğreniyor; Deve Hörgüç Allah'ın Kerîm İsmini Öğreniyor; Penguen Badi Allah'ın Hakîm İsmini Öğreniyor; Somon Simsim Allah'ın Selam İsmini Öğreniyor; Yunus Yoyo Allah'ın Rahman İsmini Öğreniyor; Ahtapot Oktopus Allah'ın Kuddüs İsmini Öğreniyor; Kunduz Kumpaz Allah'ın Kâdir İsmini Öğreniyor;* and *İpekböceği Pırpır Allah'ın Rab İsmini Öğreniyor.*

35. Sarı, "Çocuk Kitapları İllüstrasyonları," 84.

36. Schulevitz, *Writing with Pictures.*

37. Sarı, "Çocuk Kitapları İllüstrasyonları," 88–90.

38. Akgül et al., *İlköğretim Din Kültürü ve Ahlak Bilgisi 4. Sınıf,* 111.

39. Özmen, *Allah'a Teşekkür Ediyorum,*7.

40. The editors of this book, whom I interviewed, accept the inconsistency of this depiction with the current situation: teachers are forbidden from wearing the Islamic headscarf in school.

41. Özmen, *Oruç Tutmayı Seviyorum,* 6, 32; Özmen, *Dua Etmeyi Biliyorum,* 18; and Ertekin, *Ramazan Sevinci,* 4.

42. Özmen, *Oruç Tutmayı Seviyorum,* 20–21.

43. Navaro-Yashin, *Faces of the State,* 249.

44. Saktanber, "Formation of a Middle Class Ethos and Its Quotidian," 143.

45. Kıvanç, "İslamcılar & Para-Pul: Bir Dönüşüm Hikayesi," 47.

46. Tuğal, *Passive Revolution.* A recently developed children's game, Silk Road, which is the Islamic counterpart of the game Monopoly, reflects the Islamist desire to keep the capitalist motive of increasing gains but disguising it under an allegedly authentic, visual, and symbolic form: "*İPEK YOLU OYUNU: Elinizde size verilmiş 24 altın var. Bunları en iyi şekilde değerlendirecek ticaret yapacaksınız. Yaptığınız iyiliklerle ve yolculuklarla biriktirdiğiniz paralar oyunu kazanmanızı sağlayacak.*" (You are given 24 gold coins. You will make commerce in such a way that you will increase your gains. The money you will accumulate with the beneficences and trips that you will make will enable you to win the game). There are no dice in this game. Progress is

made according to correct answers given to a quiz, which includes questions about Islamic concepts and principles. As the representative of the manufacturer states, this game "belongs totally to our culture. The essence of the game is commerce." The game crystallizes the new spirit of Islamic entrepreneurship in children's world. Available at http://www.mustu.com/urun.php?ID=1581. Ozan Baştürk from Muştu Yayınları: "Tamamen bizim kültürümüze ait. Bu oyunun özünde ticaret var." Reported by CNN Turk, "'İslami Monopoly' çıktı," October 7, 2006, available at http://www.tumgazeteler.com/?a=1729481.

47. This new image of the "happy child" is a deviation not only from the earlier Islamist imagination but also from the dominant image "unhappy children" in the popular children's tales in Anatolia, collected and analyzed by Yavuz. Helimoğlu Yavuz, "Türk Masallarında Çocuk İmgeleri," 132–40.

48. Navaro-Yashin, *Faces of the State;* and Tuğal, *Passive Revolution.*

49. Tuğal, *Passive Revolution,* 11.

50. Ibid., 141, 143.

51. Ibid., 193.

52. Ibid., 212–13.

53. The popularity of these Islamic names (which are considered old-fashioned within modern Westernized and secular families) among Islam-oriented middle-class families presents another facet of Islamization of everyday life in Turkey.

54. Kadriye ve Ömer Baldık, *Allah'ın Güzel İsimlerini Biliyorum,* illustrated by Ahmet Keskin (Istanbul: TİMAŞ, 2008), 6; Çiğdem Özmen, *Namaz Kılmayı Seviyorum,* illustrated by Ahmet Keskin (Istanbul: TİMAŞ, 2008), 4–5; Çiğdem Özmen ve Ömer Baldık, *Peygamberin Kim Olduğunu Biliyorum,* illustrated by Ahmet Keskin (Istanbul: TİMAŞ, 2008), 16–17; Çiğdem Özmen, *Cenneti Merak Ediyorum,* illustrated by Ahmet Keskin (Istanbul: TİMAŞ, 2008), 16; Rabia Yıldırım, *Hayırlı Dua,* illustrated by Osman Turhan, Mübarek Gün ve Geceler Serisi, 3, Berat Kandili (Istanbul: Muştu Yayınları, 2007), 3; and Yavuz Bahadıroğlu, *Gizli Kameralar,* illustrated by Sevgi İçigen, Benim Güzel Allah'ım Serisi, 7 (Istanbul: Nesil Yayınları, 2008), 10, 12.

55. Saktanber, "Muslim Identity in Children's Picture-Books," 177. The same sexism is also a main characteristic of school textbooks. See Helvacıoğlu, *Ders Kitaplarında Cinsiyetçilik.*

56. Asım Uysal Mürşide Uysal, *Dinimi Öğreniyorum: Resimlerle ve Hikâyelerle Çocuğun Dua Kitabı* (Istanbul: Uysal Yayınevi, n.d), 15, 27.

57. Yavuz Bahadıroğlu, *Zikir Fikir Şükür,* illustrated by Sevgi İçigen, Benim Güzel Allahım Serisi, 7 (Istanbul: Nesil Yayınları, 2008), 14.

58. Helvacıoğlu, *Ders Kitaplarında Cinsiyetçilik.*

59. Melek Çe, *Kalbimin Çiçeği Cennetin Müjdesi -Çocuk ve Dua-* (Istanbul: TİMAŞ, 2008), 10.

60. Ümit Yıldırım, *Namaz Kılmayı Öğreniyorum,* illustrated by İsmail Abay (Istanbul: Muştu Yayınları, 2008), 26.

61. One example of a story that does not refer to or depict women is about a boy who is afraid of circumcision. The boy runs away from the ceremony and is finally found by his father and relatives, who tell him about the benefits of getting circumcised, such as the rewards to be gained in the paradise. His uncle confirms his brother's advice and adds, "It is also good for health, as Europeans say!" The boy overcomes his fear and wants to be circumcised as soon as possible. Gülten

Gezer, *Sünnetten Kaçılır mı?* illustrated by Gökhan Gülhan, Meraklı Bilgiler Serisi, 10 (Istanbul: Nesil Yayınları, 2007), 11, 12.

62. Özmen, *Dua Etmeyi Biliyorum,* 10, 28, 29; Rabia Yıldırım, *Üç Kardeş,* illustrated by Osman Turhan, Mübarek Gün ve Geceler Serisi, 1, (Istanbul: Muştu Yayınları, 2007), 10; and Yıldırım, *Namaz Kılmayı Öğreniyorum,* 18. Also see the figure of the devil: Belkıs İbrahimhakkıoğlu, *Hz. Eyüp,* illustrated by Cem Kızıltuğ, Peygamber Öyküleri Dizisi (Istanbul: TİMAŞ, 2008), 16.

63. Yıldırım, *Hayırlı Dua,* 13.

64. Ertekin, *Ramazan Sevinci,* 12.

65. Yıldırım, *Namaz Kılmayı Öğreniyorum,* 6.

66. Roy, "İslâmcı Hareketin Sıradanlaşması," 927–35.

CHAPTER 7

Sadrabiliyya: The Visual Narrative of Muqtada al-Sadr's Islamist Politics and Insurgency in Iraq

IBRAHIM AL-MARASHI

Since the 2003 Iraq War, religious figures in Iraq have employed various forms of visual media, from satellite television to the internet, to reach followers in national and transnational settings. The visual narrative of Muqtada al-Sadr in post–2003 Iraq provides a vibrant case study of the relationship between Islamist political elites (clerical politicians and lay figures) and their strategies for political communication in the Arab world. After 2003 the Sadrists emerged in post–Ba'athist Iraq as a religious elite that sought to protect the interests of the Shi'a masses, particularly their urban poor in Baghdad, and engaged in a religious and political competition with the returning exiled Shi'a parties Al-Da'wa and the Supreme Islamic Iraqi Council (SIIC)[1] for the loyalty of this constituency. In this elite formation process, the Sadrist movement has sought to shape the Iraqi religious and political space through a syncretic visual discourse that combines political Islam and Iraqi nationalism.

Since the rise of the secular pan-Arabist Ba'ath party in 1968, the state has attempted to fix Iraqi history by forging a notion of Iraqi citizenship; employing Iraqi nationalism imbued with contradictory iconography that invokes Mesopotamian glory and the victory of Salah al-Din (or Saladin); and stressing the Arab background of the Shi'a Imam Ali and Saddam Hussein in order to appeal to Arab Shi'a, Sunni, and Kurds alike. Since the state's monopoly on forging a hybrid identity collapsed in 2003, numerous parties have engaged in a cross-fertilization of patriotic imagery, continuing to blur the secular–Islamic binary—a trend that is particularly evident in the imagery of Islamist groups. This chapter explores Sadr's visual media through a framework that analyzes Islamist visual narratives competing for the loyalty of Iraqis, ranging from street posters to textbook stickers for juvenile audiences.

While the literature on Iraq has examined the ways in which political elites have contested national identity on various levels, few scholars have studied this issue following the 2003 Iraq war. Past studies have examined the ideological aspect of Iraqi politics and the creation of an identification or common bond between the people and the administration, bolstering the position of the state vis-à-vis the populace. Saddam Hussein's leadership employed a sustained rhetorical and visual campaign to maintain the loyalty of the Iraqi people by emphasizing the unity of Iraq's ethnic and sectarian communities during conflicts with Iran and the United States that threatened to upset the ethno-sectarian balance in Iraq—jeopardizing the minority rural, tribal, Tikrit Arab Sunni regime. Ofra Bengio's work on the Ba'ath analyzes interactions between cultural symbols, notions of Iraqi identity, and the construction of Saddam Hussein's cult of personality in the rhetoric of the state, particularly during times of crisis, such as the Iran–Iraq War.[2] The works of Amazia Baram deal with similar themes, including the re-invention of Mesopotamian identity in works of architecture and pageants, particularly during the eight-year war.[3] In *The Monument,* Kanan Makiya examines the meaning of the Victory Arch statue—of Saddam Hussein's forearms bearing two crossed swords—in relation to other public monuments dedicated to the former Iraqi leader during the Iran–Iraq War.[4] Eric Davis's work focuses on politics and collective history in Iraq from the time of the monarchy to the post–2003 period.[5] Finally, Adeed Dawisha examines the causal relationship between identity and Iraq's politics:

> In Iraq, competing sub-national, national, and supranational identities inevitably have influenced foreign policy. Similarly, the existence of competing identities has afforded the ruling elites countless opportunities to define and redefine the country's identity in accordance with their own interest and the dictates of policy at any given time.[6]

These overlapping subnational and regional identity-based loyalties continue to coexist or clash in post–2003 Iraq. As parties in post–Ba'athist Iraq have sought a broad institutional base, they have turned to mobilization efforts. These political elites contest Iraqi identities—promoting visions of an Iraq with a localized Shi'i Islamism imbued with Iraqi nationalism, a democratic Islamic Republic, an Islamist state linked to the predominantly Arab Sunni world, or Al-Qa'ida's Islamic State of Iraq as a base for a greater transnational movement—and call on the Iraqis to join their struggle.

This chapter focuses on the Sadrist imagery that emerged as the movement asserted itself on the political scene after the 2003 war. After the fall of the Ba'ath, this group began a process of defining their Shi'a movement as one that endured in Iraq under Saddam Hussein in order to legitimize themselves in opposition to the other Shi'a exiled parties that returned after the U.S. invasion. Since the invasion, the young cleric and his followers have sought to define their vision of the country's identity as part of establishing their presence and agency in a postwar Ba'athist vacuum and as a means to compete with such parties as Al-Da'wa and SIIC, which had acquiesced to the U.S. presence. In the aftermath of the invasion, Sadr had been ignored in the American plans for a post–Ba'athist government, although whether Sadr would have accepted an American offer to partake in these early discussions in 2003, and whether the other Shi'a parties would have allowed his participation, is a matter of speculation. Nevertheless, in the face of this political snub, Sadr sought to portray himself as an actor on the Iraqi political scene, and the creation of an armed militia, the Army of the Mahdi (*Jaysh al-Mahdi*), was one manifestation of this strategy. The rise of this army represented the physical assertion of Sadr's aspiring power, and violent motifs would imbue some of the visual imagery produced in tandem by his movement. The pervasiveness of violent resistance would separate Sadr's Shi'a movement from the groups that had cooperated with the American forces.

The postwar chaos that ensued after 2003 marked a period when the Arab parties inside Iraq feared that their nation would collapse into various ethno-sectarian mini-states. All of Iraq's neighbors were also wary of this scenario, fearing that a fractured Iraq would upset their ethno-sectarian balance. At the same time, some policy-makers in Washington were openly advocating a three-state solution to better manage Iraq's conflicting parties. However, none of the Shi'a parties advocated a separate mini-Shi'a state. On the contrary, the Shi'a of Iraq had found themselves at the helm of the state for the first time since its creation and had no intention of presiding over its collapse. To allay the fears of other Iraqi communal groups, the Shi'a religious parties sought to brandish their Iraqi nationalist credentials, resulting in visual narratives that combined both secular and religious imagery.

The rise of new communication technologies in Iraq after 2003 allowed Muqtada al-Sadr's followers to produce a visually rich lexicon. Identity-based struggles form the political context for analyzing the visual narratives of the Sadrists in Iraq, who have appealed to their followers with a combination of anti-imperialist (i.e., anti-American and anti-Israeli) and Iraqi nationalist messages. The Sadrist visual narrative is designed to project the power of Muqtada al-Sadr through a Shi'a metalanguage, which combines iconographic and linguistic sectarianism with Iraqi nationalism. In a Barthesian sense, visual signifiers and linguistic structures surround al-Sadr, resulting in signifieds that promote loyalty to the cleric.[7] This visual narrative in Iraq, using images of the cleric, members of the Mahdi Army, Iraqi flags, natural imagery, and quranic verses, involves techniques that Barthes describes as "parasitic messages," "trick effects," and "meanings chosen in advance."[8] Thus the Sadrists developed a code of connotation in a symbolic post–Ba'athist order, with aesthetic and ideological signifiers intended to appeal to an Iraqi society capable of receiving and reading the encoded messages.[9]

The Emergence and Evolution of the Iraqi Communication Sphere

Facing weak state institutions in the aftermath of the fall of the Ba'ath, Islamist parties in the post–2003 government, as well as the opposition, including the Sadrists and Sunni Islamist groups, augmented their power with calls to Islamist agendas infused with nationalism. These political elites, opposition leaders, and nonstate actors employed methods of patronage-based politics. Such politics have characterized the Iraqi state since its formation in the 1920s.[10] In the post–2003 context, patronage politics entailed mobilizing sectarian communities and enshrining warlordism. Alongside the rise of these political factions, media conglomerations formed in Iraq, with print, radio, and television communications at their disposal. Ethnic factions among the Arabs, Kurds, and Turkmens, along with religious-sectarian factions among the Sunni, Shi'a, and Christians, established networks of communications directed to their ethno-sectarian constituencies in Iraq and abroad. Independent media groups with no ethno-sectarian affiliations exist, but do not have access to the funds that the political parties can provide.

The fall of the Ba'ath represented the collapse of the state monopoly of the cultural sector. The result has been the accidental emergence of a pluralized media sector that has allowed a variety of actors to create a visual culture to define their visions of the state and nation. As in other contexts, in the wake of conflict and with a newly independent media, ideal internal media pluralism is hardly present. Most of the media in Iraq are now independently owned, but they operate as extensions of Islamist institutions. The dominant Arab media are owned by Iraqi Islamist parties, who deem necessary channels that convey political messages and inspire their constituents.

The Sadr Trend's media assets include the daily *Ishraqat Al-Sadr* (Splendor of Sadr), the weekly *Al-Hawza Al-Natiqa* (The Outspoken Seminary),

Al-Salam (Peace) radio station, Al-Salam television station, and a website, alsadronline.com. Rival Shi'a Islamist political factions, the Al-Da'wa Party and SIIC, also own media assets that complement or compete for the attention of Iraqis. The Da'wa Party's media organs range from the daily paper *Al-Da'wa* (The Call) to the weekly *Al-Bayan* (The Announcement), Al-Masar (Orbit) radio station, and Al-Masar television channel. SIIC owns the daily *Al-'Adala* (Justice), the weekly *Al-Wahda* (Unity), Al-Ghadir radio station, and Al-Furat (The Euphrates) satellite television channel.

Arab Sunni Islamist media include the General Dialogue Conference's *Al-'Itisam* (The Guardian) daily newspaper; the Association of Muslim Scholars' *Al-Basa'ir* (Insights) daily newspaper, its Rafidayn Satellite Channel; and the offshoot of the Iraqi Muslim Brotherhood, the Iraqi Islamic Party's *Dar Al-Salam* (House of Peace) radio station, *Dar Al-Salam* daily paper, and its Baghdad Satellite Channel.[11]

These Islamist elites have utilized the aforementioned mass media to shape their political agenda since 2003, when many Iraqis' first priority was to purchase the formerly banned satellite television dish and transponder. At the same time, such groups as the Sadrists also developed a wide range of small media, ranging from street posters to keychains, to communicate in the spheres of everyday life and thus supplement the mass-mediated messages, or to reach those Iraqi constituents who could not afford their own television and satellite.

During times of political stability, Iraq's plural media ownership reflected that calm. During periods of discord and disintegration, such as the sectarian infighting following the destruction of the Al-'Askariyya shrine in Samarra in early 2006, media polarization further undermined the capacity of the weak state to govern. Simultaneously, political parties reinforced the country's sectarian divisions. As early as 2006, Arab Iraqi Sunni Islamist factions and tribes began to oppose the strict religious parastate created by Al-Qa'ida, eventually realigning themselves against the Islamic State in Iraq. The tribes coalesced into the Reawakening Councils known as *Al-Sahwa* (The Sons of Iraq); these managed to bring relative stability to their areas, forcing Al-Qa'ida elements to disperse and seek refuge in other parts of Iraq. Once this conflict de-escalated, so did the "war of the airwaves," and by 2008 the Iraqi channels, including those owned by the Sadrists, had directly incited no party to violence. All have reasserted their claim to Iraqi nationalist credentials and the oft-repeated statement that they do recognize any differences between the Shi'a and Sunnis of Iraq. Nevertheless, there are a multitude of channels that form an ethno-sectarian media landscape, reflecting the fractured political structure that emerged in Iraq in 2003.

The Arab Islamist political movements that participated in the January and December 2005 elections, including the Sadrists, mobilized as Islamist parties that maintained their own militias. These parties, as in nearly every conflict in a deeply divided society, were the first to organize and did well in post-conflict elections. The Islamist factions, some radical in nature, rallied support among the populace on a platform of promising to protect each community's identity-based interests. One could characterize the dynamic as "mediated patronage." The Sadrists, for example, broadcast through their own media the message that they could provide security, highlighting the successes of the Mahdi Army as well as appealing to their constituents through Shi'ism and Iraqi nationalism. Political parties and movements based on non-sectarian platforms could not provide this mediated protection for their constituencies.

The Rise of the Sadrist Movement

Islamist groups in Iraq have set another bloody regional precedent on par with Algeria's Islamist violence: a relentless campaign of violence and the indiscriminate use of terror against civilians. The instability in Iraq from 2004 to 2008 has been attributed to conflicts between the factions of political Islam: the Sadrists versus other Shi'a Islamist groups, the latter collectively pitted against Iraqi Sunni Islamist groups and Al-Qa'ida-linked insurgents.[12] During this conflict, the Sadrist faction, apparently an organization concerned with a purely ideological Islamist agenda, evolved into a sectarian nationalist movement that would splinter into several factions, with the young cleric yielding tentative control over the movements fighting in his name.

After the death of Grand Ayatullah Abu al-Qasim al-Khoei in Iraq in 1993, Grand Ayatullah Muhammad Sadiq al-Sadr followed in the footsteps of his cousin Muhammad Baqir al-Sadr (the founder of the Al-Da'wa Party in Iraq in the 1960s) and emerged as the political and spiritual leader of segments of the Shi'a population in Iraq, especially those based in the east Baghdad district known as Saddam City. Sadiq al-Sadr, like his cousin, argued that the *Hawza* (the Shi'a seminary) was divided into an *al-hawza al-natiqa,* or the "outspoken Hawza," which he advocated, and the *al-hawza al-samita,* or "silent Hawza," referring to Ayatullah Ali Sistani, who had avoided confrontation with Ba'athist political authorities following the death of al-Khoei. Sadiq al-Sadr was renowned for his Friday sermons, preaching against Israel and challenging the authority of Saddam Hussein, which led to his death in February 1999, along with two of his sons, allegedly at the hands of Iraq's security forces. His surviving son, Muqtada, went into hiding and would later emerge as a pivotal force in Iraq's politics.

Muqtada al-Sadr, the "thirty-something"-year-old cleric, inherited his father's ideology, bolstered by his own credentials as a respected Shi'a cleric who had opposed Saddam Hussein. After years of hiding in an unknown location, Muqtada reappeared in Najaf when the American military occupied the town in 2003. He held a relatively junior rank among the clergy, but managed to harness the deep sympathy for his father and family. Initially his followers emerged as the "The Group of the Second Sadr," which would later assume the title of the "Al-Sadr Trend."

After the 2003 war, Muqtada's armed followers would evolve into a highly organized and motivated force known as the Mahdi Army. While chaos prevailed in other parts of Iraq, Muqtada's army formed a shadow state in areas where he enjoyed wide support, especially in the Baghdad neighborhood Sadr City (the former "Saddam City"), renamed after Muqtada's family.

The former U.S. Coalition Provisional Authority (CPA), headed by Paul Bremer, faced a dilemma over how to handle the growing power of al-Sadr. While the CPA believed that al-Sadr had little following among Iraq's Shi'a, especially among secular members of that community, his followers were nonetheless motivated and disciplined. The CPA had co-opted most of Iraq's Shi'a parties, or at least had induced them not to oppose the U.S. presence. Al-Sadr's group emerged as a focal point for discontented Shi'a opposed to the American occupation of Iraq and those Shi'a who supported the notion of *al-hawza al-natiqa*. Armed clashes broke out in Najaf and Karbala between the Sadrists and the militia affiliated with the rival SIIC party. Bremer moved against al-Sadr in April 2004, when the CPA ordered the closure of al-Sadr's newspaper *Al-Hawza*, because it allegedly carried articles that incited violence, and issued an arrest warrant for the young cleric, who allegedly played a role in the murder of Majid al-Khoie, a descendent of Abu al-Qasim who had entered Iraq in the aftermath of the 2003 war. After the arrest warrant was issued, intense fighting erupted in southern Iraq between U.S. forces and the Mahdi Army. Sadr called for cooperation between his forces and the insurgents in the predominantly Arab Sunni urban areas of Falluja and Ramadi, under the rubric of a resistant Iraqi nationalism in the face of an American occupation. This joining of forces, and the call to overcome sectarian differences, is represented in the visual media produced during this first phase of the Sadrists' rise.

A second phase can be delineated by the events following the February 22, 2006, bombing of the Al-'Askari shrine in Samarra, allegedly conducted by the Al-Qa'ida Organization in Iraq, which spiked an unprecedented level of sectarian violence. After Al-Qa'ida's previous attacks against Shi'a civilians, particularly during the emotive 'Ashura commemorations, Iraq's leaders had called for calm. The Iraqi Shi'a generally listened. However, the attack against the symbolic mosque housing the body of Imam 'Ali al-Hadi served as a critical provocation for Shi'a Islamist groups and their affiliated militias.

Iraq suffered from a spiral of retaliations after the attack, whereupon Sunni mosques were targeted and other Shi'a mosques attacked, prompting further violence against other Sunni mosques as well as civilians. Al-Sadr declared that his Mahdi Army was willing to defend the Shi'a, an indication that he could offer protection when Iraq's official security forces were incapable of doing so. The Iraqis, both Sunni and Shi'a, would then begin to look to the nonstate militias for security.

During the fighting with U.S. forces that began in April 2004, Muqtada had developed a syncretic notion of Shi'a populism imbued with notions of Iraqi nationalism that called upon Iraqi Shi'as and Sunnis to unite in the face of an occupation. In reality, his notions of Iraqi sectarian unity had been undone by his own militia during the spiral of sectarian violence that consumed the center of Iraq after February 2006. During this second phase Muqtada himself was not in firm control of all factions of the Mahdi Army, which essentially had evolved into a network of Mahdi Armies, including the splinter faction known as Asaib Ahl al-Haq (The League of the Righteous). Nuri al-Maliki, Iraq's prime minister from the Al-Da'wa Party, successfully deployed the Iraqi armed forces in 2008 to confront the Sadrists in Basra and Al-Sadr City, in what emerged as another chapter in Iraq's inter-Shi'a rivalry. A tentative peace emerged, with the Mahdi fighters promising to lay down their arms and Sadr's declarations that his followers would continue their socio-economic activities and participate in the political process. This period represents the third phase of the Sadrist movement, which resulted in the disbanding of the Jaysh al-Mahdi, Muqtada's move to Qom, Iran, to pursue religious studies, and the Sadrists' emphasis on social work rather than armed struggle. While Sadr's power waned after Maliki's crackdown, this chapter now turns to an examination of the visual narratives developed by this movement during their emergence from obscurity in 2003 and their subsequent rise to power.

Sadribiliyya: The Visual Narrative of the Sadrists

Within a few months of the fall of Ba'athist government, al-Sadr's net-works employed visual media such as videos, television, radio, pamphlets, and fliers to define a role for the young cleric in the public domain of Iraqi politics and the private sphere of individual Iraqis. Al-Sadr's ethno-sectarian "media empire" demonstrated that various media coalesced around his Trend, with print, radio, and television communications all at his disposal.

In addition to Sadr-affiliated mass media, his network also produced a vast array of what Srebreny and Mohammadi refer to as "small media,"[13] or alternative, non-mass-mediated communications ranging from fliers to the ubiquitous poster in areas where the cleric enjoyed support. Combined, these communications provide a form of mediated patronage built around al-Sadr's cult of personality. Collectively, these media stress the role of Islam in public life and anti-imperialistic zeal directed against Israel and the United States. These media also were devoted to Iraqi nationalism, cen-tered on the notion of Iraqi unity, opposed to Kurdish and SIIC's plan for a federal Iraq. While al-Sadr's militias have been blamed for conducting vio-lence against Iraq's Sunnis, his media would never admit this, instead argu-ing that Iraq's sectarian problems emerged from the "Wahhabi threat" of Saudi Arabia. This threat is articulated in a book that includes several inter-views with the cleric. In this work al-Sadr called for an Islamic state in Iraq, but with the caveat that Iraq would not replicate the Islamic Republic in Iran but rather forge close ties with their Persian co-religionists across the border.[14] Through the following images, the Sadrists negotiate their posi-tion vis-à-vis other Iraqi parties; as a faction within a new Iraqi state, they create a mesh of symbols that serve as part of the post–Ba'athist iconog-raphy. The commoditization of Sadrist culture includes media such as the video compact discs (VCDs) that were sold in shops in Sadr City. One such video included images of the Mahdi Army marching in military formation, resembling the military-style parades of Hizballah in Lebanon. Militant music with oppressive drumbeats plays in the background, accompanied by a chorus: "We will not live in oppression; we resist with our rifles." The images in the video shift from military parades to footage of the Mahdi Army militiamen in combat, interspersed with scenes from the Hollywood blockbuster *Blackhawk Down,* about nineteen American soldiers killed in Somalia in 1993. The Sadrist media department has created a montage with seamless editing, giving the impression that the Mahdi Army militiamen in the video were responsible for downing the Blackhawk helicopter depicted in the film. The Sadrists had no qualms about borrowing special effects produced in Hollywood for a video with an anti-American message. The purpose of such videos was captured by a *Christian Science Monitor* interview with Abu Mujtaba, a member of the media department of the Sadr Trend, who claims, "The TV channels always show the Americans strong, saying 'Go, Go, Go!' They never show the American deaths. So these films by the Mahdi Army show how we kill the Americans, they are not invincible."[15]

The use of the *Blackhawk Down* images demonstrates that the aesthetics of combat are not bound by a strict cultural geography. Ironically, the film also served as a reference for U.S. soldiers who were fighting in Sadr City at the same time the video was produced. One *Newsweek* article captures the sentiments of Americans who were caught in the combat there: "The red tracer trajectories lit up 'a big red V, and we were right in it,' says driver Spc. Dee Foster, 'It was just like that movie "Blackhawk Down."'" Adds one of his comrades, 'More like Blackhawk Down times five.'"[16] In the American context, the film signifies an ambush in the face of overwhelming odds, yet in the Iraqi setting the original Hollywood referent is forgotten through what Barthes deems "trick effects" and is determined by the cultural context in Iraq, particularly Sadr City and the defeat of U.S. forces.

The visual images analyzed henceforth fit under the rubric of "small media." Figures 7.1 and 7.2 are thin cardboard posters that measure 8 by 11 inches and were obtained by the author in Iraq between 2004 to 2005, when the Mahdi Army had emerged as a potent force engaging the U.S. military. Both images depict Muqtada's face, superimposed on the background of a stone structure, and an armed figure. The close-up image of al-Sadr gives the impression of a cleric larger than life, with the soldiers assumed to be members of the Mahdi Army, signifying resistance. In figure 7.1 the fighter is featured as a shadow silhouette, and in figure 7.2 (see also plate 15) a masked member of the militia holds a Kalashnikov rifle. The faces of the fighters in both images are not necessary, as the dominant personality in the resistance is Muqtada, commanding armed followers in his struggle. The images vest loyalty to the cleric at the expense of the institutions of the Sadr Trend, including the militia.

Figure 7.1 consists of Iraqi nationalist motifs, featuring the Iraq flag in the background and the words chiseled in stone, "Sayyid Muqtada, *kul ihna wiyak*" ("All of us are with you") in the Iraqi dialect, rather than the modern standard Arabic phrase, "*kuluna ma'aka*." According to Barthes's model, the photographs of Muqtada are not "isolated structures" since they are in communication with a linguistic text—in this case, the captions that accompany the image.[17] The linguistic structure, captions in the Iraqi

FIGURE 7.1. Small poster of Muqtada al-Sadr. *Purchased by author, Basra, 2004.*

dialect, cooperate with the face of al-Sadr, militia figures, and the Iraqi flag. The text, according to Barthes, in this instance is "a parasitic message," designed to "quicken" the meaning of the image, in this case resistance and solidarity with Muqtada. The text and image, according to Barthes, serve as a "remote-control" to the viewer, forcing a "meaning chosen in advance."[18] In this case, the meaning in the images conflates loyalty to the cleric with Iraqi resistance against the U.S. occupation.

Both images include dramatic stone structures and stark natural scenes opposed to the images of "paradise," such as lush forests or waterfalls, found in insurgent images associated with Al-Qa'ida in Iraq. Figure 7.2 (plate 15) is particularly interesting because the militia member and Sadr are not situated in an Iraqi location, but rather are juxtaposed under an image of Turret Arch in Arches National Park, Utah. The phrase "*Ya laytina kunna ma'akum, fanafuz fawzan 'aziman*" ("If only we were with you, we would have won a great victory"), in formal Arabic superimposed on the bottom, differs from the text in figure 7.1, which uses the Iraqi dialect. Why one image uses the colloquial, whereas a similar image invokes the modern standard Arabic, is unclear. In this case, the switch between language forms bears no resonance with the imagery; however, in other Iraqi cases, the dialect is used in an informal setting.

IBRAHIM AL-MARASHI

FIGURE 7.2.
Small poster
of Muqtada
al-Sadr.
*Purchased by
author, Basra,
2004.*

Both share an aesthetic contrast between the stark nature of the scenery used as the backdrop and the dramatic images of al-Sadr. The natural backdrops in the Sadrist images could be classified as what Barthes describes as "trick effects."[19] The abovementioned photographs have been created by artificially bringing together the face of Muqtada and a natural location in the United States. The Kalashnikov does not have fixed particular meaning and serves as another example of the erosion of the secular–Islamist binary. The rifle is invoked as a symbol by the Sadrists and other Islamist organizations ensconced in the flag of Hizballah and the Revolutionary Guard of Iran, yet it is also depicted in the flag of countries such as Mozambique, which has no relation to the aforementioned Islamist organizations. Rather than having a specific Islamic connotation, the rifle symbolizes counter-hegemonic struggles, forming part of the inherent fusion between the secular and religious. In opposition to Sistani and his religious school, which abstained from advocating violence in post–2003 Iraq, the weapon conflates Sadr, the outspoken seminarian, and resistance as an ideological package to garner legitimacy among his followers.

Other tensions are manifested by the Iraqi flag, denoting the secular strain of Iraqi patriotism and the image of Sadr in a black turban, a uniquely Shi'i signifier used to indicate descent from the Prophet Muhammad. This image was produced during the initial phase of Sadrist–Sunni cooperation and thus seeks to override the obviously sectarian background of the cleric in the context of a common struggle against the occupation—although a direct referent to the U.S. is missing in the fliers, as opposed to in the VCD. The visual rhetoric of the Sadrists fused nationalism and Islam, just as this political Islamist group would seek the advancement of an ethno-nationalist agenda during Iraq's inter-sectarian conflict, which would begin in 2006.

In Barthes's framework, the signifiers in these images—Muqtada, the militia member, and the stark background—emerge as signs for Iraqi society. He writes: "Signification is always developed by a given society and history."[20] The signs were familiar to Iraqis during the period of intense conflict following 2003, and the code of connotation in this case belongs to a period in Iraq's history (the Sadr uprising against the United States and internecine warfare from 2004 to 2008). This code of connotation is anchored in a symbolic Iraqi post–Ba'athist order, in which a stock of stereotypes has been utilized by the Sadrists. According to Barthes, these include colors (such the black and green banners relevant to Shi'ism, or red, black, and white, the colors of the Iraqi flag), graphisms (the militia fighter), gestures (the stern expression of Sadr), and the arrangements of elements (such as the natural stone structures). Thus, per Barthes, "thanks to its code of connotation the reading of the photograph is thus always historical; it depends on the reader's 'knowledge' just as though it were a matter of a real language [langue], intelligible only if one has learned the signs."[21] The Sadrist image-producers act as media "tinkerers" in the case of the *Blackhawk Down* montage and the image from Utah in figure 7.2 (plate 15). Through the technique of bricolage, the images of the Blackhawk helicopter and American settings are dislocated from their normal context within the United States and are used in a new map of anti-imperialist meaning.

Images like the aforementioned may be considered "campy" or "kitschy" according to Western sensibilities or even among Iraqi elites. In

Iraq and the Arab world, images of vast, dramatic landscapes, often with waterfalls or tropical jungles, can be found in any kebab shop or teahouse. According to Barthes, "the signified, whether aesthetic or ideological, refers to a certain 'culture' of the society receiving the message."[22] The natural imagery in this case and in other Islamist contexts often serves as a reminder of the purity of God's creation. The paradise-like images used in Al-Qaida videos that are aired during religious programs on mainstream Middle Eastern channels often depict verses from the Qu'ran against a backdrop of waterfalls, sunsets, or mountain ranges.

Determining the popular reception of the Sadrist images in Iraq can be difficult, but deductions can be made about the consumption of such images. In certain Shi'a settings he is idolized. When I visited Iraq in April 2004, Iraq was undergoing "de-Ba'athification," removing the symbols of Saddam Hussein, the personification of the party, while an opposite process of "re-Shi'afication" was occurring. During this trip I faced ethnographic hurdles in determining reception of the aforementioned images. They are not dissected as this chapter seeks to do, but consumed as a total. When asked what the images represented to them, the vendors who sold them usually provided responses such as "He is our *marja* [source of religious emulation]" or "He is the only one defending us." They found no incongruence when I pointed out that the arch was in the United States, as that detail did not detract from the message intended and perceived. (In fact, they found me, an Iraqi American struggling to understand the postwar chaos of Iraq, more of an anomaly).

Sadr City is the geographical focal point of the cleric's loyalty. However, the consumption of his image in Basra proves interesting, as it is a mixed Shi'a–Sunni city and far removed from Baghdad. Parts of Basra were undergoing re-Shi'afication, in which painted portraits of Imam Husayn replaced Saddam Hussein, and pictures of al-Sadr were prominently displayed. After passing a checkpoint in the city manned by Iraqi policemen, I noticed that one had al-Sadr's picture posted in the window of a police car. It was not displayed as a wanted poster but as an iconic depiction of a man the officers respected. The Coalition Authority had issued an arrest warrant for al-Sadr in that month and ordered the Iraqi police forces to arrest him. It appeared doubtful that the Iraqi police would have been willing to arrest an idol, as the United States had instructed them to do—perhaps those uniformed policemen were members of the Mahdi Army who had infiltrated the security forces.

Figure 7.3 is taken from my journey to Basra in 2004 and was snapped in one of the city's largest markets. The image is a wall poster of al-Sadr, flanked on three sides by images of Imam Husayn with the large words in Arabic behind the poster reading *Maktab al-Iman li-Ta'lim* (The Office of the Faith for Instruction). While Shi'a Islam has relaxed attitudes to human depictions of religious figures, what was striking was the fact that al-Sadr's image was placed in the center of the wall of the market, above a poster of Imam Husayn, almost elevating the young cleric's status above that of the beloved Imam. The fact that the poster was for sale in a bustling market indicates that there is popular consumption of these images in Basra.

In figure 7.3 a poster of al-Sadr's deceased father has been relegated to the far side of the wall. While this would first appear to relegate the father to a peripheral role, the juxtaposition has more to do with how I framed the photo, and in fact, often Sadr and his father are depicted in images together. Unlike Sadr's towering status over the militiamen, father and son are usually depicted with the same proportions. The presence of his father fits into a Shi'a Islamic iconography of martyrdom, in which each Shi'a faction claims legitimacy from a martyred cleric. Al-Da'wa often invokes the image of Muhammad Baqir al-Sadr, the cleric who founded the party in the 1960s and was executed by the Ba'ath in the 1980s. Muhammad Sadiq Al-Sadr was killed in a roadside ambush in the 1990s, and the spiritual founder of SIIC, Ayatullah Muhammad Baqir al-Hakim, was killed by a bomb in Najaf in August 2003. The image-makers are clearly drawing upon the "historical grammar" belonging to the iconographic language of Shi'ism. Thus all three parties can invoke a foundation martyr and seek legitimacy by continuing his legacy.

Moving forward, figure 7.4 (plate 16) provides further evidence of the commodification of al-Sadr's image. The image is of a laminated keychain that measures two inches by one inch. Both sides of the keychain have images of al-Sadr, with one side depicting Muqtada speaking with another cleric. The image from the other side of keychain is included in this chapter to demonstrate similarities with figure 7.1. It includes nationalist motifs, with the Iraqi flag in the shape of a heart next to an image of al-Sadr in supplication, also framed by a heart. The image of two hearts that one would find on a Valentine's Day card features the words underneath: "Allah, make this country safe." Since al-Sadr is in a state of prayer, it is assumed that the cleric is asking God to make Iraq safe in response to his love for the country, symbolized by the two hearts. The keychain is designed to be used for keys to a home or a car, the private sphere of a follower of al-Sadr, and thus is not designed for large-scale public consumption, as is a large poster, but rather for an intimate setting. While the images of Saddam Hussein that were often displayed in homes (frequently against the will of

FIGURE 7.3. Wall with posters of Muqtada al-Sadr and Imam Husayn. *Photograph by author, Basra, 2004.*

the family) represented government intrusion into the private realm, the Sadrist images represent a voluntary will to display loyalty to the cleric in an intimate setting.

The use of a heart would indicate a Western aesthetic, appropriating a signifier into an Iraqi cultural form. While the use of a heart may seem unremarkable even by Middle Eastern norms, in Iran a recent effort has been made by the state to prohibit any imagery related to Valentine's Day.[23]

Spirituality, in the Shi'a sense, is also expressed. The black turban (signifying descent from the Prophet Muhammad's family) and holding one's hands together in the middle of prayer (an action usually only practiced by the Shi'a), as seen in the "Valentine's Day" image, are relevant signifiers among the Shi'a of Iraq. Similarly, figure 7.5 is also displayed in a medium designed for a private setting: a child's textbook. It originates from a sheet of stickers used by pupils to indicate ownership of a schoolbook. The lines are for students to write their "name," "grade," and "class subject," and once that is done the sticker can be placed inside the cover of a notebook or textbook. Unlike the previous images, which communicate resistance against the backdrop of a stern cleric, figure 7.5 depicts a compassionate, smiling Sadr embracing two children. While in previous images he is

FIGURE 7.4. Key chain. *Purchased by the author, Basra, 2004.*

wearing a black *thowb,* or robe, in the image reserved for schoolchildren he is dressed in white. The production of stickers for schoolbooks inculcates Sadr's image as a patriarch. The "pose," according to Barthes, "prepares the reading of the signifieds of connotation." With the exception of the image for the textbook, the pose of al-Sadr, with a stern expression and never smiling, signifies the heavy nature of the task imposed on him: namely, leading the resistance against the enemies of Iraq and the Shi'a. The combatant imagery is not directed toward children, but the centrality of Sadr is communicated to the youth, inculcating the young to the symbolic representation of the cleric and his group.

Collectively, these images share similarities with the Islamist iconographies discussed in Umut Azak's and Özlem Savaş's contributions to this volume. However, the use of natural scenery differs in each context. Colorful pictures in Turkish children's books, which are produced for a young audience, depict nature and the countryside as a setting for contemplating God. The rocky and barren countryside in the Sadrist narrative is geared for an adult audience, with the harsh terrain here a stage for conducting resistance, itself sanctioned by God and al-Sadr.

Azak writes that children's stories with Islamist themes in the Turkish context serve as socializing agents that transmit social norms and Islamic values. While I did not find any children's book produced by the Sadrists,

FIGURE 7.5. Textbook stickers. *Purchased by the author, Basra, 2004.*

and while a textbook sticker cannot be compared to an entire book, never-theless they share a commonality in that the producers created products designed for a young audience. The Sadrist images reserved for children focus on communicating loyalty to the cleric over Islamic values. Among the various Sadrist texts and images analyzed for this study, only al-Sadr's Friday sermons dealt with issues of Islamic practice, although the same sermons would also deal with political themes involving Iraq. Materials analogous to the study of children's books in Turkey that deal with fast-ing, the Prophet, or paradise were not found in the Sadrist context. In the visual narrative of al-Sadr, it is not a forgone conclusion that the Shi'a to which they appeal are believing Muslims. The message communicated in this visual narrative has more to do with loyalty to the cleric than everyday practice of the faith.

Similarities between the Sadrist images and Özlem Savaş's study of the "Crying Boy" picture can also be found. On one level, like the crying boy image in Turkey, images of Sadr can be found displayed on the walls of middle-class and working-class homes, shops, coffeehouses, and the back windows of cars, buses, and trucks in Iraq. Moreover, the "holy *mazlumluk*" (downtrodden), which Savaş cites as the idea underpinning the image of the "Crying Boy" in the Turkish Islamist context, has some ramifications for Shi'a imagery in general as well as within the Sadrist visual narrative. The downtrodden (*madhlumun* in Arabic) is a dominant theme in Shi'i discourses, particularly during the 'Ashura commemoration ceremonies. The Sadrists take on this discourse in their videos-for-sale, conveying that the status of being *madhlum* can be overcome through loyalty to the cleric and armed resistance. They are thus part and parcel of a larger political project centered on the empowerment of the Shi'a and the followers of al-Sadr.

This chapter has portrayed the imagery of the Sadrists during the first phase of his movement's emergence, from 2004 to 2006. In April 2010 I traveled to the Shi'a shrines in Najaf, Karbala, Samarra, Kufa, and Kazimiyya, and al-Sadr's public images appeared to have retreated along with the Mahdi Army. While his images were not prevalent in the vicinity of the shrines, I did speak with his loyalists from Sadr City, dressed in black shirts and khaki pants, who worked alongside uniformed Iraqi forces in the security checkpoints outside the entrances to the holy sites, checking for mobile phones, lighters, or matches that could be used to detonate an explosive advice. By 2010 it appeared that the militant imagery of the Sadrists was redundant, as Sadr had already asserted power (although he was in Iran at the time) and the Jaysh al-Mahdi had been disbanded.

Conclusion

This chapter focused on Sadrist visual imagery from its first overt political phase, their emergence in post–Ba'athist Iraq. In this context the Sadr movement has developed a vast array of visual texts designed to direct the Shi'a of Iraq, and, in Barthes's words, the signifieds of the Sadrist images subtly seek to visualize and dispatch loyalty to the cleric. The projective power of these pictures was designed to enhance the authority of the young al-Sadr, employing a Shi'a metalanguage that emanates from a fusion of sectarian and nationalistic iconography and language.

The Sadrists have constructed a system of signs to define and redefine their vision of a post–Ba'athist Iraq, and their role in it, basing their legitimacy on a mesh of symbols and icons from Shi'ism, Iraqi nationalism, and armed struggle against the "occupiers." As a result of their elite formation process, the Sadrists have produced imagery that ranges from visual depictions of religious figures, both alive and deceased, to overt appropriation of Hollywood films to mundane commodities from Euro-American culture. Secular symbols (e.g., the Iraqi flag, flowers, and hearts), religious pictures of al-Sadr, and masked members of the Mahdi Army form part an array of images of power in a post–Ba'athist Iraqi national context. The use of icons, such as the image of al-Sadr in supplication, combative emblems such as the militia fighters, or more innocent images of children set against backgrounds of cartoon flowers or deserts, demonstrates that "popular culture" (in the Western sense of the expression) also has applications in Iraq.

The appropriation of images ranging from Kalashnikovs to stone monuments in the United States to hearts in an Iraqi Shi'i context demonstrates that flows between cultural realms undermine the supposed binaries between secular and religious, Western and Eastern, Islamic and non-Islamic. The Sadrist materials form a *Volkkitsch* that is political despite the fact that Muqtada never campaigned for political office in Iraq. The images that are embedded in student textbooks or sold from the market are clerical commodities destined for intimate, private spaces.

While al-Sadr's charismatic leadership in the Weberian sense was inherited from his father, the elder al-Sadr becomes increasingly absent in the images examined in this chapter. The images form part of a visual lexicon that seeks to cultivate loyalty to the young cleric's cult of personality, involving a day-to-day reconfiguration of power through a language of authenticity that is at once Islamic, Shi'a, and nationalistic.

NOTES

1. Known as the Supreme Council for the Islamic Revolution in Iraq (SCIRI) before 2007.

2. Bengio, *Saddam's Word*.

3. Baram, *Culture, History and Ideology*.

4. Al-Khalil, *The Monument*. Prior to the end of the 1991 Gulf War, Makiya wrote under the pseudonym Samir Khalil to conceal his identity.

5. Davis, *Memories of State*.

6. Dawisha, "Footprints in the Sand," 118.

7. Barthes, *Image, Music, Text*, 16.

8. Ibid., 21, 40.

9. Ibid., 17.

10. Tripp, *A History of Iraq* (Cambridge: Cambridge University Press, 2000).

11. Price, Griffin, and al-Marashi, *Toward an Understanding of Media Policy*.

12. Those taking part in the violence in Iraq against coalition forces, the interim Iraqi government, and civilians have been referred to as "resistance fighters," "terrorists," and "foreign jihadists." In this article, the most common term, "insurgent," has been employed.

13. Sreberny-Mohammadi and Ali Mohammadi, *Small Media, Big Revolution*.

14. Al-Musawi, *Al-Sayyid Muqtada Al-Sadr, Sadr Al-Iraq Al-Thalith*.

15. Baldauf, "Militia's Other Weapon."

16. Liu, "Mean Streets."

17. Barthes, *Image, Music, Text*, 16.

18. Ibid., 40.

19. Ibid., 21.

20. Ibid., 28.

21. Ibid.

22. Ibid., 17.

23. Open Source Center, "ILNA."

CHAPTER 8

The Martyr's Fading Body: Propaganda vs. Beautification in the Tehran Cityscape

ULRICH MARZOLPH

In 2008 a new mural was painted on the wall that borders the eastern side of Tehran's Najmiye Hospital courtyard, situated on the southern side of Jomhuri Avenue just west of where it crosses Hafez Avenue (fig. 8.1 and plate 17). The new mural replaces an old, fading image whose background depicted a blue sky poetically strewn with drifting clouds, framed on two sides by lines of poetry executed as an aesthetically appealing exercise in traditional calligraphy. The older mural's primary subject was a realistic portrait, set off against the background in a separate frame, of a man whose name was given as Doctor Mohammad-Ali Rahnamun. It was fairly obvious that this person had died as a "martyr"—a word that in the current terminology of the Islamic Republic of Iran denotes a man who has given his life to defend the country and, by extension, the country's ideological and political system. Since the martyr's death was a given fact, it was here only symbolically indicated by a red rose; moreover, a minaret of the mosque of Emam Hosein in Karbala served both to allude to the territory of Iraq (and thus the Iran–Iraq War) and to suggest the basic tenets of Shiism.

The new mural differs from the one it replaced in several respects. First, it is much larger. While the mural of Doctor Rahnamun had covered only about a third of the available space, notably the area closest to the neighboring street, the new mural covers the whole wall, even incorporating irregular extensions on the wall's top. The mural's dominant color is a light blue, particularly in its background of a clear blue sky scattered with a few white clouds. At first glance, the mural is fairly surrealistic. The image is dominated by a thin wall that covers about half of the space, to the lower right side. At second glance, however, viewers will notice that the wall obviously separates two worlds. The area to this side of the wall appears to be the world in which we live, as a spiral staircase starts at the bottom right side of the image, next to the courtyard, thereby directly linking the image with the "real" world. The staircase leads up and over the wall, where its steps gradually disintegrate and finally fade altogether. The area on the wall's other side is indicated on the mural's left side, where view-

FIGURE 8.1. Surrealistic Mural. Tehran, Jomhuri Avenue, Courtyard of the Najmiye Hospital. ©*Ulrich Marzolph, 2008.*

ers are permitted a glimpse into a scenery of fertile fields and lush green trees. This area appears to be of a different nature and, in fact, one beyond human comprehension: while the elements of this world are depicted in a fairly realistic manner, the trees in the "otherworld" are floating in air and the scenery is upside down.

Without knowing the artist's intention, if a viewer were to make sense of the two areas, the area on the wall's other side immediately suggests paradise. This interpretation can be further validated by two symbols that for many years have commonly been used in the Tehran murals to indicate the martyr's soul in heaven. On the right, the top of the fading staircase is crossed by a group of white doves heading toward the wall's other side. On the left, a swaying fold of the wall generates a series of white bubbles floating in the air. These cocoon-like balls, once matured, open, birthing white butterflies that fly up to the promised land.

In such a way this new mural replaces an older one. And yet it is much more than merely a replacement or renovation. While employing a colorful, modern style that is highly appealing in its abstraction—albeit somewhat enigmatic, as surrealistic images always are—the mural's imagery can be seen as a direct continuation of previous practice, in which butterflies and white doves were often used to symbolize the martyr's soul. Rather than simply replacing an old image with a new one (a change that may or may not imply an additional change of visual message), the new mural thus refers to and revalidates the previously propagated concepts of martyrdom by condensing them to a set of commonly accepted abstractions and symbols. In other words, the new mural retains the old mural's essential message in an abstract and depersonalized manner while adapting it to modern requirements in terms of artistic representation and public appeal.

While paintings such as this one have become fairly common in recent years, the phenomenon of murals in Tehran is by no means new. To the contrary, murals have been present in the capital city of the Islamic Republic of Iran (and, to a lesser degree, in other Iranian cities) for quite some time. In many ways they constitute the logical successors to smaller items of visual propaganda, such as the posters, postcards, photographs, stamps, and coins discussed in Peter Chelkowski and Hamid Dabashi's groundbreaking publication on the visual culture of post-revolutionary Iran.[1]

On February 10, 2009, the Islamic Republic of Iran celebrated the thirtieth anniversary of the Islamic Revolution, commemorating the historical events that led to the definitive abolishment of monarchic rule in Iran and resulted in the establishment of a radically new political system. The celebrations were undergirded by the many centuries of competition between the political rulers and the Shiite clergy concerning the legitimacy of political rule in an Islamic country. Today, the Islamic Republic of Iran for the first time in modern history has put into practice a principle that is regarded as the only legitimate one by the dominant current of contemporary Shiite clergy. This principle was formulated by Ayatollah Ruhollah Khomeini, the charismatic founder of the Islamic Republic, as *velayat-e faqih,* implying political leadership by the commonly acknowledged superior religious scholar of Shiite Islam. In the current system of the Islamic Republic, this leader (*rahbar*) is the uncontested political and military authority. His supervision alone guarantees that in case of doubt or dispute, each and every action of the state and its various institutions will be consistent with the values and norms that are regarded as "Islamic."

ULRICH MARZOLPH

The Islamic Republic of Iran's efforts in this respect cover all fields of cultural activities and are particularly visible in the large murals that adorn numerous buildings in Tehran.

The Tehran murals, many of which have been placed strategically so as to be visible from a far distance as well as to passing motorized traffic, constitute a fascinating facet of contemporary Iranian visual culture. The murals have been installed by order of the Tehran municipality, in particular its office for "beautification" (ziba-sazi), in an attempt to ease the monotony of the concrete habitat by adorning large walls (in particular those of highway bridges) with images of flowers, lush green meadows, or colorful ornaments. These murals often imitate nature, thus attempting to merge the walls with the surrounding greenery, or, conversely, to turn parts of the barren structures into virtual representations of a natural surrounding that is otherwise lacking.

The dominant theme of the Tehran murals, however, is the martyr (shahid), a term that almost exclusively implies men who have died in the course of promoting what is considered the just, "Islamic" cause. Many of the murals, particularly the more aggressive ones (such as the anti-American mural next to the flyover on Karim Khan Zand Avenue, which depicts a U.S. flag whose stripes turn into falling bombs),[2] have been used to illustrate numerous newspaper and journal reports about contemporary Iranian politics. In recent years, murals such as these also have received scholarly attention. One of the earliest studies to deal with the Tehran murals is Talinn Grigor's one-page paper in the August 2002 newsletter of the International Institute of Asian Studies,[3] and the most recent contributions to the topic are those by Houshang Chehabi and Fotini Christia, Christiane Gruber, and Pamela Karimi, published in a special volume of Persica.[4] The genesis of the murals, their overt and covert visual messages, and their development have been studied against the backdrop of both political motivations in Iran and visual culture on an international scale.

By drawing on photographic documentation covering more than a decade (1997–2009), the present contribution discusses and analyzes one particular aspect of the murals. My interpretation may or may not differ from that intended by the artists or the various institutions that ordered the murals. I read the murals according to my individual experience as a non-Iranian specialist in Iranian popular culture and folklore, while considering the backdrop of the changing political developments over the past few decades.

The aspect I have chosen for this study relates to the rhetoric of how the martyr's fate and body are represented, at times against the events that led to this person's death, or "martyrdom." Special attention will be given to recent developments in the style of the murals, particularly the change in the iconography of martyrs from the graphic and rather gory realistic mode to the abstract and symbolic mode as depicted in the mural discussed at the outset of this essay. Having documented the Tehran murals for an extensive period, I find it fascinating to witness the development of and changes to both their overt style and their more covert messages. The most recent change has occurred since about 2008, when the realistic portraits of martyrs began to be replaced by surrealistic images. Following a discussion of some older murals, the present paper will focus on the recent surrealistic images and the ways they adjust the lasting message of martyrdom to modern requirements. A limited number of new murals will be used to demonstrate that this adjustment often involves a fading of the martyr's body, which used to serve as a direct visual allusion to his cruel fate, and the replacement of it with traditional, abstract symbols of martyrdom, whose decoding is possible through a particular kind of cultural literacy.

The contemporary Iranian veneration of the martyr as a person who has given his life serving the just cause of Islam relate to the very roots of the Islamic religion. Statements regarding martyrdom are found in the Qur'an and the *hadith,* the utterances of the Prophet Muhammad. The Islamic orientation to martyrdom is also mirrored in the murals. For example, the latter half of a Qur'anic verse from *surah* 33 (*The Confederates,* verse 23) forms part of the logo of the *Bonyad-e shahid,* the Foundation of Martyrs, itself responsible for the majority of the Tehran murals. The *Bonyad-e shahid* is a powerful and influential institution founded by Khomeini's personal decree at the very beginning of the revolution in 1979.[5] The full text of the Qur'anic verse in its logo reads: "Within the believers there are men who have carried out the deeds they have promised to God. Some of them have already passed away while others still have to wait. And they have falsified nothing." These words, in the Qur'an placed after a passage discussing the historical Battle of the Trench in CE 627 and the necessity of armed defense, elevate martyrdom to a true believer's obligation toward God and the Islamic community. On another mural, an utterance of the Prophet Muhammad, albeit one whose canonical status is only acknowledged in Shiite tradition, lists three groups of persons whose intercession God will accept on the Day of Judgment: the prophets, the scholars, and the martyrs.[6] It is against this backdrop that the founder of the Islamic Republic, Ayatollah Khomeini, formulated the dictum "martyrdom is the art of the men of God" (*shahadat honar-e mardan-e khoda-st*), which is frequently quoted on murals.

The practical application of self-sacrifice in contemporary Iran ultimately relies on the pivotal martyrdom of Shiite Islam's third imam, the Prophet Muhammad's grandson Hosein, at Karbala in the year 680 CE.[7] Today, it is above all present through the large number of casualties resulting from the so-called "Imposed War," when the country defended itself against the U.S.-backed Iraqi aggression in the years 1980–88. However, in a wider interpretation, each person whose violent death is linked to the service of ideals propagated by the Islamic Republic of Iran is regarded as a martyr. Martyrs commemorated on the Tehran murals include victims of planned assassinations, including supreme judge Ayatollah Mohammad Beheshti, President Mohammad-'Ali Raja'i, and Prime Minister Mohammad Javad Bahonar, all of whom were killed in 1981 during major explosions allegedly initiated by the opposition group Mojahedin-e khalq; the group of Iranian diplomats massacred by the Taliban in the Afghani city of Mazar-e Sharif in September 1998; precursors of the Islamic Republic's ideological foundations, including Seyyed Hasan Modarres, one of Khomeini's teachers, who died in prison in 1937; and members of Hezbollah, most of whom gave their lives in the course of what Iran regards as a legitimate armed struggle for the liberation of Palestine. Finally, the title of "martyr" is also applied to individuals such as Mostafa Mazeh, the Conakry-born Lebanese Shiite Muslim who died when priming a bomb in a London hotel room in August 1989, supposedly preparing to execute Khomeini's *fatwa* against novelist Salman Rushdie.

Almost all murals of martyrs in Tehran have traditionally presented a simple, straightforward, and realistic depiction of the martyr's face or upper body along with his name. At times, the images are enhanced by symbols such as a red rose or a red tulip, both of which indicate blood and signify, by extension, the martyr's violent death. Often there is also a butterfly or white dove, symbolizing the martyr's soul. Although they aim to depict specific individuals, these portraits bear few individual traits, and their constant repetition effectively turns the martyrs into a mass phenomenon. The victims depicted thus become rather interchangeable, and, as a consequence, relatively anonymous. Yet many murals aim to provide the background to a martyr's fate or even to tell a story. Some of these murals depict the complex narrative behind the martyr's death in the nutshell of a single illustration, at times employing powerful visual allusions instead of words to indicate the particular circumstances of his death and to enable recognition by the viewer. Even so, the interpretation of these murals presupposes a certain "literacy," or knowledge of the depicted person and events, access to which is bound to fade into memory (or altogether) as time goes by and as younger generations emerge. In order to demonstrate this point, I wish to discuss a selection of murals in greater detail.

A mural depicting Sheikh Fazlollah Nuri appears on the wall of a building adjacent to the freeway bearing his name (fig. 8.2). Sponsored by the Foundation of the Martyrs, the image is dominated by the sheikh's lifelike portrait against a light blue sky filled with scattered clouds. The lower edge of the image is filled by a field of red tulips, the single buds of which transform into what looks like a sea of flowers stretching to the horizon. The few words by Khomeini that have been added to the portrait express admiration for the sheikh's erudition and sincerity. The image turns into the visual representation of a story by virtue of a barely visible object to the left of the center, a gallows from which a single rose is hanging. This scene alludes to the fact that Nuri, a stout opponent of the constitutional movement, was hanged in 1909. Out of respect, the deceased person is portrayed as he would be remembered from life, and the humiliating scene of his having been hanged is posthumously turned into a heroic act, a red rose substituted for his dead body as a common symbol of blood and martyrdom.

Further, the mural commemorating the death of director Mortaza Avini, situated on the same freeway, used to depict what appeared to be a scene from one of his war documentaries (fig. 8.3). The dark silhouettes of three soldiers are set against a generic background of water and evening sky. The soldiers are waving their guns in an apparent celebration of victory. Avini's lifelike portrait on the right is matched by a hand holding a camera, filming the scene, on the left. The celebrated cinematographer was killed by a landmine on April 9, 1993, while making a documentary about the soldiers missing from the former war fronts of southwestern Iran. The mural praises him with the exceptional honorific title of *sayyed-e shahidan-e ahl-e qalam*, "the prince of the martyred intellectuals," a direct allusion to Hosein's qualification as *sayyed al-shohada'*, or "Prince of Martyrs." Still today, Avini is celebrated as a major figure among Iran's artistic and literary community, and an extensive website commemorates his work.[8]

Probably the old mural's slightly pretentious presentation was the reason that the painting was refurbished a few years ago. The new version of the mural depicts Avini differently (fig. 8.4). He appears in the center of the image, surrounded by a frame, part of whose upper end is covered by a stream of vapor that emanates from around his head and turns into a misty sky dominated by a slogan praising the martyrs as the backbone of humanity (*shohada' sham'-e mahfal-e bashariyat-and*). Avini's identification as a martyr is clearly indicated by the flowers framing his image on both

ULRICH MARZOLPH

FIGURE 8.2. Mural of Sheikh Fazlollah Nuri. Tehran, Fazlollah Nuri Highway. ©Ulrich Marzolph, 2001.

FIGURE 8.3. Mural of director Morteza Avini. Tehran, Fazlollah Nuri Highway, old version. ©Ulrich Marzolph, 2001.

sides, while for those viewers who might not remember his profession so many years after his death the image's outer edges on both sides allude to a roll of film or cinematic frame. Furthermore, whether indicative of political change or not, it is interesting that the new mural does not include, as did its previous version, the portraits of both Khomeini and Khamenei. Their portraits could be read as an official endorsement of the martyred director's activities, as well as an act of claiming them for the interests of the Islamic Republic. The mural's new version, without the portraits of the former and present *rahbar*, suggests a stronger emphasis on Avini as an individual, while the added dictum—which is both much shorter than the previous one and more legible in its large graphic mode—suggests Avini's fate as an individual human condition rather than an affair of state.

Murals such as these depict the few individuals whose fate is well known to the average Iranian, having been widely discussed in the media. The visual exegesis of the murals has been prepared by a considerable amount of propaganda, which far exceeded the attention given to the hundreds of thousands of nameless martyrs. The common characteristic of these murals is the exemplification of martyrdom and self-sacrifice in the service of the Islamic Republic. This obvious interpretation is underlined time and again by the fact that the images are accompanied either by verbatim quotations of the former or the current leader of the Islamic Republic or by their portraits.

And yet the story of the innumerable casualties caused by the war is not a pleasant one, and aside from the relatively few individuals celebrated as heroes, the fate of most martyrs is either unknown or not told in detail. Their constant, and, in fact, overwhelming presence in the murals rather serves to remind society of their sacrifice, without which the Islamic Republic might not exist in its present form. The Tehran murals constitute a claim that, due to its visual nature, remains to a certain extent virtual. Meanwhile, President Ahmadinezhad's failed initiative (in early 2006) to exhume martyrs and rebury their bodies in the public sphere (such as in the large squares or even the university campuses in Tehran) can be read as a physically documented extension to the manner in which the murals already claim specific readings of society in public space.[9]

Moreover, the murals do not simply commemorate events or heroes of the past. By projecting historical events into the present, the murals refer to the past as the foundation of identity, a notion that is valid for the religion of Islam in general (and, as a matter of fact, probably constitutes a truism for each and every religion).[10] In Shiite Islam, for which the guilt of not having prevented Hosein's death at Karbala constitutes an everlasting theme,

ULRICH MARZOLPH

FIGURE 8.4. Mural of director Morteza Avini. Tehran, Fazlollah Nuri Highway, new version. ©Ulrich Marzolph, 2003.

this notion has been particularly strong. The murals negotiate the relation to the past not in redefining changing attitudes toward the Islamic faith, as exemplified in Yasemin Gencer's contribution to this volume. They rather underline and reaffirm a specific interpretation of the past that regards the martyrs and their sacrifice as essential for the present. Since today's present is nothing but tomorrow's remembered past, the murals also are designed to perpetuate the martyrs' lives and ideals into the future as a valid interpretation of the past and, thus, as a truly lasting foundational value. In this respect, one might add a fourth category of "history projected" to the three concepts of "history remembered, recovered, and invented" that Stefan Heidemann quotes from Bernard Lewis in introducing his discussion of the political iconography of history in the present volume.

Yet a survey of Tehran murals from the past decade demonstrates that there is no single coherent message to the images and, hence, no single coherent interpretation. Rather, the Tehran cityscape preserves a variety of murals. In fact, there are simultaneously extant examples from various periods that are fairly wide apart. Even a few of the early specimens of a socialist and/or anti-imperialist import of the late 1980s still exist—such as Iraj Eskandari's anti-American mural placed on a wall adjacent to the Felastin Square. The highly artistic murals by Firuze Golmohammadi, such as the one on the eastern side of the Vali-'Asr Square, will probably soon be replaced due to their poor state of preservation.[11]

One of the most moving martyr murals from the 1990s was replaced in 2002 (fig. 8.5).[12] This mural had been painted adjacent to one of the heavily traveled city freeways heading north. It showed a little girl covered with a black *chador* and holding a red rose in her hand, mourning her dead father, placed in front of her, with the words *Baba-ye shahidam—hich goli khoshbutar az yad-e to nist*, "My martyr father—no rose smells sweeter than your memory!" The mural's Tehran version did not specify the martyr's name, and it was only by chance that I discovered essentially the same image (probably taken from a photograph) in the city of Sirjan. Here, the martyr's name is given as Jamshid-e Zardosht. In a recent essay, Alice Bombardier has identified the mural's earlier versions and its artist as Gholam-'Ali Taheri, who executed the mural's first version, no longer extant, in 1981.[13] The lack of specificity in the mural's Tehran version was probably not coincidental, since the mural's composition elevates the martyr's fate to an abstraction whose appeal arises from its general applicability. The image was furthermore supplied with a number of stars containing invocations addressed at a group of five persons who represent the holy family revered by Shiite Islam: Mohammed, his daughter Fatima (implied in her epithet Zahra'), Ali, and their sons Hasan and Hosein; to this group was added the denomination of the hidden twelfth imam, al-Mahdi, the world's only rightful ruler. The upper-right corner contained what looked like a crack in the sky, allowing a glimpse of paradise, the future residence of all martyrs. The writing on the left side of the mural once offered comfort to the martyrs by telling them that the community will never forget their victory. In its particular composition, the mural raised the anonymous martyr's individual fate to a true Shiite believer's obligation, and the little girl's individual mourning became a general appeal to share in the martyr's fate.

The mural of Jamshid-e Zardosht was a powerful and emotionally moving celebration of martyrdom within the Shiite experience and worldview. And yet, it had to give way due to an obviously changing political agenda on the part of the Bonyad-e shahid. First, in 2003 the Bonyad had the original mural whitewashed and replaced by a mural expressing solidarity with the Palestinians (fig. 8.6). Picturing the Dome of the Rock in the middle, the image was framed on the left by the portraits of Khomeini and Khamenei and on the right by the head of an anonymous Palestinian man obviously crying out in anger and pain. The image's caption—probably one of the first in the Tehran murals to be given in both Persian and English, thus also communicating their written message to a non-Iranian audience—reproduced a

ULRICH MARZOLPH

FIGURE 8.5. Mural of Jamshid-e Zardosht. Tehran, Modarres Highway. ©*Ulrich Marzolph, 2001.*

quote from the leader of the revolution, whose English version reads: "the Islamic ummah [nation] will forever stand by the side of the Palestinians, and against their enemies." Already by 2004, the mural had been changed again, this time, however, preserving the previous subject matter. The obvious reason for the repeated change must have been the execution of Sheikh Ahmad Yasin by the Israeli army on March 22, 2004, since the Palestinian leader's portrait now figures prominently in the mural's center (fig. 8.7). It is revealing that, although Sheikh Yasin certainly fits the qualification of "martyr" as defined by the Iranian authorities, the mural does not include any of the symbols usually related to martyrdom. Instead, the mural's center is dominated by a set of three buildings representing the Iranian vision of Islam: the Dome of the Rock in Jerusalem, the Kaaba in Mecca, and the mosque of Emam Hosein in Karbala. It is also interesting to note that the towering figures of the leaders of the revolution have now been relegated to a fairly small ornamental frame on the image's right side.

The three different versions of this mural demonstrate a gradual fading of the martyr's body, from the image of a named individual via that of an unnamed Palestinian to a mere photographic portrait overshadowed by towering architectural symbols of Shiite Islam. Other, more recent murals go even further in that the martyr's body disintegrates into vague allusions and highly charged symbols.

FIGURE 8.6. Mural of an anonymous Palestinian martyr. Tehran, Modarres Highway. ©*Ulrich Marzolph, 2003.*

FIGURE 8.7. Mural of Sheikh Ahmad Yasin. Tehran, Modarres Highway. ©*Ulrich Marzolph, 2008.*

A mural on the wall of the courtyard that borders the headquarters of the Foundation of Martyrs in Tehran's central Taleqani Avenue used to depict an anonymous martyr who, after taking off his boots and putting aside his machine-gun, was humbly dressed in a white shroud, standing at the entrance to paradise (fig. 8.8). The depersonalized image was supplied with Khomeini's dictum reading *shahid avval kasi-st ke be-behest vared mishavad,* "the martyr is the first one to enter paradise." Originally executed in a style reminiscent of traditional miniature painting, the mural was replaced some years ago using bright, modern colors (fig. 8.9). While essentially depicting the same scene, the new image removes the martyr's individuality even further by more or less reducing the martyr to a pair of boots standing in front of a field of red tulips. Only an attentive viewer will notice that the martyr's body is still there. His nude feet are dangling below his swaying white shroud, which is enveloped by a pair of large white wings. Likewise, his head is vaguely discernible in the center of the image, where one hand holds it while a second loosens the red ribbon that qualifies him as a martyr ready to sacrifice his life. In this mural the martyr's body is still present, but its visibility has faded in favor of a complex design that once more draws on a common pool of symbols. If this change in the mural's style were to be seen as aiming at the larger applicability of its martyrial theme, the newly added quotation from the *maqam-e mo'azzam-e rahbari,* the Leader of the Islamic Republic, stressing the fact that society will never forget the martyrs, can also be understood to underline this fact.

The few existing interviews with viewers of the murals in Tehran have made it fairly clear that the younger generation in particular does not—to put it mildly—respond positively to the "traditional" murals that allude to the martyr's fate simply by showing portraits of the deceased.[14] Since additional data is not available, it remains unclear whether any of the sponsoring institutions ever considered taking into account the public's response, or whether the obvious propagandistic mission was deemed insufficient reason for the execution of the murals. Some of the young people Camilla Cuomo and Annaliza Vozza interviewed for their documentary *Factory of Martyrs* (2008) thought that most of the murals are badly executed and lack artistic qualities, while others admit to not even consciously noticing the murals at all. Additionally, Christiane Gruber has pondered the "expiration date" of the murals, since the "revolutionary and wartime murals [exist] in a socio-political time capsule" that apparently does not correspond to the present needs of the younger generation.[15] Of the various possibilities that Gruber envisions for future development, recent murals appear to opt for a reclaiming of the traditional core values of martyrdom while at the

FIGURE 8.8. Mural of an anonymous martyr. Tehran, Headquarters of the *Bonyad-e Shahid*, old version. ©*Ulrich Marzolph, 2000.*

same time aiming to take into account the longing of contemporary society for a less graphic representation and a greater aesthetic appeal. These changes are particularly visible in the murals designed by young artists such as Mahdi Qadiyanlu.[16] His murals replace a number of old murals of martyrs with new ones painted in bright colors, adding to their visibility and appeal. Second, the realistic mode of representation has been replaced by a surrealistic or pseudo-realistic mode in which the images are often merged with the shape or background of their surroundings, to the extent that at times they are hardly discernible as images. And yet, while some of the new murals appear to distance themselves from the traditional theme of martyrdom, many others essentially redeploy and reemphasize martyrial messages through visual abstractions and clues.

In her recent essay on Tehran's post–Iran–Iraq War murals, Pamela Karimi mentions a mural on the west side of Ferdousi Avenue, north of

ULRICH MARZOLPH

FIGURE 8.9. Mural of an anonymous martyr. Tehran, Headquarters of the *Bonyad-e Shahid*, new version. ©*Ulrich Marzolph, 2003.*

Ferdousi Square (today called Qarani Avenue), that depicts a war veteran with an amputated leg alongside a caption: "The value of you, the veteran, is more than that of the martyrs (fig. 8.10).[17] This mural was repainted in early 2009 and replaced by a mural in an updated style (fig. 8.11). The new mural, while retaining the portraits of venerated individuals on its left side, has replaced the somewhat gruesome, realistic depiction of the wartime veteran with a scene in the trompe l'œil mode that is currently popular. Here, a mother and her son bid farewell to their martyred husband and father. While previous murals, such as the ones discussed above, had already paved the way for the fading of the martyr's body, in this mural the body has completely disappeared. Since younger generations in Iran find it difficult to relate directly to a war that is long past, and tend to be "allergic" to, alienated by, or at best bored with the direct visualization of physical disability caused by the war, the new mural has obviously opted for a "hygienic" representation. This new version presents a synecdochal representation of the wounded veteran by simply depicting his wheelchair. Since the martyr's body has completely disappeared, one might also wonder whether the veteran is supposed to have died in the meantime, but the symbol of the white dove flying high up in the air—after so many years of having been employed in murals of martyrs—leaves no doubt of the image's message: the martyr's body has undergone a metamorphosis resulting in the white dove, a common symbol for the martyr's soul. Considered together with the image of the staircase, the fact that the dove is flying into a trompe l'œil oculus might also indicate an ascension of the soul and the ultimate elevation of the martyr to his promised abode in paradise.

A mural placed on the western side of a building on Tehran's busy Enqelab Avenue again tells a well-known story (fig. 8.12 and plate 19). The image used to show a burning Iraqi tank placed in front of the upper body of a young boy rising from scenery that was filled with additional approaching enemy tanks. A sad and melancholic Khomeini, looking at the boy from above, was towering in the background, while the top of the image bore a caption quoting Khomeini's historical utterance: "Our leader is that 12-year-old boy who . . . threw himself under an enemy tank, blew it up and drank the beverage of martyrdom." The boy is Hosein Fahmide, whose suicide bombing in 1982 made him an icon of the Iran–Iraq War and an Iranian national hero.[18] He was subsequently celebrated by a monument on the outskirts of Tehran and commemorated by a postage stamp issued in 1986. The fact that a statement on the mural attributed to the present leader of the Islamic Republic, Ayatollah Khamenei, used the term *hamase,* "epic," to characterize the event, added an almost mythical dimension to Hosein Fahmide's exemplary act of self-sacrifice.

The mural's new version, installed in the summer of 2009 (fig. 8.13 and plate 20), revalidates previous ideals to quite unprecedented levels. Fahmide, whose "heroic" deed is so well known in present-day Iran that it does not need an explicit illustration, is now depicted on what looks like a postcard portrait placed on a large bookshelf. The only explicit allusion to his fate as a martyr is a hand grenade placed on the shelf below. The grenade is framed by several candles whose flames are blowing in the wind, and the shelf itself is covered by a ribbon in red and white. The red on the ribbon alludes to the martyr's blood, and—together with a number of lush green cypress trees on the image's upper left that supposedly would indicate paradise—the three colors represent the colors of the Iranian national flag. The martyr's body has thus faded into a stand-in object that has been placed into a commemorative setting. The original contextual informa-

LEFT: FIGURE 8.10. Mural of a disabled war veteran. Tehran, Qarani Avenue, old version. ©Ulrich Marzolph, 2003.

RIGHT: FIGURE 8.11. Mural of a disabled war veteran. Tehran, Qarani Avenue, new version. ©Ulrich Marzolph, 2009.

tion now relies on the presupposed common knowledge of this particular martyr's deeds.

Even more fascinating than the new mode of representing the martyr is the absolutely stunning fact that the portrait of Khomeini, originally towering in the image's background, has now completely disappeared. This portrait, together with the leader's related utterance, used to suggest the image's intended interpretation in linking the martyr's individual fate with larger issues of state and religion. Whatever the vanishing of Khomeini's image implies, it is certainly unlikely to be coincidental. Without going into much speculation, it must be noted that the elimination of Khomeini's image in this mural diminishes his visual presence in the public domain. Only time will tell whether it constitutes a first step in restricting Khomeini's unquestioned authority, in a possible attempt to transfer this authority to the present *rahbar.*

The new symbolic revalidation of the concept of martyrdom is further visible in a number of other murals, such as the one on the northern side of Fatemi Square, where an oculus in the wall links to the image of a lush green area, the home of white doves (fig. 8.14 and plate 18). Without the long history of martyr murals, viewers might see this realistic depiction and assimilation to the urban surrounding as a wishful projection of real

LEFT: FIGURE 8.12. Mural of Hosein Fahmide. Tehran, Enqelab Avenue, old version. ©*Ulrich Marzolph, 2004.*

RIGHT: FIGURE 8.13. Mural of Hosein Fahmide. Tehran, Enqelab Avenue, new version. ©*Ulrich Marzolph, 2009.*

life. This suggestion is further validated by the fact that the mural previously placed on this wall was an artistic image of birds and calligraphic exercises painted many years ago by students of the Faculty of Arts at Tehran University. And yet once again, against the backdrop of antecedent martyr murals, the white doves, the oculus, and the lush green area beyond can be seen as symbolic codes that represent the quest of the martyr's soul for paradise. Considering the new surrealistic trend in the Tehran murals, the images appear to opt for an ideal combination of the "traditional" martyr mural that used to focus on the portrait and body of the actual individual and more modern artistic approaches designed to communicate with a younger audience. On the one hand, they retain the older symbols of martyrial imagery, such as clouds, white doves, and allusions to paradise. On the other, they relegate these symbols to levels of culturally encoded "literacy" that by now might rightly be presumed to be firmly anchored in Iranian viewers' subconscious by way of the hundreds of "traditional" images that have been present for several decades.

The new mode of symbolic representation reaches its apogee in a mural recently painted on top of a building bordering the southwestern side of the crossing of Kargar and Fatemi Avenues to the northwest of

FIGURE 8.14. Mural of a green countryside with doves. Tehran, Meidan-e Fatemi.
©Ulrich Marzolph, 2009.

Tehran's Lale Park area (fig. 8.15). This mural discloses its powerful meaning only against the backdrop of several decades of martyr murals. At first sight, it innocently depicts a flying white dove against a sky so blue that, considering Tehran's pollution, the sky itself seems almost surrealistic. Besides the bird's tremendous size, the only element that enables viewers to distinguish the mural as a painting from afar is a rectangular area in the dove's back, vaguely signaling another world beyond. Considering the history of symbolic cues embedded in dozens of murals in Tehran, this particular one offers itself to be read as a martyrial simile in visual form, as a corporate stand-in for the martyr's soul as couched in the image of the flying white dove.

Research into the murals of Tehran has repeatedly stressed their "significant documentary value for modern Iranian visual culture."[19] Their study allows a glimpse into the development of contemporary representations of social and religious values that are propagated as essential for an "Islamic" identity as defined in today's Islamic Republic of Iran. Moreover, their long-term examination also permits us to study changing attitudes in a society that—considering the impact of recent transitions—constitutes a fascinating and quickly evolving field of research.

FIGURE 8.15. Mural of a white dove. Tehran, Kargar, north of Lale Park. ©*Ulrich Marzolph, 2009.*

The recent murals discussed in this essay combine surrealistic representations and the trompe l'œil mode to produce attractive, eye-catching visuals. Floating trees and flying objects create an atmosphere of surprise, arousing viewers' curiosity. Fertile meadows and lush green trees, as the suggested continuation of a rather dismal, gray urban setting, present stark contrasts to a daily routine. These juxtapositions are certainly unexpected, yet they are probably appreciated all the more because they constitute the ultimate expression of a city dweller's potential longing for greener pastures. Meanwhile, considering the political and ideological climate in the Islamic Republic of Iran, it would be surprising if the surrealistic murals were just another "simple" attempt to beautify the urban habitat, and it appears unlikely that they were designed as "innocent"— that is, as being devoid of a specific message. The interpretation offered in the present contribution thus suggests that they are a direct and logical continuation of previous martyr murals, although at first sight the martyr himself appears to have faded away. The murals' primary message has, however, not changed in essence, as the martyr makes an implicit appearance in clues, most commonly in the symbol of the white dove that signals the martyr's soul on its way to paradise.

ULRICH MARZOLPH

If this interpretation holds true, the surrealistic murals with their inherent martyrial messages would constitute an even stronger medium than previous murals with direct messages. Previous martyr murals invited viewers to commemorate the martyrs and celebrate their sacrifices—an invitation that, depending on the circumstances, may or may not result in the viewers' outright rejection. The new murals, on the contrary, employ the surrealistic mode as a more subtle means of driving home their messages. By taking recourse to topics and subjects that are both visually appealing and in accordance with the viewers' inherent desire for more urban beauty, such murals veil their essentially unchanged martyrial message, which is retained through the rhetoric of symbolic expression.

NOTES

1. Chelkowski and Dabashi, *Staging a Revolution.*
2. Gruber, "The Message Is on the Wall," 23, fig. 5.
3. Grigor, "(Re)Claiming Space," 37.
4. Chehabi and Christia, "The Art of State Persuasion"; Gruber, "The Message Is on the Wall"; Karimi, "Imaging Warfare, Imagining Welfare"; and Marzolph, "The Martyr's Way to Paradise."
5. See Rahimiyan, *Dar harim-e laleha.*
6. Quoted from a (no longer extant) mural on the freeway bridge leading to Tehran's *shahrak-e Qods.* The reference on the mural was given as Majlesi's *Bihâr al-anvâr,* vol. 97.
7. For recent studies of the visual aspects of martyrdom in present-day Iran, with special reference to the martyrdom of Hosein, see Aghaie, *The Martyrs of Karbala;* Varzi, *Warring Souls;* Newid, *Der schiitische Islam in Bildern;* and Flaskerud, *Visualising Belief and Piety in Iranian Shiism.*
8. See http://www.aviny.com/; and Khosronejad, "Introduction."
9. See Esfandiari, "Iran."
10. See, e.g., Afsaruddin, *The First Muslims.*
11. Karimi, "Imaging Warfare, Imagining Welfare," 52, fig. 2.
12. Marzolph, "The Martyr's Way to Paradise," 95, fig. 5.
13. Bombardier, "La peinture murale iranienne"; see also Coyne, "Iran under the Ayatollahs," 110.
14. For a mural viewer's negative reaction, see Gruber, "The Message Is on the Wall," 45.
15. Ibid., 46.
16. Karimi, "Imaging Warfare, Imagining Welfare," 44–46.
17. Ibid., 49.
18. See Chelkowski and Dabashi, *Staging a Revolution,* 132–34; Gruber, "The Message Is on the Wall," 31, fig. 8.
19. Gruber, "The Message Is on the Wall," 46.

PART 3

Satirical Contestations

FIGURE 9.1. Ramiz Gökçe (1900–1953), Conservative Reaction gets caught in the Republic's Machine, *Akbaba*, front page, March 3, 1924, Atatürk Kitaplığı, Istanbul.

CHAPTER 9

Pushing Out Islam: Cartoons of the Reform Period in Turkey (1923–1928)

YASEMIN GENCER

A cartoon published in 1924, on the front page of the Turkish satirical journal *Akbaba* (Vulture), depicts a machine and as its operator, Mustafa Kemal, the president and leader of the recently founded Turkish Republic (fig. 9.1).[1] A second man, identifiable by his long cloak and turban as a mullah, is caught in a grinding machine. The machine is identified in the register below the cartoon as "the Republic's Machine" (*Cumhuriyet Makinesi*). Further clarifying the cartoon, its caption reads, "Conservative Reaction gets himself caught in the Modern Machine, whose meaning he did not understand." The text equates the concept of the republic with modernity, represented by the machine, and, by extension, its opposition with "Conservative Reaction," personified by the mullah figure.

The mullah, the former leader—and exemplary member—of the Muslim community, is represented as a bumbling cretin so unaware of his surroundings and out of touch with modern technology that he is incapable of avoiding injury (and perhaps even death). He is rendered as a caricature not only by his predicament but also through the style of his depiction. Indeed, in contrast to the portrait-like precision of Mustafa Kemal's facial features, the mullah peers out at the world through popped eyes and sports a gaping mouth with missing teeth. His turban looks as though it might slip off of his bald head as he jumps back with haste and surprise. The image works closely with the text to depict this man as ignorant and irrational, "conservative" and "reactionary." While his garments identify him as a Muslim cleric, within the context of the abbreviated language of the cartoon he nevertheless becomes a personification of Islam. The original meaning of the mullah as a positive symbol of Islam is only further inverted by the positioning of the figure as opposite Mustafa Kemal, the virtual savior and leader (and, later, "father") of the new republic,[2] who seems indifferent to the mullah's struggle with the machine. Moreover, the cartoonist has bypassed depicting a fully clothed version of Mustafa Kemal in favor of a shirtless portrayal that emphasizes his virility and Herculean strength: his flexed muscles draw attention to the laborious task of passing reform legislation. In addition to the realistic rendering of Mustafa Kemal's facial features, his body dwarfs the mullah's, adding visual power and charisma to the muscled hero while taking such traits away from the cartoonishly debilitated mullah, whose actions are more animal-like than human. The crazed mullah indeed becomes an example of how not to behave, think, or even dress. Thus, the symbolic embodiment of Islam is reversed from a positive sign to a negative one within the syntax and grammar of the cartoon.

Many similar political cartoons produced in Turkey during the reform period (1923–28) employ narrative dichotomies and pictorial opposites in order to illustrate and drive forward their political messages. They also provide varying degrees of realism to their protagonists in order to elevate them or caricaturize, and thus disempower their antagonists. The "Republican Machine" cartoon, and others like it, presents a message laden with cultural symbols from both the past and present. Specifically, these cartoons relay an opinion regarding Islam that was inspired by the Kemalist reforms of the period that were aimed at modernizing and secularizing the newly established Turkish Republic. However, would it be accurate to characterize these cartoons as anti-Islamic? Are these cartoons advocating for a non-religious society, in which Islam plays no role in a person's life, or do they simply depict a secular separation of religion and state? Finally, why address Islam at all? Where are religion and Islamic identity located within the construction of a supposed Turkish "identity" as promoted within new Republican ideals?

This essay argues that the cartoons dealing with the reforms of the early Republican period promote and support a certain brand of secularism that restricted the role of Islam to the private sphere by systematically depicting its removal from various public spheres in government and society, concluding that the private (and less visible) sphere was to be the place of Islam within the newly minted construct of modern national identity in Turkey. Drawing from five front-page cartoons from three prominent satirical journals, *Akbaba*,[3] *Kelebek* (Butterfly),[4] and *Karagöz* (named after a popular shadow theater character),[5] as well as the newspaper *Cumhuriyet* (Republic),[6] this essay explores illustrations responding to two of the most controversial and superficial reforms of the period 1923–28.[7] These include the abolition of the caliphate and the consequent closing of religious schools (*medreses*) in 1924, as well as the replacement of the Arabic script with Latin letters in 1928.[8] These cartoons use a variety of methods to reinforce their messages, including (but not confined to) juxtaposing Islam and modernity by reconfiguring previously positive iconic symbols of Islam to negative signs of backwardness, ridiculing Islam through the caricaturing of its leading figures, and using the image of Mustafa Kemal to justify such claims. The decision to focus on cartoons illustrating these two particular reforms is based on the fact that they relate directly to the issues of reforms and identity at stake. These cartoons attest to the key moments of controversy surrounding the reforms through the thoughts and sketches of some of their most enthusiastic supporters.

The Question of Censorship

While proponents of these reforms were able to express their support through cartoons, there remained a glaring lack of cartoons opposing or criticizing the same reforms. This lack of dissent can best be explained by addressing the question of censorship that persisted since the Ottoman era.

As Palmira Brummett's book *Image and Imperialism in the Ottoman Revolutionary Press* notes, the years 1908–11 witnessed a period of relative freedom enjoyed by the print media in the late Ottoman Empire. This second constitutional period, which followed a thirty-year period of strict censorship imposed by the administration of 'Abdülhamid II (r. 1876–1909), was a time when every opinion was voiced and few social or political criticisms were truly suppressed. The Ottoman press continued to experience relative freedom of expression; satirical publications multiplied;[9] and cartoon arts flourished from 1908 until the First World War (1914–18). Conversely, the Armistice period (1918–20) following the war and Ottoman defeat was one of restricted freedom, especially in the British-occupied capital of the empire, Istanbul.[10]

A brief period of relaxed censorship followed the Turkish War of Independence in 1922, but ended abruptly after a major Kurdish rebellion in February 1925, in which the agitators demanded the reestablishment of the caliphate and religious law and order (*shari'a*) by the Turkish government. These demands created an unstable political environment that the new government combated with the new censorship law. The *Takrir-i Sükun Kanunu* (Law on the Maintenance of Order) was passed in March 1925, allowing the government to shut down any publication considered to be a threat to law and social order, following this rebellion.[11] Shortly after the signing of this code into law, the government shut down eight major newspapers in Istanbul.[12] This law, which was intended to stay in effect for only two years, remained in force until 1929.[13]

Government censorship during the initial years of the republic was a reality—one that certainly influenced and curtailed freedoms of expression.

Moreover, even when the press was not openly censored, social self-censorship may have been taking place, especially during the years after the independence victory and before the Kurdish rebellion that sparked official censorship in the form of a law.[14] As a response to the national victory, and the close encounter with foreign occupation, the initial drive toward social unity could have resulted in a kind of self-censorship to strengthen a cultural identity under threat. This environment fostered the elevation of Mustafa Kemal as a national savior in what Jack Goldstone has called a "honeymoon" period following a major political revolution.[15] It is in this relatively restrictive arena of expression (both self- and regime-imposed) that the cartoons of the early Republican period were born: an environment conducive to messages in support of the rapidly occurring reforms—and an environment hostile to multiple viewpoints. The united messages created in the pages of these satirical journals—a positive and supportive outlook toward the Kemalist reforms—gave the impression of an equally unified front of popular approval. This objective was reached through a wide variety of recurring visual motifs.

Nation-Building and National Identity

As a result of the various state- and self-imposed censorships of the early Republican period, most of the satirical journals that remained in operation supported the new government and their reform efforts. The satirical journal *Karagöz* was the most enthusiastic supporter of the Independence Struggle and Mustafa Kemal. Despite an occasional cartoon that voiced objection to censorship,[16] the journal was a prime disseminator of some of the most nationalistic and vehemently pro-reform cartoons of the period—a stance that is perhaps best foretold by its name and history.[17] *Karagöz* was one of the earliest and longest-running journals of the period. The adoption of the name Karagöz was a clever idea when the journal first began publication in 1908, during the second constitutional period, when widespread media censorship was lifted. Karagöz was the name of a popular shadow puppet character representative of the common Turk and best known for his wit and sharp tongue. The use of the Karagöz character as the journal's mascot (and name) thereby situated the journal on the side of the people.[18] This populist subtext survived the regime change and continued through the 1920s.

Karagöz frequently employed the shadow puppet character either as a passive narrator or an active participant in its cartoons. The cartoon character Karagöz, like his shadow puppet counterpart, often uses slang and colloquial language to comment on events. This adds to his popular and populist appeal, which is further amplified by the cartoons' subject matter. For example, the March 1, 1924, issue of *Karagöz* published a front-page cartoon depicting Mustafa Kemal discarding a book whose title reads "old laws," along with Karagöz and his sidekick, Hacivat, happily discarding a skull that bears the inscription "old head" (a common Turkish expression that means outdated mentality) and a jar (fig. 9.2). All the while, a man wearing a turban looks on from behind a wall in the background. A short text placed above the cartoon—"March may enter, and the rubbish must leave"—is a popular expression referring to spring-cleaning. The caption below the cartoon quotes the character Hacivat as stating: "In celebration of the New Year, let's throw away all that is old and worn, Karagöz!" Karagöz responds, "The new Republic must make everything new. That is why we must revive our old Turkish customs and throw out all that is outdated."

The text and cartoon create a clear equation between the discarded objects and the "outdated" thoughts and practices that must be thrown away. The book of "old laws" represents *shari'a* (Islamic law) as an archaic legal system that is no longer appropriate for the emerging secular Turkish Republic, while the "old head" represents a retrograde (i.e., Islamic and Ottoman) mindset that is further stressed visually by the artist's decision to depict a skull rather than a fully fleshed head. The unmarked jar represents the Treaty of Sèvres (August 10, 1920), which was signed by the Ottoman Empire and Allied forces at the end of the First World War.[19] The treaty gave control of the empire's finances to the Allied forces, permitted them to occupy various parts of the empire at will, and required the Ottomans to dissolve their military. The Turkish War of Independence following the First World War prevented the treaty from achieving its intended goal, namely, to reduce the Ottoman Empire to a small land-locked state in the middle of Anatolia.[20]

The selection of certain protagonists is also carefully calculated: Mustafa Kemal represents national freedom and reform; Karagöz and Hacivat symbolize a cultural tradition of storytelling that is considered indigenously "Turkish"[21] rather than Ottoman or Islamic. Furthermore, within their original context of shadow theater, Karagöz and Hacivat represent two vastly different social strata: the lower and middle classes, respectively. It is thus possible to read these characters as representing cooperation across social and economic classes to change the nation and help the state. Additionally, there is a man wearing a turban in the background who is peering from over a wall with an expression of concern discernible on his face; he is obviously excluded from the events taking

FIGURE 9.2. The disposing of old mentalities and laws, *Karagöz,* front page, March 1, 1924, Atatürk Kitaplığı, Istanbul.

place in the foreground. He crowns the clutter of jettisoned objects in the center of the cartoon, thereby personifying all that must be discarded from Islamic civilization. The mullah is thus visually marginalized and symbolically incapacitated. As a result, this cartoon communicates a revolutionary message, pitting Turkishness against Islam, and Western secularism against the "antiquarian" Ottoman-Islamic legal system of *shari'a.*

The cartoon also subtly assigns duty to members of society based on the objects discarded by the protagonists. Karagöz and Hacivat, emerging from the windows and doors of a regular house, represent the people who, having already rid themselves of their foreign occupiers (the Sèvres vase), must now "clean house" of their old ways and mentalities (the skull). Mustafa Kemal, on the other hand, is depicted still wearing his military uniform and appears as the savior and leader of his community. Standing on the balcony of a more palatial building, he tackles legislative reforms, cued by the book of laws he is discarding—or, rather, "reforming."

This cartoon assigns roles to certain parts of society—the political and military elite as well as the common folk—and aligns negative and positive symbols with certain persons and ideological paths. It also assigns blame for the state of the country to Islamic law, ignorance, and poor leadership under Ottoman rule, as made apparent by the Sèvres vase. Miroslav Hroch has examined the nation-building efforts of many small European countries, observing that modern nation-states have been constructed around ideas of shared history, culture, and language.[22] It is well established that, indeed, in all cases, these very building blocks of national identities are themselves mere constructs.[23] The cartoon illustrates this process by visually molding a seemingly coherent national identity via a selective process that encourages its readers to "revive" Turkish customs while "throwing out" outdated ones. Outdated elements are equated with religious law and the putatively backward mentalities of the recent, Islamic past. Here, the modern "revival" is sought in a more distant, pre-Islamic, and thus "inherently" and "purely" Turkish, past.

In articulating a new history (or rather, a new take on history) Hroch and Malečková have noted that many nation-building projects found a culprit on which to blame their recent failures.[24] Essential to Hroch and Malečková's observation is the fact that this occurred mostly in national struggles in which the largest segment of the population were of nondominant social and political standing. The Turks of the Ottoman Empire were not oppressed and enjoyed a dominant status, as they made up the majority of the population. Yet Turks found themselves in the midst of their own "national struggle" to define, rebuild, and refine a national identity—following a path of nation-building similar to that of nations in which the majority population was non-dominant.[25] This cartoon clearly partakes in nation-building because it suggests a flaw in the recent past that can be fixed by the Turkish peoples' own efforts and distant past. The Islamic Ottoman age is thus designated as the malaise, and Islam as its cause; conversely, innately Turkish customs,[26] the new (i.e., progressive) republic, and an evacuation of the superannuated are the only remedy.

Alphabet Reform as a Source of National Pride

According to Hroch, language also has been a major factor in most European efforts at nation-building.[27] On a practical level, a common language is the most perceptible indicator of a person's national identity. Indeed, the rise of the newspaper, journal, and other publications, along with the use of (or realized need for) a common language among minorities, became a point of departure for a great number of national movements in Eastern Europe. The Turkish movement was no exception.[28]

The second half of the nineteenth century witnessed linguistic contention in the Ottoman Empire among scholars interested in Turkish culture and history. Debates emerged regarding the "Turkishness" of the Ottoman language, as well as the complex and thus largely unintelligible nature of the Ottoman language to the common people.[29] By the early 1900s, plans for purifying the Ottoman language and even changing the alphabet began to be proposed and debated at length in various journals.[30] The prevalence of Arabic and Persian words and grammatical constructs in the Ottoman language was seen by many scholars as undermining the innate richness of the Turkish language.[31] Such statements indicate a desire to symbolically break from other languages, which were perceived as having exerted dominance over the Turkish language (and, by extension, Turkish culture in general).

Prior to the language reform that would occur in the 1930s, a transformation of the alphabet was instigated in 1928, whereupon the Arabic alphabet was replaced with a system of Latin characters that was called the "Turkish alphabet."[32] The alphabet and its very name gave the people of the Turkish Republic something to claim as their own. It also allowed the new republic to symbolically break away from its Islamic neighbors and Islamic past. While the military victories of the Independence Struggle aided the emerging republic in escaping the grips of foreign political occupation to her west, this legislative victory helped the republic sever itself from the strong cultural influences from the east and southeastern regions. Thus,

YASEMIN GENCER

when the dust settled, these two events left a more politically and culturally independent Turkish Republic in their wake.

A cartoon about the alphabet reform that appeared on the front page of the satirical journal *Akbaba* on August 30, 1928, cleverly equates the magnitude of the legislative victory (alphabet reform) with the widely celebrated military victory of the Turkish army over the Greek forces six years earlier (to the day) (fig. 9.3). Here, Mustafa Kemal wears a Western-style suit while standing victoriously atop a mountain of crushed Arabic letters. The triumphant leader holds an oversized European steel-nib pen that is meant to create a contrast with the simple hand-cut reed pen traditionally used in the Muslim world.[33] Furthermore, this pen bears a crescent and star on its shaft, thus resembling a military banner.[34] It thereby establishes a further nationalistic connection between military and legislative triumphs—as led by Mustafa Kemal. The mammoth pen represents the grand action of lawmaking as well as the specific law on alphabet reform, itself intimately related to the pen. The cartoon is sandwiched between a sentence above it, which states that the cartoon "celebrates the 31 August 1922 victory," and a caption below that bluntly declares a new "31 August 1928 victory."[35] The captions above and below the cartoon indicate that the cartoon creates a direct relation between the already well-known military victory and this new legislative victory. By highlighting the multiple fronts on which wars have been waged, the cartoon heralds the progress the country has made in the last six years, militarily and even alphabetically freeing itself from unwanted foreign powers and influences.[36]

The cartoon also combines two moments: the elimination of the Arabic alphabet and the subsequent anticipated period of enlightenment. This awakening is quite literally brought about by the sun, inscribed with the words "the New Turkish Letters," that is rising behind Mustafa Kemal.[37] The sun is an object that illuminates the world while also commencing a new day; it is a symbol of enlightenment as well as renewal and rebirth. As such, it serves as a harbinger of the rebirth of the nation following the military victory of 1922 while also suggesting that it will defeat ignorance and illiteracy with its radiant light.

The new letters also become bearers of a new Age of Enlightenment, guaranteed to eliminate the darkness and illiteracy caused by the Arabic alphabet (which was argued to be very difficult to learn).[38] The contrast drawn between dark and light, ignorance and enlightenment, is coupled with a second contrast, that of order and chaos. The scrambled Arabic letters are in a state of utter disarray, while the New Turkish Letters rise above the mound in perfectly legible order and arranged in a single register.

FIGURE 9.3. Ramiz Gökçe (1900–1953), Victory over the Arab Alphabet, *Akbaba*, front page, August 30, 1928, Atatürk Kitaplığı, Istanbul.

The mound of spoliated letters visually conveys the collection, elimination, and domination over the relics of a formidable opponent—now rendered obsolete and relegated to the past.[39] Moreover, the arrangement of the Arabic letters, stacked on top of one another, constitutes criticism toward the calligraphic arts as it exaggerates and thus satirizes the often illegible forms this art took.[40] The use of scripts such as *sülüs* and a popular compositional arrangement called *istif* (whereupon letters are woven together and layered in a stylistic manner) rendered Arabic-language inscriptions aesthetically pleasing but virtually illegible, much like the jumbled mess beneath Mustafa Kemal's feet.[41] Interestingly, on the far right corner of the mound the seemingly carelessly tossed letters, *mim* and *lam-elif*, also happen to spell the word "mullah." However, this playful arrangement of letters, while appearing accidental, refers any attentive reader to the secularizing reforms of the past five years that systematically pushed Islam out of the public sphere. As will be explored below, alphabet reform was one salient aspect of Mustafa Kemal's larger secularizing agenda for the country that found its place in Turkish cartoon arts.

Secularism as Modernization

Within the context of early Republican thought and the realities of the post–World War I period, both secularism and nationalism were seen as means by which to achieve a modern state.[42] At this time, the late Ottoman and early Republican intelligentsia equated ideas of "modernness" with "Western civilization" or even "Europeanness"; thus, that which was European or Western was modern and advanced.[43]

Because a secularized state was an envisioned path to modernity, one comes across a wide array of cartoons that illustrate modernity's conflict with, and victory over, religion. The oppositional dichotomy created between modernity and the institutionalized religious establishment is demonstrated by a front-page cartoon published in the satirical journal *Kelebek* on March 13, 1924 (fig. 9.4). Here, a rather stern Mustafa Kemal is depicted operating a steamroller that is crushing domed buildings as the occupants run off, angrily shaking their fists in the air. The cartoon is adorned with the title "Real Revolution." The caption below the cartoon reads: "A strong administrative machine like this was all that was necessary for definitive reform." Both the machine and Mustafa Kemal bear the signs of modernism. The steamroller is a modern industrial creation from the West, built to pave roads and flatten rubble and rubbish. Likewise, Mustafa Kemal is depicted—as he was in life—dressed in a European-style

FIGURE 9.4. The administrative machine of definitive reform, *Kelebek,* front page, March 13, 1924, Atatürk Kitaplığı, Istanbul.

suit. Placed at the helm of the machine, he takes on the role of a modern Western leader, a path-breaker of sorts.

What, then, constitutes the old in need of crushing in this cartoon? The domes of the building and the fleeing men are what the Republic needs to eradicate. The fleeing men, like the turbaned man in figure 9.1, represent religious figures, and furthermore serve as personifications of Islam. Represented here as small and cowardly—hardly able to remain and fight—these mullah figures and Islam provide the antithesis of modernism as represented by the machine and its driver, Mustafa Kemal. Published ten days after the abolition of the caliphate and the signing of the *Tevhid-i Tedrisat* law, which closed all religious schools (*medreses*), this cartoon both commemorates and legitimizes the recent reforms while also calling for additional reforms in the caption. By generalizing the mullahs as religious figures rather than simply showing the caliph or a *medrese* teacher, it widens its message to one that is critical of Islam's role in both politics and the public sphere.

This cartoon also follows a similar formula to two previously discussed cartoons (figs. 9.1 and 9.3). Both visualize Mustafa Kemal as the savior and leader-in-chief. He wields utensils of enlightenment (the pen-banner) and modern technology (machines). In both figures 9.3 and 9.4 he triumphantly stands atop mounds of the demolished past. Both forms of rubble—the Arabic alphabet and the *medreses*—are symbols of Islam. These symbols, however, have been transformed from intellectual symbols of the past to ones of backwardness and ignorance. Finally, in all three cartoons, symbols of the recent Islamic past are juxtaposed with (and eliminated by) the symbols of modernism and nationalism.

Ahmet Davutoğlu has pointed out that secular forms of society were foreign to non-Western countries such as Turkey. Thus, the ideological importation of secularism from the West caused it to be "de-traditionalized" in that it was automatically deemed an alien—and thus inherently non-indigenous—concept. In this way, secularism became closely associated with other dynamic technological, scientific, and cultural imports from the West,[44] and was consequently placed within the conceptual sphere of modernism and progress. The Republican era's emphasis on and glorification of pre-Islamic Turkish civilization also helped in limiting the role of Islam in public life because, in Republican thought, pre-Islamic Turks were forbears to modern democracy and ideas of equality.[45] Thus, it was argued that before Islam Turks had achieved a society closer to modern European models, thereby demonstrating that there was no need for Islam to achieve internal reform and social progress. In other words, modernity could be considered but a revival of Turkish cultural traditions that not only pre-dated but also outlasted the presence of Islam in Ottoman lands.

To illustrate this modernist, secular approach to nation-building let us turn to one last cartoon that again deals with the alphabet reform. The cartoon was published on November 30, 1928, in the newspaper *Cumhuriyet* (fig. 9.5 and plate 21).[46] It portrays an automobile built of Latin letters speedily driving by a camel, formed by Arabic letters. The automobile touts a small Turkish flag on its hood. It also happens to be the only item on the front page of the newspaper that is picked out in red, other than the title of the newspaper, "*Cumhuriyet*," which is located right above the cartoon. This clever use of color almost renders the red newspaper title a label for the red automobile, effectively naming the car "Republic." The automobile, as the faster and more efficient mode of transportation, embodies advancement and modernity—as does the Latin alphabet (from which it is composed). On the other hand, the slow and stubborn camel serves as a metaphor for the Arabic alphabet, and thus sluggishness.[47] This interpretation is confirmed by the text above the cartoon, which claims that "making the transition from Arabic letters to Turkish letters is like getting off a camel and getting into an automobile."

The actions and direction of the automobile, especially in relation to the camel, signify and heighten the perceived cultural break between the Islamic Arab lands east and southeast of Anatolia and those of the more technologically advanced European countries to the west. While both "vehicles" are moving uphill toward the sun, one will most certainly reach it, and hence enlightenment, before the other. Indeed, the rays of the sun are already touching the front end of the car. Likewise, the exhaust from the automobile is almost in physical contact with the camel. Thus, the people of the new Turkish Republic are aboard the automobile and moving quickly toward modernity, whereas users of the Arabic script remain left behind in a cloud of dust.

This cartoon illustrates one of the more practical arguments put forth in favor of a new alphabet: that the Arabic alphabet was too time-consuming and hard to learn. This cartoon therefore may be pointing to the relative time it takes to learn the two scripts. However, on a more ideological level the cartoon is commenting on Islamic and perhaps even Arab culture. The Arabic script leaves whole societies—represented here by a traditional mode of transportation—behind. The cartoon, by depicting the new script as a sleek automobile, places the new alphabet within the realm of the modern and the progressive, moving westward toward the sun.

YASEMIN GENCER

FIGURE 9.5. Ramiz Gökçe (1900–1953), The Turkish Alphabet leaves the Arabic Alphabet in the dust, *Cumhuriyet,* November 30, 1928, Atatürk Kitaplığı, Istanbul.

The leap from Arabic to Latin script was even more significant than it may appear at first glance. It truly constituted a symbolic break with Islamic culture, as the Arabic language is considered to be the language of God, and therefore the written words in the Qur'an are seen as God's inerrant Logos. The Arabic script since the first centuries of Islam enjoyed an exalted status as the script transmitting the "word of God." Indeed, in the Ottoman Empire, for most people, the very act of learning to read and write began with the Qur'an in *medreses;* thus, the Qur'an and literacy went hand in hand. The adoption of the new "Turkish Alphabet" broke this link, effectively secularizing the act of learning to read and distancing literacy proper from holy scripture. Alphabet reform also served to create an even more visually secularized society, as newspapers, signs, monumental inscriptions, and other forms of public writing would no longer "look" Islamic or Arabic to Westerners who often lumped the two identities together. The public spaces of the new Republic of Turkey, with the adoption of its new alphabet, appeared more secular and modern to visitors from Europe; Turkey separated itself from the rest of the Muslim Middle East while simultaneously drawing itself closer to the "West."[48]

One Message, Multiple Messengers

The political cartoons of the early Republican period present to their readers a wealth of information through a number of expressive vehicles, the most obvious of which is the satirical journal itself. Any given visual message—be it a photograph in a newspaper or an advertisement—communicates through many elements, ranging from the name of the publication in which it appears to the very medium used to spread it.[49] Each artistic and compositional decision made for the communication of a visual message is calculated and rarely accidental.[50] Such is the case with the cartoons discussed in this essay.

The cartoons examined here all present various aspects of the constructed national identity of the Turkish Republic. Their messages revolve around newly articulated ideas of modernity, secular life, and "Turkish" nationalism embodied by the Westward-looking republic. These messages begin to be communicated through the medium of the printed satirical journal, which itself is a transmitter of a message of modernity and technological advancement, especially in a society that was initially so slow to adopt the printing press.[51] The prominent placement of these cartoons within their respective journals only serves to amplify their messages, as they all serve as front-page illustrations. Thus, they take on the secondary function of advertisement for that particular issue and for the journal in general. Those who agreed with or admired the cartoon would ideally buy that issue, and hopefully become regular consumers of the product from that point onward.

In addition to the printed medium and the placement of these cartoons within the journals, their messages were communicated visually from within the confines of their frames, further strengthened by text. It quickly becomes apparent that both visual and textual vehicles transmit the message of modernization and secularization. Most frequently, cartoonists used the realistic depiction of Mustafa Kemal to convey their messages. Following the victory in the Independence Struggle, Mustafa Kemal garnered a great amount of admiration, gratitude, and respect from the public at large, which translated into political capital and an almost indisputable mandate for change. His face and persona were thus deployed in the task of leading the people in the direction of his desire. As a result,

YASEMIN GENCER

Mustafa Kemal is employed as the main communicator of positive change in these cartoons, and his idealized physical likeness symbolizes determination, leadership, agility, modernity, and victory. Additionally, depictions of Mustafa Kemal in these cartoons become representative of the nation as well, as he is shown leading by example, and the nation is expected to follow his lead.

For every reforming change, there must be a policy in need of change or oppression in need of suppression—in other words, a conflict in need of resolution. There must be an antagonist to Mustafa Kemal: a new enemy to replace the old foes of the battlefields. In each of these cartoons the conflict and solution co-exist within a single, nonlinear narrative. The internal opposition to Mustafa Kemal was to be the object of his secularizing and modernizing reforms: Islam. An important tool for the creator of a visual message is the culturally recognizable icon. The cartoon, advertisement, or poster needs to take advantage of shorthand references and symbols in order to conserve space: saying the most with a limited amount of room.

Barthes points out the importance of utilizing such a visual language in advertisements, whose main goal is to communicate a message accurately and clearly.[52] This is the case with Republican-period cartoons, too. Just as Mustafa Kemal is being used to symbolize a number of ideas and ideals, so are images (such as the mullah, camel, Arabic script, and domed buildings) used to allude to Islam. Most significant, though, is the reversal of many of these images, from previously revered symbols of Islam to caricaturized icons of backwardness. These Islamic icons, adopted by the cartoonists of this period, are repeatedly reconfigured to signify the antimodern by their systematic juxtaposition to Mustafa Kemal and his machines of progress.

Subverting Islam: Pushing it Out from Where and Why?

Overt censorship and journalistic editing can never be completely eliminated from the process of satirical cartoon production and the messages such cartoons are meant to convey, especially in the cases of publications from the 1920s and 1930s, when many governments were closely involved in overseeing and censoring the press.[53] While it is almost impossible to gauge the extent of editing and censorship that occurred in the cartoons of the reform period, it is clear that there are indeed certain boundaries that the cartoonists were reluctant to cross.

Secularism as a modern, national drive is a recurring theme in these cartoons. While they advocate for the "pushing out" of Islam through their narrative lines and imagery, however, the cartoons also do not advocate for a non-Islamic society. The brand of secularism advocated by the new Republican government is indeed reflected in the cartoons, as they do not comment on private practices of faith such as prayer or fasting. A prime example of this distinction can be seen in the cartoon from the journal *Karagöz* (fig. 9.2), in which a book marked "old laws" is being discarded. While the old laws referred to are clearly *shari'a* laws derived from the Qur'an itself, it would have been inconceivable for the artist to depict a Qur'an being discarded.

Similarly, the *Kelebek* cartoon depicting the destruction of buildings by a steamroller refrains from showing average citizens running from the buildings; instead, men who are clearly identifiable as mullahs are used as representations of institutional and public Islam—the type of Islam that requires a leader (e.g., a caliph or religious school teacher). The buildings themselves are not explicitly identifiable as mosques, but rather resemble buildings of religious instruction such as *medreses,* as they lack prominent minarets.[54] These two examples constitute the expressive boundaries that were so critical to maintain at this time. Although the secularization reforms were revolutionary, the cartoonists, like the legislators, were careful not to interfere in the personal spheres of the Muslim faith.

The two reforms discussed in this essay—the abolition of the caliphate and the alphabet reform—possess strong symbolic components that speak to the new constructs of Turkish national identity that leaders of the Republic were keen to verbalize. This raises the following questions: whom do these reforms (and the cartoons that illustrate them) target and what do such visually elaborated reforms aim to accomplish? The answer to these questions can be explained in part through both Hroch and Davutoğlu's approaches to national movements and secularism. Hroch has observed that the process of nation-building largely consists of identity politics based on a community's shared history, language, and culture. The Kemalist reforms of the 1920s, including the abolition of the caliphate and the adoption of the "New Turkish Alphabet," were part of a nation-building program intended to create a national identity that was modern, Turkish, and secular.

Davutoğlu, on the other hand, has noted that present-day approaches to secularism have sought to reincorporate religious identity into the discussion in a renewed attempt at cultural self-assertion within the global community.[55] This self-assertive attitude, adopted in tandem with the project of constructing a new "Turkish" identity in the 1920s, worked in the opposite direction, as it aimed to assert itself as non-Islamic and hence declare itself modern to the rest of the world.

Turkish Republican leaders' desire to prove Turkey a modern nation divorced from its Islamic and Ottoman past is reflected in Turkish newspaper articles that celebrate foreign approval of the Republican reforms. This was usually done by republishing European and American articles that bear titles such as "The Marvel of the Near East: Country Civilized in Four Years."[56] Similarly, Mustafa Kemal himself betrayed his own preoccupation with appeasing the West by conforming to modernity with these words: "There is no way to be successful with turbans and robes, now we have proven to the world that we are a civilized nation," a statement that adorned the front page of an issue of *Cumhuriyet* in 1928.[57]

These reforms—symbolic as they seem—are therefore aimed at transforming the new Turkish society from within, while also transforming the international image of Turkey from Ottoman, Islamic, and backward to Turkish, secular, and modern. Mustafa Kemal and the leaders of the new Republic sought to cut off cultural ties to the previous political entity that occupied the same core territories as the new one. The brand of secularism envisioned by the reformers and cartoonists alike was one that subverted Islam, pushing it out of public visibility and relegating it to the private sphere of life, where it would effectively remain out of public and international view. The excitement and anxieties that accompanied such reconfigurations of identity on the national scale were then poured into visual imagery. Through cartoons, the many reforms passed by the new Republican government gained a second level of visibility that was achieved by rationalizing, promoting, and illustrating what were already very visible social changes.

NOTES

The author would like to thank the helpful staff of the Atatürk Library in Istanbul; Chris Murphy and Martha Kennedy for their assistance with materials at the Library of Congress in Washington, D.C.; Bret Rothstein, H. Erdem Çıpa, Tobias Heinzelmann, and Sune Haugbolle for their insightful feedback and comments; the Netherlands Institute in Turkey (NIT), the Research Center for Anatolian Civilizations (RCAC), and the Kluge Center in the Library of Congress for their hospitality, excellent facilities, and services; the American Institute of Iranian Studies (AIIrS) for the generous grant that allowed for travel to Istanbul to carry out field research during the summer of 2009; and the Swann Foundation Fellowship (Library of Congress, Prints and Photographs Division) for the generous grant funding my research at the Library of Congress at various intervals in 2009 and 2010; and, last but not least, Christiane Gruber for her invaluable comments, advice, and guidance throughout the duration of this project.

1. The cartoon was published in the upper left corner of the front page, immediately below the title head of the journal. The cartoon occupies about one-sixth

of the front page, not including the rather large title head that is typical of these kinds of satirical journals.

2. For a discussion of theories of the concept of Atatürk as "progenitor," see Özyürek, "Miniaturizing Atatürk," 382–83.

3. *Akbaba* was published twice weekly (on Mondays and Thursdays) in Istanbul from December 7, 1922, to January 1977. It consisted of a single broadsheet-style folio, folded in half to create a four-page format. A single issue of *Akbaba* featured between seven and twelve cartoons or illustrations. Usually, the back page contained two to three republished cartoons from a European or American publication.

4. *Kelebek* was published once a week (Thursdays) in Istanbul from April 12, 1923, to September 5, 1924. A single issue consisted of eight folios (sixteen pages) and featured anywhere between fourteen and twenty cartoons or illustrations. Like *Akbaba*, most issues included several foreign cartoons republished on the back page.

5. *Karagöz* was published twice a week (Wednesdays and Saturdays) in Istanbul from August 10, 1908, to January 26, 1935. This publication consisted of a single broadsheet-style folio, folded in half to create a four-page format. Between two and five cartoons appeared per issue. Although often elaborate and detailed, the cartoons in *Karagöz* were generally not as aesthetically pleasing or artistically executed as those of *Akbaba* and *Kelebek*.

6. *Cumhuriyet* is a daily newspaper that is still published today. It began publication in Istanbul on May 9, 1924, as a six-page newspaper. Around the end of 1925 the newspaper occasionally increased to eight pages during the weekends. In the summer of 1928 the newspaper became eight pages long every day, until the alphabet reform at the end of 1928, at which time the number of pages dropped back to six. As a newspaper, it is heavy on photographic content but contains fewer cartoons than the satirical journals.

7. The most visible and violent opposition to the abolition of the caliphate was the Sheikh Said Rebellion of 1925, which took place in the eastern parts of Anatolia, especially in cities such as Diyarbakır and Bingöl. A discussion on the somewhat unclear and tentative role of the caliph during the very beginning of the new Turkish state's existence (before the caliphate was abolished) can be found in Zürcher, *Turkey*, 167–68. The Sheikh Said Rebellion is also covered on pages 169–72. The following publication, however, focuses on the abolition of the caliphate in particular: Satan, *Halifeliğin Kaldırılması.*

8. Between 1924 and 1928 other modernizing reforms also took place. These included the hat and clothing reform (November 25, 1925), the closing of the *tekkes* and *zaviyes* or dervish lodges (November 30, 1925), the adoption of the Gregorian calendar (enforced after January 1, 1926), the acceptance of the *Türk Medeni Kanunu* (the Turkish civil code on February 17, 1926), and the removal of a clause from the Constitution stating that the religion of the Turkish state is Islam (April 10, 1928). However, due to space constraints, this discussion will only focus on two such reforms. For more information on all of the early Republican period reforms, see Kili, *Türk Devrim Tarihi.*

9. Brummett, *Image and Imperialism in the Ottoman Revolutionary Press, 1908–1911.* 3–4. Between the years 1879 and 1907 the number of Turkish gazettes published in Istanbul was 103. In the single year following the Second Constitutional Revolution,

240 were published. Also, see Brummett's Appendix I (333–34), which lists 68 different satirical journals published during the years of the Second Constitutional period.

10. Kayalı, "Liberal Practices in the Transformation from Empire to Nation-State," 175–94.

11. See Zürcher, *Turkey*, 178–79; and Öngören, *Cumhuriyet Dönemi Türk Mizahı ve Hicvi, 1923-1983*, 89.

12. See Zürcher, *Turkey*, 179–80. The journal *Vatan* (Motherland), for instance, was one of the Istanbul periodicals to be closed. It was shut down just months after publishing a cartoon against government censorship and amid growing rumors of increased governmental crackdowns on the freedom of the press. Cartoons about censorship, however, were not at all uncommon. Journals such as *Akbaba* and *Karagöz*, which survived through the environment of increased censorship brought about by the *Takrir-i Sükun Kanunu*, continued to periodically publish anti-censorship cartoons, usually by depicting a personification of the press muted by means of a mouth-gag or padlock of some sort.

13. Ibid., 184.

14. It is difficult to prove if this was at all happening (and, if so, to what extent) given the lack of extant primary sources, such as the memoirs or personal notes of writers and cartoonists publishing in these satirical journals. Research concerning this topic awaits in-depth scholarly attention.

15. See Goldstone, "Rethinking Revolutions," 18–32.

16. One very interesting cartoon, published on the back page of *Karagöz* on March 8, 1925, confronts the pivotal Law on the Maintenance of Order. It depicts a large hand holding an oversized sword over an urban landscape, with mountains and fields in the background, while Karagöz and Hacivat stand on a balcony in the lower right corner. The hand has the word "Republic" written on it, whereas the sword is labeled as "Law on the Maintenance of Order." Below the cartoon is a dialogue between Hacivat and Karagöz, in which Hacivat asks Karagöz whether the sword held above them would pose any threat to them. Karagöz responds by saying that the sword is not dangerous as it is there to protect them. He continues by explaining, quite ambiguously, that the sword will protect them because it is a "sword of justice that demolishes modernity, civilization, dignity, honor, protection, evil, mischief-making, and corruption."

17. For a study that deals more closely with *Karagöz* (in addition to other journals) and that explores the extent to which *Karagöz* was a vehicle in spreading Turkish nationalistic feelings within the context of the Balkan Wars, see Heinzelmann, *Osmanlı Karikatüründe Balkan Sorunu (1908-1914)*.

18. This journal was not, however, the first to make use of the Karagöz character in its cartoons. A much earlier journal, first published in 1873, was named *Hayal* ("Fantasy/Dream"), which was the most common generic name for Turkish shadow theater plays. This particular journal often featured in its cartoons Karagöz and Hacivat in their original, two-dimensional form: directly transcribing the images from shadow puppet format to cartoon. This is not the case with the *Karagöz* journal, in which the characters are rendered in a more realistic style relative to their shadow puppet counterparts.

19. The city of Sèvres is best known for its exquisite porcelain vases. Such vases appear both in Turkish and European cartoons as a symbol of the Treaty of Sèvres.

For instance, in the May 10, 1923, issue of *Akbaba* a cartoon originally published in the German newspaper *Jugend* ("Youth"), was republished (no. 45, p. 4). It depicts a cat wearing a fez tipping over a vase from its pedestal. The caption below reads: "The leap of the Angora cat toppled the Sèvres Vase." Another cartoon, published in *Karagöz* on February 18, 1922, (no. 1453, p. 4), illustrates Karagöz handing a vase to Mustafa Kemal or a group of national representatives. Karagöz's words are written in the caption: "Oh representatives, have a good trip. But I have just one request from you: two years ago a delegation that was leaving here brought me this vase from Europe. They call it 'Sèvres' or something . . . I was never able to use it and I cracked it. Bring me back a sturdy gift when you return." All of these cartoons draw on the idea that porcelain, like a treaty, is fragile. For more information on Sèvres porcelain, see Préaud et al., *The Sèvres Porcelain Manufactory.*

20. See B. Lewis, *The Emergence of Modern Turkey*, 1st ed., 234–49.

21. An elaborate and rich mythology has developed around the characters of Karagöz and Hacivat and the origins of the shadow theater tradition. These stories are mostly maintained by *hayalis,* or professional performers of the shadow play, and are closely linked with the early periods of the Ottoman Empire. These tales persist despite more convincing evidence pointing to an importation of this performing art from Egypt in the sixteenth century. See And, *Yıktın Perdeyi Eyledin Viran,* 17; and Tietze, *The Turkish Shadow Theater and the Puppet Collection of the L. A. Mayer Memorial Foundation,* 16–17. In particular, the popular myth of Karagöz places him in the service of Orhan Bey, the second Ottoman sultan, during a time when the state still maintained a more Turkish, and less overtly Islamic, identity. Karagöz, as the shadow theater character best known for his sharp tongue and social commentary, thus gave his name to this political satirical journal. He serves as a mascot since he frequently appears in cartoons as either an active participant or witty commentator.

22. See Hroch, "The Social Interpretation of Linguistic Demand in European National Movements," 67–68; and Hroch, "Real and Constructed: the Nature of the Nation," 93–95.

23. See Anderson, *Imagined Communities.*

24. Hroch and Malečková, "Historical Heritage," 33–34. See Davutoğlu, "Philosophical and Institutional Dimensions of Secularisation," 197.

25. Hroch and Malečková, 15, 25.

26. Pre-Islamic Turks were believed to have had held "modern" values, including women's equal status in society and democracy brought upon by their nomadic lifestyle. Ibid., 30, 35. See also Durakbaşa, "Kemalism as Identity Politics in Turkey," 139.

27. See Hroch, "The Social Interpretation of Linguistic Demand in European National Movements," 67–95.

28. Ibid., 77–78. Also see Karpat, "A Language in Search of a Nation," 453–55; and Köroğlu, *Propaganda and Turkish Identity,* 25.

29. Süleyman Paşa (1838–78), author of *Sarf-ı Türki* (Turkish Grammar), asserted that although the language spoken in the Ottoman court was composed of three languages (Turkish, Persian, and Arabic) it must not be called "Ottoman" but rather "Turkish," as Ottoman refers to the state and not the nation or language. See Göçek, "Decline of the Ottoman Empire and the Emergence of Greek, Armenian, Turkish, and Arab Nationalisms," 37; and Karpat, *The Politicization of Islam,* 337–38.

YASEMIN GENCER

30. Köroğlu, *Propaganda and Turkish Identity*, 40–43. For early references to alphabet reform in particular, see Çeviker, *Gelişim Sürecinde Türk Karikatürü-III*, 143; and Koloğlu, *Kim Bu Mustafa Kemal?* 145. Celal Nuri (1877–1939), who was the head writer for the daily newspaper *İleri* ("Forward," published between 1919 and 1927), often wrote of the need to change the alphabet. Also, Hüseyin Cahid (a writer) called for the Ottomans to abandon the Arabic script as early as the 1910s.

31. Ibid., 40. Also see Gökalp, *Türkleşmek, İslamlaşmak, ve Muasırlaşmak*, 12–14. This work is a compilation of nine articles written by Gökalp and published in the journal *Türk Yurdu* between the years of 1913 and 1914.

32. More information on this language reform can be found in Aytürk, "Turkish Linguists against the West" 1–25; Aytürk, "The First Episode of Language Reform in Republican Turkey," 275–93; and Ertürk, "Phonocentrism and Literary Modernity in Turkey," 155–85.

33. See Heinzelmann, "The Hedgehog as Historian," 206–207, for a 1910 account illustrating the differences between the two writing traditions and these two very different writing implements as experienced by a European-educated Ottoman. Heinzelmann summarizes the message of the story as "even the worst scrawl produced with a steel nib is a match for the traditional style of Ottoman official handwriting."

34. The interpretation of the crescent and star at the top of the pen-banner can be expanded to include a number of visual references. This motif itself resembles the Arabic letter *nun*. This letter is featured at the beginning of the sixty-eighth chapter of the Qur'an, called "The Pen" (*Surat al-Qalam*). The initial verse of this chapter reads: "Nun. I call to witness the pen and what they inscribe." See Ali (trans), *Al-Qur'an*, 497. According to Devellioğlu's *Osmanlıca-Türkçe Ansiklopedik Lûgat*, 845, a relevant meaning for the letter *nun* draws upon a common interpretation of this Qur'anic reference, giving it the meaning "ink well." Thus, the letter *nun* that symbolizes the inkpot that becomes an accomplice to the pen in recording all of life until the day or Resurrection. The *Osmanlıca-Türkçe Ansiklopedik Lûgat* also lists another relevant meaning in its entry for *nun*, which is "sword." If one chooses to see the crescent and star motif as doubling as the Arabic letter *nun*, then within the context of the cartoon it holds great potential for the reading of a number of additional layers of meaning. The cartoonist, by depicting Mustafa Kemal as the wielder of the pen (and ink pot), may be positioning him as the proverbial creator of the new republic. Similarly, as wielder of the "sword," he can also be seen as the protector of the republic. That said, in a relatively more literal way the placement of the crescent and star on the pen could also be meant to create a resemblance to the rifles that often bore these motifs.

35. This cartoon may also be visually quoting a newly erected statue of Mustafa Kemal in Saraybunu (1926). See Gezer, *Cumhuriyet Dönemi Türk Heykeli*, 319, 347.

36. Although the importation of these very modernizing innovations and social reforms would seem at first to constitute its own form of "foreign influence," it was not considered as such. This is the case because the decision to modernize and reform society was made from within; that is, it was considered a voluntary endeavor taken up by the leaders of a now free people who are (at least in theory) ruling themselves—a people who, in the aftermath of the First World War, came very close to losing this right. See Poulton, *Top Hat, Grey Wolf, and Crescent*, 90.

37. Mustafa Kemal himself was often metaphorically likened to the sun in cartoons. Özyürek mentions in "Miniaturizing Atatürk," 381, that such an equation had started as early as the 1930s. Indeed, it seems to have begun even earlier, in the 1920s, within cartoons. Furthermore, this equating of both the new alphabet and Mustafa Kemal with a bright, rising sun may indeed be imagery that later inspired the naming of the Turkish-centric language theory championed by Mustafa Kemal himself in the 1930s, called "the Sun-Language Theory." For information on the Sun-Language Theory see Aytürk, "H. F. Kvergić and the Sun-Language Theory," 23–44; and Ertürk, "Phonocentrism and Literary Modernity in Turkey," 177–81.

38. There were a handful of practical (as opposed to ideological) arguments made at this time against the Arabic alphabet, ranging from the time it took to learn the alphabet to its inadequacy in representing the needs of the Turkish language (which has fewer consonants and more vowels than Arabic). One cartoon (*Akşam*, 1928, by Cemal Nadir, dedicated to "the children of the republic who have learned to read so well in two months") illustrates the difficulties of reading this script, which has no representation for short vowels. A child with a book in his hand is depicted frame after frame, asking various people how a certain word may be read; each person gives him a different answer (some of the suggestions are *malaska, mülaska, müllasıka,* and *melasakka*). Finally, he approaches a mullah and asks if the word is read as *melasakka.* The toothless mullah yells back at him: "how can you not recognize the name Mullah Saka! For that, you shall receive a beating!" Also see n.48 for a description of another cartoon that "illustrates" the relative difficulty of learning the Arabic script.

39. The mound motif also resembles Roman triumphal mounds of spolia, as seen on such monuments as the Arch of Titus in Rome. Perhaps, then, it is no coincidence that the cartoon's frame takes on an arched shape in its upper half, making it appear that Mustafa Kemal is standing beneath a possible "triumphal" arch. However, while the use of the word "spolia" within the Roman context suggests that the mounds were made of valuable objects worthy of transport and subsequent display, the "spolia" of this cartoon should be read in a more nuanced fashion. It seems more plausible that the Arabic letters are considered more of a "worthy opponent" that is difficult to overcome because of its long and rooted history. Such an opponent therefore can only be defeated by the strength and will of the Turkish people.

40. See n.34.

41. *Sülüs* (thuluth) and *nastalik* (nasta'liq) were the most common calligraphic scripts used for monumental inscriptions. Both are quite stylized and more difficult to read than scripts such as *nesih* (naskh), which were favored in newspapers, journals, and other printed materials due to their relative clarity.

42. See Akman, "From Cultural Schizophrenia to Modernist Binarism," 85.

43. Davutoğlu, "Philosophical and Institutional Dimensions of Secularisation," 173.

44. Ibid., 199.

45. See n.27.

46. The cartoon was published in the middle of the upper half of the front page, immediately below the title head of the newspaper. It occupies about one eighth of the front page.

47. The widespread view of camels as stubborn animals, prevalent in Turkey, is best expressed by the popular comparison "more difficult than getting a camel to jump a moat," in regard to measuring a task's relative difficulty. In fact, another cartoon was published in *Cumhuriyet* in 1928 (by Mahmud Arif) depicting a man attempting in vain to get a camel to jump a moat. Its caption reads: "Learning the Arabic alphabet is more difficult than getting a camel to jump a moat, whereas the new alphabet can be learned in just three to five lessons." Likewise, the contrast between camel and modern machinery was used as a rhetorical tool to compare the Latin and Arabic alphabets as early as 1922 in the Azeri publication, *Gelecek* ("Future"). See I. Baldauf, *Schriftreform und Schriftwechsel bei den Muslimischen Russland- und Sowjettürken*, 625.

48. A frequently cited Mustafa Kemal quote about alphabet reform underlines this emphasis. In speaking for the Turkish nation, he stated that it wanted to "show with its script and mentality that it is on the side of world civilization"; see Karpat, "A Language in Search of a Nation," 457.

49. See Barthes, "The Photographic Message," 16–19.

50. Ibid., 31.

51. The first Ottoman Turkish printing press was established in 1727 by İbrahim Müteferrika in Istanbul, almost three centuries after the initial development of the technology in Europe. The most comprehensive analysis of the various theories concerning the reasons for the late adoption of printing technology by the Ottoman Turks can be found in Sabev, *İbrahim Müteferrika ya da İlk Osmanlı Matbaa Serüveni*, 56–65. Also see my study, Gencer, "İbrahim Müteferrika and the Age of the Printed Manuscript," 181.

52. See Barthes, *Image, Music, Text*, 35–40. Barthes also warns of the "repressive value" of too much text. Thus, too much text has the potential to exclude and/or deter a portion of the audience (28–30).

53. See Morley, *Writing on the Wall*, 93.

54. Large *medreses* usually existed as dependencies to mosques and mosque complexes in major cities; however, *medreses* could also exist as separate buildings. For some examples of both independent and mosque-dependant *medreses* see Ettinghausen, Grabar, and Jenkins-Madina, *Islamic Art and Architecture*, 215, 225–27, 234–41; Blair and Bloom, *The Art and Architecture of Islam*, 45, 70–73, 196–97, 215–18, 222; also see Pereira, *Islamic Sacred Architecture*, 195–96.

55. Davutoğlu, "Philosophical and Institutional Dimensions of Secularisation," 207–208.

56. Republished in *Cumhuriyet*, July 5, 1928 (no. 1492, p. 1). The article was republished in its original form and within its own small frame. Turkish commentary on the article itself surrounds the inserted column. Later, on July 27, 1928 (no. 1514, p. 1), *Cumhuriyet* featured a lengthy article noting that a "foreign journalist" had called Mustafa Kemal a "source of light for the East."

57. *Cumhuriyet*, September 17, 1928 (no. 1566, p. 1).

FIGURE 10.1. Murat Süyür (b. 1984), *Darkness,* http://muratsuyur.com, February 19, 2009.

CHAPTER 10

Blasphemy or Critique?: Secularists and Islamists in Turkish Cartoon Images

JOHN VANDERLIPPE AND PINAR BATUR

Two iconic images used in Turkish political debates, the light bulb and the headscarf, can be read as representing political opposites: thought and enlightenment versus fanaticism and obscurantism. But what does it represent when the two are joined in an image, as in a depiction in which the light bulb, the symbol of the ruling Justice and Development Party (Adalet ve Kalkınma Parti, or AKP), wears a headscarf (fig. 10.1)?[1] Is this the smothering of critical, enlightened thought by fanatics determined to impose rigid religious dogma, or is this the liberation of the human mind from the rigid secularist dogma imposed by the Kemalist state? The juxtaposition of two competing icons reflects the contentious issues at the forefront of Turkish political debate in the twenty-first century.

Focusing on political cartoons, we are interested in the role of metaphors and icons in the rhetorical lexicon surrounding political Islam in Turkey. Political cartoons perform as conduits between intellectuals and the people. Whether these images are created by cartoonists or by other artists, they are formulated within cultural discourse and change with it. These images shape popular culture, and are shaped by it. We are interested in the ways in which cartoons and images "bracket" issues to present an adherent view of an argument, embodying both attacks and counterattacks that are displayed visually. In modern Turkish visual rhetoric, cartoons contain the icons and metaphors that are challenged by changing and contested debates, such as the discourse on secularism and Islamism. We focus on political cartoons as image-based narratives of the conflict between secularists and Islamists to explore how icons and metaphors have evolved over time in response to the fluctuating political situation in Turkey. While Yasemin Gencer in her contribution to this volume focuses on images from the early Republican period, this chapter concentrates on contemporary debates, in particular those that have developed during the period marked by the emergence and rule of the AKP (Adalet ve Kalkınma Partisi—Justice and Development Party) and Prime Minister Recep Tayyip Erdoğan since 2002.

The struggle represented in the political cartoons of both periods is an integral part of what we term the "nexus of contention," representing the debates between agents of the state, intellectuals, and the people, with an emphasis on the politics of changing terms of legitimization for institutions, senses of belonging, and the future. By "nexus of contention" we mean not so much the public sphere, which Habermas describes as a space in which people agree to debate and dialogue within certain parameters of civility, but rather the struggle for dominance among various groups that use public space to assert their own vision of past, present, and future. Cartoons, by enabling the flow of discourse as a visual summary, illustrate this ongoing contention in the domain of popular culture.

Paul Ricoeur distinguishes between different levels of hermeneutic adaptation by giving weight to both the transparency and opaqueness of icons and metaphors.[2] According to Ricoeur, "double intentionality," which defines disparate elucidations of similar or seemingly similar images, is integrated into the formulation, transformation, and redefinition of images. Transparency and opaqueness shape "double intentionality." We argue that there is also a tertiary level of complexity, which includes debate and struggle over control of icons and metaphors, leading to the creation and recreation of images according to the historical context of popular culture. Thus, while icons have an immediate transparency, their metaphors are opaque due to the multiplicity and situational nature of their meaning, which is further complicated at a tertiary level. This necessitates an unpacking of the image, the historicity of its debate, and the struggle to control the terms of its integration in the nexus of contention. The aim is to seize the image. We are suggesting that this struggle to control is shaped by debate within the nexus of contention.

Political cartoons reveal the visual iconography that has evolved since the founding of the Turkish republic in 1923,[3] with a marked intensification of contention between secularist and anti-secular Islamist forces. Since the 1990s, Islam, and its place in institutions and everyday life, has become a more compelling aspect of Turkish political discourse.[4] Since 2000 it has become an official political reality. While we are interested in the historical continuity and discontinuity of the icons and metaphors that influence the visual vernacular of the nexus of contention, for the purpose of this chapter we concentrate on the debate regarding Islam and secularism by studying cartoons of the recent period.[5] The level of intensity of imagery reveals the power struggle in the nexus of contention.

JOHN VANDERLIPPE AND PINAR BATUR

The Politics of Icons and Metaphors
in the "Nexus of Contention"

What enables us to find and decipher layers of meaning packed into the small frame of a cartoon? Icons are representations integrated into the visual lexicon of everyday life and popular culture. As images they can remain stable, but metaphors, which give meaning to icons, can change over time.[6] Icons and metaphors also generate a counterattack by those who find themselves placed in the category of "other." In the struggle to dominate the discourse, the opposition, besides inventing a new iconography, can utilize the existing dominant icons for the counter position by challenging and transforming the metaphor. The context in which this transformation and redefinition takes place is the nexus of contention.

The debates within the Turkish nexus of contention evolved out of the nineteenth-century ideas of the Tanzimat reformers and later Young Ottoman and Young Turk intellectuals, who shared similar goals: to modernize the state and protect the "motherland."[7] The central issue of contention was the role of Islam. The reformers of the Tanzimat and later the Kemalist and post-Kemalist Republicans, agreed that public expressions of religion must be remodeled into a new form, to serve a broader agenda of creating a modern, secular, progressive, and Westernized state. This effort aimed at separating the traditional past from the modern future, and, most importantly, at delineating a new trajectory away from the "East" to the "West." Men with full facial hair, a dark complexion, and religious attire, and women covered head to toe in black—an *abaya* or *çarşaf*—primarily came to represent the face of Islam, icons of the past, and metaphors used to depict the barrier to progress into the modern future.[8]

Such figures also have a secondary function. Cartoon images from the late Ottoman and early Republican periods that represent individuals in religious and "Eastern" attire also depicted them as collaborators of British and French encroachment, and agents of Western domination.[9] They are illustrations of those willing to join with colonial forces to maintain their ideological hegemony and political power, and use Islamic discourse to popularize their position. This imagery again emerged in the recent period, first in the late 1960s and 70s, with Justice Party figures draped in the American flag, and continuing in the 1990s and especially after 2000, with the ruling pro-Islamist AKP leaders and religious figures as collaborators willing to give away Turkey to the European Union and United States.

But during the late Ottoman Empire and early Republic periods, and again more recently, the iconography of images of Islam and religious people was challenged by those who saw, and depicted, the secularist Kemalist elite as aloof, enamored with Western culture, and as bad Muslims or anti-Muslims, collaborating with the West to destroy authentic Turkish-Muslim culture and traditions, and, moreover, jeopardizing Turkish sovereignty.

Turhan Selçuk's cartoon (see fig. 10.4 below) depicting a woman with a headscarf of an American flag with "AKP" emblazoned across her forehead is an excellent example of secularist imagery. The woman—wearing an "American Turban" over a dark coat resembling a *çarşaf*, against a white background—provides a statement about the political leaning and affiliation of the ruling party, as well as the oppression of patriarchy and the colonial domination of the United States. Thus, the ways in which different articulations of domination complement one another is personified as a woman in a headscarf. We are now looking at an icon, altered historically and contextually to criticize the current ruling elite's use of patriarchy and Islam to maintain its hegemony and the colonial backing of its power. The cartoon was published in *Cumhuriyet,* a left-leaning independent daily newspaper. The award-winning cartoonist, Turhan Selçuk, drew mostly for left-leaning newspapers and periodicals in Turkey, such as *Akbaba, Yön, Devrim, Toplum,* and *Cumhuriyet.* He is famous for his mastery of using historical images to allude to contemporary conflicts. His serial, "Abdülcanbaz," begun in 1952, depicts an Ottoman intellectual confronting the modern political and economic realities of Turkey. When he ended the serial in 1987, public outcry forced him to resurrect "Abdülcanbaz" in 1994 for a series that ran until his death in 2010. The cartoon of the woman in a headscarf is from Selçuk's editorial corner, called "Söz Çizginin" (The Word Belongs to the Image).

A contrasting image to Selçuk's woman in the "American Turban" is a woman in a *çarşaf,* drawn by İbrahim Özdabak (fig. 10.2 and plate 22) and published in the right-leaning, religiously oriented daily, *Zaman.*[10] The image shows six arrows shooting through the back of a woman with a head covering and black *çarşaf*-like overcoat. The six arrows that pierce her body are emblematic of the major opposition party in Turkey, representing the Republican People's Party's (CHP) six principles of republicanism, nationalism, populism, statism, secularism, and reformism, adopted in 1931. The six principles, the cornerstones of Kemalism and the official ideology of the Turkish state during the single-party period of the People's Party, were always represented as six arrows, radiating out from the crescent and star on the party's banner.

JOHN VANDERLIPPE AND PINAR BATUR

FIGURE 10.2. İbrahim Özdabak (b. 1957), *Untitled,* www.ibrahimozdabak.com,
February 19, 2009.

The original articulation of the six arrows came in large part as a response to criticism that the People's Party, despite its name, was a dictatorial rather than representative institution, more responsive to state power than to the needs of the population. The articulation of the six arrows, and their incorporation into the Turkish constitution during the single-party period, did not alter this perception of the People's Party, and with the advent of multiparty politics in 1945, during the presidency of İsmet İnönü, the six arrows—and by extension Kemalism itself—became the subject of political contention. Of the six, secularism proved to be the arrow subjected to the most debate and disagreement, both within and outside of the People's Party. Today, secularists tend to view any questioning of the six principles as an attack on all six arrows, and thus on Kemalism, the founding ideology of the Turkish Republic. Islamists tend to see the six arrows as weapons used to stifle any and all democratic debate on the meaning of any aspect of Kemalism. The image of a woman pierced by the six arrows of Kemalism indicates how this struggle is conceptualized by AKP sympathizers and right-leaning political cartoonists. Furthermore, it is important to note that the arrows are striking her in the back—a depiction of a cowardly, dissembling attack on an unsuspecting public. Özdabak's cartoon can be interpreted as arguing that the Kemalist republic is not only destroying the rights of women, but also striking at the heart and soul of the motherland—depicted as a devout Muslim woman— an attack enabled by the party that represents Kemalist oppression.

Both cartoonists, Selçuk and Özdabak, used an image of a woman as a symbol of vulnerability, a common practice in patriarchal societies. Their primary objective is to visualize the debate regarding the sovereignty of the state and the origins of its power. Both use secondary imagery, such as "AKP" or arrows, as well as the attire of the women, to display the popular lexicon of contention between Islamists and secularists. Both ask the reader to ponder the continuity of this struggle over legitimacy, belonging, and the future.

Struggle of Imagery in the Nexus of Contention

Kemalism promised a future of modernity, democracy, and progress, as well as a state that represented the will of the people and was based on the struggles against the backwardness of the Ottoman, "Eastern," Islamic past and the threat of foreign intervention and its domestic collaborators, especially communists. But as the Kemalist vision of modernity, democracy, and progress came under challenge from the 1940s onward, an alternative vision claimed legitimacy by portraying the Kemalist state and Kemalist elite as static, oppressive, and mired in an irrelevant past. The challenge came from left and right—the socialist future and the Islamist future, together with ultra-nationalists. The nexus of contention included three overlapping debates: on the state's contract with citizens; the political, economic, and social alteration of institutions and sense of community; and alternative models for the future. The iconography of cartoons evolved through this contention. The uneasy iconography of contention focuses on three articulations of Kemalist ideology: nationalism, democracy, and secularism, pronounced separately or superimposed on each other to elucidate warring ideologies and potential allies.

Certain iconic images of Turkish nationalism—the flag, the map-shaped image of the motherland, Atatürk, and the word "Democracy"—are used to represent competing interpretations of the Kemalist principles of reformism, populism and republicanism, and especially secularism. The flag, as a metaphor, is malleable, and it is possible to use the symbol joined with other iconic images to present competing metaphors. For example, a red flag with three crescents, or the flag with a wolf image superimposed over the crescent and star, indicate ultra-nationalism, while the crescent and star over a green background means pro-Islamist militarism, in contrast to a flag with the superimposed image of Atatürk, which indicates Kemalist nationalism.[11] Interpretations of the flag vary. Some argue that the flag represents the War of Independence and the Turkish Republic, while others suggest that the red color represents blood; the crescent, God; and the star, Muhammad. The elasticity of metaphors cannot permeate the iconography of cartoons. Since 1937, a Turkish Flag Decree (renewed in 1982) has regulated the ways in which the flag can be displayed or depicted. Yet, even if undistorted, the image of the flag in cartoons has come to represent vulnerability as well as strength. This may be why a cartoon depicting the Turkish flag that was published outside Turkey was republished in Turkish newspapers under the rubric of "news," rather than "political commentary,"[12] which allowed the papers to avoid prosecution under the flag law.

The image, by Turkish cartoonist Selçuk Demirel and published on April 17, 2008, in *Le Monde,* replaces the crescent with a headscarf, and the star with a bow (fig. 10.3). The cartoon carried no caption, leaving viewers to interpret the meaning of the image. But who was the intended audience? Because the image was published outside of Turkey, was the cartoonist using Turkish popular culture as the main context of the narrative, or utilizing globalized discourse on what this image represents? The complexity of this image-based narrative, whether or not it represents challenges to the iconic flag, and hence the national sovereignty of Turkey, demonstrates how the discourse on nationalism does not exist in isolation, interacting only with the discourse on democracy and secularism in Turkey, but also resonates globally.

Viewers of Demirel's image of the flag as headscarf are left with a variety of possible interpretations: is he saying that the Turkish nation is threatened by Islamism, or that adherence to Islamic principles is patriotic? Is this a warning of an imminent threat, and a call to action, or is it a celebration of victory? Another interpretation might be that Islamists are veiling their political agenda in Turkish nationalist rhetoric. Viewers are also left to ponder whether Islamism poses a threat to Kemalism and democracy in Turkey, and, if so, what kind of threat—is it the threat that the light of democracy will be smothered by the veil of obscurantism, or is the threat more localized in the grasping claws of AKP leaders and their supporters?

Selçuk Demirel argues that he prefers neutrality on political issues. In an interview with *Vatan Gazetesi* in 2008 he said that in the secular versus religious discussion, he prefers not to take sides because both sides are trying to tear Turkey apart. He also said that the focus on the headscarf obscures other important issues confronting Turkey.[13] Demirel is a freelance cartoonist who publishes mostly in left-leaning publications, such as *Cumhuriyet* and *Yüzyıl,* along with *Le Monde,* the *Guardian,* and the *New York Times.* While some see his flag-as-headscarf as a colonial attack from France on the sanctity of Islam—and the sovereignty of Turkey—by a traitor, others see it as a critical voice of the intellectual in exile. The complexity of the interpretation of these narratives comes from the fact that the images can be used simultaneously by opposing groups: to represent the destruction of Kemalism, or the liberation of Kemalism from its followers' tyranny; the fulfillment of democracy or the destruction of the foundations of the republic; Islamist domination or Islamic liberation. In this way, the struggle moves away from the icon and the metaphor's double intentionality of transparency and opaqueness to a tertiary level of struggle over the icons themselves. In the case of this cartoon, the image moves the debate on a global level by complicating its narrative. Not only is the image targeted at multiple audiences, it is also seized globally and utilized for alternative positions in different struggles.

The Tertiary Struggle over the Turban

As an extension of the secularization project, the Turkish "Hat Law" of 1925 encouraged Western-style clothing and forbade the wearing

JOHN VANDERLIPPE AND PINAR BATUR

FIGURE 10.3. Selçuk Demirel (b. 1954), *Untitled, Le Monde,* April 17, 2008.

of religious garb in public, outside of religious institutions.[14] The law restricted the personal expression of piety in the public sphere, limiting it to thoughts, words, and deeds. Later, in its everyday interpretation and adaptation to the realities of cultural life and expression, wearing an article of clothing associated with religion continued to be restricted in public buildings, such as schools, government offices, and the Turkish parliament.

The Kemalist initiative to encourage adoption of European fashion focused on the elite of the cities and large towns, but largely ignored the peasants and urban working classes. Traditional clothing was less an issue than the politics of dress. Thus, there has always been a great distinction between the *başörtüsü,* village women's traditional head coverings, and urban working-class women's use of an *eşarp* (scarf), which have never been regulated, and the *çarşaf* (abaya), *peçe* (veil), and *turban* (headscarf), which have come to represent political expressions of Islam. The struggle is over the use of the head coverings in public, particularly at state institutions like universities and government offices where space is regulated by the state. The wearing of a particular head covering, called the turban, has become a way of challenging restrictions on public expression as well as the secularist principles of the Kemalist republic.

One of the incidents of struggle over this distinction came in 1967, when female students of the Faculty of Divinity tried unsuccessfully to enter the university with their heads covered with the turban. In 1982 the Higher Education Commission (YÖK) forbade the wearing of headscarves in universities, thus defining a space of contention. Later, in 1984, YÖK lifted the ban, only to reinstate it in 1987. In 1988 it repealed the reinstatement of the ban, only to reverse itself once again in 1989 and prohibit headscarves. The following year brought a law allowing headscarves in public spaces, which was repealed in 1997.[15] In 1998 Hayrünnisa Gül, wife of President Abdullah Gül, wanted to register at Ankara University, but her head covering was prohibited. She sued the Turkish government, both in Turkey and at the International Court at The Hague, for violation of her individual and human rights.[16] On February 9, 2008, the Turkish Assembly voted to abolish the restriction on head coverings, a decision that was overturned by the Turkish constitutional court in June.[17] No wonder cartoonists use the headscarf in general, and the turban in particular, to depict the struggle over secularism and democracy, especially after Prime Minister Tayyip Erdoğan was quoted as saying, "what if the turban is a symbol of Islam? Even if it were a political symbol it should not be forbidden."[18] Head cover-

JOHN VANDERLIPPE AND PINAR BATUR

ing has always been a political statement. Yet, the turban has become a political image associated with AKP supporters.

Thus, Murat Süyür's presentation of a light bulb wearing a black turban is a very controversial image (fig. 10.1). Süyür defines himself as a creative photographer, and he likes to bring images together to ask questions.[19] Two iconic and well-known images, the headscarf and light bulb, ask the question of whether a political party has the right to be anti-secularist or to politicize the headscarf for its own legitimization. Opponents of the AKP claim that the party has supported the use of the headscarf as a symbol of protest in order to increase its own political appeal and to generate followers. Yet the turban, as an icon and metaphor, lends itself to a multiplicity of positions. It represents devotion to Islam, yet a particular articulation of Islam. It is an act of obedience, as well as a form of resistance. Wearing it designates one as part of a group, yet denotes assertion of individual rights. It is an old symbol, but utilized in a new and alternative way. It is a private decision, but a public act. It is an intervention into local discourses on piety, cultural expression, and political stance, but its exertions are global in scale. The struggle over control of this icon—as a symbol of backwardness or progress, oppression or democracy—has become a defining feature of the nexus of contention.

Why Has the AKP Become an Icon and Metaphor of Struggle?

The visual iconography of the contemporary secularist-Islamist struggle concentrates on three main areas—accountability of the state, changing institutions and sense of belonging, and definition of the future—that embody older struggles over nationalism, democracy, and secularism. With the electoral success of religiously oriented parties in the 1990s and 2000s, the arena of struggle has shifted as well. The AKP was established in 2001, claiming to embody the synthesis of almost all center-right pro-Islamic parties that have existed since the foundation of the Republic and have claimed to be the voice of political alternatives since the 1960s. The AKP also has the distinction of having received overwhelming support in the 2002, 2004, and 2007 elections. Yet, accusations of betrayal of public trust, absence of accountability, and publicly scorned duplicity have been integral to the secularist representation of the ruling pro-Islamist party, especially targeting their claims of being the "people's voice," and a legitimate political articulation of the Islamist project.

The acronym of the ruling party, AKP, and the light bulb as its symbol have become political icons as much as the headscarf. One event that political cartoonists have focused on began on March 14, 2008, when Turkey's chief prosecutor, Aburrahman Yalçınkaya, asked the Constitutional Court to close and ban the AKP for betraying the republic by engaging in anti-secular activities. The indictment charged the AKP, and especially Prime Minister Tayyip Erdoğan, along with President Abdullah Gül, with undertaking activities to establish a new regime and a new state structure influenced by Islamic, rather than republican and democratic, principles, thereby causing a division of Turkish society into two camps: pro- and anti-Islam. On July 30, 2008, the court ruled against disbanding the party by one vote, but decided that the party had engaged in anti-secular activities and reduced its government funding. This was Erdoğan's second indictment; in 1997 he had been convicted of anti-secular activities (and served time in jail), in particular for advocating struggle between those he claimed blindly follow Atatürk's reforms and those Muslims who will unite under Islam and favor the sharia.[20] Cartoonists such as İbrahim Özdabak targeted these events in cartoons, and depicted Chief Prosecutor Yalçınkaya as an owl, a relic of the Kemalist past, and one who lives in the dark, without light (i.e., a light bulb). He was indicted, and further indictments followed, for insulting public officials in the press. Özdabak argues that his cartoons are a nightmare for the oppressive regime, and he represents cartoonists as those who search for more democratic expression. He points out that oppressive regimes produce more cartoonists and reduce the number of images they can use in their vocabulary.[21]

Another contested articulation of AKP rule comes from the AKP's support of American foreign policy. In recent years, the AKP has been targeted by opponents for violating two sets of contracts: failing to make Islam a more prevalent aspect of state institutions and everyday life, as well as bringing an anti-secular stance into politics within a secular, democratic republic. Consequently, some cartoonists depict AKP leaders and supporters with two faces, or split down the middle, to reveal the ambiguity embedded in being a ruling party in an oppositional setting.

The disparate paths of secularists and Islamists have crossed, especially over "ılımlı Islam" (moderate Islam), a concept supported by the George W. Bush and the Barack Obama administrations as an antidote to "radical Islam" in the Middle East. Both secularists and Islamists have denounced the concept as a form of interference by the West, and advocating "secular-Islam" has been long discredited by secularists and Islamists alike. Secularist and anti-secularist intellectuals both point out that the issue is not the presence or absence of contentious ideologies in the Middle East. Rather, the concept of "moderate Islam" indicates the limits of the West's tolerance of Islam as a political, social, and cultural force, and its expression in a given country. Thus, regardless of Erdoğan's assertion that there is only one true articulation of Islam, and his claim that the notions of moderate or extreme Islam are meaningless, the AKP's support from Western powers means that the party has come to represent ılımlı Islam. Both sides of the debate in Turkey have targeted this stance, and constructed it as a betrayal of their secularist and anti-secularist ideals simultaneously. Such disclaimers mean that when it comes to this issue, there is no middle ground, no compromise, and no easy synthesis.

In cartoons, the Turkish face of ılımlı Islam is drawn as someone with an American flag. Selçuk's portrayal of a woman wearing a headscarf in the form of the American flag leaves viewers to interpret whether the image means that the AKP is America's puppet, or if it is Americans whose vision is obstructed by the veil of "moderate" Islamists (fig. 10.4).[22] The image might be the same, but its transparency might be obscured, giving alternative meanings according to context and different levels of struggle. Because conflicting discourses overlap, and competing perspectives claim the legitimization crises of each other, cartoons utilize icons that mix metaphors. The tertiary struggle in the nexus of contention is where the struggle for control of icons carries forth the struggle for hegemony and legitimization.

Collectively Laughing at Our Confusion and Sorrow: Iconography and the Struggle

As suggested by the popular saying in Turkish, "güleriz ağlanacak halimize," we laugh at our sorrowful condition.

Being a cartoonist is a dangerous occupation in Turkey. The cartoonists' wit and might is continually challenged in the courts, and the Turkish government's claims of commitment to freedom of speech sag under the burden of putting cartoonists in jail.[23] Just recently, the cartoonist Ertan Aydın served two consecutive sentences for two different cartoons, and Ahmet Erkanlı was jailed for ten months. The editor of Lemon, a weekly political satire magazine, was jailed for three and half months, while GırGır, another weekly, was ordered closed for a month. The record goes to Ratıp Tarık Burak, a Kemalist secular democratic political cartoonist, who was tried fifty-four times between 1950 and 1960; he served time in jail, but was later elected to parliament.[24] In 1973 Turhan Selçuk was beaten by the state police for questioning his own arrest. He was one of the founding

FIGURE 10.4. Turhan Selçuk (1922–2010), *Untitled*, *Cumhuriyet*, September 27, 2008, p. 6.

members of the Association of Cartoonists, established in Turkey in 1969. The association's webpage includes many names of cartoonists indicted, jailed, or currently serving sentences for images they utilized in place of spoken words.[25] One of the latest is Muammer Şengöz, who was sentenced to eleven months in jail and a fine of seven thousand Turkish lira for his depiction of a public official. After the sentencing, he said, "no one can stop my pen. I will continue to draw."[26]

Icons and metaphors cannot be understood in isolation, but only in the context of struggles to seize the image and its meaning. But why use similar images? This blockage is the result of the unfinished agenda of the opposing ideologies as well as the narrowness of discourses locked in the nexus of contention. While the secularists perpetuate the discourse inherited from the Ottoman intellectuals, Islamists, in reacting, are unable to invent and introduce a new visual lexicon to claim new icons representing the contention. Also, using similar images provides a stable vocabulary shaped in the nexus of contention.

The visual articulation of antagonism might have provided a reason to raise new antagonisms and widen the form of the conflict. But even when confronted with the iconography of globalization, Islam in the visual lexicon of the cartoons depicts new and old forms of both domination and subordination within an existing vocabulary, thereby maintaining its familiar position in hegemony and in counter-hegemony. This elasticity results in a general poverty of the visual rhetoric. Thus, both sides of the secularism debate perpetuate the icons and the metaphors as acts, mimicry, and response, and the cartoonists continue to bracket them into the registry of contention. The Turkish public is challenged to decipher them at a tertiary level, to join the struggle and the debate at the nexus of contention, and to witness the legitimization crisis of secular and anti-secular discourse locked into the not-so-small square of a cartoon.

NOTES

We are grateful to Sulhiye Batur and Professor Sevinç Karol for their help in locating images for this chapter, and to Ertuğ Tombuş, Ashley Tay, Dylan Cate, and Danielle Falzon for their assistance with research and editorial comments. We are thankful to the organizers of and participants in the conference Rhetoric of the Image for their generosity and critiques. We thank Vassar College and the New School for Social Research for their institutional support for this ongoing project.

1. *Mizah Haber.*

2. Ricoeur, *The Symbolism of Evil;* Ricoeur, *The Rule of Metaphor;* and Ricoeur, *A Ricoeur Reader.*

3. Akman, "From Cultural Schizophrenia to Modernist Binarism," 83–132; and M. Göçek, "Political Cartoons as a Site of Representation and Resistance," 1–12.

4. Gülalp, "Modernization Policies and Islamist Politics in Turkey," 52–63; Gülalp, "Globalization and Political Islam," 433–48; and Gülalp, "Enlightenment by Fiat," 351–72.

5. Taş and Uğur, "Roads 'Drawn' to Modernity," 311–14; and Tunç, "Pushing the Limits of Tolerance," 47–62.

6. Batur-VanderLippe and Feagin, *The Global Color Line;* VanderLippe, "Racism and International Relations," 47–63; and al-Azmeh, "Islamic Studies and the European Imagination," 122–45.

7. Batur-VanderLippe and VanderLippe, "Young Ottomans and Jadidists," 59–82.

8. Ahmad, *The Young Turks;* Berkes, *The Development of Secularism in Turkey;* and Zürcher, *Turkey.*

9. Çeviker, *Gelişim Sürecinde Türk Karikatürü* (Turkish Caricatures in the March of Development: The Second Constitutional Period, 1908–1918); Çeviker, *Meşrutiyet İmzasız Karikatürler Antolojisi* (Anthology of Unsigned Caricatures of the Constitutional Period);Okay, *Dönemin Mizah Dergilerinde Milli Mücadele Karikatürleri, 1919-1922* (Caricatures of the National Struggle in the Period's Satirical Journals, 1919–1922); Asthana, "Religion and Secularism as Embedded Imaginaries," 304–23; Maden, "Cartoons Tell Political Journey of Turkey."

10. Özdabak, "Karikatür Baskıcı Yönetimlerin Korkulu Rüyasıdır"; Kasaba, "Kemalist Certainties and Modern Ambiguities," 15–36; and Göle, "The Quest for the Islamic Self within the Context of Modernity," 81–94.

11. Erdem, "MHP Hep Turbancıydı" (MHP Always Supported the Turban); and Keyman, "MHP ve Türk-İslam Sentezi Kıskacında" (MHP and Turk-Islam Synthesis at the Crossroads).

12. "Türban Motifli Türk Bayrağı Le Monde'da" (Turkish Flag with Turban Motif in *Le Monde*).

13. "Selçuk Demirel'le bir Konuşma" (A Conversation with Selçuk Demirel).

14. Lewis, *The Emergence of Modern Turkey*, 268–71.

15. "The Battle for Turkey's Soul."

16. "Gül'ün Eşi Türban için AİHM'e Gitmişti."

17. "Başörtüsü Düzlenlemesi TBMM'de."

18. Karakuş, "Yeni Turban Çıkışı" (New Turban Event); Erdem, "MHP Hep Turbancıydı"; Asad, *Formations of the Secular.*

19. For more of Murat Süyür's work, see his webpage at http://muratsuyur .com.

20. "Okuduğu Şiir Erdoğan'ın Başını Ağrıtmaya Devam Ediyor" (Poem Read by Erdoğan Continues to Give Him Headaches).

21. Özdabak, "Karikatür Baskıcı Yönetimlerin Korkulu Rüyasıdır."

22. Selçuk, "Söz Çizginin" (The Word Belongs to the Image), 6.

23. Coşgun, "Desen Bir Türlü, Demesen Bir Türlü" (Damned If You Say It, Damned If You Don't); "Erdoğan Şimdi de 'Kedi Tom'" (Now Erdoğan's a Tomcat); "Semiramis Aydınlık'ı Yitirdik" (We've Lost Semiramis Aydınlık); and Tunç, "Pushing the Limits of Tolerance."

24. Özer, "Karikatür ve Siyaset" (Caricature and Politics).

25. Karikatürcüler Derneği/The Association of Cartoonists in Turkey, http:// www.karikaturculerdernegi.org/i.asp?id=2.

26. "Muamer Sengoz'e Hapis Cezası" (Jail Sentence for Muamer Şengöz).

CHAPTER 11

Naji al-Ali and the Iconography of Arab Secularism

SUNE HAUGBOLLE

You put yourself in his shoes when you see his drawings.
—a fan of Naji al-Ali, Ramallah, February 2010

Art can do a very simple, but very powerful thing: it can mirror our lives by creating poignant stories, images, and sounds that are at once familiar and strange. Or, as a dedicated fan of the Palestinian cartoonist Naji al-Ali explained his popularity to me: "Naji avoided clichés" (the un-strangely familiar) and instead "held on to the one broken image he had in his head when he left his house" at the age of ten. "He took that boy, who was himself, and placed him in front of the injustices of the Arab world," as the one who observes and archives what others ignore and forget. The character Handhala, he explained, is a condensation of the pain, longing, and love experienced by millions of Palestinians and Arabs in the late twentieth century. "He never left that image of a boy leaving his village. And you put yourself in his shoes when you see his drawings."[1]

Here, my informant—a professor at Birzeit University on the West Bank in Palestine—must have referred to Naji al-Ali and not his iconic trademark figure Handhala, who is notoriously barefoot. Handhala was created in 1969 to memorialize the moment when al-Ali left Palestine in 1948, at the age of ten.[2] Like al-Ali then, and like thousands of kids in the Palestinian refugee camps, Handhala is ragged and dirty, with spiky, unkempt hair, but he is also proud and staunch, resisting by observing the calamities taking place around him. Handhala (the word in Arabic means a small, bitter fruit) can therefore be seen both as a metaphor for Palestinian and Arab *sumud* (steadfastness), as well as an alter ego for al-Ali himself, who refused to forget his initial experience throughout his artistic career.[3] That initial experience was one of eviction from Palestine in 1948 and a youth spent in the Lebanese refugee camp of Ayn al-Hilwa. Later, in 1961, the Palestinian author Ghassan Kanafani discovered al-Ali's talent and helped him launch a career as a cartoonist in left-leaning journals and newspapers, first in Beirut, then in Kuwait, and, between 1974 and 1982, again in Beirut, before the Lebanese Civil War forced him to move back to the Gulf and later to London, where he was assassinated in 1987. His murder remains unresolved but is widely attributed to agents of either the PLO (Palestinian Liberation Organization) or Israel.[4] Over these three decades, al-Ali produced more than forty thousand cartoons,[5] many of which were published in leading Arab newspapers. He was widely read and loved for his satirical commentaries on Arab politics.

Naji al-Ali is today more than just a beloved cartoonist whose political views and use of familiar images make him easy to identify with. He belongs to a group of select few artists who have been so influential in Arab thought and sensibilities that they have arguably become cultural icons, in the sense that their work provides an aesthetic language through which the diverse historical memory of the Arab twentieth century is articulated and negotiated.[6] Taking Naji al-Ali as an example, this article explores the social life of such cultural icons. Some, like the divas Fairuz and Umm Kulthum, embody moments or aspects of nation-building. Others merit attention for the ways in which they have circulated and developed secular ideologies, not as manifestos written by important thinkers, nor as the slogans of political parties, but as entertaining, attractive, humanist art reflecting the life and emotions of ordinary people.

By Arab secular ideologies I refer to variants of Nasserist, Marxist, Ba'athist, and socialist ideas and movements—collectively known as the Arab left (al-yasar al-'arabi)[7]—that privilege the separation of religion and politics and materialist interpretations of history. Together, they constitute an Arab tradition of secular thought and activism that I see as a secularism among many "secularisms,"[8] rather than a straightforward local adaptation of Western secular tradition (which itself, of course, includes several strands). Prior to the Islamic awakening of the late twentieth century, these ideologies dominated most Arab countries. Musicians such as the Egyptian Shaykh Imam and the Lebanese Marcel Khalife and Ziad al-Rahbani, and such writers as Palestinians Ghassan Kanafani and Mahmoud Darwish, gave Arab nationalism, socialism, and the Palestinian struggle an artistic expression, which has had lasting impact on cultural production as well as the taste and worldview of millions.

Coming after a generation of Arab writers like Sati al-Husri and Taha Hussein, who, during the 1940s, 50s, and 60s, invented and buttressed the idea of social commitment (iltizam) until the crucial turning point of the Arab defeat in the 1967 war[9]—many of whom subsequently lost belief in the power of the word to change the world—al-Ali's generation created an art that was, and remains, popular. The subversive but also mass-consumed genres of songs and caricature were particularly well suited for the cultural criticism that developed after 1967.[10] The artists of this generation, who have become iconic, share a preoccupation with low-income classes and their life worlds, vocabulary, humor, and socio-political critique. Eschewing the often programmatic approach of Marxist writers and of the social realism (*waqi'iya ishtiraqiya*) that was in vogue during the 1960s—not to speak of the formalism of classicist art, music, and poetry—their artistic production is not bound by strict aesthetic prescriptions, but rather by the artist's individual sense of responsibility,[11] by quotidian language, and daily-life images. Their work deals with social justice, revolution, and resistance against Israel, Western powers, and the powerful classes in Arab society, often termed "the bourgeoisie." Religion, if it figures at all in their work, is usually one among many components of national culture, and sometimes even a signifier of reactionary thought and conservative social structures.

Social and political critique is a mainstay in Naji al-Ali's work. From the moment he first appeared in the Arab press to today, Arab readers have appreciated his subtly satirical critique of the powers that be in the Middle East and outside. He made fun of Arab and Western leaders, he exposed the hypocrisy of the rich, and he gave hundreds of thousands of readers a window into the life worlds of the poorest and most vulnerable members of Arab societies. Most of all, his cartoons revolved around the predicament of Palestine, as he filled them with nostalgic images of the homeland to which he never returned after 1948.

His trademark figure Handhala is a cultural icon of the late twentieth century in the sense that he has become an easily recognizable nonreligious symbol for Palestinian resistance. However, the iconic nature of Naji al-Ali's work is not restricted to Handhala. For leftists in Palestine and other Arab countries, al-Ali's images retain a particular resonance. As I demonstrate in this study, they are part of a body of art constitutive of what it means to be a leftist (*yasari*). By keeping alive the images of cultural struggle during the 1970s and 1980s, fans of Naji al-Ali produce and maintain the validity of a secular anchoring for Arab cultural and political identity. In the context of this volume on visual culture in the modern Middle East, the present article examines the role that cultural production plays in the reproduction of secular ideology. Building on ethnographic fieldwork in Beirut and Ramallah, I investigate how and why Naji al-Ali became an icon of the Arab secular left. In doing so, I go beyond the (sparse) existent research on Naji al-Ali written in English, most of which focuses on content analysis of his cartoons.[12] My concern here is less with individual cartoons, although I do analyze some, and more with Naji al-Ali's meaning for Arab public culture. I am interested in the factors that have transformed his images into iconic, easily recognizable signifiers for the interpretive community of Arabs in general and leftists in particular. Why do certain images attain a role as signifiers of collective experiences? To what extent does al-Ali reproduce secular iconography in his work, and to what extent does he invent it? What *is* secular iconography, and what is its role in an Islamizing Middle East today?

To start with the last question, I use the term "secular iconography" to refer to nonreligious images, tropes, and themes that feature prominently in particular cultural, political, and national public spheres. In the twentieth century, the original meaning of "icon," an image preserving the divine, gradually has been secularized to mean "representations that inspire some degree of awe—perhaps mixed with dread, compassion, or aspiration—and that stand for an epoch or a system of beliefs."[13] Secular icons supply our modern experience of history as "social action in profane time"[14] with signposts that allow individuals to perceive time as "epochs" and "systems of beliefs." Reproduced in the marketplace of mass mediation, and in "the secularist theology of the nation-state,"[15] secular icons become simulacra of an original work of art, an actual person, or an event imbued with (secularized) religious significance. Phrased in terms of Peircean semiotics, iconic signs stand for extant objects to interpreters who constitute the sign as such in the act of interpretation.[16] Although they are often open symbols that engender a range of interpretations, it is their ability to mark *specific* frameworks for collective understandings that distinguish them as icons. Secular icons are crucial for the constitution of what Peirce calls sign communities,[17] social formations based on common knowledge of "objects or persons in the real world that through time accrue to themselves a certain exemplary cultural status."[18] For social historians, therefore, secular icons provide important pointers to the semiotic coherence of social groups and societies, but also to the cultural logic or taken-for-grantedness, what Webb Keane calls semiotic ideology, that resides within and permeates language and visual culture.[19]

In the Arab Middle East, Gamal Abdel Nasser has become *the* iconic signifier of the age and system of beliefs referred to as Arab nationalism. Although Arab nationalist ideologies predate Nasser and include clusters of diverse political and social ideas, Nasser became their chief signifier because his political project epitomized the conviction that modern Arab history moves toward the telos of a unified, modern, secular state. Therefore, the Arab defeat in the 1967 war stands as a dividing line between the "radical" political projects of the early post-independence period and the ensuing rise of Islamist ideologies from the 1970s onward, even if, as Gelvin and Browers note, the hegemony of Islamism and the decline of Arab nationalism, and the ostensibly sharp divide between these two categories, have arguably been overstated in recent historiography.[20] Because of a number of factors related and unrelated to the legacy of Nasserism, secular ideologies have lost their position as the guiding light for Arab modernization. In that sense, Nasser's defeat sounded the decline, if not defeat, not only of Arab nationalism, but also of secular ideologies more broadly.

A caveat is necessary here to explain what I mean by ideologies. My approach to ideology is influenced by theorists like Slavoj Žižek and Terry Eagleton, who have followed Althusser's assertion that ideologies should not be seen as descriptions of the world, but rather embodied and often unconscious practices constitutive of political subjectivity.[21] In this tradition of what Herzfeld calls "cultural ideology,"[22] ideologies do not primarily reside in books, tracts, or party programs. Rather, they become meaningful objects of social analysis in their adaptation and mediation. The important question, in this optic, is not whether ideologies are accurate descriptions of social reality, but how they establish themselves through everyday practices and aesthetic experiences that often bypass disputation or even conscious identification. Icons are the "quilting points" of ideologies, the master signifiers that tie communities together.[23] They form part of practices that inscribe the individual or political subject in a relation with the specificities of a community, its *Thing*, in Žižek's term.[24] This sense of shared references and shared aesthetics is sine qua non for any *sensus communis*. By enjoying ("jouissance") the shared *Thing*, political subjects also establish themselves as a group vis-à-vis outsiders who do not have access to their cultural codes.[25] This line of thinking about ideology is particularly suited to describe nationalism and comes close to Herzfeld's conceptualization of cultural intimacy as a zone of internal codes produced in a dialectical fantasy of insiders in contraposition to the gaze of outsiders.[26] However, I also find it a useful way to think about the embodied modalities of Arab secular tradition, and an important addendum to the bulk of work on ideology in the Middle East focusing squarely on big thinkers and political movements.

Naji al-Ali was never a member of a political movement, although he was close to the Popular Front for the Liberation of Palestine (PFLP). He saw himself as a leftist (*yasari*), even a Marxist,[27] and belonged to a leftist Arab milieu in Kuwait, Beirut, and London. However, there is little in accounts of his life to suggest that al-Ali considered himself a secular or secularist artist.[28] In fact, one could argue that secular art and cultural production only becomes a relevant analytical category with the Islamic revival in the late twentieth century, and the emergence of "clean cinema" in Egypt and other examples of pious art, exemplified in this book by Christa Salamandra's article on Syrian television series, and by influential recent biographies by Abu-Lughod and Hirschkind, among others.[29] In other words, "secular art" only becomes visible once it no longer occupies the entire ocular field, and this only happens once something else—namely the *tathqif* agenda (dominance of the cultural field) of the Islamic trend—begins to crowd it out of the frame. This may explain why today many Arab artists and producers see the cultural industries as the last bastion of Arab secularism in a way they would not have formulated as secular/ist thirty years ago. There is no escaping the fact that Islamic revivalism has made its mark on cultural production today in Arab countries.[30] Seen from the vantage point of this new reality, Arab art and cultural production must be historicized differently than they were during a time when "secular art" was a given as the dominant (and therefore largely unarticulated) truth regime in Arab cultural production, and hence often uncritically equated with "nationalist art" both by Arab artists and by scholars.

In this article, I focus on how, in an age when Arab secularism has become a contested, unstable, sometimes even nostalgic notion, its meaning is negotiated through particular icons from a time when secular art was a given. Following the conceptual cues of "cultural ideology" sketched in the previous pages, I am interested in how Naji al-Ali emerged as a secular icon shaping everyday ideologies from the 1970s to today. I do this by, first, examining ideological positions in his work, including his relation to Arab secular critique. Second, I trace the emergence of his popularity in Palestine and the Arab world. Finally, I analyze his position as a marker of leftism and secular critique today.

Naqd and Nahda in al-Ali's Early Work

Naji al-Ali's life spanned the decline of Arab secularism. He fled Palestine in 1948, at the age of ten, and later started his professional career in the shadow of the Six Day War. He was a child of the *Nakba* (catastrophe) of 1948 and the *Naksa* (setback) of 1967, and his work can be seen as a meditation on both events. Indeed, in the cartoon from 1969 that first introduces Handhala, the boy presents himself as "a child of 1967."[31] In the course of al-Ali's career, Nasser's dreams suffered serious setbacks because of military defeats to Israel in 1967, 1973, and 1982, as well as a new moderate line initiated by Egyptian president Anwar Sadat and adopted by Jordan, Saudi Arabia, and the Gulf countries. These political events gave rich occasion for an art of resistance and subversion that dovetailed with Palestinian art in formulating a general cultural critique of mainstream Arab politics.[32] Trapped between the hopes of revolutionary Arab nationalism and Palestinian liberation movements on one side, and the rhetoric of compromise and normalization on the other, many Palestinians and other ordinary Arab citizens in the 1970s and 1980s lived with a bitter experience of failed dreams. Obviously, none of the regimes nor their associated media and cultural industries conceded defeat, which meant that the processes of publicly expressing a widespread sense of humiliation and negotiating its meaning were left to art and popular culture, to the extent that critical art was tolerated in different national publics. Al-Ali's work gave this common experience an expression.

Today, many Internet fan-sites buttress the ways in which Naji al-Ali's cartoons "exposed the brutality of the Israeli occupation of the Palestinians and the Arab world regimes' corruption and hypocrisy."[33] As an internationally recognizable symbol of Palestinian resistance, Handhala has become a mainstay of Arab popular culture, and is today recycled in a number of artifacts, from key chains, amulets, and T-shirts to the logos of political groups.[34] Undoubtedly, Palestine was the central theme in his work; it was the injustice at the heart of his own personal life and the life of the region as he saw it. However, what gets lost in this appropriation of al-Ali as an "Intifada artist" is his correlation to wider Arab issues, and to a secular leftist Arab tradition. I believe that his work must also be read in the context of secular critics like Sadallah Wannous, Abdallah Laroui, Constantine Zurayq, and Sadiq al-Azm. These writers and many others like them in the leftist milieus of Cairo, Damascus, Beirut, and other Arab intellectual centers called for the traumatic experience of the 1967 defeat to be turned into a cultural project of soul-searching with the aim of comprehending how the hopes of freedom and emancipation, embodied by the first reformers of the *nahda* and later by the post-independence governments, had ended in frustration. It was of central importance to what some have called the second *nahda* to invent a language for secular critique and for fostering historical awareness, in order to avoid mythical-metaphysical illusions of Islamic purity or national heritage.[35] Instead they urged the Arabs to return to the rational analysis of Arab history and identity that, in their eyes, had been the key to the *nahda*'s success, as a necessary first step toward historical awareness, enlightenment, political reform, and progress.

Similar to large swaths of Arab intelligentsia in the post-1967 period, al-Ali was preoccupied with *naqd* (critique) and *nahda* (rebirth). Far from the lofty ideological critique of the second *nahda,* his point of departure was always at street level. He lambasted Arab leaders, corrupt state officials, businessmen, capitalists, Westerners, and particularly the double standards of those who professed to represent "the Arab cause" but ignored the interests of the poor. In doing so, he also constructed—or fed into—a discourse of victimization and populism, which in some ways runs counter to the absolute self-critique leveled at Arab societies by, for example, Sadiq al-Azm. However, as I demonstrate in the following pages, other aspects of al-Ali's early work from the late 1960s and early 1970s dovetail with the laicist "fundamentalist secularism" (in the sense of going back to the fundamentals of the early Enlightenment) that we find in Sadiq al-Azm's two famous books, *Naqd al-fikr al-dini* (Critique of Religious Thought) and *Naqd al-dhati ba'd al-hazima* (Self-Critique after the Defeat) from 1969 and 1970. In the style of the European Enlightenment, al-Azm in these books attacks the modes of reactionary thought of the heirs of the *nahda,* who in his view never fully confronted the superstructures of Arab society such as patrimonialism and clientelism. Instead, Nasser and his generation of Arab nationalists had bowed to the forces of Islamic authority and traditional leadership, which had resulted in a half-cooked revolution that eventually backfired. In this view, the rise of Saudi Arabia's power in Arab politics embodies the ills of Arab modernity.[36]

Naji al-Ali agreed with al-Azm in the assessment of a deep Arab ailment, but differed over the precise diagnosis. He retained a deep admiration of Nasser, but he never stopped critiquing the ways in which Nasser's ideals were betrayed after his death.[37] Particularly the years 1967–75 felt to him like the end of an era. His idols in politics (Nasser), intellectual debate (Sati al-Husri), literature (Ghassan Kanafani), and culture (Umm Khultum) all died within a short time span.[38] Meanwhile, he sensed the emergence of a new class uninterested in Arab renaissance and political struggle. The weakness and consent of this new class is represented in al-Ali's cartoons as a rotund conservative Arab leader or businessman, who is sometimes rendered without any feet, as a slug-like, cross-eyed creature with an affable smile. He is often paired with *al-Zalame* (the fellow/guy), the archetypical poor refugee.

The result is always a pictographic rhetoric of victimization, as in figure 11.1, in which the crucifixion of the poor during the Lebanese Civil War is ignored by the rich. In the midst of the fiercely sectarian war, the cartoon maintains that there is a close connection between Islam and Christianity: the cross and the crescent intersect in the moon (as the naturally given), and poor Christians and Muslims suffer alongside each other, while the fat cats in the background, regardless of faith, stand face to face but refuse to confront the suffering *Zalame*. Here, and in many other al-Ali cartoons, he makes use of religious symbols like the crucifix to tell the story of social injustice. The most famous example, perhaps, is his rendering of a rock-throwing Jesus resisting from his cross, or of Jesus as the refugee wearing a key to his birthplace of Bethlehem.[39] These cartoons abound with religious symbols, like the cross and the crescent, but al-Ali's use effectively secularizes them. Jesus becomes another stranger, hit by the condition of strangeness and exile (*ghurba*) that runs through all of al-Ali's work. His characters are driven from their homeland, situated in a wasteland, and longing for the return. This wasteland is strewn with objects from cultural history, including religious signifiers—which, however, are never used to activate religious sentiments, or to draw boundaries between religious communities within the Arab realm. Rather, they are secularized kegs in the arsenal of social and political critique.

In figure 11.1, the two corpulent, conservative Arabs are marked as Muslim and Christian, respectively. Later, al-Ali standardized this character as the Slug, a turncoat wealthy Arab with no feet of his own to stand on, and no particular religious marker.[40] In several of al-Ali's early drawings, before the Slug found his final form in the late 1970s, he depicted similar rotund characters as conservative Gulf Arabs mired in sexual repression, double standards, ignorance, and subservience to the West. In fact, the genesis of al-Ali's critique of the bloated, capitalist Arab can be traced to his years in the Gulf. As an engaged leftist Palestinian artist, he was repulsed by much of the new wealth that surrounded him in the Gulf and the uses it was being put to, and these sentiments spilled over into his work. Figure 11.2, an unpublished drawing from the late 1960s,[41] juxtaposes a young woman with free-flowing hair with the new oil riches, symbolized by two drilling towers. The drawing carries the richly ambiguous title *nahdat al-sa'il al-aswad* (rise/rebirth of the black fluids), which probably refers to the oil discoveries that, in the late 1960s, were rapidly changing the power structures of the Arab world. At the same time, there is a sense of rebirth surrounding the young woman, rising organically out of the desert landscape as a sphinx or a timeless figure of beauty. Although the meaning is far from self-evident, the tension between the organic and the mechanic is palpable, and could be interpreted as a tension between a natural order and the new age of oil riches.

In a very similar drawing from 1975 (fig. 11.3b) with Handhala in the foreground, the (previously liberated) Arab woman has been moved from the corner to the center and is now veiled with bars in front of her eyes and shrouded in a black *aba'ya,* the traditional dress of Gulf women. The text reads "International women's year" (declared by the United Nations in 1975). Rising monumentally from the desert, similar to the woman in figure 11.2, a woman with a face obscured by bars has been commoditized, locked in a mechanized position, and reduced to nothing more than a drilling tower among others. Handhala, and with him the reader, observes in silence the surreal injustice of women in the Gulf, or perhaps in the Arab countries more generally.

Naji al-Ali first moved to Kuwait in 1963 in order to raise money. He became part of a vibrant Palestinian artistic milieu, and it was there, as cartoonist for the newspaper *al-Siyassa,* that he developed his style. However, despite residing in the Gulf for more than a decade of his life, he never viewed it as his home,[42] and he reserved the right to attack "the rise of the black fluids" in Arab politics: American confluence with conservative regimes and the influence of conservative social mores on Arab society, a pungent cocktail sometimes referred to as "petro-Islam." His unequivocal critique of the oppression of women in the Gulf is elaborated in many other drawings that expose Gulf Arab men as sex-hungry simpletons. The drilling towers recur in these cartoons as the backdrop to Gulf Arabs, as in figure 11.3a, in which a deluged Arab region and outstretched hands waving for help are met with fantasies about bare legs (which the American cartoonist Joe Sacco interprets as fantasies of leisurely swimming),[43] or as in figure 11.4, in which an Arab man is licking his lips at the thought of the Venus de Milo pregnant. Faced with the needs of his Arab brethren living in poverty, the conservative Arab man cannot see clearly because of his own repressed desires (or, alternatively, his wish for a life of excess), and, confronted with one of the icons of European aesthetic culture, he thinks of reproduction. As Nabulsi writes, the aim of this criticism is to expose not only sexual repression, "the imprisoned body," but also "the imprisoned mind/reason [*aql*]."[44] In this way, al-Ali's cultural critique is always directly related to a political critique, namely the various means through which Arabs are being made incapable of seeing and reacting to injustice, or, in Marxist terms, the ubiquitous false consciousness imposed by petro-fueled capitalism.

SUNE HAUGBOLLE

نهضة السائل الاسود

ABOVE:
FIGURE. 11.1. Poor Christians and Muslims united in suffering during the Lebanese Civil War, while rich Christians and Muslims are united in ignoring them, and Handhala observes. Unpublished drawing, 1978. *From the personal collection of Kefah Fanni.*

LEFT:
FIGURE 11.2. "Rebirth of the Black Fluids," undated. *From the personal collection of Kefah Fanni.*

FIGURES 11.3a (1972) and b (1973). Critiquing the conservative Arab order, the texts read "The Arab region" (a) and "International women's year !!" (b). *From the personal collection of Kefah Fanni.*

Figures 11.2, 11.3a, 11.3b, and 11.4 are examples of Naji al-Ali's use of juxtaposition, not only between the ostensible values of the Gulf and the ideals of gender equality and intellectual freedom, but also between the portrayed Gulf Arabs and the implicit reader, symbolized in figure 11.3b by the observant boy Handhala, who became a recurrent feature in all of Naji al-Ali's cartoons from around 1972. Handhala and his readers know that the situation is absurd and they lament it, or try to laugh about it.[45] Truth about the political and social realm is embodied by the poor and by a political—progressive, socialist, Arab nationalist—order that identifies with them. By consequently exposing the rich and the powerful, while placing the ability to tell right from wrong with the poor and powerless, al-Ali set a standard for subversive social and political analysis in Arab media, which won him many enemies but also an unparalleled popular following.

FIGURE 11.4. "Venus," 1972. *From the personal collection of Kefah Fanni.*

The Making of an Icon

How did Naji al-Ali's status evolve from that of a popular cartoonist into a cultural icon? As mentioned, al-Ali first invented Handhala in 1969, and over the next five years experimented with his form and shape. By 1974, when al-Ali returned to Lebanon, Handhala had become the signature of his increasingly widely read daily cartoons. In Beirut, al-Ali joined a group of young Arab nationalists who established the newspaper *al-Safir* in 1975. Over the next eight years, until he was forced to flee Beirut in 1983, al-Ali became closely associated with its pro-Palestinian, Arab nationalist line, and an important reason for its great popularity.[46] In the words of his previous editor at al-Safir, Talal Salman, "Naji was the first thing people read in al-Safir, including us journalists. We would flip straight to his cartoon to see what he had come up with. Which was good for readership reasons, of course, but also for our identity as a newspaper. Naji was a fix point."[47] Through the turbulent early years of the Lebanese Civil War, al-Ali established himself as a voice of the poor in Lebanon—including of course his own Palestinian people. Mirroring al-Safir's editorial line, his cartoons sympathized with the Shiite South, raged against the Christian Right and the United States, and were fiercely supportive of the Palestinian fighters in Lebanon, if not always the Palestinian leadership. During these years, he invented a genre of monumental, expressionist cartoons with no humorous point, which nonetheless worked formidably as political cartoons. He became a chronicler of the war as seen from the viewpoint of the secular left, and he produced many haunting images that remain mnemonic icons—places of memory in Pierre Nora's term—for the Palestinian struggle and Lebanese Civil War.

In Palestine, meanwhile, Naji al-Ali was known throughout leftist milieus, particularly by members of the PFLP, from the early 1970s. However, it was not always easy to acquire copies of his cartoons. Inside Israel his drawings were forbidden, which of course only added to their popularity. According to one informant in Ramallah, who was a student in Galilee in the late 1970s, university students from around 1976 began using Handhala as a symbol of Palestinian identity, along with such symbols as the flag and the territory of Palestine, which would be worn around the neck or stenciled on bags, cars, and clothes. On the West Bank Naji al-Ali became a symbol of Palestinian national identity in general, and of the particular group who rejected the "normalization" process initiated by Egypt, Jordan, and Saudi Arabia, and later formalized in a Palestinian context by the PLO under Yassir Arafat.[48]

During a time of severe media regulations in the occupied territories, it was never easy to acquire his cartoons. Before the second intifada, photocopy machines were banned and very rare. Some drawings were reproduced in the newspapers al-Mithaq, al-Quds, and al-Nahar,[49] but his daily cartoon in al-Safir or al-Qabbas, available to an Arab audience in London, Paris, Amman, Beirut, and other capitals, had to be collected outside Palestine, copied, and distributed through personal channels. Reading Naji al-Ali therefore became a game of collecting, which was possible for those in the right circles and those who were able to travel, but for others

SUNE HAUGBOLLE

remained very difficult. Nevertheless, drawings did circulate and hence became a way to establish social and political connections. In the words of a Palestinian man who grew up in a refugee camp close to Bethlehem during the 1980s, "we were all raised on Naji al-Ali. Knowing his characters was a natural part of life. Naji lived with us, not just his images but also his words. He was very smart [shatir] with his use of words, you know."[50] My informant was an aspiring young member of the PFLP, and, for boys like him, owning a collection of Naji al-Ali cartoons and being able to quote from them was a sign of distinction, of being an accepted member of a community and its Thing, to invoke Žižek's term.[51] The jouissance, enjoyment, surrounding al-Ali consisted equally in the collecting, the comparing, and the quoting of his cartoons, as well as the feelings of familiarity and proud sumud that his work stoked in people. It was also an outright provocation aimed at the Israeli occupation.

The outbreak of the first intifada in December 1987, a few months after the death of Naji al-Ali, once again changed his status. Al-Ali was now a shahid (martyr) of the Palestinian cause, and during the intifada Handhala became the symbol par excellence of popular resistance and of readiness to die for "the cause" (al-qadiya).[52] As is the case for religious and secular saints, his premature death is foundational for his quasi sainthood, and arguably also for the status of Handhala as a secular icon. According to several informants in Ramallah, it was not before the late 1980s and early 1990s that Naji al-Ali became property of the whole Palestinian population. Not only had his death added to his popularity, access to television had also become much more widespread, and people who did not or could not read newspapers were now able to watch frequent reruns of a popular film from 1991 about the life of Naji al-Ali, starring the Egyptian actor Nour al-Sharif and directed by 'Atif al-Tayyib, by far the most politically outspoken Egyptian director of the late 1980s and early 1990s. The film was also shown at public screenings in the camps. It is a realistic, if rather eulogizing, tribute to Naji al-Ali, and is still shown every so often on Arab television networks. During this time, study circles and culture clubs were organized to discuss al-Ali's work. Several exhibitions in Palestine, as well as in Arab and European capitals, added to his fame. Most importantly, people kept reading his work, and, with the arrival of the internet in the late 1990s, were able to exchange drawings more freely. Through exhibitions, passed-down collections, and the internet, a new generation of admirers, who do not remember Naji al-Ali—or the time he wrote about—has learned to love his cartoons. It is to the contemporary appreciation of Naji al-Ali that we now turn.

Naji al-Ali and the Arab Left

That Naji al-Ali remains so popular today is perhaps remarkable given the fact that his art was produced for the notoriously transient medium of journalism. Who still reads editorials by Talal Salman, very popular when published in *al-Safir* in the late 1970s? The texts of that period are all but gone, while the images are continuously reproduced in today's media-saturated world. An explanation may be found in the truism that media technologies favor sound and image over the written word. However, media alone cannot sustain a cultural icon; doing so also requires appreciation, resonance, and agency. In the case of Naji al-Ali, that agency, I argue, is located particularly among people who see themselves as leftists (*yasariun*). Here, I briefly consider two groups of leftist Naji-lovers in Beirut and Ramallah—an older generation who were active in the 1970s and 1980s, and a younger generation of aspiring leftists today—in order to illustrate that Naji al-Ali has become a marker for social practices of leftist ideology over the course of two generations since his death.

In Beirut, Naji al-Ali has nostalgic connotations for aging leftists. A particular stronghold is the newspaper *al-Safir,* where I carried out fieldwork in 2008 and 2009. In 2010 *Al-Safir* still was edited by Talal Salman, and its staff writers continued to see their paper as leftist, Panarabist, and Nasserist in orientation. Today, *al-Safir* is no longer the strong focal point of leftist opinion-making that it was during its heyday in the late 1970s and early 1980s: first, because the left is less of a force in Lebanese and Arab politics; and second, because gravity in the Arab public sphere of mass media has swung from newspaper toward satellite television. Moreover, during the 2006 war between Israel and Hizbollah, a group of its journalists, with the now deceased *al-Safir* veteran Joseph Samaha at its helm, founded a competing leftist daily, *al-Akhbar.* In doing so, Samaha took part of *al-Safir*'s dwindling readership with him. Prior to 2006, circulation numbers had already fallen sharply from those of the 1980s, as they have among most Arab dailies, and *al-Safir* is, at the time of writing, fighting for survival. The worn interior of the building mirrors the general mood among the staff. Despite the fact that this period is obviously hard, the paper's journalists take pride in its illustrious history and its role during the civil war. In the late 1970s it was, in the words of one journalist, "an incredible hub of pan-Arabists and Arab socialists from every Arab country. *Al-Safir* was a school of Arab leftist journalism, where some of our greatest thinkers found a space to develop their talent: Joseph Samaha, Elias Khoury, Ibrahim al-Amin, Hazim Saghie, and Naji al-Ali."[53]

SUNE HAUGBOLLE

The inclusion of the artist Naji al-Ali in this pantheon of leftist Arab intellectuals may seem remarkable. During my visits to the newspaper in 2008 and 2009,[54] however, I heard repeatedly about the importance of Naji al-Ali from al-Safir journalists, who always invoked him with immense pride. Inside the editorial rooms of al-Safir, the position of Naji al-Ali as a patron saint of the paper was underlined by a framed front page adorning the wall. The page is taken from the August 5, 1982, edition of al-Safir, during the height of Israeli bombardment during its 1982 invasion of Beirut, and features one of Naji al-Ali's famous drawings, "Sabah al-khayr ya Beirut" (Good Morning Beirut). The drawing shows Handhala standing next to shrapnel, handing a flower to a beautiful young woman who symbolizes Beirut. Peering out through a shot hole, she receives the flower as a token of love and sympathy from the Palestinian people. Handhala here is wearing the kaffiyeh, the Palestinian headscarf, to mark him as a fida'i, a popular fighter.

The framed image celebrates Naji al-Ali's role at al-Safir, and fondly commemorates the close alliance between the secular left—on the cusp of the rise of the Islamic left in the resistance fight against Israel after 1982[55]—and the Palestinian liberation movement. The cartoon is famous and has been recycled in popular culture. A striking example of this phenomenon is another cartoon by the talented Lebanese artist Mazen Kerbaj (fig. 11.5), whose comic strips have appeared since 2009 in al-Akhbar, al-Safir's competitor. Mazen Kerbaj (born 1975) is known for satirical strips that routinely expose the dark side of Lebanese society: sectarian divisiveness, snobbish pretension, and social inequality. Like many other young Lebanese artists, Kerbaj is secular, anti-sectarian, and, although not formally a member of any political group, leftist in orientation. The drawing is from a series called "NEW WAR?"[56] produced in May 2008 during a spout of fighting between Hizbollah and Sunni/Druze groups, which many people at the time feared would be a prelude to full-blown civil war.

At a time of immense tension, Kerbaj's cartoon subtly integrates the older drawing by al-Ali and intersects with its messages. The top text reads, "When I woke up this morning, I thought about this drawing by Naji al-Ali." Below, a figure representing Mazen Kerbaj remarks, "go hide yourself Handhala, it seems Beirut is going insane these days." On one level, the cartoon communicates what many Lebanese feared in May 2008: that their country was going down the road of another civil war. But at the same time, it wryly rejects the possibility of the same sort of heroism that the older cartoon represents. By asking Handhala to go and hide, the cartoon seems to be saying that he would be wasting his efforts today. Beirut is

FIGURE 11.5. Naji al-Ali's cartoon "Sabah al-khayr ya Beirut," used by Mazen Kerbaj, May 8, 2008. *From Mazen Kerbaj's blog, http://www.flickr.com/photos/ kerbaj/2478452281/.*

simply not worth fighting for anymore, it seems, in the way that it was twenty-six years earlier. Rather than facing an external enemy, it is—once again—turning the gun on itself.

The two reproductions of "Sabah al-khayr ya Beirut" offer snapshots of the many social uses Naji al-Ali is being put to in Lebanon today. Whereas older "comrades" use Naji al-Ali's images to maintain a link to personal memories of a time when their political and cultural project felt in ascendance rather than in decline, younger leftists connect with the ideals that they see embodied in Naji al-Ali's work. However, they do so skeptically, rather than heroically. They know, and live with a daily experience of, the sidelined status of secular groups and parties in Lebanon vis-à-vis sectarian groups such as the Shiite Hizbollah and Amal, the Christian al-Kata'ib and Lebanese Forces, the Druze Progressive Socialist Party, and the Sunni Mustaqbal Movement. They also live in a neoliberal economy that has exacerbated economic disparities since 1990.

Furthermore, the Lebanese left has been split over how best to address this reality, some siding with the pro-Western March 14 group and others with the pro-Hizbollah March 8 coalition since 2005. This split has accentuated other, older rifts in the leftist milieu going back to the civil war.[57] In such a situation, which for many young leftists seems an impossible predicament, heroes of a bygone age can serve as guiding lights and standard bearers for ideals, like social justice and secular resistance, that they wish to maintain for a secular left. Naji al-Ali and other icons of Arab secularism, including the singer Ziad al-Rahbani, connect them to the historical memory of their fathers' generation through images and sounds that have become familiar through their upbringing in leftist milieus. In that way, icons of Arab secularism become bearers of what Hirsch calls postmemory: a form of residual memory that relies on passed-down accounts and is therefore not personally experienced, but socially felt.[58]

In Palestine, Handhala is more present in the public sphere than he is in Lebanon, where he is mostly seen on campuses, on occasional T-shirts and key rings. Around the city center of Ramallah and in the old city of Jerusalem, shops sell Handhala paraphernalia, and close to Ramallah a whole arts and crafts center is dedicated to Naji al-Ali knickknacks. Beyond the activist/tourist commoditization, appreciation of Naji al-Ali has more specific political connotations in Palestine than in Lebanon. Generally, his images form a mnemonic iconography that serves as an all-embracing national symbol of the suffering of ordinary people and the struggle of *fida'yeen*. At the same time, as Laleh Khalili has remarked, the resolute insistence on uncompromising resistance in his work inevitably serves as a reminder of the ensuing squandering of the Palestinian liberation struggle under Yasser Arafat's leadership of the PLO.[59] Because of Naji al-Ali's well-known confrontations with Yassir Arafat—whose growing talk of normalization al-Ali viewed as capitulation and lambasted in several cartoons shortly before his death[60]—his work from the early 1980s on was increasingly adopted by PFLP members and by the party as a marker of political belonging. Much like their communist colleagues in Lebanon, the PFLP today is sidelined in the Fatah-dominated Palestinian National Authority (PNA). This is not to say that Fatah supporters do not appreciate al-Naji's drawings, but the Naji fanatics I met in Ramallah were exclusively sympathetic to the PFLP or communist groups. They use Handhala and Naji al-Ali generally to signal resistance against the current line of the Palestinian leadership. At Birzeit University, I spent time with a young man active in student politics. He also happened to know everything about Naji al-Ali, and had worked as a consultant on a recent exhibition of his cartoons at the Birzeit Ethnographic and Art Museum.[61] Although he had been raised in a religious family in which Naji al-Ali had never been mentioned, as an adolescent he had become attracted to the PFLP. Part of this shift had involved acquiring new cultural heroes. Today, he is a member of the PFLP. Naji al-Ali, he explained,

> is part of the package for us leftists. We read him together and so we know . . . ya'ni, we see the lies [al-kidhb] of our politicians, of the system, and of Arab politics. We remember the people, how they suffer. And the history, [the fact] that it is still the same. Naji was a prophet; when you read his cartoons today you see that he was really a prophet, he knew what would happen. How did he know that? Wollah, he was smart [shatir].

The explanation that he was shatir enough to see behind the façade of superficial politics, to expose the truth behind the lies, recurred both in Lebanon and in Palestine when I asked people why they liked Naji al-Ali so much. The more particular insight my informant referred to was, of course, Naji al-Ali's ability to foreshadow the Oslo peace process in the 1990s, as well as its ensuing unraveling in the 2000s and eventual deadlock. The overwhelming sense among Palestinians that "normalization" has brought them no political or material gain finds a succinct and satirical expression in the cartoons. By reading his work, young PFLP stalwarts are able to connect their emotions and their tangible experience of occupation with previous times—with the experience of their fathers. They attach to a

SUNE HAUGBOLLE

condensed social memory and see "that it is still the same," and that action is still needed to address the situation.

The older generation of activists whom I met had a more direct relationship with Naji al-Ali. Some of them had known him personally. They had lived the modern history of Palestine and in many cases suffered long imprisonments at the hands both of the Israeli occupation and of the *sulta* ("the power," a euphemism for the PNA). Naji al-Ali had followed them in their political struggle. Their offices were adorned with images from his cartoons, Handhala mouse pads and coffee coasters (fig.11.6), and, in one case, a drawing with a personal dedication from Naji al-Ali (fig. 11.7). One man recounted that one of his friends in prison had constructed an amazing Handhala figure in his cell from little pieces of straw. It was an elaborate work that took months, but focusing on this project gave him strength. He completed it because Handhala symbolizes an ideal, the informant explained, but sometimes also a reality:

> In a way, we all need to be Handhala. Sometimes, we feel that we are. It gives us power to remember that he stands tall, that way we can resist. When we suffer, we must be Handhala, be strong and not give up. When we can act, we must act. Like in the cartoons where he suddenly stops looking and throws a stone.[62] That is why he built the straw [figure]. We must be patient like Handhala.[63]

However, as my informant freely admitted, most of the time he and others were not like Handhala. With "the situation being as it was, with the occupation being so strong and the Palestinian leadership so corrupted," he understood those who either escaped to the West or became part of "normalization." If Handhala embodies the qualities that a Palestinian activist must ideally possess, the reality was much more muddled. "The left is so weak and divided. It invested so much in the civil society movement [in the 1990s]. And it merged with normalization. People want to live, and this [giving up armed resistance and activism] is understandable. And what can we say about Hamas? They resist, but this is not the Arab world that we want. Our ideals are secular, like Naji al-Ali was secular." Reading Naji al-Ali took him back to the ideals of his leftism, he explained, but he rejected my suggestion that Naji al-Ali could be compared to a nostalgic fix:

> No. Not nostalgia. Because even during Naji's time the situation was bad. You see it in his cartoons, if you read them well. Arab politics was corrupted. He lived after the fall, if you will. We still do. Nothing has changed. This is what his drawings tell us. Nothing has changed, but it should, if we can be patient.[64]

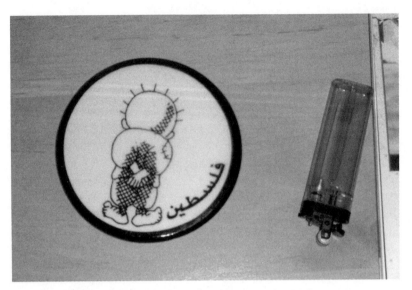

FIGURE 11.6. Handhala coaster in the office of activist Kefah Fanni. Ramallah, February 2, 2010. *Photo by Sune Haugbolle.*

The fall or point of no return, here, is the 1967 war and the crisis of Arab secularism that came with it. These comments may not be representative of the Palestinian left, or even a faction within it. They are of course personal reflections on modern Arab history. But they are striking nonetheless, because they confirm the reading of history that we find in a leftist intellectual tradition, from the second *nahda* through Naji al-Ali to today. Handhala, then, both inspires hope and serves as a reminder of social injustice, occupation, and Western hegemony in the Middle East, a reality that is of course inescapable in Palestine today; for Naji al-Ali's most devoted fans it is a reality that is not addressed by their political leaders. On a daily basis they put themselves in Handhala's shoes—even if he isn't wearing any.

Conclusion:
On the Possibility of a Secular Reading of History

As any form of mass culture, the political cartoon has a status somewhere between cultural fast food and highly priced artistic production. Naji al-Ali is a remarkable, if not the sole, example of an Arab cartoonist whose work has been elevated to the status of art, eliciting exhibitions of and a critical literature about his work. More than two decades after al-Ali's death, his cartoons continue to be popular with Arabs in Palestine,

SUNE HAUGBOLLE

FIGURE 11.7. Poster-sizes drawing with personal dedication to economist 'Adil Samara from Naji al-Ali, 1985. *Photo taken by Sune Haugbolle in 'Adil Samara's office, Ramallah, February 6, 2010.*

in the larger Arab world, and in diaspora communities. The current-day adaptation of Handhala is a triumph for the artistic ambitions of Naji al-Ali. From the beginning, he sought to create a visual language that engaged the reader in a more direct way than traditional painting could do.[65] His images engage Arabs, I have suggested here, because they speak powerfully of collective experiences refracted through public culture.

Those experiences are not particular to nonreligious or even secular Arabs. As a very drunk Egyptian Palestinian woman well into her sixties told me in a Ramallah bar: "*min al-maghreb lal-Iraq, miin ma by'arif Nagi el-Ali?*" (from Morocco to Iraq, who doesn't know Naji al-Ali?). Many Arabs who lived during the 1970s and 1980s have vivid memories of reading his cartoons. They have become what Aleida Assmann calls external memory anchors, symbols that ex post facto create historical moments in one's consciousness.[66] To leftists in Lebanon and Palestine, Naji al-Ali's work and persona signify a set of social relations and sensuous experiences, a shared reading of his work, and a particular ethical reading of history that highlights the structural injustices perpetrated against the poorest members of Arab societies, and the cynicism of official politics. In this article, I have tried to show how the reproduction and material exchange of his work maintains that experience in the physical world. In other words, while Islamists may well love Naji-Ali equally for his anti-Western, anti-Israeli, and socialist viewpoints, secularists claim a particular ownership of his work. Whether in the revering of Naji al-Ali as a patron-saint of *al-Safir*, through the clandestine circulation of copies of his cartoons in the West Bank, in reading clubs on campuses, or the construction of a straw Handhala in prison, leftists do not merely read Naji al-Ali's work: they use it as an ideological fix point in a time of extreme ideological adversity for the secular left. His iconography binds people together in shared understandings, and through shared icons and actions.

The explanation for his iconic status, this article has suggested, can be found in his solid grasp of popular rhetoric. As a refugee, Naji al-Ali grew up with refugees, spoke their language, and was able to use this embodied knowledge in his visual creations. As Batur and VanderLippe note in their article on Turkish cartoons in this volume, the power of political cartoons depends on their ability to make use of icons—or representations that are integrated into the visual lexicon of everyday life and popular culture—playing with them, breaking them down, and reinventing them. Part of al-Ali's success is undoubtedly related to his direct personal access to subaltern aesthetics and discourse.

Not everyone claiming to speak on behalf of the less articulate, the less empowered, has direct access to their imaginaries. Islamist intellectuals have blamed the distance between intellectuals and the people they supposedly represent for the failing of secular leftist ideologies from the 1950s to today.[67] This critique recurs as self-critique in leftist circles. As an Egyptian veteran activist, quoted by Marilyn Booth, put the problem of representation with regard to another leftist icon, the *sha'bi* (popular) singer Shaykh Imam, he and his poet sidekick Ahmad Fu'ad Nigm, "were the oral facet of the leftist movement and therefore their impact was huge," unlike the political movement of the Egyptian left, which was "fundamentally a movement of intellectuals."[68]

Far from the champagne socialist camp and the over-theorizing Marxist and post-Marxist camp of the Arab left, Naji al-Ali was an organic intellectual who kept the causes and the images dearest to ordinary people in close view by constructing archetypes and stereotypes that reappear throughout his work. The artistic flipside of such sharp dichotomies is of course a certain simplistic bent, a discourse of victimization, and an inability to critique social structure, or "the people," as the critical project of the second *nahda* would have prescribed. The world of ordinary people is staged through the eternal refugee family: the common man al-Zalame, his wife Fatima, their poor children, and in particular the ragged child Handhala.[69] Opposing these characters we find the traditional subjects of political cartoons, namely bloated politicians and leaders. In addition to the Slug, al-Ali poked fun at Sadat, Sharon, Ford, Nixon, Kissinger, Arafat, and many others. Had he still been alive, he would probably have had a field day with today's Arab leaders and cheered the demise of Mubarak, Ben Ali, and Ghaddafi.

Al-Ali's stereotypes and archetypes have become mnemonic icons for the Palestinian struggle, as well as for the era—the 1970s and 1980s—when they were produced. This time of internal Arab wars and disunity, autocratic regimes, repression, and violence may have been the age of despair for many, but it was also a period of reorientation and vital artistic, political, and intellectual attempts to reinvent the project of Arab rejuvenation of the earlier twentieth century.[70] If it is true, as several scholars have recently argued, that crucial moments of Arab liberal thought and action in the first part of the century have been marginalized in Middle East studies,[71] it is equally true for the period after 1967. Even as we recognize the growing importance of Islamic discourses in the Middle East, we should not belittle the heritage of secular ideologies, but rather engage with the foundational role they play for ideological contentions in Arab societies today.[72]

Pieces of this historiography must be sought in political, intellectual, and social histories of the Arab countries. Along with Swedenburg, Stein, and others, I call for public and popular culture to be central to this historiography, both because cultural production is a crucial terrain of power that interacts with broader social and political processes,[73] but also—as I have argued elsewhere—because public culture and media form part of the day-to-day negotiation of the broad, common-sense conceptions of the world that ultimately determine how a society reads its past and orientates itself toward the future.[74] Al-Ali's work is part of a media history as well as an art history and social history of the late twentieth century in the Arab world. His is an art for, of, and about the popular.

Contentions over the precise definition of the popular are always at the heart of ideological debates. In Naji al-Ali's time it was possible, indeed natural, to use religious symbols to denote the national struggle. As I have shown, al-Ali secularized the redemptive significations of both Christian and Muslim symbols by drawing on them to express the aspirations of Palestinians and Arabs as a whole. In his work, they become *cultural* symbols in line with the kaffiyeh, the peasant dress, the key to abandoned houses in Palestine, the moustache, and Handhala for that matter. Religion in Naji al-Ali's work is part of the historical ballast of stories and identity markers that make up the Arab cultural realm as identified from a secular Arab nationalist viewpoint. Today it is often the other way around: the national is inscribed in religious narratives about Arab identity. Visual culture and other forms of public culture have indeed become imbedded in a matrix of Muslim-speak, as Francois Burgat has described.[75] Maintaining the possibility of a secular reading of history is one of the challenges facing the Arab left, and perhaps a challenge that seems more manageable in light of the uprisings since 2011. On the level of everyday ideology, such readings make use of icons that refer back to a time when secular readings of history were taken for granted.

NOTES

1. Conversation with Mohsen Kana'an, Birzeit University, Palestine.
2. Nabulsi, *Akalahu al-dhi'b* (The Wolf Ate Him), 5–32.
3. Ibid., 139–45.
4. Ibid., 423–42.
5. Countless collections of his cartoons were published in Arabic. In this article I refer mostly to al-Ali, *Karikatur Naji al-'Ali,* and *A Child in Palestine.*
6. Scott and Tomaselli, "Cultural Icons," 7–24.
7. For recent Arab debates on the Arab left, see special issue of *al-Adab* (2), 2010.

SUNE HAUGBOLLE

8. Jakobsen and Pellegrini, *Secularisms*.

9. Klemm, "Different Notions of Commitment *(Iltizam)* and Committed Literature *(al-adab al-multazim),*" 51–62.

10. Nabulsi, *Akalahu al-dhi'b,* 102.

11. Klemm, "Different Notions of Commitment *(Iltizam)* and Committed Literature *(al-adab al-multazim),*" 57.

12. Yaqub, "Gendering the Palestinian Political Cartoon," 187–213; Najjar, "Cartoons as a Site for the Construction of Palestinian Refugee Identity," 255–85; al-Shaykh, "Historiographies of Laughter," 65–78; and Boullata, *Palestinian Art,* 137–39.

13. Vicky Goldberg quoted in Brink, "Secular Icons," 136.

14. Taylor, *A Secular Age, 194.*

15. *Herzfeld, Cultural Intimacy,* 2nd ed., 93.

16. Zitzewitz, "The Secular Icon," 13.

17. Peirce, *The Collected Papers,* 1:210–13.

18. Scott and Tomaselli, "Cultural Icons," 18.

19. Keane, *Christian Moderns,* 16–23.

20. Gelvin, "Modernity *and* Its Discontents," 71–89; and Browers, *Political Ideology in the Arab World.*

21. Eagleton, *Ideology;* Žižek, *Tarrying with the Negative;* Žižek, "Introduction," 3–7; and Sharpe, "The Aesthetics of Ideology," 95–120.

22. Herzfeld, *Cultural Intimacy,* 2nd ed., 95.

23. Sharpe, "The Aesthetics of Ideology," 117.

24. Žižek, *Tarrying with the Negative.*

25. Sharpe, "The Aesthetics of Ideology," 113–16.

26. Herzfeld, *Cultural Intimacy,* 2nd ed.

27. Conversation with Naji al-Ali's personal friend, the economist 'Adil Samara, Ramallah, February 4, 2010.

28. Shakir Nabulsi, perhaps al-Ali's foremost biographer in Arabic, only mentions secular ideals in relation to al-Ali's depiction of veiled women (in *Akalahu al-dhi'b,* 215–22).

29. Abu-Lughod, *Dramas of Nationhood;* and Hirschkind, *The Ethical Soundscape.*

30. Van Nieuwkerk, "Creating an Islamic Cultural Sphere," 169–76; and Winegar, *Creative Reckonings,* 77–78.

31. Nabulsi, *Akalahu al-dhi'b,* 144.

32. Boullata, *Palestinian Art.*

33. See http://www.najialali.com/articles.html (site discontinued).

34. The short film *al-Iquna* (The Icon) by Hana Ramli documents the multiple ways in which Handhala is used in daily life, and his meaning for young Palestinians. See http://najialali.hanaa.net/film-TheIcon-Handala.html (site discontinued).

35. Kassab, *Contemporary Arab Thought,* 48–115.

36. Kassab, *Contemporary Arab Thought,* 74–82.

37. Nabulsi, *Akalahu al-dhi'b,* 214.

38. Ibid.

39. Al-Ali, *A Child in Palestine,* 4, 116.

40. Ibid., 34, 57, 89, 90.

41. The style would suggest that it is from around 1966–69.

42. Nabulsi, *Akalahu al-dhi'b,* 212–36.

43. Al-Ali, *A Child in Palestine,* 77.

44. Nabulsi, *Akalahu al-dhi'b*, 221.

45. Arab political cartoons have a tradition of black humor mixed with satire, represented by the likes of Ali Farzat and Mahmoud Kahil, a friend and contemporary of al-Ali.

46. In the early 1980s, *al-Safir* had a daily circulation of seventy to eighty thousand copies, making it one of the most-read Arab newspapers.

47. Conversation with Talal Salman, Beirut, October 14, 2008.

48. Conversation with Ala' al-Azzeh, Ramallah, February 3, 2010.

49. The Palestinian, not the Lebanese, *al-Nahar*.

50. Conversation with Shafiq Abdallah, Ramallah, February 3, 2010.

51. Žižek, *Tarrying with the Negative*.

52. Conversation with Moslih Kanaan, Ramallah, February 1, 2010.

53. Conversation with Hanady Salman, October 13, 2008.

54. I met with *al-Safir* journalists in Beirut in October 2008, February 2009, and October 2009.

55. Hizbollah was formed in reaction to the 1982 invasion and subsequently challenged the Lebanese left for leadership of the resistance against Israeli occupation, a struggle Hizbollah eventually won.

56. See Mazen Kerbaj's Photostream,, "NEW WAR?" set, May 2008, http://www.flickr.com/photos/kerbaj/sets/72157604969493202/.

57. Haugbolle, *War and Memory in Lebanon*, 210–12.

58. Hirsch, *Family Frames*.

59. Khalili, *Heroes and Martyrs of Palestine*, 133–34.

60. The most famous (al-Ali, *A Child in Palestine*, 93) is a January 1984 cartoon of Arafat showing a V for Victory sign formed by outstretched arms in surrender rather than by two fingers.

61. See Birzeit University, Virtual Gallery, http://virtualgallery.birzeit.edu/.

62. Handhala in some cartoons throws stones at Israeli soldiers (al-Ali, *A Child in Palestine*, 113, 114).

63. Conversation with Kefah Fanni, Ramallah, February 3, 2010.

64. Conversation with Kefah Fanni, Ramallah, February 3, 2010.

65. Boullata, *Palestinian Art*, 137.

66. A. Assmann, "Three Memory Anchors," 43.

67. Browers, *Political Ideology in the Arab World*, 33–40.

68. Booth, "Exploding into the Seventies," 39–40.

69. For a discussion of Fatima, al-Zalame, and Handhala, see Yaqub, "Gendering the Palestinian Political Cartoon."

70. Kassab, *Contemporary Arab Thought*, 48–115.

71. Schumann, *Nationalism and Liberal Thought in the Arab East*.

72. Browers, *Political Ideology in the Arab World*, 3–4.

73. Stein and Swedenburg, "Popular Culture, Transnationality, and Radical History," 7.

74. Haugbolle, *War and Memory in Lebanon*, 29–32.

75. Burgat, *Islamism after al-Qaida*.

PART 4

Authenticity and Reality in Trans-National Broadcasting

CHAPTER 12

Arab Television Drama Production and the Islamic Public Sphere

CHRISTA SALAMANDRA

Syrian drama creators find themselves at the forefront of a pan-Arab satellite television industry with a global reach. Their key product, the dramatic miniseries (*musalsal*) dominates public culture in the Arab world. This is particularly true during Ramadan, which has given the genre its form and has in turn been shaped by it. In the months leading up to this peak broadcast season, the city of Damascus becomes a film set, as producers rush to finish their thirty-episode series. Every evening of holy month, streets across the Arab world empty as families gather around television sets in homes, restaurants, and cafés, partaking in what has become known as the "drama outpouring" (*al-fawra al-dramiyya*). Dramatic depictions of Arab and Muslim politics and society, traditions and values, customs and practices—past and present—are discussed and debated in conversation and in the media. Drama series have become sites where Islamic revivalism, terrorism, and *takfir* are invoked and criticized.[1]

This paper aims to map the crucial terrain where politics, religion, and markets converge in the current of Islamism. It examines Islamization, economic liberalization, and globalization through the lens of visual culture, and explores the ways in which television drama creators (writers, directors, actors, producers, programming executives, and others) both shape the Arab world's most powerful mass medium and reconcile an increasingly Islamized public sphere with their own largely secular agendas. My research addresses the ways in which the demise of socialism, the perceived failures of secular nationalism, and the rise of Islamism are reshaping popular culture. I argue that despite—and, indeed, because of—these conditions and constraints, Arab drama creators produce alternative, liberal interpretations of religion and religiosity. The immense popularity of their products among transnational audiences suggests that drama allows for alternative political, social, and religious envisioning.

The *Musalal*

Eagerly anticipated, obsessively followed, yet vastly understudied, the drama miniseries has become the Arab world's dominant cultural form. The *musalsal* has played a crucial role in the rise of pan-Arab television stations and the spread of satellite access that has transformed and expanded Arabic-language media. In societies in which overt public political and religious debate is stifled, and civil society curtailed, drama becomes a permissible, although beleaguered, mode of alternative political and religious expression. This holds true for those who create series, those who write about them, and the audiences who watch and discuss them. Continual attempts by Arab regimes, religious authorities, and Islamist groups to block some series and commission others, confirm that television drama is far from mere entertainment.[2] Death threats against directors and broadcasters underscore the *musalsal*'s influence.[3]

Nor are television-drama makers mere entertainers. Some of the Arab world's leading intellectuals have become drama creators. Syrian informants note that when political parties were banned in the 1960s, activists became journalists, but constraints on the press and employment opportunities have now rendered them television-show makers. Many see themselves as the vanguard of a modernizing, secularizing project, and believe in the transformative potential of mass culture. Arab leaders and religious authorities also understand well what a *New York Times* reporter refers to as drama series' "extraordinary public reach and their power to challenge accepted ideas or traditions."[4]

Several factors underlie television drama's centrality. In a tradition in which the written word is highly valued and the major forms of expressive culture have, until recently, been literary (specifically poetic), low readership figures and meager book production reflect what some Arab scholars see as a deep crisis of intellectual life.[5] Books are relatively expensive; satellite dishes are increasingly affordable, and television has largely supplanted older popular culture forms. A vibrant culture of cinema and theatergoing flourished until the 1980s, when videocassette recorders expanded viewers' choices beyond Syria's two state-run television channels. Most of the cinema houses that middle-aged Syrians recall fondly have closed; the remaining few show martial arts movies to young male audiences.[6] A once thriving amateur and professional theater tradition survives as a small elite preserve.[7] The spread of satellite access has heightened this trend.

In addition, pan-Arab satellite television stations, particularly those owned by the wealthy governments and individuals of the Gulf Cooperation

CHRISTA SALAMANDRA

Council (GCC), have proliferated. Syrians produce much of the drama material filling these new outlets. Satellite networks air an average of thirty Syrian *musalsals* on consecutive evenings each Ramadan and rebroadcast them throughout the year. Syrian dramas now reach the entire Arab world and numerous diasporic communities beyond. Their creators and audiences contend with a new set of constraints imposed by the conservative Islamic markets of the GCC.

The Politics of Production

The confluence of economic liberalization and Islamic revivalism is reshaping the work of drama production. Throughout most of its history, Syrian television was state owned as well as state controlled, its employees uniformly low in status, socially marginal, and relatively impoverished. A move toward economic liberalization in 1991 opened the door to private production companies, which emerged in the most Syrian of ways: owned by individuals with strong links to the regime.

The rise of satellite broadcasting has swelled the industry. Television drama work now encompasses much of the Syrian intellectual and artistic community. The industry attracts—and, to varying degrees, employs—writers, directors, photographers, visual artists, designers, composers, musicians, and actors from various sectarian, regional, and socioeconomic backgrounds. Cultural producers use television work to support their more "serious" artistic endeavors; hairdressers, tailors, and technicians use it to supplement poorly paid trade labor.

For television creators, the drama outpouring entails the steep cost of economic liberalization, a process rife with bittersweet consequences. The flow of capital is vertiginous and uneven: the rise of a star system has produced increasing economic fragmentation, making a few wealthy and famous and leaving many more struggling. A transnational industry of fan literature, in print and on the internet, bestows social legitimacy, even prestige, on a lucky few.[8] The rest endure the insecurities of a flexible labor market and an unstable geopolity.

Syrian television drama is increasingly transnational but must operate within the confines of a state whose attitude toward the medium remains ambivalent. Sometimes the regime embraces television as an emblem of Syrian national culture or a safety valve for oppositional voices. At others it tightens the reins on television's potential subversion. Most frequently, television drama is a low priority on the state's agenda. While government censorship persists, public sector involvement in other aspects of production shrinks. Most television-show makers must compete for funding from, and thus please, an exacting set of censors in the conservative GCC states. Gulf stations fund most series and receive exclusive rights for a Ramadan broadcast in return. On occasion, private producers, often from the GCC, will fund series and subsequently market them to stations. Another significant development is the emergence of the star/executive producer, the actor with enough name recognition and industry clout to attract large-scale funding from sources in Saudi Arabia or Dubai, someone who also, insiders suggest, pockets much of the budget. Tales of price undercutting and other cutthroat tactics abound. Syrian producers argue that the lack of state regulation exposes them to the caprice of Gulf business practice. While Egypt's foreign ministry has taken up the role of distributor, marketing packages of series to Gulf channels, the Syrian state has left its television-drama makers to fend for themselves in a competitive market for coveted Ramadan first-run airings.

Despite the state's laissez-faire approach to distribution, Syrian drama sells, finds vast audiences, and is taken seriously enough to provoke social, political, and diplomatic tensions at local, national, and international levels. Yet, given the torrent of drama in the satellite era, censors and regimes need worry less; as individual series join a flow, audiences fragment and channel surfing prevails. Increased production and expanded access have obliterated the annual media sensations that once united the Syrian nation in the act of viewing and responding, and created space for subnational identity expression.[9] The mediascape now encompasses the entire Arab world, but many drama makers argue that as the industry has grown, and its products have been commodified, drama's progressive potential has been diffused. Syrian television creators are aware of—indeed, perhaps exaggerate—the power of their medium to transform Syrian society. They feel that GCC domination of the market has usurped this important role. It is difficult to gauge how pan-Arab audiences themselves view GCC influence on fictional television. Most of the major GCC stations operate through state subsidies or private patronage; few rely on advertising revenues. In addition, the *musalsal's* structure—thirty episodes airing on consecutive evenings—would render ratings obsolete as soon as they appear.[10] In the absence of viewership research, it is GCC station managers, often Arab expatriates, who decide what is aired. The leading Saudi and Emirati entertainment channels represent the socially liberal end of the Gulf's ideological spectrum, and their owners often find themselves at odds with state and nonstate conservative forces in their own countries.[11] Yet

CHRISTA SALAMANDRA

Syrian industry figures argue that the potential for promoting progressive political or social agendas has decreased with satellite dominance. Syrian drama creators, like other Arab secular elites, elide the conservative Islam of the Gulf ruling elites, and the political Islam of movements such as the Muslim Brotherhood, as forces against art and progress. They argue that economic liberalization without democratization leaves them vulnerable to both Syrian censors and Gulf buyers.

Such dissatisfactions reveal a nostalgia for the Ba'thist socialist project and the accompanying Syrian state support; they also point to an underlying faith in the benefits of a strong state, a belief that deregulation leads to disaster, and a fear that the form this disaster will take is political Islam. Here representatives of the Syrian television industry employ a mode of expression akin to what Michael Herzfeld refers to as "structural nostalgia." In Herzfeld's formulation, both state and nonstate actors refer to an edenic age of harmonious social relations, a time before social disintegration and moral decay mandated state intervention. This imagining legitimizes accommodation with the state as a necessary evil.[12] Syrian drama makers invoke what might be called a structural nostalgia in reverse, harkening back to a more recent era of state support for "art," cushioning cultural producers from the vicissitudes of market forces, and what they see as a growing Islamization of public culture.

The Growth of an Islamic Public Sphere

In much of the Arab world, notions of cultural authenticity are increasingly conflated with Islam. In contemporary Arab intellectual discourses, authenticity, *asala,* is associated with religion and with revivalist Islam in particular, where it refers to fundamentalism in the literal sense, to a return to a pure Islam of scripture, of Qur'an and *hadith,* and the era of the Prophet Muhammad.[13] The conflation of authenticity with religion is a hallmark of local modernity, and marks a shift in twentieth-century Islamic thought, from the jurisprudential to the cultural and symbolic. The era of the Prophet Muhammad and early Islamic history form an authentic golden age. Both subsequent Islamic historical experience and traditions and non-Islamic cultures are rejected by some contemporary Islamists, who are concerned less with whether acts or ideas are legal or illegal—as was the case for earlier Muslim jurists—but rather whether they are sacred or profane. Much revivalist Islam adopts a method of authentication, *ta'sil,* reflecting the belief that the Qur'an contains a comprehensive guide to proper conduct for individuals, organizations, and governments.[14]

Constructs of Islamic authenticity have become the dominant mode of anti-colonial, anti-imperial critique. The "clash of civilizations" discourse prevails,[15] and Arab intellectuals—including television drama creators—face pressure to defend their secular viewpoints against charges of Westernization. This trend marks a significant departure for leftist and liberal thinkers, many of whom once saw Islam as irrelevant to their notions of modernity.[16] Just as Islamists reconfigure Islam in nationalist terms,[17] secularists inflect secularism with Islam. Drama series compete for audiences amid a transnational satellite "flow," to adopt Raymond Williams' term for the stream of television broadcasting, that includes specialized religious channels and Islamic televangelists.[18]

In addition to promoting religious programming, both state and nonstate forces seek to cleanse the satellite airways of imagery deemed non-Islamic. For example, the leader of Saudi Arabia's Supreme Judicial Council recently suggested that satellite television network owners who ignore warnings to remove "immodest" programs from the airways during Ramadan could face execution.[19] Drama makers self-censor treatments that might be considered Islamically inappropriate, and heed religiosity, but their versions of religion and Muslim polity and society often clash with the puritanism of Saudi Arabia's Salafi Islam and the conservative nature of Islamic revivalism.

Islamizing Strategies

Marwan Kraidy (in this volume) describes a shift in Saudi Islamist discourse about television, from a rhetoric of censorship to one of critical engagement. Syrian drama creators have mirrored this trajectory. After years of avoiding religious reference, they now adopt a range of strategies to reconcile calls for Islamic authenticity and modesty with their own, largely secular, proclivities.[20] Some have chosen to enter the debate in religious terms, explicitly distinguishing "true" Islam from fanaticism. For instance, eminent director Najdat Ismail Anzour broaches the timely topic of religiously inspired suicide bombings with *The Beautiful Maidens (al-Hur al-'Ayn)* of 2005 and *Renegades (al-Mariqun)* of 2006. Direct treatment of current events marks a departure for Anzour, who created the popular "fantasy" (*fantaziya*) genre, fantastical adventure stories "with no time or place" (*la makan wa la zaman*), in the late 1990s. He cites the extremists' tarring of Islam as a prime motivation for this thematic shift:

> I see that we are in need of clarification on this matter. Is it really rising from within the society, or is somebody inventing it? We see

CHRISTA SALAMANDRA

that there are many reasons for it, and without going into political details, we can say that the reasons are the struggle, the cold war between America and the former Soviet Union, and how they [the Americans] were able to attack [the Soviets] by supporting the groups in Afghanistan. One way or another, they invented the character called Bin Laden. Maybe they now have changed their way of thinking towards the region, and we are suddenly faced with a phenomenon called terrorism. And Islam is implicated, considered a religion of terrorism. We have tried, as far as we were able—we're not religious or committed, we're secularists. But at the same time, we see that this is affecting our society. Drama is very useful in this, because it clarifies things. Drama does not solve problems, but it can sheds light on matters like this phenomenon, and can begin to get into details—like where did this phenomenon come from, what are the reasons behind it, what is its history—not in a didactic way, but in a dramatic way, one that is pleasing (*muhabbab*), close to the people.[21]

Much of the hype surrounding *The Beautiful Maidens,* in the Arab and Western media and in conversations among television creators and critics, revolved around its terrorism subplot. While its condemnation of militant Islam echoes that of the Saudi state, the series also levies a powerful critique of Saudi society and its treatment of foreign Arabs, particularly women. Anzour reveals a claustrophobic world of highly educated, upper-middle-class women who have left university study and successful careers in Jordan, Egypt, Syria, Lebanon, and Morocco to accompany their husbands to the Saudi kingdom, where restrictions on women in public life exceed those of any other Arab or Muslim majority nation. Most scenes take place in the luxurious yet sterile apartment complex to which the wives are largely confined. Pampered but bored, deprived of meaningful work and intellectual stimulation, torn from family support networks, they pester their husbands and betray one another. The hothouse environment renders wives vulnerable to their husbands' physical and emotional abuse. *The Beautiful Maidens* depicts terrorists perverting Islam, but also censures Saudi Arabia's religious custodianship.

A series of car bombings forms a menacing backdrop to ongoing warfare in and among the cloistered families of *The Beautiful Maidens.* Infighting extends to the workplace, where sociopaths like the Syrian engineer Samer find a niche in which to mistreat coworkers and conduct shady business deals. One thread follows an antiterrorism poster campaign commissioned by Samer's company, in which Lebanese artist Jamal educates his employers in the semiotics of shape and color, signifying both Arab creative potential and the Arab world's inability to nurture its talent. In order to work, Jamal, like his neighbors and colleagues, must endure *ghurba,* a stifling exile. His wife 'Abir paints from their apartment and dreams of the world beyond.

The Saudis' polished professionalism in addressing the bombing of the housing complex tempers this critique. A suspect is rapidly arrested, and humanely treated. An investigator insists on time-consuming, rapport-building interrogation methods, despite pressure from his superiors, and treats his family with affection and respect. His inquiry uncovers links to the Afghan mujahidin and drug running, thus implicating United States foreign policy and undermining the militants' claim to moral authority.

Islamic references are infrequent and didactic. A few characters are shown praying, and all fast during Ramadan. An Egyptian professor's humanism provokes accusations of secularism and blasphemy but also attracts admirers and acolytes. Pondering the causes of terrorism over tea with a neighbor, the professor cites misunderstanding of Islam along with unemployment, poverty, and despair. Direct discussion of religion is largely confined to the minor subplot of Abdul-Rahim's religious radicalization. Fatherless and unemployed, the twenty-something Saudi attends lessons with the gentle and aptly named Sheikh Abdul-Latif,[22] who emphasizes compassion, tolerance, and the common good, and denounces contemporary militants' understanding of jihad, a message that proves no balm for Abdul-Rahim's frustrations. A shadowy figure overhears the young man lamenting the plight of Palestinians, lures him from mosque to cave and then to a training camp. In the final episode, we see the young recruit driving an explosive-laden car through midday traffic in a Saudi city. Remembering the kind sheikh's words, he changes his mind and detonates the bomb in the desert. Through voiceover and text, the audience learns that Abdul-Rahim "returned to his society as a citizen, found work in a corporation, and attends lessons with Sheikh Abdul-Latif, in search of knowledge and the true path of Islam."

Terrorism features in other drama series. In many of these treatments, would-be bombers are thwarted, or, like *The Beautiful Maiden*'s Abdul-Rahim, have a change of heart before carrying out their deeds and adopt a more liberal interpretation of Islam in the end. These depictions are subject to censorship from both states—Syria and GCC—and stations. The forms of religiosity advocated in such series appear to be in keeping with both Syrian and GCC state ideology; given the range of viewpoints at play in the field of cultural politics, however, these programs may easily run afoul of powerful forces. Drama creators are neither entirely controlled nor completely free. They try to exploit, and their critics seek to curtail, or co-opt, this limited autonomy. During the key broadcast season of Ramadan in particular, creators and broadcasters push the limits; state censors and Islamist groups attempt, with varying degrees of success, to rein them in. Fearing this margin of freedom, the Arab League—an association of largely authoritarian Arab states—recently produced a charter calling upon media makers to show "respect for the dignity and national sovereignty of states and their people, and refraining [sic] from insulting their leaders or national and religious symbols."[23]

Critical depictions of politics, society, and religiosity surface through layers of creative interference. In addition to terrorism, less militant forms of Islamic revivalism are critiqued, and religious scholarship is used to censure extremist practice. The growing women's piety movement in urban Syria features in director Hatim Ali's 2005 series, Unable to Cry ('Asiy al-Dam'a). The series refers to, but does not name, the Qubaisiyat, a network of home-based women's prayer groups. Here, secular critique of Islam is itself Islamized. The story, written by Ali's wife Dal'a Mamduh al-Rahbi, revolves around an up-and-coming lawyer who files charges against a man who harasses her in the street. Throughout the series, she draws on a wealth of textual knowledge to argue that abuse of women conflicts with correct interpretations of Islamic precepts. Ali himself plays her friend and would-be suitor, Samir, who cites both classical Islam—the acts and deeds of the Prophet Muhammad—and the early twentieth-century friendship between Christian writer May Ziadeh and Sheikh of Al-Azhar Mustafa 'Abd al-Raziq, to argue for a more progressive religiosity than that of his mother, leader of a piety group. The pious young judge advocates women's emancipation and debates the sharia's gender laws with his mother. Samir agonizes when forced to render decisions on custody cases that contradict his own belief—that Islamic law should evolve with changing circumstances—and sympathies, which lie with divorced mothers who lose their children upon remarriage. In the final episode, Samir resigns from the bench, unable to reconcile his own conception of a fluid Islam with the rigidity of Syria's personal status law. When a former colleague visits his newly opened clock repair shop and asks if he still enjoys fixing clocks, Samir ponders the metaphor:

> Sometime I watch people passing by, and I'm filled with despair. It's like our clock has stopped at the beginning of the last century—the same questions, and the same problems. Look around

you, listen to a news broadcast, and judge for yourself. The modernization and reform projects, the search for identity, and I don't know what else, they all failed. Look at where we were, and where we are now: the ignorance, illiteracy, fanaticism, close mindedness [*inghilaq*], backwardness, and *takfir.*

Like *Unable to Cry's* hero Samir, drama creators operate in the space between the publics they seek to reach and the state and nonstate forces that try to silence or use them. Drama makers represent the state and speak through its institutions. Their products are consumed in an increasingly Islamized public sphere. Yet many feel alienated from and disapprove of both secular Arab regimes and political Islam. The potential for co-optation, and the possibility of resistance, form a subject of debate among industry figures and audiences alike.

Anzour and Ali criticize Islamism in Islamic terms. Other drama creators opt to aestheticize Islam as costume history, or folklorize it as antiquated tradition. Television series serve as an important source of Islamic history for many Arabs. Big-budget historical epics, set in the golden ages of Islamic empires, combine elaborate period sets, luxurious costumes, and sweeping battle scenes with themes of good and evil, Muslim community against foreign enemy. Yet by invoking al-Andalus (Islamic Spain), as Ali has in a trilogy of epics, dramas recreate a cherished instance of Muslim tolerance. This use of history allows drama to reconfigure a cosmopolitan disposition in Islamic terms. Anzour adopts a similar strategy in *Ceiling of the World* (*Saqf al-'Alam*) of 2007, contrasting the recent Danish cartoon controversy with a tale of tenth-century Muslim tolerance.

Series set in the more recent past take a folkloric turn, celebrating the customs and traditions of the *hara,* the old city quarter. Director Bassam al-Malla employs this strategy to great success in *The Quarter Gate,* (*Bab al-Hara*), parts 1–5 of 2006–2010. Al-Malla has been dramatizing Old Damascus since his 1993 *Damascene Days* (*Ayyam Shamiyya*), yet his more recent treatments feature lingering prayer scenes, depictions of pilgrimage, and exemplary sheikhs.[24] Audiences noted the series' religiosity. In an article posted on *islamonline,* Nabil Shabib, writing from Germany, argues that *The Neighborhood Gate's* creators "were bound by neither a religious nor a secular position, but depicted the contradictions of both viewpoints at the same time."[25] Prominent Syrian cleric Salah al-Kuftaru "honored" the series and its creators for "returning us to morality, nobility, tradition and authenticity."[26] Kuftaru shared other critics' displeasure with *Bab al-Hara's* passive, voiceless women characters, but also argued that the series did a "great service to Islam" by "confronting the aggressive Hollywood globalization that is commanding the attention of our young men and women."[27] Yet by associating Islamic references with a bygone era, al-Malla's work betrays a secularist agenda; making the *hajj* becomes, like wearing a fez or riding a donkey, an antiquated practice.

Nostalgic historical projects, and those channeling contemporary Islamist sentiments into state-sanctioned forms, attract large-scale funding from private and public GCC—primarily Saudi and United Arab Emirate—sources. Contemporary social drama with little Islamic reference—a time-honored, much-loved *musalsal* genre—is increasingly difficult to finance, as Syrian state involvement in production shrinks and regional market forces prevail. These works that focus on "our problems," as Syrian viewers say, appear to reflect Ba'thist ideology; they also subvert it by highlighting the shortfalls of state practice. Producers continue to fund such series, often on the strength of a few successful directors and writers. Works co-authored by Najib Nusair and Hassan Sami Yusuf form an important exception to the Islamizing trend. Journalist Nusair and novelist Yusuf are the highest-paid screenwriters in Syria. Sought by producers and directors, they command loyal followings and critical respect. After a decade of screenwriting, the pair has garnered a reputation for artistic "depth" (*'umq*), yet their depictions of quotidian struggles in poor urban areas now contrast ever more sharply with the heroic and the folkloric offerings crowding the Ramadan airways. Their 2006 series *Waiting (al-Intizar)* provides a case in point. Directed by Laith Hajjo, best known for his biting satirical comedy sketch series *Spotlight (Buq'at Daw')*,[28] *Waiting* revolves around a Robin Hood figure and a low-level journalist. Both are sons of the impoverished neighborhood in which most of the action takes place. The series begins with a pulsating set of establishing images that take viewers from the heart of middle-class downtown Damascus through increasingly downscale areas and finally to the dilapidated suburb of Dweila'a. Here 'Abbud, a foundling whose house the camera never visits, steals clothing from boutiques in the city's wealthy districts and distributes it among his neighbors in the dead of night. Journalist Wa'il waxes romantic about the neighborhood's goodness and humanity; his wife rails against its dirt and danger, a position the series producers share and underscore in its dramatic turning point. While playing soccer in the neighborhood's only available clearing—a rubble-strewn lot at the edge of a busy highway—the couple's youngest son is struck by a minivan and blinded. The series' central concept is a myth of departure: most characters are waiting to move from a neighborhood, and a state of being, they perceive as a mere way station to a better life; most, it is implied, will never leave. This frustrating limbo symbolizes what *Waiting*'s creators see as the Arab condition.

Waiting failed to win a coveted Ramadan time slot on any of the GCC stations, although it appeared on Syria's satellite station, where it garnered an enthusiastic local following. *Waiting*'s competition included MBC's celebratory biopic of Khalid bin al-Walid, a hero of the Islamic conquests. Here the broadcast flow undermines authorial intent. The juxtaposition of *Waiting*'s quietly desperate present with the splendor of Islamic empire appears to buttress the Islamist cause. Contemporary social dramas do not paint pretty pictures. Seen collectively, Syrian drama contrasts a degraded present with a magnificent past.

Some television-drama makers reject the subtle Islamization of folkloric Old Damascus and golden-age epics. Many industry "have-nots," those who either refuse to join or were left out of the most lucrative projects, argue that these series pander to two dreaded, seemingly opposed enemies: the Syrian regime and political Islam. They accuse big-budget epic producers of selling out to what screenwriters Mazen Bilal and Najib Nusair call "prevailing values in the societies of the oil states."[29] Claims of compromise become part of the competitive fray among cultural producers, reflecting a mode of sociability common among elite groups in Syria, to which I have referred elsewhere as a "poetics of accusation."[30] Themselves largely secular Muslims, Syrian cultural producers argue that historical dramas bolster these two seemingly opposed forces, both united by non-urban orientations. A director argues:

> These works reviving the glories of the past amount to indirect support for the Islamists. The project is to make money, but the results play into the hands of the Islamists: look to the past, look to our own values, which should be revived. Their major crime is that they glorify the past, falsify the present, and ignore the future. This trend goes along with the Arab regimes. Tribal relations and values are promoted. Islam provides a framework for this: "obey those who are leading you." It promotes regressive social values. This is all very much blessed by the people in charge, who want everything to remain as it is. This is why we see that there is no effort to deal with the actual lives of people. This is society as expressed by the ruling system, not society as it really is.[31]

CHRISTA SALAMANDRA

Conclusion

Television drama production provides a valuable point of access into the complexities and contradictions of Arab and Muslim modernities. The waning of socialism, the rise of Islamism, and the unfulfilled promise of democracy produce a sense of ambivalence and uncertainty that media professionals share with the wider Arab and Muslim worlds. The tensions that these forces engender emerge in the discourses of industry figures, in the works they produce, in the media debates surrounding them, and in their reception by a global Arab audience.

Drama can go where politics—narrowly defined—cannot. Unlike the heated, often sensational and polarizing discussion programs on news networks like al-Jazeera, television series create a space for creative critique of religious conflict. Drama represents both a liberal Islamic impulse and an enduring tradition of Arab secularism emerging through and despite the GCC dominion of the satellite airways. Market conditions prove both constraining and generative, as drama makers take up Islam-inflected themes that they might otherwise avoid and imbue them with progressive and secularist messages. Their enormous following indicates that millions of Arabs value such alternative visions.

NOTES

This chapter is a revised and expanded version of an article originally published as "Creative Compromise: Syrian Television Makers between Secularism and Islamism," in *Contemporary Islam* 2/3 (2008), 177–89.

1. *Takfir* is the practice of denouncing fellow Muslims as heretics and threatening them with execution.

2. Ambah, "A Subversive Soap Roils Saudi Arabia"; Worth, "Arab TV Tests Societies' Limits," A6; Aji, "Syrian Director Faces Death Threats"; Slackman, "Damascus Journal"; and Abu-Nasr, "Anti-Terrorism TV Show Assailed by Some Arabs."

3. Reuters, "World Briefing"; Hammond, "Unholy Row as Saudi Clerics Slam Ramadan TV"; and Aji, "Syrian Director Faces Death Threats."

4. Worth, "Arab TV Tests Societies' Limits."

5. United Nations Development Programme, *The Arab Human Development Report 2003.*

6. On Mandate era cinemagoing, see Thompson, "Politics by Other Screens"; and Thompson, *Colonial Citizens.* On the demise of cinema houses in the 1980s, see Ghanam,"Tigers on the Ninth Day," 67–77.

7. On twentieth-century theater, see Wannous and Mohammed, "Syria," 234–49.

8. Weyman, "Empowering Youth or Reshaping Compliance?"

9. Salamandra, "Creative Compromise," 177–89; Salamandra, *A New Old Damascus;* Salamandra, "Television and the Ethnographic Endeavor"; and Salamandra, "Moustache Hairs Lost," 227–46.

10. Author's communication with Rami Omran, Syrian advertising executive, January 13, 2007.

11. On the politics of pan-Arab satellite broadcasting, see Kraidy, *Reality Television and Arab Politics.*

12. Herzfeld, *Cultural Intimacy,* 1st ed., 109–38.

13. Kubba, "Towards an Objective, Relative and Rational Islamic Discourse," 132.

14. Al-Sayyid, "Islamic Movements and Authenticity," 109–10.

15. Huntington, *The Clash of Civilizations and the Remaking of the World Order.*

16. This is particularly true of Syrian intellectuals.

17. Asad, *Formations of the Secular.*

18. Williams, *Television and Cultural Form.*

19. Reuters, "World Briefing."

20. Salamandra, "Creative Compromise." For a discussion of Islamism in Egyptian media, see Abu-Lughod, *Local Contexts of Islamism in Popular Media.*

21. Interview with the author, December 27, 2006.

22. Literally, "worshiper of the Kind," one of the ninety-nine names of God.

23. League of Arab States, "Arab League Satellite Broadcasting Charter."

24. For a discussion of *Damascene Days,* see Salamandra, "Moustache Hairs Lost"; and Salamandra, *A New Old Damascus.*

25. Shabib, "The Neighborhood Gate."

26. Nayyuf, "Da'iya bariz intiqada tariqat taswir al-nisa'" [Prominent Authority Criticizes the Depiction of Women: The Religious Trend in Syria Honors the Series *Bab al-Hara*].

27. Ibid.

28. For more on *Spotlight,* see Dick, "Syria under the Spotlight."

29. Bilal and Nusair, *Syrian Historical Drama.*

30. Salamandra, *A New Old Damascus,* 147.

31. Conversation with Syrian filmmaker Nabil Maleh, Damascus.

CHAPTER 13

Saudi-Islamist Rhetorics about Visual Culture

MARWAN KRAIDY

In *The Transparent Society,* the Italian philosopher Gianni Vattimo writes that in late modernity "reality . . . cannot be understood as the objectives given lying beneath, or beyond, the images we receive of it from our media," concluding that "reality is rather the result of the intersection . . . of a multiplicity of images, interpretations and reconstructions circulated by the media in competition with one another and without any 'central' coordination."[1] Vattimo's vision of social reality as a constellation of colliding and intersecting images is relevant to contemporary Arab societies that, since the early 1990s, have been bombarded by a plethora of images emanating from a global array of sources and beamed by a growing satellite television industry that by late 2009 numbered approximately five hundred Arabic-language channels.[2] Privately owned, eclectically themed, and mostly unregulated, the pan-Arab satellite television scene also echoes Vattimo's claim of the absence of central coordination of the myriad processes of reality construction. A visual and visible proof of the declining role of the state in controlling the production and flow of images, the anarchy of the pan-Arab airwaves has led to wide-ranging debates about the impact of visual media on Arab societies, often centering on the notion of authenticity.

Nowhere in the Arab world have anxieties about social and cultural change been as intensely discussed as in Saudi Arabia, where the Salafi doctrine of Wahhabiyya sits at the heart of the Saudi system as a sacrosanct vision of authenticity grounded in cultural and religious purity and gender separation. The advent of "reality television" in the mid-2000s has activated these debates in the kingdom. Notably, *Star Academy,* a popular Arabic-language reality show broadcast by the Lebanese Broadcasting Corporation (LBC) via satellite from Lebanon since December 2003, achieved record Saudi ratings and provoked an intense controversy in Saudi Arabia,[3] emptying city streets and animating mosque sermons, opinion pages, and talk shows. Elsewhere I have mapped the process by which the show became the locus of a battle between Saudi radicals, conservatives, and liberals.[4] Here I trace overlapping Saudi-Islamist discourses about television, including various rhetorics of censorship and critical engagement, drawing on a variety of primary texts, most centrally a widely circulated sermon titled "Satan Academy" by Shaykh Muhammad Saleh al-Munajjid. Heeding Mieke Bal's warning against artificially separating visual culture from its broader societal context,[5] I focus on the ways in which public controversies about a visual culture genre like reality television have crystallized new episodes of longstanding debates.

Censoring Visual Media, Preserving Authentic Culture

Saudi national identity is deeply imbued with Wahhabiyya's focus on purifying Saudi Islam of "foreign" influence.[6] Anxieties about the social impact of technology, with its ability to move ideas and images across national boundaries, are common in Saudi history, regularly causing contention since "modernization" was declared a national objective in the 1930s.[7] The introduction of visual media—photography, television, and film—was fiercely resisted. The royal family of Saud, whose religious legitimacy rests on the backing of the al-Shaykh family of clerics, has pushed an aggressive program of modernization since the 1950s. So in the early 1960s, King Ibn Sa'ud

> summoned his detractors and convened the ulema . . . and put forth questions: Painting and sculpture are idolatry, but is light good or bad? The judges pondered and replied that light is good; Allah put the sun in the heavens to light man's path. Then asked the King, is a shadow good or bad? There was nothing in the Qur'an about this, but the judges deduced and ruled that shadows are good, because they are inherent in light, and even a holy man casts a shadow. Very well then, said the King, photography is good because it is nothing but a combination of light and shade, depicting Allah's creatures but leaving them unchanged.[8]

The king introduced television in 1960, to modernize the country and to retaliate against Nasser's hostile media campaign against the al-Sa'ud. Clerics dropped objections to television when they gained a media policy-making role, tightening censorship to prohibit "scenes which arouse sexual excitement," "women who appear indecently dressed, in dance scenes, or in scenes which show overt acts of love," "women who appear in athletic games or sports," "alcoholic drinks or anything connected with drinking," "derogatory references to any of the 'Heavenly Religions,'" "treatment of other countries with praise, satire, or contempt," "references to Zionism," "material meant to expose the monarchy," "all immoral scenes," "references to betting or gambling," and "excessive violence."[9]

Media regulations focus on women, alongside political and religious issues, because the separation of men and women lies at the heart of social order in Saudi Arabia. In the Wahhabi worldview, the pious woman is the bearer of authentic Islamic principles and thus is central to Saudi identity. Saudi social space is therefore compartmentalized in order to prevent *ikhtilat* (illicit mixing between men and women), and a sharp boundary between private and public space governs male–female interactions.[10] Imported films shown on television are crudely censored, and until recently movie theaters were prohibited (although the comedy *Menahi* demonstrated that Saudi-produced movies could be shown on Saudi soil, albeit for male-only audiences).[11] By focusing on protecting the ideal Islamic woman as bearer of the nation's identity, television censorship reflects the importance of gender segregation as a public display of Islamic piety. Television is thus crucial to the house of al-Sa'ud, which uses it to exalt the royal family's piety by broadcasting religious rituals like the Hajj prayers in Mecca or ceremonies of royal power transfer. "The repetitiveness and regularity" of these programs, al-Rasheed explains, "confirm Saudi society as obsessively concerned with the ritualistic aspect of Islam . . . [reducing] a world religion to a set of prohibited and permissible actions for the sake of demonstrating the religiosity of power."[12] Television is a potent ritual tool in the hands of the rulers.

Media and Modernity, Reality and Image

The media have historically played a crucial role in Arab experiences with modernity. A recurrent story in Albert Hourani's classic *Arabic Thought in the Liberal Age, 1798–1939* is the importance of newspapers as platforms for nineteenth-century Arab and Muslim reformers advocating creative synthesis with Western modernity.[13] This trend continued into the early twentieth century, when newspapers in Ottoman cities like Aleppo featured intense debates about what it meant to be modern.[14] In his book *Fractured Modernity*, the Moroccan poet Muhammad Bennis considers the Arab press to be the midwife of modernity, spreading the "alphabet of light" to the Arab population.[15] The Saudi literary and social critic 'Abdallah al-Ghaddhami argues that the advent of the newspaper column in Saudi Arabia in the 1950s constituted "a foundation for the constitution of an independent, individual opinion,"[16] an emancipation that, by enabling dissent, is central to modernity.

These struggles are driven by a complicated process of cultural translation in which Arabs and Muslims have to grapple with Western sway over their world. Timothy Mitchell argued that modernity is born out of the distinction between the West and the non-West;[17] each time the distinction is made, the modern risks contamination by the non-modern. As I argue at length elsewhere, the Saudi debate about reality television enabled the elaboration of the reverse: a presumptive modern polluting the non-modern, most acutely in the ways in which reality television subverted Saudi Wahhabiyya's insistence on cultural and religious purity.[18] In this context, the claims of television channels to represent "reality" clash with local understandings of authenticity, whose guardians—in Saudi Arabia, these include both clerics of establishment Wahhabiyya and radical firebrands of the Sahwa Islamiyya—rejected *Star Academy*'s claims to the real by arguing that the program depicted a foreign reality imposed by a genre of visual culture that is unequivocally alien and polluting.

In effect, the polemic over how to adapt Western modernity turns public space into a battlefield of beliefs and values, a process that in Saudi Arabia unfolds between an understanding of authenticity defended by the cleric-political status quo on the one hand and notions of reality advanced by a commercial television industry on the other. The creation of European modernity, wrote Mitchell, is based on "the way in which the modern is staged as representation."[19] Mitchell explains:

> To claim that the modern is always staged as representation is not to argue that modernity is concerned more with image-making than with reality . . . Representation does not refer here simply to the making of images or meanings. It refers to forms of social practice that set up in the social architecture and lived experience of the world what seems an absolute distinction between image (or meaning, or structure) and reality, and thus a distinctive imagination of the real. This dualism of the real . . . has been generalized. . . . In sphere after sphere of social life, the world is rendered up in terms of the dualism of image and reality.[20]

Generating acute conflict over representation, the reality television controversies highlight contrary views of the Arab experience with *al-hadatha*—modernity. What it means to "be modern" in the Arab context has been vigorously contested since the 1850s, but the debate took on a renewed poignancy in the 1990s, with the rise of pan-Arab commercial television. The commotion over reality television exacerbated tensions associated with modernity—the relationship between religion and the state, the development of representative forms of governance, the rise of nationalism, and conflict over gender roles.[21]

In the 1980s and 1990s, Saudi Arabia witnessed fierce public battles between advocates and adversaries of modernity, resuscitating debates that emerged initially in subdued forms during the formative years of modern Saudi Arabia in the mid-1920s and reappeared throughout the twentieth century in disputes over poetry. The new modernity war was more intense, exacerbated by the 1991 Gulf War, and involved a wider circle of participants. The publication of *al-Khati'a wal-Takfir* (Sin and Excommunication) by al-Ghaddhami provoked strong reactions in the country's intellectual circles. The upheaval uncannily foreshadowed the reality television scandal explained in this chapter. The book, al-Ghaddhami writes,

> became a topic to which were attributed all the problems of the nation and all the dangers of the future, till it reached mosques' pulpits, animated Friday sermons, and became material for preachers, missionaries, fatwa makers, cassette-tapes, publications and posters; books were published and *fatwas* were issued, and [Sin and Excommunication] became the talk of councils and . . . Saudi society for five full years.[22]

Attacks began with a widely circulated cassette tape, *al-Hadatha fi Mizan al-Islam* (Modernity in the Scale of Islam), which was later published as a book prefaced by 'Abdulaziz Bin Baz, a prominent arch-conservative cleric who would become Grand Mufti of Saudi Arabia in 1993. From that experience, al-Ghaddhami developed the notion of the "symbolic event" (*al-hadath al-ramzy*), when new ideas threaten the prevailing order by challenging what he calls the "conservative mode" (*al-Nasq al-Muhafizh*) and spawning heated polemics.[23] The battle became unruly to the point that the Minister of Information banned the use of the word "modernity" in the media, though the prohibition was implemented only temporarily.[24]

The battle over Saudi modernity overlapped with post-1991 political activity, in which Sahwi, liberal, and other activists submitted petitions to the king advocating various reforms.[25] These "Memoranda of Advice" urged the royal family to acknowledge diverging opinions, eventually leading the then-regent Abdullah to launch the National Dialogue Forum in June 2003, two years before he became the sixth king of Saudi Arabia in August 2005. Participation in the National Dialogue Forum is restricted to a group of individuals personally selected by the king to discuss issues framed by the royal agenda and under the auspices of the King 'Abdul 'Aziz Center for National Dialogue. In contrast to this highly selective forum, controversies over popular culture can become protracted public contests that draw a large number of clerics, intellectuals, journalists, and even members of the royal family.

To understand the intensity of the debate, it is helpful to recall the consolidation of pan-Arab media ownership in Saudi hands, combined with the fact that the kingdom is the largest national Arab media market, with more than twenty million comparatively wealthy Arabic speakers.[26] Also fueling the polemic is what I call the Saudi–Lebanese connection, which consists of Lebanese professionals occupying key industry ranks in advertising, journalism, and, more visibly, entertainment television production, all bankrolled by Saudi capital.[27] The "conspicuous liberalism" manifest in LBC shows regularly stirs polemics in Saudi Arabia, but competing business interests have prevented Saudi media moguls from dictating conservative programs across the board.[28] These factors polarized Saudi opinion because they subverted Wahhabi notions of social order and individual piety that have long shaped Saudi media policy. At the heart of the dispute were rival rhetorics of what constituted "reality"—that is, authentic, true and pure—and what was merely "image," that is, foreign, make-believe, and contaminated. Visual culture thus becomes a primary site for contentious discourses of authenticity and reality.

Visual Culture from Rejection to Multiple Engagements

The polemic over reality television reflects a spectrum of discourses about visual culture, ranging from a *rhetoric of censorship* to a *rhetoric of critical engagement.* The gamut involves overlapping degrees of rejection and engagement, although the trend is clearly toward a more systematic engagement with the epistemology of television. An early polemic occurred after *al-Ra'is,* the Arabic version of *Big Brother* produced in Bahrain by Saudi-owned, Dubai-based MBC, was shut down after pressures from the Saudi clerical establishment.[29] Ahmad Mansour, the Islamist (Muslim Brotherhood) al-Jazeera talk-show personality, aired two episodes of *Bila Hudud* about reality television in March 2004. In the first episode, he hosted Lebanese advertising personality Ramsay Najjar, who adroitly maneuvered to disconnect reality television from "reality" because that connection was at the heart of Islamist attacks against reality television. In the second episode, Mansour hosted Muhammad al-'Awadhi, of the World Islamic Media Committee affiliated with the Mecca-based League of the Islamic World. Like Najjar, this Wahhabi activist objected to reality television's claim to represent reality. In contrast to Najjar's, al-Awadhi's objection was not semantic, but religious, as reflected in this exchange:

> *Ahmad Mansour:* . . . supporters . . . claim that [reality TV] is an expression of human reality, of feelings, a spontaneous expression devoid of artifice, imitation, acting, and fake emotions that most people have?
>
> *Muhammad al-'Awadhi:* . . . Which reality are they talking about? You chose a certain reality, you create an ambience, you put it under the spotlight, and you tell people this is reality. It is an artificial reality but it is (promoted as) an ideal reality. But what does this reality put under the spotlight? Moments of weakness, instinct, prohibited relations, illegitimate and immoral situations, all that in a society already afflicted (by many problems).[30]

It is tempting to see in Najjar and al-'Awadhi's questioning of the "reality" of reality television a continuation of previous panics about the impact of "foreign" television. In this view, the new genre exacerbates already extant anxieties about television's representational power, in line with the argument by media scholar Justin Lewis that reality television brought to the surface inconsistencies that were long implicit in television viewing.[31] While this applies somewhat to the Arab context, reality television struck raw nerves in Arab countries for other reasons. Al-'Awadhi's words reflect deep anxieties about reality television's potential for subverting the ritual bases of the Saudi clerico-political order.

This skirmish anticipated a larger battle. Anger against *Star Academy* was widespread. An Imam at Mecca's Great Mosque called it a "Weapon of Mass Destruction."[32] Even the relatively liberal newspaper *Al-Riyadh* published guest op-eds with such titles as "Destructive Academy Is Harmful to the Family"[33] and "Star Academy . . . The Other Terrorism," whose author wrote that "modesty and morals vanish when . . . young men and women get together, wearing clothes that provide modesty for very few parts of their bodies . . . [and] reflect confusion about . . . authentic identity and culture."[34]

In the winter of 2004, as *Star Academy* became the talk of the country, Sahwi activists began peddling on city streets, for one riyal, or a quarter of a U.S. dollar, a cassette tape titled *Satan Academy,* which they claimed sold one million copies.[35] The tape featured a thirty-six-minute and forty-one-second sermon by Muhammad Saleh al-Munajjid, a Syrian-born cleric who has a weekly Saturday afternoon show on Qur'an Radio and is active on the internet. The *Satan Academy* sermon presents the most analytical and conceptually systematic critique of reality television from a Wahhabi perspective—*a rhetoric of critical engagement in action.*[36] The intensity of the polemic reflected the popularity of the show with wide swaths of the Saudi public, especially young people. As I have shown, many Saudi columnists, especially women, also exploited *Star Academy* "positively" to make arguments for reforming the Saudi system, especially regarding youth issues and social policy.[37]

The commotion compelled the "Permanent Committee for Scientific [or Academic] Research and the Issuing of Fatwas"—a subcommittee of the Higher Council of 'Ulamas supervised by the Ministry of Religious Affairs—to issue a dedicated *fatwa.* It prohibited watching, discussing, voting in, or participating in *Star Academy,* and exhorted businessmen not to finance this type of program. The committee's main charge was that *Star Academy* violated and subverted Islamic principles because it carried "a number of serious evils" such as:

> *Free mixing of the sexes* . . . the main idea of [*Star Academy* and similar shows] is mixing between the sexes and removing all barriers between them, as well as the wanton display and unveiling on the part of women displaying their charms, which leads to much evil . . . *Blatant promotion of immorality* . . . by making [Muslims] get used to seeing these shameful scenes that provoke desires and by distancing them from good morals and virtue.[38]

Like Saudi censorship rules, the *fatwa* was most concerned with women and their interactions with men.[39] Unlike media regulations, which apply to institutions, however, the *fatwa* called upon believers directly and as individuals to actively oppose *Star Academy:* "It is not sufficient for you to abstain from watching these shows," the 'ulamas stipulated, "[y]ou should also advise and remind those whom you know watch them or take part in them in any way, because that comes under the heading of cooperating in righteousness and piety, and forbidding one another to engage in sin and transgression."[40] One of the most remarkable aspects of the *fatwa* is the visual lexicon it invokes—"display," "unveiling," "scenes"—to warn of the danger of *Star Academy,* confirming visual culture as a central field of contention between guardians of authenticity and popular entertainment programs produced by an increasingly commercial media industry.

Grappling with Modernity

The incomplete shift toward a rhetoric of critical engagement with television can be discerned in al-Munajjid's opinion on the issue. He begins by expressing a strategic perplexity:

Why do these programs become greatly popular? Why do people become preoccupied by them? Why do people gravitate towards these programs and why do these programs attract them? Why do [people] spend God knows how much time following these shows?[41]

At the center of the Saudi–Lebanese connection sits the relationship between LBC and Saudi society. Since LBC went on satellite in 1996, Saudi viewers have boosted its ratings and Saudi investments have fueled its growth.[42] Nonetheless, LBC's screen aesthetic reflects the socially liberal extreme of segments of the Lebanese creative class, characterized by ostensible mimicry of Western consumer lifestyles; slick production values; informality in newscasts and talk-shows; language switching between Arabic, French, and sometimes English; and, most importantly, the ubiquity of alluringly dressed women—LBC's essentially visual signature of *conspicuous liberalism.*

If the Islamic ideal of the pious woman is central to Saudi Arabia's national identity, the consumer ideal of the "Western-looking," uninhibited woman is central to LBC's corporate identity. When I asked LBC general manager Pierre al-Daher to distill his channel's profile, he said, "We are a general entertainment channel without social inhibitions."[43] An unsubtle social liberalism has been manifest since the channel's launch in 1985, with variety shows featuring provocative fashion and behavior and commercial breaks full of suggestive advertisements for lingerie and cosmetics. Commoditized femininity became central to LBC's pan-Arab brand in the satellite era. LBC's commoditization of the female form is central to its ability to create programs mixing high production values, lightheartedness, boldness, and titillation, because these characteristics lure audiences, most importantly the prized Gulf and Saudi viewers. Controversies ensue in Saudi Arabia because the *hyper-visibility* of women's bodies on LBC clashes head-on with Wahhabiyya's compulsive *invisibility* of the female body in public space.[44]

The paradoxical relationship between the Arab world's most socially liberal media institution (LBC) and its most socially conservative clerico-political regime (Saudi Arabia) has been one catalyst of the Saudi debate over authenticity. Images of young Arab and mostly Muslim men and women, alluringly dressed, dancing, hugging, and singing together on stage or in their common house, featured nightly on *Star Academy,* have provoked controversy because the program depicts a lifestyle that breaches the Saudi prohibition on *ikhtilat.* Women not only dress immodestly, but they also touch men physically, and sing and dance; further, they publicly disagree and argue with the men on the show, compete with them, and even sometimes beat them in various competitions. By being, in the words of one Saudi critic, "A Sincere Invitation to *Ikhtilat*,"[45] *Star Academy* offers an alternative social reality, with fluid gender boundaries and imbued with women's agency—albeit contrived and commoditized—inimical to Wahhabi definitions of social order.[46] As discussed earlier, this problematic portrayal is compounded by LBC promotions touting the "real" aspect of the "*reality* television" show, which provoked vehement objections from clerics infuriated by the claim that *Star Academy represents reality.*

Inasmuch as it claims to represent reality, *Star Academy* reflects a blend of multiple realities. It is a highly public, and therefore controversial, cultural hybrid. *Star Academy* confounds the boundaries between the "domestic" and the "foreign," between what is "Arab" or "Islamic" and what is alien. It violates Wahhabi diktats on gender segregation and cultural purity, enforced through ritualistic behavior in prayer, dress, and social relations. A culturally ambiguous category that muddles notions of identity and authenticity, *Star Academy* threatens the core of Wahhabiyya in two specific ways: it reflects a radically pluralistic world, and it compels participants to enact alien social norms.

As the Arabic version of a European television "format," *Star Academy* is a mixture of multiple cultural predilections. The contestants' demeanor reflects the socially liberal extreme of the Lebanese spectrum (although there is something "authentically Lebanese" about *Star Academy*). Several contestants spoke an Arabic peppered with French; they frequently sang French, English, Spanish, even Hindi (Bollywood) songs. English is the show's logistical lingua franca, as the terms "star academy" and "nominee," and even the notion of "star" itself, are quintessentially American. The show's "primes" are carnivalesque spectacles, mixing Lebanese Rahbani musicals, *khaliji* (Arabian Gulf) songs, Broadway musicals, French cancan, Russian circus numbers, and the like. From the point of view of Wahhabiyya, this radical and hybrid eclecticism invokes the *jahiliyya*, the chaotic pre-Islamic era characterized by fragile tribal orders and fluid gender boundaries.

By grafting an Arabic language program on a Western format, *Star Academy* is what the literary theorist Mikhail Bakhtin calls an "intentional" hybrid. Unlike organic hybridity, which is an unintentional product of intercultural contact, intentional hybridity is "*concrete and social,*" resulting from the perception of one cultural system through the language of another culture, the latter being "*taken as the norm.*"[47] Since Western standards set production norms for Arab reality television programs, *Star Academy* depicts not merely a fantasy world that viewers watch, but a social world that viewers recreate through such rituals as nominating and voting for contestants. Because reality television claims to represent reality, *Star Academy* posits a *normative* social world. As a cultural hybrid, the show exposes within the Arab world what the media scholar Jesús Martín-Barbero, writing about Latin America, describes as "the sense of continuities in discontinuity and reconciliations between rhythms of life that are mutually exclusive."[48]

As a widely popular program that is culturally hybrid, *Star Academy* exposes the tension between the official dogma of cultural purity and the effective reality of cultural fusion. *Star Academy* draws Saudi viewers to participate in rituals—watching, voting, and so forth—that enact a syncretistic identity, subverting the notion of cultural purity that is cardinal to Saudi identity. The ensuing polemic exposes Wahhabiyya's fear and rejection of the outside world, all the more so because the show ritually enacts, and therefore upholds, alien norms, values, and behaviors.

Star Academy undermines the prevalent notion of authenticity in a more fundamental way due to formal elements of the reality television genre, whose success largely depends on its ostensible liveness. The claim to represent reality—which activates the modern conundrum between "reality" and "image"—is based on the premise that what viewers watch is spontaneous and unrehearsed. Key moments in reality television occur when participants are caught (by cameras) being their *real selves*—it is precisely when contestants lose sight of the cameras that reality television reaffirms its claims to reality. While from the audience's point of view, this feature represents one of reality television's main attractions, in the Saudi context these moments signal a redefinition of authenticity from obedience to Wahhabi diktats to an individual performance. *Star Academy* not only conjures up a social order inimical to Wahhabiyya, it also features the individual body—which Wahhabiyya sees primarily as an instrument of sin—as the locus of identity.[49]

This personally experienced, individually performed authenticity lies at the heart of reality television's presumptive connection to reality. Clerics fiercely contested *Star Academy*'s reality claims because establishment Wahhabiyya seeks to preserve its monopoly on representing social reality. In contrast, *Star Academy* turns viewers into *witnesses* of a reality created by a television genre that itself claims to represent reality. This was a central theme in al-Munajjid's *Satan Academy* sermon:

> These programs do not consist of acting, lying and pretending;
> rather they are in the realm of reality. These are unrecorded

shows. . . . People desire the natural, the self tends towards the natural more than the acted. So they [television producers] thought: Why don't we then make this immorality [*fujur*][50] toward which we want to attract people, why don't we make it [*Star Academy* is] . . . a real thing practiced realistically . . . not a written script that actors have rehearsed, but a real thing whose events occur in reality. It is also live . . . it is transmitted to people live and people are attracted by fresh things more than they are attracted by old things. No wonder people follow these shows breathlessly.[51]

Witnessing involves searching one's memory to extract the details of that eventful moment when the witness was present in space (there) and time (then), and then rendering the event to those who were not present. Media institutions derive a great deal of their social authority from their role as witnesses. Unlike news or documentary, however, reality television ostensibly relinquishes some of the power-to-witness to its viewers. Al-Munajjid succinctly captured this in *Satan Academy* when he sermonized:

In the past events used to be reported . . . to those who did not see or live them. In contrast today [in reality television shows] events are witnessed and attended [*mashhuda wa mahdura*].[52] The media have shifted from "it happened" to "it is happening." [*min hadatha ila yahduthu*] . . . The public and the viewers intervene to determine things, so it is an interactive process. [In the past, v]iewers did not intervene in films or televisions serials except by watching; but today [reality television] programs entail contributions from viewers who nominate, comment, and send text messages or emails that appear immediately on the television screen.[53]

Viewers experiencing *Star Academy* as a continual flow await the eventful moment—the moment of authenticity—with anticipation. They are, in a sense, witnesses in reverse. Unlike witnessing, which as John Peters reminds us is "retroactive,"[54] the ritualized watching of *Star Academy* is *proactive*. Whereas witnesses are compelled to produce a verisimilar rendering of a past event, reality television viewers are enthralled by the future possibility of the program going "off-script." The former calls for a narrowing of alternatives to come as close as possible to a necessary "truth," the latter proliferates alternatives whose "authenticity" rests on their liveness, hence their contingency. Viewers wait for contestants to forget the cameras and "come out" as their true, authentic selves at the moment when authenticity comes into being (although some contestants become adept actors, with contrived "spontaneous" outbursts). Reality television viewing in this case is a kind of intense, vigilant, intentional—albeit reverse—witnessing.

Reality television's treatment of viewers as witnesses to manufactured situations is controversial because a witness creates a version of an event that is more legitimate than other versions. *Star Academy* viewers therefore are complicit in a social reality that clashes with regnant Saudi definitions of authenticity. Viewing as witnessing entails the ritual diffusion of the power to define social reality. Ritualistic Islam is a dominant preoccupation in Saudi Arabia because Saudis as a community engage in conspicuous worship rituals that are punctiliously regulated and intolerant of variation. *Star Academy* depicts alternative rituals of engagements on a popular television show at a time when Wahhabi clerics, in al-Rasheed's description, have turned "[p]rayer, fasting and pilgrimage . . . into spectacles regularly dramatized on local and satellite television channels."[55] By establishing alluring rituals that rival those described above, reality television poses a threat to Wahhabi governance. As al-Munajjid stated:

> Learning and proselytizing through images is more potent than face-to-face. If someone is told: be corrupted! Be corrupted! Be corrupted! Come to corruption! Come to corruption! Come to corruption! Take this number! Take this number! Take this number! Call! Call! Call! All this will have an effect. But when you see the images with your own eyes and interactivity occurs, the effect on the self is more.[56]

This, according to al-Munajjid, is *tazyeen,* which means "adorning," "decoration," or "ornamentation," but also connotes manipulation, as in "make-believe," "pretense," or "sham." Reality television, according to al-Munajjid, is *"tazyeen lil-munkar li-yabdu bi-a'yan al-nas hasan,"* "adorning evil so that it appears good in people's eyes," with obvious implications for reality TV's image dichotomy of modernity.

Visual Culture as a Field of Contention

Based on the reality television polemic in Saudi Arabia, this chapter has explored visual culture as a field of contention in a modern Muslim national context. Contradictory yet overlapping rhetorics about television and its social impact on Saudi Arabia illustrate the different ways in which a variety of local actors engage, negotiate, and resist genres of visual culture that appear to threaten the prevailing status quo. In this case, *Star Academy* undermined the core principles of Wahhabi governance by suggesting an alternative reality that proved popular with Saudi viewers, threatening such core pillars of Wahhabiyya as the prohibition on *ikhtilat* and the preservation of a Saudi culture uncontaminated by foreign influence. By creating an environment of unbridled gender and cultural mixing, *Star Academy* posed a direct affront to vital building blocks of Saudi authenticity. When viewers are lured into fandom, mobilization, and voting, and, according to critics, away from prayer, fasting, and pilgrimage, visual culture contributes to the articulation of a fluid social reality and thus emerges as a *field of contention.*

By introducing into public debate "images" that clash with a "reality," visual culture becomes an important space in which various elements of modernity, many emanating from a nebulously defined "West," are selectively adapted in modern Muslim contexts. Al-Munajjid's critical engagement with the formal characteristics of reality television—discussing and rejecting its claims to representing reality—suggests an understanding of new kinds of agency. These agencies are enabled by participatory forms of visual culture that are grounded in ritualistic viewer engagement in an environment that stifles participation in public life because the status quo preserves its hegemony precisely through mass-mediated rituals in which the visual plays a central role. Clearly, "critical engagement" does not suggest acceptance of television genres that Islamists find objectionable. Rather, it signals that Islamists are compelled to understand and interpret television in increasingly sophisticated and systematic ways, indicating that Saudi-Islamist rhetorics about visual culture are varied and evolving.

Although iconoclasm—or anti-ocularism—may have played a role in Saudi controversies about reality television, the primary evidence scrutinized in this chapter does not suggest that the fear of images per se was a major issue in the polemics under study. During the reign of King Faisal, the decision to ban movie theaters in Saudi Arabia was made not because of film's visual nature, but because movies are projected in large and dark theaters that might encourage *ikhtilat* among moviegoers. The reason that television was allowed in the Faisal era, despite its visual content, was precisely because it did not pose the same risk of illicit interaction between men and women.[57] Finally, the fact that Arab music videos, brief audiovisual blurbs containing a plethora of provocative images, have not generated controversies in Saudi Arabia as heated as those caused by reality television lends credence to the view that anti-ocularism was at most a minor factor in the Saudi reality television wars.

As a field of contention, Arab visual culture expands the scope of social and political actors who traffic in various definitions of reality, authenticity, and therefore politics. On the one hand, the importance of the battle over *Star Academy* is that it widened the circle of participation and illustrates the important public role that popular culture can take in the absence of public institutions for debate and deliberation.[58] This reflects the increasing importance of popular visual culture; the definition of visual culture is therefore expanded beyond modern institutions like the museum to include symbolic and material artifacts from *contemporary everyday life*. On the other hand, if, as Göle argued, "Islamism, in its pursuit of the establishment of religious boundaries, gives priority to *the visual, corporal,* moral regulation of social relations"[59] (emphasis added), then the contentious politics of Arab reality television help us comprehend the shifting modalities of the moral regulation of social expectations in modern Muslim contexts. Studying visual culture as a field of contention may help us develop a truly global theory of visuality, one "focusing on questions of what is made visible, who sees what, how seeing, knowing and power are interrelated."[60]

NOTES

This chapter is based on my *Reality Television and Arab Politics: Contention in Public Life* (Cambridge: Cambridge University Press, 2009).

1. Vattimo, *The Transparent Society,* 7.

2. Kraidy and Khalil, *Arab Television Industries.*

3. Author's interviews with Jihad Fakhreddine, Director of Research, Pan-Arab Research Center (PARC), June 1, 2004, Dubai, United Arab Emirates; and Shadi Kandil, Director of Research, IPSOS-STAT, June 2, 2004, Dubai, United Arab Emirates.

4. Kraidy, "Reality Television, Gender, Authenticity in Saudi Arabia," 345–66.

5. Bal, "Visual Essentialism and the Object of Visual Culture," 5–32. At the same time, I find Mark Poster's argument that "visual studies . . . is most productively conceived as media studies" ("Visual Studies as Media Studies," 67) to be sweeping, if only because media and communication scholars have difficulty defining what "media studies" is exactly.

6. This includes not only the West but also non-Sunni Saudi Muslims—notably the Shi'a. See al-Rasheed, "The Shi'a of Saudi Arabia," 121–38.

7. See Kraidy, "Governance and Hypermedia in Saudi Arabia." For a broader scope, see al-Ghaddhami, *The Tale of Modernity in the Kingdom of Saudi Arabia.*

8. Eddy, "King Ibn Sa'ud," 258.

9. Boyd, *Broadcasting in the Arab World,* 164.

10. Two cautionary notes are in order here. First, gender separation can be found worldwide, but it is more intense in Saudi Arabia. Second, there were also concerns over privacy that echo those raised in the West, although these were overshadowed by social-religious worries.

11. Saudis flock to neighboring Bahrain to attend movie theaters, an experience captured in "Cinema 500 Km," a Saudi docu-drama about the three-hundred-mile, movie theater–seeking journey from Saudi Arabia to Bahrain. Saudi film production is nascent: the first Saudi-produced movie, *Keif al-Hal* (How Is It Going?), was shot in Dubai and released in non-Saudi Arab locations in 2006. A project of Prince al-Waleed Bin Talal, the film featured Hind Muhammad, the first Saudi film actress, in a leading role. See "Saudis Become Refugees Cinematically." A more recent treatment can be found in Fawwaz, "Saudi Cinema Gambles on the Future."

12. Al-Rasheed, "The Shi'a of Saudi Arabia," 60.

13. Hourani, *Arabic Thought in the Liberal Age*, 95.

14. Watenpaugh, *Being Modern in the Middle East*.

15. Bennis, *Fractured Modernity*, 121.

16. Al-Ghaddhami, *The Tale of Modernity*, 126.

17. T. Mitchell, *Questions of Modernity*, 26.

18. Kraidy, *Reality Television and Arab Politics*, chap. 4.

19. T. Mitchell, *Questions of Modernity*, 16.

20. Ibid., 17.

21. See Cole, *Modernity at the Millenium*.

22. Al-Ghaddhami, *The Tale of Modernity*, 207.

23. Ibid., 100. In addition to "mode," *nasq* can be translated as "system," "order," "disposition," or "alignment."

24. Al-Ghaddhami, *The Tale of Modernity*.

25. See al-Rasheed, "The Shi'a of Saudi Arabia"; Dekmejian, "The Liberal Impulse in Saudi Arabia," 381–99; and Fandy, *Saudi Arabia and the Politics of Dissent*.

26. Saudi holdings include two London-based pan-Arab daily newspapers, *al-Hayat* and *Asharq al-Awsat*, the multichannel MBC group based in Dubai, and several religious radio and television stations, in addition to stakes in various Egyptian and Lebanese channels. See Kraidy and Khalil, "The Middle East," 79–98.

27. With the exception of drama, chiefly an Egyptian and Syrian province. For a detailed explanation of the Saudi–Lebanese connection, see chapter 3 of Kraidy, *Reality Television and Arab Politics*.

28. A diversity of outlooks within the Saudi elite has spawned channels airing various programs, ranging from titillating music videos (Rotana) to puritanical religious sermons (al-Majd). For that perspective, dissimilarity in programs on Saudi-owned channels is not as paradoxical as some have argued; for example, see Mellor, "Bedouinisation or Liberalisation of Culture?" 353–74.

29. The episode is analyzed in detail in chapter 2 of Kraidy, *Reality Television and Arab Politics*.

30. "Mimicking Western Programs and Imposing Them on Arabs," episode 2.

31. J. Lewis, "The Meaning of Real Life," 290.

32. "Star Academy 'Weapon of Mass Destruction.'"

33. Al-Dakhil, "Destructive Academy Is Harmful to the Family."

34. Al-'Enezi, "Star Academy."

35. Abbas, "Satan's Academy." The tape features a speech by Shaykh Muhammad Saleh al-Munajjid, in which he presents a systematic case against *Star Academy* grounded in Wahhabi doctrine.

36. Another cleric recorded a tape titled *SARS Academy*, in reference to the deadly virus of the same name (Severe Acute Respiratory Syndrome), in which he

told the story of a little girl who lost her innocence and decided to become a pop star after watching *Star Academy*, at which moment the sound of an explosion can be heard. Both *Satan Academy* and *SARS Academy* tapes were cleared by the Ministry of Information, indicating official approval.

37. Kraidy, *Reality Television and Arab Politics*, chap. 4.

38. "Fatwa on *Star Academy*."

39. Two verses from the Qur'an focus on women's dress code to preempt the sexual temptation of men: verse 31, Sura 24 (The Light), and verse 59, Sura 33 (The Clans). For more, see Dabbous-Sensenig, "To Veil or Not to Veil," 60–85.

40. "Fatwa on *Star Academy*."

41. Al-Munajjid, *Akademiyat al-Shaytan wal Superstar.*

42. In addition to a news-gathering joint operation with the pan-Arab daily *Al-Hayat*, owned by Saudi prince Salman Bin-'Abdulaziz, governor of Riyadh, LBC's association with al-Waleed bin Talal culminated in July 2008 when al-Waleed raised his stake to 85 percent.

43. Author's interview with Pierre el-Daher, General Manager, Lebanese Broadcasting Corporation, June 30, 2004, Adma, Lebanon.

44. *Star Academy* producers do not show Saudi contestants (all male) dancing or touching female contestants; nor do they show them in the swimming pool introduced in later seasons.

45. Al-Dawyan, "*Star Academy*."

46. I am not using "gender" to mean "women," but rather to connote the constructed reality of both femininity and masculinity and the ways the relationship between them is socially organized. In interviews with *Star Academy* staff I was told that during production every attempt was made not to show male contestants dancing or acting in ways that could be seen as "effeminate" or "gay." Opponents in Saudi Arabia and elsewhere in the Gulf often criticized *Star Academy* for promoting *muyu'a*, which means "unsteadiness," "effeminacy," and "softness," from the verb *ma'a*, which means "to become soft" and "to be indulgent," connoting concerns about masculinity. Clearly, anxieties related to gender concern the instability of *both* femininity and masculinity.

47. Bakhtin, *The Dialogical Imagination*, 359–60.

48. Martín-Barbero, *Communication, Culture and Hegemony*, 188.

49. This is accomplished by exhortations to participate, call, nominate, etc., as al-Munajjid argued in the *Satan Academy* sermon: "Learning and preaching with images is more potent than face-to-face. If you are told ' . . . be corrupted, be corrupted, be corrupted; take this [phone] number, take this number, take this number; call, call, call;' you will be influenced somewhat; but when you see the scenes yourself and interactivity occurs, its impact on the self is more potent" (*Akademiyat al-Shaytan wal Superstar.*).

50. "*Fujur*" can also be translated as debauchery, iniquity, depravation, fornication, etc.

51. Al-Munajjid, *Akademiyat al-Shaytan wal Superstar.*

52. "*Mahdura*" comes from the verb "*hadara*," which means "attended" or "watched," connoting presence. "*Hadar*" refers to sedentary or settled peoples (as opposed to nomads); "*hadaara*" means "civilization."

53. Al-Munajjid, *Akademiyat al-Shaytan wal Superstar.*

54. Peters, "Witnessing," 722.

55. Al-Rasheed, "The Shi'a of Saudi Arabia," 59.

56. Al-Munajjid, *Akademiyat al-Shaytan wal Superstar.*

57. Kraidy, *Reality Television and Arab Politics,* chap. 3.

58. In Wedeen, *Peripheral Visions,* the author develops a concurrent view, arguing that the absence of state institutions can actually foster popular democratic practices.

59. Göle, "Snapshots of Islamic Modernities," 115.

60. Hooper-Greenhill, *Museums and the Interpretation of Visual Culture,* 14, quoted in Bal, "Visual Essentialism," 19.

Abbas, Faisal. "Satan's Academy." *Asharq al-Awsat,* June 8, 2005. [Arabic].

Abd al-Badi', Ahmad Lutfy. "Al-Fann." *Al-Ikhwan Al-Muslimun,* November 20, 1943, 6.

Abduh, Muhammad. *Al-A'mal al-kamila lil-Imam Muhammad 'Abduh.* Collected and edited by Muhammad 'Imara. Beirut: Al-Mu'assasa al-arabiya lil-dirasat wal-nashr, 1972.

Abisaab, Rula Jurdi. *Converting Persia: Religion and Power in the Safavid Empire.* London: I. B. Tauris, 2004.

Abrahamian, Ervand. *Iran between Two Revolutions.* Princeton, N.J.: Princeton University Press, 1982.

Abu-Lughod, Lila. *Dramas of Nationhood: The Politics of Television in Egypt.* Chicago: University of Chicago Press, 2004.

———. "Finding a Place for Islam." *Public Culture* 5 (1993): 493–513.

———. *Local Contexts of Islamism in Popular Media.* Amsterdam: Amsterdam University Press/ISIM Papers, 2006.

———. "Movie Stars and Islamic Moralism in Egypt." *Social Text* 42 (Spring 1995): 53–67.

———. "Writing against Culture." In *Recapturing Anthropology,* edited by Richard D. Fox, 137–62. Santa Fe: School of American Research, 1991.

Abu-Nasr, Donna. "Anti-Terrorism TV Show Assailed by Some Arabs." *Seattle Times,* October 11, 2005. http://seattletimes.com/html/nationworld/ 2002553111_syria11.html.

Açıkel, Fethi. "Kutsal Mazlumluğun Psikopatolojisi." *Toplum ve Bilim* 70 (1996): 153–99.

Afsaruddin, Asma. *The First Muslims: History and Memory.* Oxford: Oneworld, 2008.

Aghaie, Kamran Scot. *The Martyrs of Karbala: Shi'i Symbols and Rituals in Modern Iran.* Seattle: University of Washington Press, 2004.

Ahmad, Feroz. *The Young Turks: The Committee of Union and Progress in Turkish Politics, 1908-1914.* Oxford: Oxford University Press, 1969.

Aji, Albert. "Syrian Director Faces Death Threats." *Washington Post,* September 26, 2006. http://www.washingtonpost.com/wpdyn/content/article/2006/09/ 26/AR006092600643.html.

Akgül, M., et al. *İlköğretim Din Kültürü ve Ahlak Bilgisi 4. Sınıf.* Ankara: MEB, 2008.

Akman, Ayhan. "From Cultural Schizophrenia to Modernist Binarism: Cartoons and Identities in Turkey (1930–1975)." In *Political Cartoons in the Middle East,* edited by Fatma Müge Göçek, 83–131. Princeton, N.J.: Markus Weiner Publishers, 1998.

Aktay, Yasin, ed. *Modern Türkiye'de Siyasi Düşünce: 6, İslamcılık.* Istanbul: İletişim, 2004.

al-Ali, Naji. *Karikatur Naji al-'Ali.* Beirut: Al-markaz al-'arabi lil-ma'lumat, 2007.

———. *A Child in Palestine: The Cartoons of Naji al-Ali.* London: Verson, 2009.

Ali, Ahmed, trans. *Al-Qur'an: A Contemporary Translation by Ahmed Ali.* Princeton, N.J.: Princeton University Press, 1993.

Ali, F. A. "Šauqi, der Fürst der Dichter." In *Orientalistische Studien. Enno Littmann zu seinem 60sten Geburtstag,* edited by Rudi Paret, 139–48. Leiden: Brill, 1935.

Ali, Wijdan. *Modern Islamic Art: Development and Continuity.* Gainesville: University Press of Florida, 1997.

———. "The Status of Islamic Art in the Twentieth Century." *Muqarnas* 9 (1992): 186–88.

Alpöge, Gülçin. "Günümüz Çocuk Kitaplarında Çocuk İmgesi." In *Çocuk Kültürü: 1. Ulusal Çocuk Kültürü Kongresi, 6–8 Kasım 1996,* edited by Bekir Onur, 286–300. Ankara: Ankara Üniversitesi Çocuk Kültürü Araştırma ve Uygulama Merkezi, 1997.

Ambah, Faiza Saleh. "A Subversive Soap Roils Saudi Arabia." *Washington Post,* August 3, 2008. http://www.washingtonpost.com/wp-dyn/content/article/2008/08/02/ AR2008080201547.html.

Amir-Moezzi, Mohammad Ali. "L'Imam dans le ciel: ascension et initiation (aspects de l'Imāmamologie duodécimaine III)." In *Le voyage initiatique en terre d'Islam,* edited by Mohammad Ali Amir-Moezzi, 99–116. Louvain: Peeters, 1996.

———, ed. *Le voyage initiatique en terre d'islam: ascensions célestes et itinéraires spiri-tuels.* Louvain: Peeters, 1996.

And, Metin. *Yıktın Perdeyi Eyledin Viran: Yapı Kredi Karagöz Koleksiyonu.* Istanbul: Yapı Kredi Kültür Sanat Yayıncılık, 2004.

Anderson, Benedict. *Imagined Communities.* London: Verso, 2006.

Appadurai, Arjun. *Modernity at Large: Cultural Dimensions of Globalization.* Minneapolis: University of Minnesota Press, 1996.

Appleby, Timothy. "Jihad Is Not Just a Word for War." *The Globe and Mail,* September 20, 2001. http://www.theglobeandmail.com.

Ariès, Philippe. *History of Childhood: A Social History of Family Life.* New York: Alfred A. Knopf, 1962.

Armbrust, Walter. "Audiovisual Media and History of the Arab Middle East." In *Middle East Historiographies: Narrating the Twentieth Century,* edited by Israel Gershoni, Amy Singer, and Y. Hakan Erdem, 288–314. Seattle: University of Washington Press, 2006.

———. "Islamists in Egyptian Cinema." *American Anthropologist* 104, no. 3 (2002): 922–31.

———. *Mass Culture and Modernism in Egypt.* Cambridge: Cambridge University Press, 1996.

Arvasi, M. Sacid. "Gözlerinden Hayat Akan." *Sızıntı* 299 (2003).

Asad, Talal. *Formations of the Secular: Christianity, Islam, Modernity.* Stanford, Calif.: Stanford University Press, 2003.

———. "Thinking about Religion, Belief, and Politics." In *The Cambridge Companion to Religious Studies,* edited by Robert Orsi, 36–57. Cambridge: Cambridge University Press, 2012.

Assmann, Aleida. "Three Memory Anchors." In *Crisis and Memory in Islamic Societies,* edited by Angelika Neuwirth, 43–58. Beirut: Ergon, 2001.

———. "Zur Mediengeschichte des kulturellen Gedächtnisses." *Media and Cultural Memory* 1 (2004): 45–60.

Assmann, Jan. "Collective Memory and Cultural Identity." *New German Critique* 65 (1995): 125–33.

———. *Das kulturelle Gedächtnis, Schrift, Erinnerung und politische Identitat in frühen Hochkulturen.* Munich: Beck, 1992.

Asthana, Sanjay. "Religion and Secularism as Embedded Imaginaries: A Study of Indian Television Narratives." *Critical Studies in Media Communication* 25 (2008): 304–23.

Atacan, Fulya. *Kutsal Göç: Radikal İslamcı Bir Grubun Anatomisi.* Istanbul: Bağlam, 1993.

Atkinson, Rick. *Crusade: The Untold Story of the Gulf War.* Boston: Houghton Mifflin, 1993.

Atwood, Robert. "Looters in the Temple." *Lost Magazine* 5 (April 2006). http://www.lostmag.com/issue5/looters.php.

Ay, Mehmet Emin. "Çocuklarımıza Allah'ı Nasıl Anlatalım?" Istanbul: TİMAŞ. http://www.timas.com.tr/index.php?key=tkg&id=237.

Aytürk, İlker. "The First Episode of Language Reform in Republican Turkey: The Language Council from 1926 to 1931." *Journal of the Royal Asiatic Society,* 3rd ser., 18 (2008): 275–93.

———. "H. F. Kvergić and the Sun-Language Theory." *Zeitschrift der Deutschen Morgenländischen Gesellschaft* 159 (2009): 23–44.

———. "Turkish Linguists against the West: The Origins of Linguistic Nationalism in Atatürk's Turkey." *Middle Eastern Studies* 40 (2004): 1–25.

al-'Azm, Khalid. *Mudhakkirat Khalid al-'Azm.* 3 vols. Beirut: al-Dar al-Muttahida lil-Nashr, 1973.

al-Azmeh, Aziz. "Islamic Studies and the European Imagination." In *Islams and Modernities,* 122–45. London: Verso, 1993.

Bakhtin, Mikhail M. *The Dialogic Imagination: Four Essays.* Edited by Michael Holquist. Translated by Caryl Emerson and Michael Holquist. Austin: University of Texas Press, 1981.

Bal, Mieke. "Visual Essentialism and the Object of Visual Culture." *Journal of Visual Culture* 2, no. 1 (2003): 5–32.

Baldauf, Ingeborg. *Schriftreform und Schriftwechsel bei den Muslimischen Russland- und Sowjettürken (1850-1937): Ein Symptom Ideengeschichtlicher und Kulturpolitischer Entwicklungen.* Budapest: Akadémiai Kiadó, 1993.

Baldauf, Scott. "Militia's Other Weapon: Videos." *Christian Science Monitor,* August 25, 2004. http://www.csmonitor.com/2004/0825/p01s03-woiq.html.

al-Banna', Hasan. *Five Tracts of Hasan al-Banna'.* Translated by Charles Wendell. Berkeley: University of California Press, 1978.

Baram, Amatzia. "A Case of Imported Identity: The Modernizing Secular Ruling Elites of Iraq and the Concept of Mesopotamian-Inspired Territorial Nationalism, 1922-1992." *Poetics Today* 15 (1994): 279-319.

———. *Culture, History and Ideology in the Formation of Ba'thist Iraq: 1968-1989.* London: St. Martin's Press, 1991.

———. "Territorial Nationalism in the Middle East." *Middle Eastern Studies* 26 (1990): 425-48.

Barthes, Roland. *Image, Music, Text.* New York: Hill and Wang, 1977.

———. "The Photographic Message." In *Image, Music, Text,* edited by Stephen Heath, 15-31. New York: Hill and Wang, 1977.

———. "Rhetoric of the Image." In *Image, Music, Text,* edited by Stephen Heath, 32-51. New York: Hill and Wang, 1977.

"Başörtüsü Düzlenlemesi TBMM'de." http://www.tumgazeteler.com/?a=2516299.

"The Battle for Turkey's Soul." European Stability Initiative, April 2008. http://www.esiweb.org/pdf/esi_picture_story_-the_battle_for_turkey%27s_soul_-_april_2008.pdf.

Batur-VanderLippe, Pınar, and Joe Feagin, eds. *The Global Color Line: Racial and Ethnic Inequality and Struggle from a Global Perspective.* Stamford, Conn.: JAI Press, 1999.

Batur-VanderLippe, Pınar, and John VanderLippe. "Young Ottomans and Jadidists: Past Discourse and the Continuity of Debates in Turkey, the Caucasus and Central Asia." *Turkish Studies Association Bulletin* 18 (1994): 59-82.

Bauer, Janet. "Corrupted Alterities: Body Politics in the Time of the Iranian Diaspora." In *Dirt, Undress, and Difference: Critical Perspectives on the Body's Surface,* edited by Adeline Masquelier, 233-53. Bloomington: Indiana University Press, 2005.

Al Bawaba. "Protests against Seductive Music Videos Erupt in Egypt." March 6, 2005. http://www.albawaba.com/en/main/180979/&searchWords=alexandria%20university.

Behdad, Sohrab. "Islamic Utopia in Pre-Revolutionary Iran: Navvab Safavi and the Fada'ian-e Eslam." Middle Eastern Studies 33, no. 1 (1997): 40-65.

Belge, Murat. *Tarihten Güncelliğe.* Istanbul: Alan, 1980.

Bengio, Ofra. *Saddam's Word: Political Discourse in Iraq.* Oxford: Oxford University Press, 1998.

Benjamin, Walter. "The Work of Art in the Age of Mechanical Reproduction," *Illuminations* (1968): 217–51.

Bennis, Muhammad. *Fractured Modernity.* Casablanca: Toubqal Press, 2004. [Arabic].

Berkes, Niyazi. *The Development of Secularism in Turkey.* Montreal: McGill University Press, 1964.

Bhabha, Homi. "Another Country." In *Without Boundary: Seventeen Ways of Looking,* edited by Fereshteh Daftari, 30–35. New York: Museum of Modern Art, 2006.

Bilal, Mazen, and Najib Nusair. *Syrian Historical Drama: The Dream of the End of an Era (al-drama al-tarikhiyya al-suriyya: hilm nihiyat al-'asr).* Damascus: Dar al-Sham, 1999.

Blair, Sheila, and Jonathan Bloom. *The Art and Architecture of Islam (1250–1800).* New Haven, Conn.: Yale University Press, 1995.

Bombardier, Alice. "La peinture murale iranienne: Genèse et évolution. Enjeux de la spatialisation artistique dans le processus d'affirmation et de pacification des pays du Moyen-Orient." In *Eternal Tour 2010 Jerusalem,* 112–22. Geneva: Labor et Fides/Black Jack Edition, 2010.

Booth, Marilyn. "Exploding into the Seventies: Ahmed Fu'ad Nigm, Sheikh Imam, and the Aesthetics of New Youth Politics." In *Political and Social Protest in Egypt,* edited by Nicholas S. Hopkins, 19–44. Cairo: American University of Cairo Press, 2009.

Boozari, Ali. "Persian Illustrated Lithographed Books on the *Mi'raj:* Improving Children's Shi'ite Beliefs in the Qajar Period." In *The Prophet's Ascension,* edited by Christiane Gruber and Frederick Colby, 252–68. Bloomington: Indiana University Press, 2009.

Boullata, Kamal. *Palestinian Art 1850–2005.* London: Saqi Books, 2009.

Bourdieu, Pierre. *On Television.* London: New Press, 1999.

Bourriaud, Nicholas. *PostProduction. Culture as Screenplay: How Art Reprograms the World.* New York: Has and Sternberg, 2005.

Boyd, Douglas A. *Broadcasting in the Arab World: A Survey of the Electronic Media in the Middle East.* 2nd ed. Ames: Iowa State University Press, 1993.

Brink, Cornelia. "Secular Icons: Looking at Photographs from Nazi Concentration Camps." *History and Memory* 12 (2000): 135–50.

Browers, Michaelle L. *Political Ideology in the Arab World: Accommodation and Transformation.* Cambridge: Cambridge University Press, 2009.

Brummett, Palmira J. *Image and Imperialism in the Ottoman Revolutionary Press, 1908–1911.* Albany: State University of New York Press, 2000.

Buccianti, Alexandra. "Turkish Soap Operas in the Arab World: Social Liberation or Cultural Alienation?" *Arab Media and Society* 10 (Spring 2010). http://www.arabmediasociety.com/?article=735.

Bulaç, Ali. "İslâm'ın Üç Siyaset Tarzı veya İslâmcıların Üç Nesli." In *Modern Türkiye'de Siyasi Düşünce: 6, İslamcılık,* edited by Yasin Aktay, 48–67. Istanbul: İletişim, 2004.

Burgat, Francois. *Islamism after al-Qaida.* Austin: University of Texas Press, 2007.

Campo, Juan E. *The Other Side of Paradise: Explorations into the Religious Meanings of Domestic Space in Islam.* Columbia: University of South Carolina Press, 1991.

Çankaya, Erol. *İktidar Bu Kapağın Altındadır: Gösteri Demokrasisinde Siyasal Reklamcılık.* Istanbul: Boyut, 2008.

Cavanagh, Dermot, and Tim Kirk. "Introduction: Subversion and Scurrility in the Politics of Popular Discourses." In *Subversion and Scurrility: Popular Discourse in Europe from 1500 to the Present,* edited by Dermot Cavanagh and Tim Kirk, 1–10. Aldershot: Ashgate, 2000.

Çayır, Kenan. *Islamic Literature in Contemporary Turkey: From Epic to Novel.* London: Palgrave Macmillan, 2007.

Çelik, Zeynep. *Displaying the Orient: Architecture of Islam at Nineteenth-Century World's Fairs.* Berkeley: University of California Press, 1992.

Centlivres, Pierre, and Micheline Centlivres-Demont. "Une étrange rencontre: la photographie orientaliste de Lehnert et Landrock et l'image iranienne du Prophète Mahomet." *Etudes Photographiques* 17 (2005): 5–15.

Çeviker, Turgut. *Gelişim Sürecinde Türk Karikatürü: II Meşrutiyet Dönemi 1908–1918.* Ankara: Anadolu Yayıncılık, 1988.

———. *Gelişim Sürecinde Türk Karikatürü—III.* Istanbul: Adam Yayınları, 1991.

———. *Meşrutiyet İmzasız Karikatürler Antolojisi.* Ankara: Anadolu Yayıncılık, 1989.

Chalcraft, John, and Yaseen Noorani. "Introduction." In *Counterhegemony in the Colony and Postcolony,* edited by John Chalcraft and Yaseen Noorani, 1–16. Basingstoke: Palgrave Macmillan, 2007.

Chehabi, Houchang E. *Iranian Politics and Religious Modernism: The Liberation Movement of Iran.* London: I. B. Tauris, 1990.

Chehabi, H[oushang] E., and Fotini Christia. "The Art of State Persuasion: Iran's Post-Revolutionary Murals." *Persica* 22 (2008): 1–13.

Chelkowski, Peter, and Hamid Dabashi. *Staging a Revolution: The Art of Persuasion in the Islamic Republic of Iran.* New York: New York University Press, 1999.

Clark, Arthur. "The Art of Satire and the Satiric Spectrum." In *Studies in Literary Modes,* 31–49. London: Oliver and Boyd, 1958.

Clarke, David. "The Curse of the Crying Boy: Could A Kitsch Print Bring Fiery Disaster To Its Owners?" *Fortean Times.* July 2008. http://www.forteantimes. com/features/articles/1308/the_curse_of_the_crying_boy.html.

Cline, Eric L. "Does Saddam Think He's a Modern-Day Saladin?" *History News Network,* October 3, 2003. http://hnn.us/articles/1305.html.

Colby, Frederick. "The Early Imami Shi'i Narratives and the Contestation over Intimate Colloquy Scenes in Muhammad's *Mi'raj.*" In *The Prophet's Ascension,* edited by Christiane Gruber and Frederick Colby, 141–56. Bloomington: Indiana University Press, 2009.

Cole, Juan. *Modernity at the Millenium: The Genesis of the Baha'i Faith in the Nineteenth-Century Middle East.* New York: Columbia University Press, 1999.

Colston, James. *History of the Scott Monument.* Edinburgh: Printed for the Magistrates and Town Council, 1881.

Conermann, Stephan. "Muslimische Ritter—gibt es das? Die Saladin-Rezeption in europäischen Werken des Mittelalters." In *König Artus lebt! Eine Ringvorlesung des Mittelalterzentrums der Universität Bonn,* edited by Stefan Zimmer, 221–72. Heidelberg: Winter, 2005.

Cook, Michael. *Commanding Right and Forbidding Wrong in Islamic Thought.* Cambridge: Cambridge University Press, 2000.

Coşgun, Kürşat. "Desen Bir Türlü, Demesen Bir Türlü." *Karikatür ve Mizah Dünyası,* April 23, 2008. http://kursatcosgun.blogcu.com/desen_14169171.html.

"Country Profile: Afghanistan, August 2008." *Library of Congress Country Studies.* Available online at: lcweb2.loc.gov/frd/cs/profiles/Afghanistan.pdf.

Coyne, Michael. "Iran under the Ayatollahs." *National Geographic* 168, no. 1 (1985): 110.

Dabbous-Sensenig, Dima. "To Veil or Not to Veil: Gender and Religion on Al-Jazeera's Islamic Law and Life." *Westminster Papers in Communication and Culture* 3, no. 2 (2006): 60–85.

Daftari, Fereshteh. "Islamic or Not." In *Without Boundary: Seventeen Ways of Looking,* edited by Fereshteh Daftari, 10–27. New York: Museum of Modern Art, 2006.

———. *Without Boundary: Seventeen Ways of Looking.* New York: Museum of Modern Art, 2006.

Dagher, Sam. "Rewriting History in Bronze." *New York Times,* October 8, 2008. http://atwar.blogs.nytimes.com/2008/10/08/rewriting-history-in-bronze/.

Dağlı, Nihat. "Erkek Adam Ağlar." *Sızıntı* 212 (September/Eylül 1996). http://www.sizinti.com.tr/konular/ayrinti/erkek-adam-aglar.html.

al-Dakhil, Munira M. "Destructive Academy Is Harmful to the Family." *Al-Riyadh,* February 27, 2005. [Arabic].

Davis, Eric. *Memories of State: Politics, History and Collective Identity in Modern Iraq.* Berkeley: University of California Press, 2005.

———. "The Museum and the Politics of Social Control in Iraq." In *Commemorations: The Politics of National Identity,* edited by John R. Gillis, 90–104. Princeton, N.J.: Princeton University Press, 1994.

Davutoğlu, Ahmet. "Philosophical and Institutional Dimensions of Secularisation." In *Islam and Secularism in the Middle East,* edited by Azzam Tamimi and John Esposito, 170–208. New York: New York University Press, 2000.

Dawisha, Adeed. "Footprints in the Sand: The Definition and Redefinition of Identity in Iraq's Foreign Policy." In *Identity and Foreign Policy in the Middle*

East, edited by Shibley Telhami and Michael Barnett, 117–36. Ithaca, N.Y.: Cornell University Press, 2002.

al-Dawyan, Wafa' M. "*Star Academy:* A Sincere Invitation to *Ikhtilat.*" *Al-Riyadh,* March 22, 2005. [Arabic].

Debord, Guy. *The Society of the Spectacle.* New York: Zone Books, 1995.

Deeb, Lara. *An Enchanted Modern: Gender and Public Piety in Shi'i Lebanon.* Princeton, N.J.: Princeton University Press, 2006.

de Groot, Joanna. *Religion, Culture, and Politics in Iran: From the Qajars to Khomeini.* London: I. B. Tauris, 2007.

Dekmejian, Richard. "The Liberal Impulse in Saudi Arabia." *Middle East Journal* 57, no. 3 (2003): 381–99.

Deringil, Selim. *The Well-Protected Domains: Ideology and the Legitimation of Power in the Ottoman Empire, 1876–1909.* London: I. B. Tauris, 1998.

Determann, Matthias. "The Crusades in Arab School Textbooks." *Islam and Christian-Muslim Relations* 19 (2008): 199–214.

Devellioğlu, Ferit. *Osmanlıca-Türkçe Ansiklopedik Lûgat.* Ankara: Aydın Kitabevi Yayınları, 2006.

Dick, Marlin. "Syria under the Spotlight: Television Satire that is Revolutionary in Form, Reformist in Content." *Arab Media and Society* 3 (2007). http://www.arabmediasociety.com/countries/index.php?c_article=120.

Dikmen, Halit. "Masum Çocuk." *Sızıntı* 88 (1986).

Dikovitskaya, Margaret. *The Study of the Visual after the Cultural Turn.* Cambridge, Mass.: MIT Press, 2005.

"Diyanet 11 milyon kitap dağıttı." *Yeni Şafak,* November 3, 2007. http://yenisafak.com.tr/KulturSanat/?i=79107.

Djaroueh, Adnan. *Mawsu'at al-'umlat al-waraqiyya al-suriyya / Encyclopedia of Syrian Paper Money.* Beirut: Dar al-Mourad, 2005.

Donaldson, Bess Allen. *The Wild Rue: A Study of Muhammadan Magic and Folklore in Iran.* London: Luzacand Co., 1938.

Douglas, Mary. *Purity and Danger: An Analysis of Concepts of Pollution and Taboo.* Harmondsworth: Penguin, 1970.

"A Dream Role: Ghassan Massoud on Salah al-Din, Syrian Actor and Making It Big." In *Emerging Syria,* 160–61. Oxford: Oxford Business Group, 2006.

Duben, Alen, and Cem Behar. *Istanbul Households: Marriage, Family and Fertitliy, 1880–1940.* Cambridge: Cambridge University Press, 1991.

Durakbaşa, Ayşe. "Kemalism as Identity Politics in Turkey." In *Deconstructing Images of "the Turkish Woman,"* edited by Zehra F. Arat, 139–55. New York: St. Martin's Press, 1998.

Eagleton, Terry. *Ideology: An Introduction.* London: Verso, 1991.

Eddé, Anne-Marie. *Saladin.* Paris: Flammarion, 2008.

Eddy, William. "King Ibn Sa'ud: Our Faith and Your Iron." *Middle East Journal* 17, no. 3 (1963): 257–63.

Eickelman, Dale F., and Jon W. Anderson. "Redefining Muslim Publics." In *New Media in the Muslim World*, edited by Dale F. Eickelman and Jon W. Anderson, 1–18. Bloomington: Indiana University Press, 1999.

Ekhtiar, Maryam. "Infused with Shi'ism: Representations of the Prophet in Qajar Iran." In *Picturing Prophetic Knowledge: The Prophet Muhammad in Cross-Cultural Literary and Artistic Traditions*, edited by Christiane Gruber and Avinoam Shalem. Berlin: De Gruyter, 2014.

Elahi, Maryam. "The Rights of the Child under Islamic Law: Prohibition of the Child Soldier." In *Children in the Muslim Middle East*, edited by Elizabeth Warnock Fernea, 50–57. Austin: University of Texas Press, 1995.

Elkins, James. *Visual Studies: A Skeptical Introduction*. New York: Routledge, 2003.

Ende, Werner. "Kollektive Identität und Geschichte in der islamischen Welt der Gegenwart." In *Die fundamentalistische Revolution: Partikularistische Bewegungen der Gegenwart und ihr Umgang mit der Geschichte*, edited by Wolfgang Reinhart, 151–64. Reihe Historiae 7. Freiburg: Rombach, 1995.

———. "Wer ist ein Glaubensheld und wer ist ein Ketzer? Konkurrierende Geschichtsbilder in der modernen Literatur islamischer Länder." *Die Welt des Islams* 23–24 (1984): 70–94.

al-'Enezi, Hamed A. "Star Academy . . . The Other Terrorism." *Al-Riyadh*, March 19, 2005. [Arabic].

Erdem, Özgür. "MHP Hep Turbancıydı." *Türksolu* (2008): 171. http://www.turksolu.org/172/erdem172.htm.

Erdoğan, Necmi. "Ağlayan Çocuk . . . Gerçekleşmeyen Hayallerimizin Sembolü." *Birikim* 124 (1999): 39–41.

"Erdoğan Şimdi de 'Kedi Tom.'" *Radikal*, April 1, 2008. http://www.radikal.com.tr/haber.php?haberno=148291.

Erickson, Edward J. *Ordered to Die: A History of the Ottoman Army in the First World War*. Westport, Conn.: Greenwood Press, 2001.

Ertekin, Betül. *Ramazan Sevinci*. Istanbul: Muştu Yayınları, 2005.

Ertürk, Nergis. "Phonocentrism and Literary Modernity in Turkey." *Boundary 2* (2010): 155–85.

Esfandiari, Golnaz. "Iran: Students Protest Burials of War Dead on Tehran Campuses." *Payvand Iran News*, March 15, 2006. http://www.payvand.com/news/06/mar/1138.html.

Ettinghausen, Richard, Oleg Grabar, and Marilyn Jenkins-Madina. *Islamic Art and Architecture (650–1250)*. New Haven, Conn.: Yale University Press, 2001.

Fandy, Mamoun. *Saudi Arabia and the Politics of Dissent*. New York: Palgrave Macmillan, 1999.

Faris, Nabih Amin. *The Mysteries of Purity: Being a Translation with Notes of the Kitab Asrar al-Taharah of Al-Ghazzali's Ihya 'Ulum al-Din*. Beirut: American University of Beirut, 1966.

al-Faruqi, Lois Ibsen. "Music, Musicians, and Muslim Law." *Asian Music* 17, no. 1 (1985): 3–36.

"Fatwa on *Star Academy*." Standing Committee for Scientific Research and the Issuing of Fatwas. Saudi Arabia, 2004. [Arabic].

Fawwaz, 'A. "Saudi Cinema Gambles on the Future." *al-Akhbar,* August 25, 2008. [Arabic].

Flaskerud, Ingvild. *Visualising Belief and Piety in Iranian Shiism.* London: Continuum, 2010.

Fox, Richard D., and Barbara J. King, eds. *Anthropology beyond Culture.* Oxford: Berg, 2002.

Freedman, Leonard. *The Offensive Art: Political Satire and its Censorship around the World from Beerbohm to Borat.* Westport, Conn.: Praeger, 2009.

Freitag, Ulrike. "In Search of 'Political Correctness': The Baath Party in Syria." *Middle Eastern Studies* 35 (1999): 1–16.

Frishkopf, Michael, ed. *Music and Media in the Arab World.* Cairo: American University in Cairo Press, 2010.

Geertz, Clifford. *The Interpretation of Cultures.* New York: Basic Books, 1973.

Gelvin, James. "Modernity and Its Discontents: On the Durability of Nationalism in the Arab Middle East." *Nations and Nationalism* 5, no. 1 (1999): 71–89.

Gencer, Yasemin. "İbrahim Müteferrika and the Age of the Printed Manuscript." In *The Islamic Manuscript Tradition: Ten Centuries of Book Arts in Indiana University Collections,* edited by Christiane Gruber, 154–93. Bloomington: Indiana University Press, 2009.

Gerber, Haim. *Remembering and Imagining Palestine: Identity and Nationalism from the Crusades to the Present.* New York: Macmillan, 2008.

Gezer, Hüseyin. *Cumhuriyet Dönemi Türk Heykeli.* Ankara: TİSA Matbaasi, 1984.

al-Ghaddhami, 'Abdullah Muhammad. *The Tale of Modernity in the Kingdom of Saudi Arabia.* Beirut: Arab Cultural Center, 2005. [Arabic].

Ghanam, Oussama. "Tigers on the Ninth Day: Cinema in a Quarter Century." In *Insights into Syrian Cinema: Essays and Conversations with Contemporary Filmmakers,* edited by Rasha Salti, 67–77. New York: Rattapallax Press and ArteEast, 2006.

al-Ghazali, Abu Hamid Muhammad b. Muhammad. *Ihya' 'Ulum al-Din (The Revival of the Sciences of Religion).* Cairo: Mu'assasa al-Halabi, 1967.

Giladi, Avner. "Concepts of Childhood and Attitudes towards Children in Medieval Islam." *Journal of the Economic and Social History of the Orient* 32, no. 1 (1989): 121–52.

Göçek, Fatma Müge. "Decline of the Ottoman Empire and the Emergence of Greek, Armenian, Turkish, and Arab Nationalisms." In *Social Constructions of Nationalism in the Middle East,* edited by Fatma Müge Göçek, 15–83. Albany: State University of New York Press, 2002.

Göçek, Fatma Müge. "Political Cartoons as a Site of Representation and Resistance in the Middle East." In *Political Cartoons in the Middle East,* 1–12. Princeton, N.J.: Markus Wiener, 1998.

Gökalp, Ziya. *Türkleşmek, İslamlaşmak, ve Muasırlaşmak.* Ankara: Serdengeçti, 1963.

Goldstone, Jack A. "Rethinking Revolutions: Integrating Origins, Processes, and Outcomes." *Comparative Studies of South Asia, Africa and the Middle East* 29 (2009): 18–32.

Göle, Nilüfer. "Islamic Visibilities and Public Sphere." In *Islam in Public: Turkey, Iran and Europe*, edited by Nilüfer Göle and Ludwig Ammann, 3–43. Istanbul: Bilgi University Press, 2006.

———, ed. *İslamın Yeni Kamusal Yüzleri.* Istanbul: Metis, 2000.

———. "Snapshots of Islamic Modernities." *Daedelus* 129, no. 1 (2000): 91–117.

———. "The Quest for the Islamic Self within the Context of Modernity." In *Rethinking Modernity and National Identity in Turkey*, edited by Sibel Bozdoğan and Reşat Kasaba, 81–94. Seattle: University of Washington Press, 1997.

Gombrich, E. H. "The Cartoonist's Armoury." In E. H. Gombrich, *Meditations on a Hobby Horse and Other Essays on the Theory of Art*, 127–42. London: Phaidon Publishers, 1963.

Grabar, Oleg. "Islam and Iconoclasm." In *Iconoclasm: Papers Given at the Ninth Spring Symposium of Byzantine Studies, University of Birmingham, March 1975*, edited by Anthony Bryer and Judith Herrin, 45–52. Birmingham: University of Birmingham, 1977.

———. "What Makes Islamic Art Islamic?" In Oleg Grabar, *Islamic Art and Beyond, Constructing the Study of Islamic Art*, 3:247–51. Aldershot, Vt.: Ashgate Variorum, 2006.

Grabar, Oleg, and Mika Natif. "The Story of Portraits of the Prophet Muhammad." *Studia Islamica* 96 (2003): 19–37.

Graham, William. "Qur'an as Spoken Word: An Islamic Contribution to the Understanding of Scripture." In *Approaches to Islam in Religious Studies*, edited by Richard Martin, 23–40. Tucson: University of Arizona Press, 1985.

Gramsci, Antonio. *Selections from the Prison Notebooks.* London: International Publishers.

Grandin, Thierry. "Introduction to the Citadel of Salah al-Din." In *Syria, Medieval Citadels between East and West*, edited by Stefano Bianca, 139–80. Turin: Allemandi, 2007.

Grigor, Talinn. "(Re)Claiming Space: The Use/Misuse of Propaganda Murals in Republican Tehran." *IIAS Newsletter* 28 (August 2002): 37.

Gruber, Christiane. "Between Logos (*Kalima*) and Light (*Nur*): Representations of the Prophet Muhammad in Islamic Painting." *Muqarnas* 26 (2009): 1–34.

———. "Jerusalem in the Visual Propaganda of Iran." In *Jerusalem: Idea and Reality*, edited by Tamar Mayer and Suleiman Ali Mourad, 168–97. London: Routledge, Taylor and Francis, 2008.

———. "Me'raj ii. Illustrations." *Encyclopaedia Iranica.* Published February 20, 2009. http://www.iranica.com.

——. "The Message Is on the Wall: Mural Arts in Post-Revolutionary Iran." *Persica* 22 (2008): 15–46.

——. *The Timurid Book of Ascension (Mi'rajnama): A Study of Text and Image in a Pan-Asian Context.* Valencia: Patrimonio Ediciones, 2008.

——. "When *Nubuvvat* Encounters *Valayat:* Safavid Paintings of the Prophet Muhammad's *Mi'raj,* ca. 1500–1550." In *The Art and Material Culture of Iranian Shi'ism: Iconography and Religious Devotion in Shi'i Islam,* edited by Pedram Khosronejad, 46–71. London: I. B. Tauris, 2011.

Gruber, Christiane, and Frederick Colby, eds. *The Prophet's Ascension: Cross-Cultural Encounters with the Islamic Mi'raj Tales.* Bloomington: Indiana University Press, 2009.

Gülalp, Haldun. "Enlightenment by Fiat: Secularization and Democracy in Turkey." *Middle Eastern Studies* 41 (2005): 351–72.

——. "Globalization and Political Islam: The Social Bases of Turkey's Welfare Party." *International Journal of Middle East Studies* 33 (2001): 433–48.

——. *Kimlikler Siyaseti: Türkiye'de Siyasal İslamın Temelleri.* Istanbul: Metis, 2003.

——. "Modernization Policies and Islamist Politics in Turkey." In *Rethinking Modernity and National Identity in Turkey,* edited by Sibel Bozdoğan and Reşat Kasaba, 52–63. Seattle: University of Washington Press, 1997.

Gülen, Fethullah. "Allah Karsisindaki Durusuyla Mü'min." *Sızıntı* 328 (2006).

——. "Bence Tam Ağlama Mevsimi." *Sızıntı* 361 (2009).

——. "Bu Ağlamayı Dindirmek İçin Yavru." *Sızıntı* 1 (1979).

——. "Çile." *Sızıntı* 36 (1982).

——. "Garipler." *Sızıntı* 45 (1982).

——. "Tears." http://www.fethullahgulen.org/broken-plectrum/1849-tears.html.

"Gül'ün Eşi Türban için AİHM'e Gitmişti," http://arsiv.ntvmsnbc.com/ news/406259.asp.

Gürbilek, Nurdan. *Kötü Çocuk Türk.* Istanbul: Metis, 2001.

Halim, Hala. "The Signs of Saladin: A Modern Cinematic Rendition of Medieval Heroism." *Journal of Comprative Poetics* 12 (1992): 78–94.

Hall, Stuart. "Encoding, Decoding." In *The Cultural Studies Reader,* edited by Simon During, 90–103. London: Routledge, 1993.

Hammond, Andrew. "Unholy Row as Saudi Clerics Slam Ramadan TV." *Reuters,* September 15, 2008. http://uk.reuters.com/article/televisionNews/ idUKLC20580020080915.

Hanioğlu, Şükrü. *A Brief History of the Late Ottoman Empire.* Princeton, N.J.: Princeton University Press, 2008.

Hasu, 'Abd al-Nasir. "Salah al-Din al-Ayyubi shakhsiyyat al-marhala bayna sha-shatay al-sinima wal-tilifiziyun." *Al-Thawra,* August. 9, 2005. http://thawra .alwehda.gov.sy/_print_view.asp?FileName=41367847420050811130717.

Haugbolle, Sune. *War and Memory in Lebanon.* Cambridge: Cambridge University Press, 2010.

Hebdige, Dick. "From Culture to Hegemony." In *The Cultural Studies Reader*, edited by Simon During, 359–67. London: Routledge, 1993.

Heikal, Yousef. "Jaffa . . . As It Was." *Journal of Palestinian Studies* 13 (1984): 3–21.

Heinzelmann, Tobias. "The Hedgehog as Historian—Linguistic Archaism as a Means of Satire in the Early Work of Refik Halid Karay." In *The Middle Eastern Press as a Forum for Literature*, edited by Horst Unbehaun, 195–211. Frankfurt: Peter Lang, 2004.

———. *Osmanlı Karikatüründe Balkan Sorunu (1908–1914)*. Istanbul: Kitap Yayınevi, 2004.

Helimoğlu Yavuz, Muhsine. "Türk Masallarında Çocuk İmgeleri." In *Çocuk Kültürü: 1. Ulusal Çocuk Kültürü Kongresi, 6–8 Kasım 1996*, edited by Bekir Onur, 132–40. Ankara: Ankara Üniversitesi Çocuk Kültürü Araştırma ve Uygulama Merkezi, 1997.

Helvacoğlu, Firdevs. *Ders Kitaplarında Cinsiyetçilik (1928–1995)*. Istanbul: Kaynak, 1996.

Herzfeld, Michael. *Cultural Intimacy: Social Poetics in the Nation-State*. 1st ed. New York: Routledge, 1997.

———. *Cultural Intimacy: Social Poetics in the Nation-State*. 2nd ed. London: Routledge: 2005.

Hillenbrand, Carole. *The Crusades: Islamic Perspectives*. Edinburgh: Edinburgh University Press, 1999.

———. "The Evolution of the Saladin Legend in the West." *Mélanges de l'Université Saint-Joseph* 58 (2005): 497–510.

Hirsch, Marianne. *Family Frames: Photography, Narrative, and Postmemory*. Cambridge, Mass.: Harvard University Press, 1997.

Hirschkind, Charles. *The Ethical Soundscape: Cassette Sermons and Islamic Counterpublics*. New York: Columbia University Press, 2006.

———. "The Ethics of Listening: Cassette-Sermon Audition in Contemporary Egypt." *American Ethnologist* 28, no. 3 (2001): 623–49.

Hobsbawm, Eric J. "Inventing Tradition." In *The Invention of Tradition*, edited by Eric J. Hobsbawm and Terrence Ranger, 1–14. Cambridge: Cambridge University Press, 1983.

———. "Mass-Producing Traditions: Europe 1870–1914." In *The Invention of Tradition*, edited by Eric J. Hobsbawm and Terrence Ranger, 263–307. Cambridge: Cambridge University Press, 1983.

Holland, Patricia. *Picturing Childhood: The Myth of the Child in Popular Imagery*. London: I. B. Tauris, 2004.

Holmes, James R. "Did Saddam Mimic Saladin." *The American Thinker*, November 8, 2004. http://www.americanthinker.com/2004/11/did_saddam_mimic_saladin.html.

Hooper-Greenhill, Eilean. *Museums and the Interpretation of Visual Culture*. London: Routledge, 2000.

Hourani, Albert. *Arabic Thought in the Liberal Age, 1789-1939*. Cambridge: Cambridge University Press, 1983.

Hroch, Miroslav. *"Real and Constructed: The Nature of the Nation."* In Miroslav Hroch, *Comparative Studies in Modern European History: Nation, Nationalism, Social Change*, 91–106. Burlington, Vt.: Ashgate Variorum, 2007.

———. "The Social Interpretation of Linguistic Demand in European National Movements." In Miroslav Hroch, *Comparative Studies in Modern European History: Nation, Nationalism, Social Change*, 67–96. Burlington, Vt.: Ashgate Variorum, 2007.

Hroch, Miroslav, and Jitka Malečková. "Historical Heritage: Continuity and Discontinuity in the Construction of National Histories." In Miroslav Hroch, *Comparative Studies in Modern European History: Nation, Nationalism, Social Change*, 15–36. Burlington, Vt.: Ashgate Variorum, 2007.

Hudson, Leila. *Transforming Damascus: Space and Modernity in an Islamic City*. London: I. B. Tauris, 2008.

Hunt, Lynn, and Victoria E. Bonnell. "Introduction." In *Beyond the Cultural Turn*, edited by Lynn Hunt and Victoria E. Bonnell, 1–34. Berkeley: University of California Press, 1999.

Huntington, Samuel P. *The Clash of Civilizations and the Remaking of the World Order*. New York: Simon and Schuster, 1998.

"III. Dini Yayınlar Kongresi Sonuç Bildirgesi." October 30, 2005. http://www.diyanet.gov.tr/yayin/sicerik.asp?id=1243&sorgu=13.

'Imara, Muhammad. *Al-Islam wal-Funun al-Jamila*. Beirut: Dar al-Shuruq, 1991.

Işıtan, Sonnur. "Resimli Çocuk Kitaplarının Benlik Kavramıyla ilgili Konuları İçermesi Yönünden İncelenmesi." M.A. thesis, Hacettepe Üniversitesi Sağlık Bilimleri Enstitüsü Çocuk Gelişimi ve Eğitimi Programı, 2005.

Israeli, Raphael. *Islamikaze: Manifestations of Islamic Martyrology*. London: Frank Cass, 2003.

Issa, Naji. "Despite Oil and Greenery, Iraq Was Still Very Impoverished." *Alternative* 1, no. 5 (2003): 7. http://www.alternative-online.org.

Jakobsen, Janet, and Ann Pellegrini, eds. *Secularisms*. Durham, N.C.: Duke University Press, 2008.

Jankowski, James, and Israel Gershoni. *Redefining the Egyptian Nation, 1930-1945*. Cambridge: Cambridge University Press, 1995.

Jaschinski, Klaus. "Des Kaisers Reise in den Vorderen Orient 1898, ihr historischer Platz und ihre Dimensionen." In *Des Kaisers Reise in den Orient, Gesellschaft Geschichte-Gegenwart 27*, edited by Klaus Jaschinski and Julius Waldschmidt, 17–36. Berlin: Travo Verlag, 2002.

Jay, Martin. "Scopic Regimes of Modernity." In *Vision and Visuality, Discussions in Contemporary Culture* 2, edited by Hal Foster, 3–38. Seattle: Bay Press, 1988.

Jubb, Magaret. *The Legend of Saladin in Western Literature and Historiography*. Studies in Comparative Literature 34. Lewiston, N.Y.: Edwin Mellen Press, 2000.

Kalam, Ali Javahir. "*Rakhtshui* Iranian." *Khandaniha* 4 (Shanbeh, 9 Urdibihisht, 1323/Saturday, May 9, 1944): 9–10.

Karakuş, Abdullah. "Yeni Turban Çıkışı." *Milliyet*, January 15, 2008. http://www .milliyet.com.tr/2008/01/15/siyaset/axsiy01.html.

Karimi, Pamela. "Imagining Warfare, Imaging Welfare: Tehran's Post Iran–Iraq War Murals and Their Legacy." *Persica* 22 (2008): 47–63.

Karpat, Kemal. "A Language in Search of a Nation: Turkish in the Nation-State." In Kemal Karpat, *Studies on Turkish Politics and Society: Selected Articles and Essays*, 435–65. Leiden: Brill, 2004.

———. *The Politicization of Islam: Reconstructing Identity, State, Faith, and Community in the Late Ottoman State*. Oxford: Oxford University Press, 2001.

Kasaba, Reşat. "Kemalist Certainties and Modern Ambiguities." In *Rethinking Modernity and National Identity in Turkey*, edited by Sibel Bozdoğan and Reşat Kasaba, 15–36. Seattle: University of Washington Press, 1997.

Kashani-Sabet, Firoozeh. "Hallmarks of Humanism: Hygiene and Love of Homeland in Qajar Iran." *American Historical Review* 105, no. 4 (2000): 1171–1203.

———. "The Politics of Reproduction: Maternalism and Women's Hygiene in Iran, 1896–1941." *International Journal of Middle East Studies* 38, no.1 (2006): 1–29.

Kassab, Elizabeth. *Contemporary Arab Thought*. New York: Columbia University Press, 2010.

Kayalı, Hasan. "Liberal Practices in the Transformation from Empire to Nation-State: The Rump Ottoman Empire, 1918–1923." In *Liberal Thought in the Eastern Mediterranean: Late 19th Century until the 1960s*, edited by Christoph Schumann, 175–94. Leiden: Brill, 2008.

Keane, Webb. *Christian Moderns: Freedom and Fetish in the Mission Encounter.* Berkeley: University of California Press, 2007.

Kedar, Benjamin Z. "The Battle of Hattin Revisited." In *The Horns of Hattin: Proceedings of the Second Conference of the Society of the Crusades and the Latin East,* edited by Benjamin Z. Kedar, 190–207. Jerusalem: Yad Izhak Ben-Zvi, Israel Exploration Society, 1992.

Keddie, Nikki R. *Roots of Revolution: An Interpretive History of Modern Iran.* New Haven, Conn.: Yale University Press, 1981.

Keshmirshekan, Hamid. "Discourses on Postrevolutionary Iranian Art: Neotraditionalism during the 1990s." *Muqarnas* 23 (2006): 132–57.

———. "Modern and Contemporary Iranian Art: Developments and Challenges." In *Different Sames: New Perspectives in Contemporary Iranian Art*, edited by Hossein Amirsadeghi, 10–37. London: Thames and Hudson, 2009.

Keyman. E. Fuat. "MHP ve Türk-İslam Sentezi Kıskacında." *Radikal*, February 16, 2008. http://www.radikal.com.tr/ek_haber.php?ek=r2&haberno=8118.

Khalid, 'Amr. "Culture, Art, Media . . . and Making Life." http://www.amrkhaled .net/articles/articles406.html.

al-Khalil, Samir [Kanan Makiya]. *The Monument: Art, Vulgarity, and Responsibility in Iraq.* Berkeley: University of California Press, 1991.

Khalili, Laleh. *Heroes and Martyrs of Palestine.* Cambridge: Cambridge University Press, 2006.

Khatib, Lina. "Nationalism and Otherness: The Representation of Islamic Fundamentalism in Egyptian Cinema." *European Journal of Cultural Studies* 9, no. 1 (2006): 63–80.

Khomeini, Ruhollah. *Imam Khomeini's New Risaleh.* Vol. 1: *Worship and the Development of the Self.* Edited by Abdol Karim Biazar Shirazi. Tehran: Moassisey-i Anjam Kitab, 1980.

——. *Imam Khomeini's New Risaleh.* Vol. 2: *Economic Issues.* Edited by Abdol Karim Biazar Shirazi. Tehran: Moassisey-i Anjam Kitab, 1980.

——. *Imam Khomeini's New Risaleh.* Vol. 3: *Family Matters.* Edited by Abdol Karim Biazar Shirazi. Tehran: Moassisey-i Anjam Kitab, 1982.

Khosronejad, Pedram. "Introduction." In *Iranian Sacred Defence Cinema: Religion, Martyrdom and National Identity,* edited by P. Khosronejad, 1–57. Wantage: Kingston, 2012.

Kili, Suna. *Türk Devrim Tarihi.* Istanbul: Türkiye İş Bankası Kültür Yayınları, 2001.

Kılıçbay, Barış, and Mutlu Binark. "Consumer Culture, Islam and the Politics of Lifestyle: Fashion for Veiling in Contemporary Turkey." *European Journal of Communication* 17, no. 4 (2002): 495–511.

King, David A. "Two Iranian World Maps for Finding the Direction and Distance to Mecca." *Imago Mundi* 49 (1997): 62–82.

Kıvanç, Ümit. "İslamcılar and Para-Pul: Bir Dönüşüm Hikayesi." *Birikim* 99 (1997): 39–58.

Klausen, Jytte. *The Cartoons That Shook the World.* New Haven, Conn.: Yale University Press, 2009.

Klemm, Verena. "Different Notions of Commitment (*Iltizam*) and Committed Literature (*al-adab al-multazim*) in the Literary Circles of the Mashriq." *Middle Eastern Literatures* 3, no. 1 (2000): 51–62.

Koloğlu, Orhan. *Kim Bu Mustafa Kemal?* Istanbul: Boyut Kitapları, 1997.

Kömecoğlu, Uğur. "Kutsal ile Kamusal: Fethullah Gülen Cemaati Hareketi." In *Islamın Yeni Kamusal Yüzleri,* edited by Nilüfer Göle, 148–94. Istanbul: Metis, 2000.

Köroğlu, Erol. *Propaganda and Turkish Identity: Literature in Turkey During World War I.* London: Tauris Academic Studies, 2007.

Kraidy, Marwan. "Governance and Hypermedia in Saudi Arabia." *First Monday* 11, no. 9 (2006). http://firstmonday.org/issues/special11_9/kraidy/index.html.

——. *Reality Television and Arab Politics: Contention in Public Life.* Cambridge: Cambridge University Press, 2009.

——. "Reality Television, Gender, Authenticity in Saudi Arabia." *Journal of Communication* 59 (2009): 345–66.

Kraidy, Marwan, and Joseph Khalil. *Arab Television Industries*. London: British Film Institute/Palgrave Macmillan, 2009.

———. "The Middle East: Transnational Arab Television." In *The Media Globe: Trends in International Mass Media*, edited by L. Artz and Y. Kamalipour, 79–98. Lanham, Md.: Rowman and Littlefield, 2007.

Kreiser, Klaus. "Ein Freiheitsdenkmal für Istanbul." In *Istanbul. Vom imperialen Herrschersitz zur Megalopolis. Historiographische Betrachtungen zu Gesellschaft, Institutionen und Räumen*, edited by Yavuz Köse, 296–314. Munich: Meidenbauer, 2006.

———. "War Memorials and Cemeteries in Turkey." In *The First World War as Remembered by the Countries of the Eastern Mediterranean*, edited by Olaf Farshid, Manfred Kropp, and Stephan Dähne, 183–201. Beiruter Texte und Studien 99. Würzburg: Ergon, 2006.

Kris, Ernst. "The Psychology of Caricature." In Ernst Kris, *Psychoanalytic Explorations in Art*, 173–203. New York: International Universities Press, 1952.

Kubba, Laith. "Towards an Objective, Relative and Rational Islamic Discourse." In *Cosmopolitanism, Identity and Authenticity in the Middle East*, edited by Roel Meijer, 129–44. London: Curzon, 1999.

Kubler, George. *The Shape of Time: Remarks on the History of Things*. New Haven, Conn.: Yale University Press, 1962.

League of Arab States. "Arab League Satellite Broadcasting Charter." Unofficial English translation. *Arab Media and Society*, March 2008. http://www.arab mediasociety. com/?article=648.

Lefebvre, Henri. *The Production of Space*. Oxford: Wiley-Blackwell, 1992.

Lewis, Bernard. *The Emergence of Modern Turkey*. 1st ed. London: Oxford University Press, 1966.

———. *The Emergence of Modern Turkey*. 3rd ed. New York: Oxford University Press, 2002.

———. *History: Remembered, Recovered, Invented*. Princeton, N.J.: Princeton University Press, 1975.

Lewis, Justin. "The Meaning of Real Life." In *Reality TV: Remaking Television Culture*, edited by S. Murray and L. Ouellette, 288–302. New York: New York University Press, 2004.

Libal, Kathryn R. "Childhood: Premodern-Modern. Turkey." In *Encyclopedia of Women and Islamic Cultures: Family, Body, Sexuality and Health*, edited by Suad Joseph and Afsaneh Najmabadi, 86–87. Leiden: Brill, 2006.

Lincoln, Andrew. *Walter Scott and Modernity*. Edinburgh: Edinburgh University Press, 2007.

Liu, Melinda. "Mean Streets: Inside the Brutal Battle of Sadr City." *Newsweek*, April 24, 2004. http://www.uslaboragainstwar.org/article.php?id=4421.

Lockman, Zachary. *Contending Visions of the Middle East: The History and Politics of Orientalism*. Cambridge: Cambridge University Press, 2004.

Long, Jerry Mark. *Saddam's War of Words: Politics, Religion, and the Iraqi Invasion of Kuwait.* Austin: University of Texas Press, 2004.

Lowry, Glenn. *Oil and Sugar: Contemporary Art and Islamic Culture.* Toronto: Royal Ontario Museum, 2009.

Maden, Esra. "Cartoons Tell Political Journey of Turkey." *Today's Zaman,* October 12, 2008. http://www.todayszaman.com/tz-web/detaylar .do?load=detay&link=155666.

Mahmoud, Saba. *The Politics of Piety: The Islamic Revival and the Feminist Subject.* Princeton, N.J.: Princeton University Press, 2005.

——. "Secularism, Hermeutics, and Empire: The Politics of Islamic Reformation." *Public Culture* 19/2 (2006): 323–47.

Majlesi, Muhammad Baghir. *Hilyat al-Muttaqin.* Tehran: Peyman del-Agah Publishers, 1384/2006.

Malti-Douglas, Fedwa. *Medicines of the Soul: Female Bodies and Sacred Geographies in a Transnational Islam.* Berkeley: University of California Press, 2001.

Martín-Barbero, Jesus. *Communication, Culture and Hegemony: From the Media to Mediations.* London: Sage, 1993.

Marzolph, Ulrich. "The Martyr's Way to Paradise: Shiite Mural Art in the Urban Context." *Ethnologia Europaea* 33/2 (2003): 87–98. Also published in *Sleepers, Moles and Martyrs: Secret Identifications, Societal Integration, and the Differing Meanings of Freedom,* edited by Regina and John Bendix, 87–98. Copenhagen: Museum Tusculanum Press/University of Copenhagen, 2004.

Maskoob, Shahrokh. *Iranian National Identity and the Persian Language.* Washington, D.C.: Mage Publishers, 1992.

Matthews, Weldon C. *Confronting an Empire, Constructing a Nation: Arab Nationalists and Popular Politics in Mandate Palestine.* Oxford: Palgrave Macmillan, 2006.

McGeough, Paul. "A Visit to a Street of a Thousand Saddams." *The Age,* March 4, 2003. http://www.theage.com.au/.

M'Daghri, Muhammad Abdulkebir Alaoui. "The Code of Children's Rights in Islam." In *Children in the Muslim Middle East,* edited by Elizabeth Warnock Fernea, 30–41. Austin: University of Texas Press, 1995.

——. "Der andere Islam. Zum Bild vom toleranten Sultan Saladin und neuen Propheten Schah Ismail." In *Die Begegnung des Westens mit dem Osten,* edited by Odilo Engels and Peter Schreiner, 131–56. Sigmaringen: Jan Thorbecke 1993.

Meeker, Michael E. "The Muslim Intellectual and His Audience: A New Configuration of Writer and Reader among Believers in the Republic of Turkey." In *Cultural Transitions in the Middle East,* edited by Şerif Mardin, 153–88. Leiden: E. J. Brill, 1994.

Meital, Yoram. "Deliberately Not Empty: Reading Cairo's Unknown Soldier Monument." In *Material Evidence and Narrative Sources: Interdisciplinary Studies of the History of Islamic Societies,* edited by Daniella Talmon-Heller and Katia Cytryn-Silverman. Leiden: Brill, forthcoming.

Mellor, Noha. "Bedouinisation or Liberalisation of Culture? The Paradox in the Saudi Monopoly of the Arab Media." In *Kingdom without Borders: Saudi Arabia's Political, Religious and Media Frontiers,* edited by M. al-Rasheed, 353–74. New York: Columbia University Press, 2008.

"Mimicking Western Programs and Imposing Them on Arabs." Episode 2, *Bila Hudud* (Ahmad Mansour, Host). Doha: Al-Jazeera, March 10, 2004. [Arabic].

Mirsepasi, Ali. *Intellectual Discourse and the Politics of Modernization: Negotiating Modernity in Iran.* Cambridge: Cambridge University Press, 2000.

Mitchell, Richard P. *The Society of the Muslim Brothers.* London: Oxford University Press, 1969.

Mitchell, Timothy. *Colonizing Egypt.* Berkeley: University of California Press, 1991.

———, ed. *Questions of Modernity.* Minneapolis: University of Minnesota Press, 2000.

Mitchell, W. J. T. *Picture Theory.* Chicago: University of Chicago Press, 1994.

———. "The Pictorial Turn." *ArtForum* 30, no. 7 (1992): 89–94.

———. *What Do Pictures Want?* Chicago: University of Chicago Press, 2005.

Mizah Haber. July 31, 2007. http://mizahhaber.blogspot.com/2007_07_01_archive.html.

Möhring, Hannes. "Der andere Islam. Zum Bild vom toleranten Sultan Saladin und neuen Propheten Schah Ismail." In *Die Begegnung des Westens mit dem Osten,* edited by Odilo Engels and Peter Schreiner, 131–56. Sigmaringen: Jan Thorbecke, 1993.

———. *Saladin: The Sultan and His Times.* Baltimore: Johns Hopkins University Press, 2008.

———. "'Saladin, der edle Heide' Mythisierung und Realität." In *Konfrontation der Kulturen? Saladin und die Kreuzfahrer,* edited by Heinz Gaube, Bernd Schneidmüller, and Stefan Weinfurter, 160–75. Mainz: Philipp von Zabern, 2005.

Molavi, Afshin. *Persian Pilgrimages: Journeys across Iran.* New York: W. W. Norton, 2002.

Moll, Yasmin. "Islamic Televangelism: Religion, Media and Visuality in Contemporary Egypt." *Arab Media and Society* 10 (Spring 2010). http://www.arabmediasociety.com/?article=732.

Momen, Moojan. *An Introduction to Shi'i Islam: The History and Doctrines of Twelver Shi'ism.* New Haven, Conn.: Yale University Press, 1985.

Morley, Simon. *Writing on the Wall: Word and Image in Modern Art.* Berkeley: University of California Press, 2003.

"Muamer Sengoz'e Hapis Cezası." Karikatürcüler Derneği/The Association of Cartoonists in Turkey. http://www.karikaturculerdernegi.org/detay.asp?id=6718.

al-Munajjid, Muhammad Saleh. "*Akademiyat al-Shaytan wal Superstar.*" March 19, 2004. http://www.islamway.com/?iw_s=Lesson&iw_a=view&lesson_id=28385.

al-Musawi, Muhsin Al-Nuri. *Al-Sayyid Muqtada Al-Sadr, Sadr Al-Iraq Al-Thalith: Ahdafahu, Muwaqifahu, Mashru'ahu* Baghdad: Markaz Wali Allah, 2004.

Myers, Steven Lee. "A New Role for Iraqi Militants: Patrons of the Arts." *New York Times,* February 13, 2009. http://www.nytimes.com/2009/02/14/world/middleeast//14baghdad.html?pagewanted=2&_r=1&ref=middleeast.

Nabulsi, Shakir. *Akalahu al-dhi'b.* Beirut: Al-Mu'assasat al-'arabiyya lil-dirasat wal-nashr, 2007.

Naef, Silvia. "Reexploring Islamic Art: Modern and Contemporary Creation in the Arab World and Its Relation to the Artistic Past." RES 43 (Spring 2003): 164–74.

Najjar, Orayb Aref. "Cartoons as a Site for the Construction of Palestinian Refugee Identity: An Exploratory Study of Cartoonist Naji al-Ali." *Journal of Communication Inquiry* 31 (2007): 255–85.

Navaro-Yashin,Yael. *Faces of the State: Secularism and Public Life in Turkey.* Princeton, N.J.: Princeton University Press, 2002.

———. "The Market for Identities: Secularism, Islamism and Commodities." In *Fragments of Culture: The Everyday of Modern Turkey,* edited by Deniz Kandiyoti and Ayse Saktanber, 221–53. London: I. B. Tauris, 2002.

Nayyuf, Hayyan. "Da'iya bariz intiqada tariqat taswir al-nisa': Al-tayyar al-dini fi suriya yukarrim musalsal *Bab al-hara." alarabiya.net,* October 11, 2007.

Nelson, Kristina. *The Art of Reciting the Qur'an.* Austin: University of Texas Press, 1985.

Nelson, Robert. "The Map of Art History." *Art Bulletin* 79, no. 1 (1997): 28–40.

Newid, Mehr Ali. *Der schiitische Islam in Bildern: Rituale und Heilige.* Munich: Edition Avicenna, 2006.

Neydim, Necdet. "Çocuk Edebiyatının Ölüm Fermanı." *Cumhuriyet Kitap,* May 22, 2004.

Nodelman, Perry. *Words about Pictures: The Narrative Art of Children's Picture Books.* Athens: University of Georgia Press, 1988.

Ocak, Ahmet Yasar. *Türkler, Türkiye ve İslam: Yaklaşım, Yöntem ve Yorum Denemeleri.* Istanbul: İletişim, 1999.

Okay, Cüneyd. *Dönemin Mizah Dergilerinde Milli Mücadele Karikatürleri, 1919-1922.* Ankara: Kültür ve Turizm Bakanlığı, 2004.

———. *Eski Harfli Çocuk Dergileri.* Istanbul: Kitabevi, 1999.

———. *Osmanlı Çocuk Hayatında Yenileşmeler 1850-1900.* Istanbul: Kırkambar Yayınları, 1998.

"Okuduğu Şiir Erdoğan'ın Başını Ağrıtmaya Devam Ediyor." *Habervitrini,* October 27, 2002. http://www.habervitrini.com/haber.asp?id=54733.

Olgun, Ayşe. "Birdirdir oynayalım dinimizi kavrayalım." *Yeni Şafak,* April 30, 2007. http://yenisafak.com.tr/Pazar/?t=30.04.2007&i=42857.

Öngören, Ferit. *Cumhuriyet Dönemi Türk Mizahi ve Hicvi, 1923-1983.* Ankara: Türkiye İş Bankası Kültür Yayınları, 1983.

Önis, Ziya. "The Political Economy of Turkey's Justice and Development Party." In *The Emergence of a New Turkey: Democracy and the Ak Parti*, edited by M. Hakan Yavuz, 207–34. Salt Lake City: University of Utah Press, 2006.

Onur, Bekir. *Çocuk, Tarih ve Toplum*. Istanbul: İmge Kitabevi, 2007.

——, ed. *Çocuk Kültürü: 1. Ulusal Çocuk Kültürü Kongresi*. 6–8 Kasım 1996. Ankara: Ankara Üniversitesi Çocuk Kültürü Araştırma ve Uygulama Merkezi, 1997.

Open Source Center. "ILNA: Iran Bans Printing Valentine Postcards, Posters." Iranian Labor News Agency, OSC Document Number IAP20110103950036, January 3, 2011.

Özdabak, İbrahim. "Karikatür Baskıcı Yönetimlerin Korkulu Rüyasıdır." *Cafesiyaset.com*, October 29, 2008. http://www.ibrahimozdabak.com/ basindan/91-roportajlar/246-brahim-oezdabak-qkarikatuer-baskc- yoenetimlerin-korkulu-rueyasdrq.

Özer, Atilla. "Karikatür ve Siyaset." *Bianet*, 2004. http://www.bianet.org/bianet/ kategori/bianet/44187/karikatur-ve-siyaset.

Özmen, Çiğdem. *Allah'a Teşekkür Ediyorum*. Istanbul: TİMAŞ, 2008.

——. *Dua Etmeyi Biliyorum*. Istanbul: TİMAŞ, 2008.

——. *Oruç Tutmayı Seviyorum*. Istanbul: TİMAŞ, 2008.

Özyürek, Esra. "Miniaturizing Atatürk: Privatization of State Imagery and Ideology in Turkey." *American Ethnologist: The Journal of American Ethnological Society* 31 (2004): 374–91.

Pancaroğlu, Oya. "Serving Wisdom: Contents of Samanid Epigraphic Pottery." In *Studies in Islamic and Later Indian Art from the Arthur M. Sackler Museum, Harvard University Art Museums*, 64–65. Cambridge, Mass.: Harvard University Art Museums, 2002.

Peirce, Charles Sanders. *The Collected Papers of Charles Sanders Peirce*. Vols. 1–6. Cambridge, Mass.: Harvard University Press, 1966.

Peled, M. "Annals of Doom: Palestinian Literature 1917–1948." *Arabica* 29 (1982): 143–83.

Pereira, José. *Islamic Sacred Architecture: A Stylistic History*. New Delhi: Books and Books, 1994.

Peters, John Durham. "Witnessing." *Media, Culture and Society* 23, no. 6 (2001): 703–23.

Pinney, Christopher. "Things Happen: Or, From Which Moment Does That Object Come?" In *Materiality*, edited by Daniel Miller, 256–72. Durham, N.C.: Duke University Press, 1995.

Popper, Karl. "Against Television." http://www.mediamente.rai.it/mmold/ english/bibliote/intervis/p/popper.htm.

Porter, Venetia. *Word into Art: Artists of the Modern Middle East*. London: British Museum Press, 2006.

Poster, Mark. "Visual Studies as Media Studies." *Journal of Visual Culture* 1, no. 1 (2002): 67–70.

Poulton, Hugh. *Top Hat, Grey Wolf, and Crescent: Turkish Nationalism and the Turkish Republic.* New York: New York University Press, 1997.

Préaud, Tamara, Derek E. Ostergard, Bard Graduate Center for Studies in the Decorative Arts, et al. *The Sèvres Porcelain Manufactory: Alexandre Brogniart and the Triumph of Art and Industry, 1800–1847.* New Haven, Conn.: Yale University Press, 1997.

Price, Monroe, Douglas Griffin, and Ibrahim al-Marashi, eds. *Toward an Understanding of Media Policy and Media Systems in Iraq.* Center for Global Communication Studies Occasional Paper no. 1. Annenberg School for Communication, University of Pennsylvania, May 2007.

"Q&A: Depicting the Prophet Muhammad." Published by the British Broadcasting Corporation on February 2, 2006. http://news.bbc.co.uk/2/hi/middle_east/4674864.stm.

al-Qaradawi, Yusuf. *Al-Islam wal-Fann.* Beirut: Mu'assasat al-Risala, 2001.

Qutb, Muhammad. *Manhaj al-Fann al-Islami.* Beirut: Dar al-Sharuq, 1981.

Rahimiyan, Mohammad Hasan. *Dar harim-e laleha: moruri bar resalat-e Bonyad-e shahid dar nezam-e eslami.* Tehran: Nashr-e Shahed, 1380/2001.

al-Rasheed, Madawi. "The Shi'a of Saudi Arabia: A Minority in Search of Cultural Authenticity." *British Journal of Middle Eastern Studies* 25, no. 1 (1998): 121–38.

Reid, Donald Malcolm. "The Postage Stamp: A Window on Saddam Hussein's Iraq." *The Middle East Journal* 47 (1993): 77–89.

Reinhart, Kevin. "Impurity/No Danger." *History of Religions* 30, no. 1 (1991): 1–24.

Reuters. "World Briefing: Middle East. Saudi Arabia: Clean TV Shows, or Else." *New York Times,* September 13, 2009, A8.

Richard, Jean. "Les transformations de l'image de Saladin dans les sources occidentales." *Revue des Mondes Musulman et de la Méditerranée* 89–90 (2000): 177–87.

Ricoeur, Paul. *A Ricoeur Reader: Reflection and Imagination.* Edited by Mario J. Valdés. Toronto: University of Toronto Press, 1991.

———. *The Rule of Metaphor: Multi-Disciplinary Studies of the Creation of Meaning in Language.* Translated by Robert Czerny. Toronto: University of Toronto, 1977.

———. *The Symbolism of Evil.* Translated by Emerson Buchanan. Boston: Beacon, 1967.

Rida, Rashid. "Dhikra Salah al-Din wa-ma'rakat Hattin." *Manar* 32 (September 1932): 593–606.

———. *Fatawa al-imam Muhammad Rashid Rida.* Collected and edited by Salah al-Din al-Munajjid and Yusuf Khuri. Beirut: Dar al-Kitab al-Jadid, 1970.

Riley-Smith, Jonathan. "Islam and the Crusades in History and Imagination, 8 November 1898–11 September 2001." *Crusades* 2 (2003): 151–67.

Robb, Brian J. *Ridley Scott.* Harperden: Pocket Essentials, 2005.

Roumani, Rhonda. "A Modern Saladin Speaks His Mind." *Beliefnet* 5 (2005). http://www.beliefnet.com/Entertainment/Movies/2005/05/A-Modern-Saladin-Speaks-His-Mind.aspx.

Roy, Olivier. "İslâmcı Hareketin Sıradanlaşması." In *Modern Türkiye'de Siyasi Düşünce: 6, İslamcılık,* edited by Ahmet Çiğdem, 927–35. Istanbul: İletişim, 2004.

Sabev, Orlin. *İbrahim Müteferrika ya da İlk Osmanlı Matbaa Serüveni (1726–1746).* Istanbul: Yeditepe Yayınevi, 2006.

Sadeghi, Arash. "Infrastructure: Institute for the Intellectual Development of Children and Young Adults (Kanoon)." *Bidoun: Art and Culture from the Middle East: Kids* (Winter 2009): 34–39.

Sakr, Naomi. *Arab Television Today.* London: I. B. Tauris, 2007.

Saktanber, Ayşe. "Formation of a Middle Class Ethos and its Quotidian: Revitalizing Islam in Urban Turkey." In *Space, Culture and Power: New Identities in Globalizing Cities,* edited by A. Öncü and P. Weyland, 140–56. London: Zed Books, 1997.

———. "Muslim Identity in Children's Picture-Books." In *Islam in Modern Turkey: Religion, Politics and Literature in a Secular State,* edited by R. Tapper, 171–88. London: I. B. Tauris, 1991.

Salamandra, Christa. "Creative Compromise: Syrian Television Makers between Secularism and Islamism." *Contemporary Islam* 2, no. 3 (2008): 177–89.

———. "Moustache Hairs Lost: Ramadan Television Serials and the Construction of Identity in Damascus, Syria." *Visual Anthropology* 10, no. 2–4 (1998): 227–46.

———. *A New Old Damascus: Authenticity and Distinction in Urban Syria.* Bloomington: Indiana University Press, 2004.

———. "Television and the Ethnographic Endeavor: The Case of Syrian Drama." *Transnational Broadcasting Studies* 14 (Spring/Summer 2005). http://www.tbsjournal.com/Archives/ Spring05/abstractsalamandra.html, or http://www.arabmediasociety.com/ topics/ index.php?tarticle=83.

Sander, Ake. "Images of the Child and Childhood in Religion." In *Images of Childhood,* edited by Philip Hwang, Michael E. Lamb, and Irving E. Sigel, 14–25. Mahwah, N.J.: Lawrence Erlbaum Associates, 1996.

Sarı, Nihan. "Çocuk Kitapları İllüstrasyonları Üzerine Bir Araştırma ve Bir Örnekleme." M.A. thesis, Eylül Üniversitesi Eğitim Bilimleri Enstitüsü, 2006.

Satan, Ali. *Halifeliğin Kaldırılması.* Istanbul: Gökkubbe Yayınevi, 2008.

"Saudis Become Refugees Cinematically as They Celebrate *Keif al-Hal* as the First Popular Release Movie." *Al-Riyadh,* November 12, 2006. [Arabic].

Savage-Smith, Emilie. "Memory and Maps." In *Culture and Memory in Medieval Islam: Essays in Honor of Wilfred Madelung,* edited by Farhad Daftari and Jesef W. Meri, 109–27. London: I. B. Tauris, 2003.

al-Sayyid, Radwan. "Islamic Movements and Authenticity: Barriers to Development." In *Cosmopolitanism, Identity and Authenticity in the Middle East,* edited by Roel Meijer, 103–14. London: Curzon, 1999.

Schubel, Vernon James. *Religious Performance in Contemporary Islam: Shi'i Devotional Rituals in South Asia.* Columbia: University of South Carolina Press, 1993.

Schultze, Reinhard. "Mass Culture and Islamic Cultural Production in the 19th Century." In *Mass Culture and Popular Culture, and Social Life in the Middle East,* edited by Georg Stauth and Sami Zubaida, 189–222. Boulder, Colo.: Westview, 1987.

Schumann, Christoph, ed. *Nationalism and Liberal Thought in the Arab East: Ideology and Practice.* London: Routledge, 2010.

Scott, David, and Keyan G. Tomaselli. "Cultural Icons." In *Cultural Icons,* edited by David Scott and Keyan G. Tomaselli, 7–24. Walnut Creek, Calif.: Left Coast Press, 2009.

Séguy, Marie-Rose. *The Miraculous Journey of Mahomet: Miraj Nameh, BN, Paris Sup Turc 190.* Translated by Richard Pevear. New York: G. Braziller, 1977.

"Selçuk Demirel'le bir Konuşma." *Vatan,* April 20, 2008, A1.

Selçuk, Turhan. "Söz Çizginin." *Cumhuriyet,* September 27, 2008, 6.

"Semiramis Aydınlık'ı Yitirdik." *Mizah Haber,* March 30, 2008. http://mizahhaber .blogspot.com/2008_03_01_archive.html.

Sever, Sedat. *II. Ulusal Çocuk ve Gençlik Edebiyatı Sempozyumu: Gelişmeler, Sorunlar ve Çözüm Önerileri.* 4–6 Ekim 2006. Ankara: Ankara Üniversitesi Eğitim Bilimleri Fakültesi, 2007.

Shabib, Nabil. "Bab al-hara . . . wa abwab al-ibda'." *Islamonline.net,* October 21, 2007. http://www.islamonline.net/servlet/Satellite?c=ArticleA_C&page name=Zone-Arabic ArtCulture%2FACALayout&cid=1190886520200 (site discontinued).

Shafik, Viola. *Arab Cinema: History and Cultural Identity.* Cairo: American University in Cairo Press, 2003.

———. *Popular Egyptian Cinema: Gender, Class, Nation.* Cairo: American University in Cairo Press, 2007.

———. "Prostitute for a Good Reason: Stars and Morality in Egypt." *Women's Studies International Forum* 24, no. 6 (2001): 711–725.

"Sharikat Jawzy Film." *Al-Ikhwan al-Muslimun.* September 28, 1946, 11.

Sharpe, Matthew. "The Aesthetics of Ideology, or 'The Critique of Ideological Judgment' in Eagleton and Žižek." *Political Theory* 34, no. 1 (2006): 95–120.

al-Shaykh, Abdul-Rahim. "Historiographies of Laughter—Poetics of Deformation in Palestinian Political Cartoon." *Third Text* 21, no. 1 (2007): 65–78.

Shehadi, Fadlou. *Philosophies of Music in Medieval Islam.* Leiden: E. J. Brill, 1995.

Shulevitz, Uri. *Writing with Pictures: How to Write and Illustrate Children's Books.* New York: Watson-Guptill Publications, 1985.

Silberman, N. A. *Between Past and Present: Archaeology, Ideology, and Nationalism in the Modern Middle East.* New York: Henry Holt and Company, 2004.

"Sızıntı Celebrates 30th Year as 'Magazine of Love and Tolerance.'" *Sunday's Zaman,* January 4, 2009.

Skovgaard-Petersen, Jakob, and Hans Chr. Korsholm Nielsen, eds. *Middle Eastern Cities 1900-1950: Public Places and Public Spheres in Transformation*. Aarhus: Aarhus University Press, 2001.

Slackman, Michael. "Damascus Journal: For Ramadan Viewing, a TV Drama against Extremism." *New York Times*, July 6, 2006. http://www.nytimes .com/2006/07/06/world/middleeast/06syria.html?_r=1&scp=1&sq= damascus%20journal%20for%20ramadan%20viewing&st=cse&oref=slogin.

Sontag, Susan. "The Image-World." In Susan Sontag, *A Susan Sontag Reader*, 349-67. New York: Farrar, Straus, Giroux, 1982.

Soucek, Priscilla P. "Nizami on Painters and Painting." In *Islamic Art in the Metropolitan Museum of Art*, edited by Richard Ettinghausen, 9-21. New York: Metropolitan Museum of Art, 1972.

Srathern, Marilyn. "Artefacts of History: Events and the Interpretation of Images." In *Culture and History in the Pacific*, edited by Jukka Siikala, 25-44. Helsinki: Finnish Anthropological Society, 1990.

Sreberny-Mohammadi, Annabelle, and Ali Mohammadi. *Small Media, Big Revolution: Communication, Culture, and the Iranian Revolution*.Minneapolis: University of Minnesota Press, 1994.

"Star Academy 'Weapon of Mass Destruction,'" *Middle East Online*, April 3, 2004. http://www.middle-east-online.com/english/?id=9498=9498&format.

Starret, Gregory, "The Margins of Print: Children's Religious Literature in Egypt." *Journal of the Royal Anthropological Institute* 2, no. 1 (1996): 117-39.

Stein, Rebecca L., and Ted Swedenburg. "Popular Culture, Transnationality, and Radical History." In *Palestine, Israel, and the Politics of Popular Culture*, edited by Rebecca L. Stein and Ted Swedenburg, 1-23. Durham, N.C.: Duke University Press, 2005.

Sturken, Marita, and Lisa Cartwright. *Practices of Looking: An Introduction to Visual Culture*. New York: Oxford University Press, 2001.

Swedenburg, Ted. *Memories of Revolt: The 1936-1939 Rebellion and the Palestinian National Past*. Fayetteville: University of Arkansas Press, 2003.

Takim, Liyakat. "From *Bid'a* to *Sunna*: The *Wilaya* of 'Ali in the Shi'i *Adhan*." *Journal of the American Oriental Society* 120, no. 2 (2000): 166-77.

Talima, 'Isam. *Hasan al-Banna' wa-tajribat al-fann*. Cairo: Maktabat Wahba, 2008.

Tartoussieh, Karim. "Pious Stardom: Cinema and the Islamic Revival in Egypt." *Arab Studies Journal* 15, no. 1 (2007): 30-43.

Taş, Hakkı, and Meral Uğur. "Roads 'Drawn' to Modernity: Religion and Secularism in Contemporary Turkey." *PS Online* (2007): 311-14. http://www .apsanet.org.

Taylor, Charles. *Modern Social Imaginaries*. Durham, N.C.: Duke University Press, 2004.

——. *A Secular Age*. Cambridge, Mass.: Harvard University Press, 2007.

Thompson, Elizabeth. *Colonial Citizens: Paternal Privilege, Republican Rights, and Gender in French Syria and Lebanon.* New York: Columbia University Press, 2000.

——. "Politics by Other Screens." *Arab Media and Society* 7 (2009). http://www .arabmediasociety.com/index.php?article=699&p=0.

Tietze, Andreas. *The Turkish Shadow Theater and the Puppet Collection of the L. A. Mayer Memorial Foundation.* Berlin: Gebr. Mann Verlag, 1977.

al-Tirmidhi. *Shamaa-il Tirmidhi: Characteristics of the Holy Prophet Muhammad.* Translated by Muhammad bin 'Abdurrahmaan Ebrahim. Karachi: Idaratul Quran, 1993.

Toprak, Binnaz. "Islamist Intellectuals of the 1980s in Turkey." *Current Turkish Thought,* no. 62 (1987): 2–19.

Tripp, Charles. *A History of Iraq.* Cambridge: Cambridge University Press, 2000.

Tuğal, Cihan. *Passive Revolution: Absorbing the Islamic Challenge to Capitalism.* Stanford, Calif.: Stanford University Press, 2009.

Tuğrul, Belma, and Nihan Feyman. "Okul Öncesi Çocukları için Hazırlanmış Resimli Öykü Kitaplarında kullanılan Temalar." In *II. Ulusal Çocuk ve Gençlik Edebiyatı Sempozyumu: Gelişmeler, Sorunlar ve Çözüm Önerileri,* 4–6 Ekim 2006, edited by Sedat Sever, 387–92. Ankara: Ankara Üniversitesi Eğitim Bilimleri Fakültesi, 2007.

Tunç, Aslı. "Pushing the Limits of Tolerance: Functions of Political Cartoonists in the Democratization Process: The Case of Turkey." *International Journal for Communication Studies* 64 (2002): 47–62. http://gaz.sagepub.com.

"Türban Motifli Türk Bayrağı Le Monde'da." April 19, 2008. http://www.milliyet .com.tr/default.aspx?aType=HaberDetay&ArticleID=518744; http://kursat cosgun.blogcu.com/desen_14169171.html.

"Türkiye I. Dini Yayınlar Kongresi Sonuç Bildirgesi." November 4, 2003. http://www.diyanet.gov.tr/yayin/sicerik.asp?id=1241&sorgu=13.

Tusi, Khajih Nassir al-din. *Akhlaq-i Naseri.* Edited by Mojtaba Minavi and Alireza Heidari. Tehran: Kharazmi Publishers, 1369/1990.

United Nations Development Programme, Arab Fund for Economic and Social Development. *The Arab Human Development Report 2003: Building a Knowledge Society.* New York: United Nations Publications, 2003. http://hdr.undp.org/ en/reports/regionalreports/arabstates/name,3204,en.html.

Vahidi, Mohammad. *Ahkam-i Abha: Motahharat va Nijasat.* Qom: Markaz-i intisharat daftar-i tablighat-i islami hoziye islmiy-i Qom, 1990.

VanderLippe, John. "Racism and the Making of American Foreign Policy: The'Terrible Turk' as Icon and Metaphor." In *The Global Color Line: Racial and Ethnic Inequality and Struggle from a Global Perspective,* edited by Pınar Batur-VanderLippe and Joe Feagin, 47–63. Stamford, Conn.: JAI Press, 1999.

Van Nieuwkerk, Karin. "Creating an Islamic Cultural Sphere: Contested Notions of Art, Leisure and Entertainment. An Introduction." *Contemporary Islam* 2, no. 3 (2008), 169–76.

———. "From Repentance to Pious Performance." *ISIM Review* 20 (Autumn 2007): 54–55.

———. "'Repentant' Artists in Egypt: Debating Gender, Performing Arts and Religion." *Contemporary Islam* 2 (2008): 169–96.

———. *"A Trade Like Any Other": Female Singers and Dancers in Egypt.* Cairo: American University in Cairo Press, 1996.

Varzi, Roxanne. *Warring Souls: Youth, Media, and Martyrdom in Post-Revolution Iran.* Durham, N.C.: Duke University Press, 2006.

Vattimo, Giannni. *The Transparent Society.* Baltimore: Johns Hopkins University Press, 1992.

Wallerstein, Immanuel. "The National and the Universal: Can There Be Such a Thing as World Culture?" In *Culture, Globalization, and the World System: Contemporary Conditions for the Representation of Identity,* edited by Anthony D. King, 91–105. Minneapolis: University of Minnesota Press, 1997.

Wannous, Sa'dallah, and Nadim Mohammed. "Syria." Translated by Maha Chehade and Tony Chehade. In *World Encyclopedia of Contemporary Theatre, vol. 4: The Arab World,* edited by Ghassan Maleh, 234–49. London: Routledge, 1999.

Watenpaugh, Keith David. *Being Modern in the Middle East.* Princeton, N.J.: Princeton University Press, 2006.

Weber, Max. *From Max Weber: Essays in Sociology.* Edited by H. H. Gerth and C. W. Mills. London: Routledge and Kegan Paul, 1974.

Weber, Stefan. *Damascus: Ottoman Modernity and Urban Transformation (1808–1918).* Proceedings of the Danish Institute in Damascus 5, 2 vols. Aarhus: Aarhus University Press, 2009.

———. "Ottoman Damascus of the 19th Century, Artistic and Urban Development as an Expression of Changing Times." In *Art Turc / Turkish Art, 10th International Congress of Turkish Art, Genève-Geneva 17–23 September 1995,* edited by François Deroche, 731–40. Geneva: Fondation Max Van Berchem, 1999.

———. "Zeugnisse kulturellen Wandels. Stadt, Architektur und Gesellschaft des osmanischen Damaskus im 19. und frühen 20. Jahrhundert." *Electronic Journal for Oriental Studies* 9, no. 1 (2006): I–X, 1–1014.

Wedeen, Lisa. *Ambiguities of Domination: Politics, Rhetoric and Symbols in Contemporary Syria.* Chicago: University of Chicago Press, 1999.

———. *Peripheral Visions: Publics, Power, and Performance in Yemen.* Chicago: University of Chicago Press, 2008.

Weyman, George. "Empowering Youth or Reshaping Compliance? Star Magazine, Symbolic Production, and Competing Visions of Shabab in Syria." M.Phil. thesis, Oxford University, 2006.

White, Jenny. *Islamist Mobilization in Turkey: A Study in Vernacular Politics.* Seattle: University of Washington Press, 2002.

Williams, Raymond. *Television and Cultural Form.* New York: Schocken Books, 1975.

Winegar, Jessica. *Creative Reckonings: The Politics of Art and Culture in Contemporary Egypt.* Stanford, Calif.: Stanford University Press, 2006.

——. "The Humanity Game: Art, Islam, and the War on Terror." *Anthropological Quarterly* 81, no. 3 (2008): 651–81.

——. "Purposeful Art between Television Preachers and the State." *ISIM Review* 22 (Autumn 2008): 28–29.

Wolff, Janet. "The Global and the Specific: Reconciling Conflicting Theories of Culture." In *Culture, Globalization, and the World System: Contemporary Conditions for the Representation of Identity,* edited by Anthony D. King, 161–73. Minneapolis: University of Minnesota Press, 1997.

Woods, Kevin M. *The Iraqi Perspectives Report: Saddam's Senior Leadership in Operation Freedom.* Minneapolis: U.S. Naval Institute Press, 2006.

Worth, Robert F. "Arab TV Tests Societies' Limits with Depictions of Wine, Sex and Equality." *New York Times,* September 27, 2008, A6.

Yaqub, Nadia. "Gendering the Palestinian Political Cartoon." *Middle East Journal of Culture and Communication* 2 (2009): 187–213.

Yavuz, M. Hakan. *Islamic Political Identity in Turkey.* New York: Oxford University Press, 2003.

Yavuz, M. Hakan, and John L. Esposito, eds. *Turkish Islam and the Secular State: The ŽižekGülen Movement.* Syracuse, N.Y.: Syracuse University Press, 2003.

Yıldız, Zafer. "Diyanet Çocuk Dergisi'nin Din Eğitimi Açısından Değerlendirmesi." M.A. thesis, Ankara Üniversitesi, 2004.

Yılmaz, Hakan, and Emine Dolmacı. "Ve yayıncılar çocuğu keşfetti." *Zaman,* May 6, 2006.

Zayani, Mohamed, ed. *The al-Jazeera Phenomenon: Critical Perspectives on New Arab Media.* Boulder, Colo.: Paradigm Publishers, 2005.

Zaydan, Jurji. *Salah al-Din Ayyubi.* Beirut: Dar al-Jil, n.d.

Zirinski, Michael. "A Presbyterian Vocation to Reform Gender Relations in Iran: The Career of Annie Stocking Boyce." In *Women, Religion, and Culture in Iran,* edited by Sarah Ansari and Vanessa Martin, 51–56. London: Curzon Press, 2002.

Zitzewitz, Karin. "The Secular Icon: Secularist Practice and Indian Visual Culture." *Visual Anthropology Review* 24, no. 1 (2008): 12–28.

Žižek, Slavoj. "Introduction: The Spectre of Ideology." In *Mapping Ideologies,* edited by Slavoj Žižek, 3–7. London: Verso, 1994.

——. *Tarrying with the Negative.* Durham, N.C.: Duke University Press, 1993.

Zürcher, Erik J. *Turkey: A Modern History.* London: I. B. Tauris, 1993.

UMUT AZAK is Assistant Professor in the Department of International Relations, Okan University, Istanbul. Her research focuses on the transformation of secularism and Islamism in Turkey. She is the author of *Islam and Secularism in Turkey: Kemalism, Religion and the Nation State*.

PINAR BATUR is Professor of Sociology and Director of Environmental Studies at Vassar College. Her research interests include global racism, anti-racist social movements, urban environment and movements, the relationship between knowledge and policy-making, and the meaning of risk in the twenty-first century. Her recent work includes *The Global Color Line*, edited with Joe Feagin, and *White Racism*, co-authored with Joe Feagin and Hernan Vera.

YASEMIN GENCER is a Ph.D. candidate in the Department of Art History at Indiana University, Bloomington. She specializes in Ottoman and early Republican print culture. She is the author of "İbrahim Müteferrika and the Age of the Printed Manuscript," in *The Islamic Manuscript Tradition: Ten Centuries of Book Arts in Indiana University Collections,* ed. Christiane Gruber. She is presently conducting research for her dissertation, entitled "Delivering the Satirical Punch: Reform, Secularism, and Nationalism in Cartoons of the Early Republican Period in Turkey (1923–1928)."

CHRISTIANE GRUBER is Associate Professor of Islamic Art at the University of Michigan, Ann Arbor. Her fields of research include Islamic book arts, paintings of the Prophet Muhammad, ascension tales and images, and Iranian visual culture of the post-revolutionary period. She is the author of *The Timurid Book of Ascension (Mi'rajnama): A Study of Text and Image in a Pan-Asian Context* (2008) and *The Ilkhanid Book of Ascension: A Persian-Sunni Devotional Tale* (2010). She also has edited several volumes on Islamic books arts, ascension tales and images, and Islamic and cross-cultural visual culture.

SUNE HAUGBOLLE is Associate Professor in Global Studies and Sociology at the Department for Society and Globalization at Roskilde University. His work deals with social memory, cultural production, and ideology in the modern Middle East. He is the author of *War and Memory in Lebanon,* and he co-edited the volume *The Politics of Violence, Truth and Reconciliation in the Arab Middle East* (2009). He is currently leading a research project about secularism and ideology in the Middle East.

STEFAN HEIDEMANN is Professor of Islamic Studies at Hamburg University and former Curator of Islamic Art at the Metropolitan Museum of Art. He is the author of *Die Renaissance der Städte in Nordsyrien und Nordmesopotamien* (2002), a study of early Islamic cities and settlement patterns. His other interests include social, economic, and cultural transformations in the Middle Islamic Period, as well as cultural memory in modern visual culture. He has worked in several excavations in Syria and the wider Middle East.

PAMELA KARIMI is Assistant Professor of Art History at the University of Massachusetts, Dartmouth. She is the author of *Domesticity and Consumer Culture in Iran: Interior Revolutions of the Modern Era* (2013), as well as co-editor of a special issue, "The Image of the Child and Childhood in Modern Muslim Contexts," for the journal *Comparative Studies of South Asia, Africa, and the Middle East* (2013).

MARWAN KRAIDY is Professor of Global Communication at the Annenberg School for Communication at the University of Pennsylvania and the Edward Said Chair of American Studies at the American University of Beirut. His research focuses on contemporary media, culture, and politics in the Arab world. His books include *Reality Television and Arab Politics: Contention in Public Life; Arab Television Industries* (with J. Khalil); and *Hybridity, or, The Cultural Logic of Globalization*. He also co-edited *Global Media Studies: Ethnographic Perspectives* and *The Politics of Reality Television: Global Perspectives*.

PATRICIA KUBALA is a doctoral candidate in the Department of Anthropology, University of California, Berkeley. She is the author of several articles on satellite television, music, and religion in the Arab world, which have appeared in *Arab Media and Society* and *ISIM Review*. Her current research project explores visual aesthetics and modern Islamic reform movements in Egypt.

IBRAHIM AL-MARASHI is Assistant Professor of Middle East History at California State University, San Marcos. His primary research focuses on the history of the Iraqi state. He is the co-author of *Iraq's Armed Forces: An Analytical History*. He also has written several articles on Ba'athist-era security services in Iraq and political factions that emerged after the 2003 Iraq War.

ULRICH MARZOLPH is Extraordinary Professor of Islamic Studies at the Georg August-University and a senior member of the editorial board of the Enzyklopädie des Märchens in Göttingen, Germany. His particular field of interest is the narrative culture of the Muslim world. He has published numerous books and articles on folktales and popular literature, particularly in Arabic, Persian, and Turkish. In the field of Muslim visual culture, he has a strong interest in nineteenth-century Persian lithographed books as well as graffiti and murals in contemporary Iran.

CHRISTA SALAMANDRA is Visiting Professor at the Center for Middle Eastern Studies, Lund University, Sweden, and Associate Professor of Anthropology at Lehman College and the Graduate Center, the City University of New York. Her research focuses on visual, mediated, and urban culture in the Middle East. She is the author of *A New Old Damascus: Authenticity and Distinction in Urban Syria*, and numerous articles on Arab media. Her current book project explores the cultural politics of Arab television drama production in the satellite era.

ÖZLEM SAVAŞ is Assistant Professor in the Department of Communication and Design at Bilkent University, Ankara. Her research interests include visual culture, taste, and aesthetic and politics of the everyday. She has published on Turkish diasporic material and visual cultures in Vienna. Her current project focuses on lifestyle media and the politics of taste in Turkey.

JOHN VANDERLIPPE is Associate Professor of History and Associate Dean of Faculty and Curriculum at The New School for Social Research. His research interests include the role of stereotypes in international relations, American relations with the Middle East, and democracy and authoritarianism in the Middle East. His recent work includes *The Politics of Turkish Democracy: İsmet İnönü and the Formation of the Multi-Party System, 1938-1950*. He also served as the editor of the *Middle East Studies Association Bulletin* (2002-2007).

Page numbers in italics indicate illustrations.

and post-Marxists, 255. *See also* secularism, Arab

Arab Radio and Television (ART) network, 86

Arabic language, 11, 36, 37, 154; biographies of Saladin in, 63; influence on Ottoman Turkish, 196; media in, 262; satellite television channels in, 275, 283

Arabic language, Turkish alphabet reform and, 212n38, 212n41; Arabic alphabet as slow camel, 202–204, *203*, 205, 213n47; Mustafa Kemal's victory over Arabic letters, 196–97, *198*, 199, 211n34

Arabic Thought in the Liberal Age, 1798–1939 (Hourani), 277

Arafat, Yassir, 244, 250, 255, 258n60

architecture, xvi, 145

Ariès, Philippe, 129

Arif, Mahmud, 213n47

art history, xvii–xx, 256

Arvasi, M. Sacid, 115

al-Asad, Bashar, 72, 74, 79n77, 80n88

al-Asad, Hafiz, 67–69, 74, 79n73, 79n76

Asad, Talal, xx, 84, 90

Asharq al-Awsat (newspaper), 290n26

Al-'Askariyya shrine, bombing of (2006), 148, 151

Assmann, Aleida, 254

Assmann, Jan, 57

Association of Muslim Scholars (Iraq), 148

Atacan, Fulya, 120

Atatürk, Mustafa Kemal, 207, 213n47, 213n56; as iconic image of Turkish nationalism, 221; as national savior, 192, 201

Atatürk, Mustafa Kemal, cartoon depictions of, 204–205; alphabet reform and, 197, *198*, 199, 211nn34–35, 212n39; disposal of old mentalities and laws, 193, *194*, 195; "Republican Machine" crushing conservative reaction, *188*, 189–90, 191; steamroller of modernization, 199, *200*, 201; sun linked to, 197, *198*, 212n37

authenticity, xiii, 12, 163, 282; debate on visual media in Arab societies and, 275, 278; Islamic talk shows and, xiv; revivalist Islam associated with, 265–66; witnessing the moment of, 286–87

authorship, xv

Avini, Mortaza, 170, *171*, 172, *173*

al-'Awadhi, Muhammad, 280–81

Aydın, Ertan, 227

Azak, Umut, 160

Al-Azhar University (Cairo), 83, 85

al-Azm, Sadiq, 237, 238

Ba'ath Party, in Iraq, 64, 144, 145, 147, 157, 232

Ba'ath Party, in Syria, 58, 232, 271

Bahar al-Anvar [Oceans of Light] (Majlesi II), 37

Bahayi, Sheykh, 37

Bahonar, Mohammad Javad, 169

Bahrain, movie theaters in, 290n11

al-Bahth 'an Salah al-Din (Syrian television series), 81n92

Bakhtin, Mikhail, 284

Bal, Mieke, xvii, xxv, xxvin5

Balkan Wars (1912–1913), 62

Balkhi School, 55n41

Bamiyan Buddhas, Taliban destruction of, 96

Baniasadi, Muhammad 'Ali, 27

al-Banna', Hasan, 93, 100n27

banners, xvi, xxi, 156

Barakat, 'Abd Allah, 87–88, 89

Baram, Amazia, 145

Barthes, Roland, xxiv, 147, 153–54, 160, 162, 213n52; on signification, 156, 157; on "trick effects," 155; on visual language of advertisements, 205

Al-Basa'ir [Insights] (newspaper), 148

Batur, Pinar, xxiv, 254

Baybars, Sultan, 59, 61, 73, 75n16, 77n34

Beautiful Maidens, The [al-Hur al-'Ayn] (Anzour, television series), 266–67

Beheshti, Ayatollah Mohammad, 169

Beirut, city of, 233, 237; al-Ali in, 232, 235, 243; Israeli invasion (1982), 247, 258n55

Belge, Murat, 106

"Bence Tam Ağlama Mevsimi" [I think, It Is Just the Time for Crying] (Gülen), 114–15

Bengio, Ofra, 145

Benjamin, Walter, xviii

Bennis, Muhammad, 277

Bhabha, Homi, 12

Bilal, Mazen, 272

billboards, ix

Bin Baz, 'Abdulaziz, 279

Bin Laden, Osama, 267

Birdirbir magazine, 130

al-Biyali, Ahmad, 63

Bize Nasıl Kıydınız? [How Did You Harm Us?] (film), 120

Blackhawk Down (film), 152–53, 156

Bollywood, 284

Bonyad-e shahid (Foundation of Martyrs), 168, 170, 174, 177

Book of Ascension [*Mi'rajnama*] (Séguy), 6

Booth, Marilyn, 255

Bouquet of Flowers from the Ascent, A [*Dast-i Gul-i az 'Uruj*] (Rahmati). *See* Muhammad, Prophet, mural painting of (Rahmati)

Bourdieu, Pierre, xiii

bourgeoisie, Arab, 233

Bourriaud, Nicholas, 13

Bremer, Paul, 150

bricolage, xvi, 12

Browers, Michaelle L., 235

Brummett, Palmira, 191

Buddhism, 10–11, 12

Burak, Ratıp Tarık, 227

Buraq (Muhammad's flying steed), 3, *7*, *27*

Bureau of Beautification (Tehran), 5, 17, 167

Burgat, François, 256

Bush, George W., 226

Cairo, city of, 86, 98n9, 237

caliphate, abolition of, 190, 206, 208n7

Campo, Juan Eduardo, 44–45

capitalism, 120, 134, 135–36, 141n45, 239, 240

cartoons, Arab/Palestinian. *See* al-Ali, Naji; Handhala (cartoon character)

cartoons, Turkish, xxi, *188*, 189–91, 215–16, 228–29, 254; advocacy of "pushing out" Islam, 205–207; AKP as icon and metaphor in, 225–27; on alphabet reform, 197, *198*, 199, 202–204, *203*, 211nn34–35, 212n39; cartoonists sentenced to jail, 227–28; censorship and, 191–92; icons and metaphors in nexus of contention, 217–18, *219*, 220; national identity and, 192–93, *194*, 195–96; secularism as modernization, 199, *200*, 201–204, *203*; struggle of imagery in nexus of contention, 220–22; *223*; Turkish Republic and, 204–205

Cartoons That Shook the World, The (Klausen), 31n41

Ceiling of the World [*Saqf al-'Alam*] (Azour, television series), 270

censorship, xv, 96; of Saudi television, 276–77, 280, 282; of Syrian television, 264, 265, 268; of Turkish cartoons, 191–92, 209n12, 209n16

Centlivres, Pierre, 22

Centlivres-Demont, Micheline, 22

Chaghatay Turkish language, 10

Chahine, Youssef, 64

Chehabi, Houshang, 167

Chelkowski, Peter, 166

Child in Palestine, A (al-Ali), 256n5

children's picture books, in Turkey, xxiii, 127–30, 137, 139; Sadrist images in Iraq compared with, 160–61; visual imagery in, 131–32, *133–35*, 134–37, *139*; women depicted in, *134*, 136–37, *138*

Christians/Christianity, 5, 23, 41; in al-Ali cartoons, 239, *241;* in Iraq, 147; in Lebanon, 249; as modern "Crusaders," 65; in Syria, 68, 80n84; as "visual" religion, 92

Dubai, 264, 290n11
Durmuş, Alpaslan, 130

Eagleton, Terry, 235
Eddé, Anne-Marie, 59
Egypt, xiv, 46, 97, 264; British colonial rule in, 93; "clean cinema" in, 236; debate over music videos in, 86–92, 99n18; Islamic art in, 94–95; Islamic reform movement in, 83–84; Islamic Revival era, 85, 94; leftist activists in, 255; liberalism and secularism in, xxi; "normalization" process and, 244; October War (1973) and, 69, 237; Rotana network protested in, 82–83, *83*; Saladin as historical and memory figure in, 58, 59, 61, 75n12; Six Day War (1967) and, 237; Syria united with (1959), 64
Egyptian Radio-Television Union, 94
Ende, Werner, 59
England, 32
English language, 174–75, 283, 284
Enlightenment, European, xi, 238
Enver Pasha, 62
Erdoğan, Necmi, 106
Erdoğan, Recep Tayyip, 215, 224, 226, 227
Erkanlı, Ahmet, 227
"Erkek Adam Ağlar" [Man Cries] (Dağlı), 125n35
Eroğlu, Emine, 130
Ersoy, Mehmet Akif, 109, 124n26
Ertekin, Betül, 133
Eskandari, Iraj, 173
ethnicity, 10, 11, 58
European Union, 217
everyday life, ix, xx, 49, 216, 226; construction of space in, xvi; definition of visual culture and, 289; icons in, 217, 254; ideology and, 235; Islamization and de-Islamization of, 136, 142n53; Sadrist media and, 148

Factory of Martyrs (documentary film, 2008), 177
Fadaian Islam, 32
Fahmide, Hosein, 180–81, *182*
Faisal, King, 288
Farzat, Ali, 258n45
Fatima (daughter of Prophet Muhammad), 174
Fatimid caliphate, 59
Fazilet (Virtue) party (Turkey), 111
femininity, 283, 291n46
feminism, 136
flags, 155–56
Ford, Gerald, 255
Foucault, Michel, xii, xiii
Fractured Modernity (Bennis), 277
Frankfurt School, xiii
Frederick Barbarossa (Frederick I), 61, 77n35
Freitag, Ulrike, 68
French language, 283, 284
Freud, Sigmund, xi
fundamentalism, Islamic, xiv, 265
Al-Furat (The Euphrates) satellite television channel, 148

"Garipler" [Wretched Ones] (Gülen), 118
gaze, gender and, xi, 85, 97n6
Geertz, Clifford, xii
Gelvin, James, 235
Gencer, Yasemin, xxi, 173, 215
gender, 97, 127, 136, 242; gender separation in Saudi Arabia, 277, 289n10; gender studies, ix; Saudi conflict over modernity and, 279, 291n46. See also *ikhtilat* (illicit gender mixing); men; sexuality; women
General Dialogue Conference (Iraq), 148
Genghis Khan, 10
Germany, Turkish emigrants in, 120, 128
Ghaddafi, Muammar, 255
al-Ghaddhami, 'Abdallah, 277, 279
Al-Ghadir radio station, 148

al-Ghazali, Abu Hamid Muhammad, 36, 85

GırGır (Turkish weekly), 227

globalization, 127, 228, 261, 271

Gökçe, Ramiz, cartoons by, *188, 203*

Göle, Nilüfer, 127, 289

Golmohammadi, Firuze, 173–74

Gombrich, Ernst, 24

Gourand, Henri, 62

Grabar, Oleg, 11, 29n13

graffiti, x, xvi

Gramsci, Antonio, xii, xxviin51

gravesites, xvi

Gruber, Christiane, xv, 167, 177

Gül, Abdullah, 224, 226

Gül, Hayrünnisa, 224

Gülen, Fethullah, 108, 109–10, 115; crying in sermons and speeches of, 112, 118; Ottoman Empire as "ideal period" for, 121–22; politicization of suffering and, 121–22; "Tears," 124n34; on tears in Islamic context, 114–15

Gülen movement (Turkey), 108–11, 112, 115, 122, 124n24

Gulf Arab states, 232, 239, 242

Gulf Cooperation Council (GCC), 262–63, 264, 268, 271, 273

Gulf War (1990–1991), 65, 74, 78n58, 79n68, 279

Gürbilek, Nurdan, 106, 107

Guy de Lusignan, 70, *71*

Habermas, Jürgen, 216

Hacivat (shadow puppet character), 193, 195, 210n21

al-Hadatha fi Mizan al-Islam [Modernity in the Scale of Islam] (cassette tape and book), 279

al-Hadi, Imam 'Ali, 151

hadith literature, 36–37, 39, 54n7, 91–92, 168, 265

al-Hakim, Ayatullah Muhammad Baqir, 158

halal (accepted) vs. *haram* (forbidden), 51, *52*, 56n43, 88

Hall, Stuart, xiii, xxiv

Hamas, 251

Hammurabi, 58, 64, 75n8

Hanan 'Atiyya, 87–88

Handhala (cartoon character), xxii, 240, *241, 242*, 250, 252; in Arab popular culture, 237, 257n34; as cultural icon, 233, 245, 249, *252*, 254, 256; introduction of, 236, 243; origins of, 232; as popular fighter, 247, *248*, 251, 258n62; as recurrent presence in al-Ali's cartoons, 242, 243; refugee family of, 255; as symbol of Palestinian identity, 244. *See also* al-Ali, Naji

Hanioğlu, Şükrü, 60

haram. See *halal* (accepted) vs. *haram* (forbidden)

Hasan (grandson of Prophet Muhammad), 174

Hasu, 'Abd al-Nasir, 72–73, 81n96

Hattin, Battle of (1187), 59, 65, 68, 69, 75n13

Al-Hawza Al-Natiqa [The Outspoken Seminary] (newspaper), 150

Hayal [Fantasy/Dream] (journal), 209n18

al-Hayat (newspaper), 290n26

headscarf, Islamic: as iconic image in Turkish political debates, *214*, 215; tertiary struggle over, 222, 224–25; in Turkish children's picture books, 132, *134*, 136, 141n40; as Turkish national flag, 221–22, *223*

hegemony/hegemonic discourses, xiv, xv, xxiv, 227, 229, 252

Heidemann, Stefan, xvii, 173

Herzfeld, Michael, 235, 265

Hillenbrand, Carole, 59, 67, 80n84

Hirsch, Marianne, 249

Hirschkind, Charles, xi, 46, 90, 99n23, 236

historicism, xxv, 61

history, political iconography of, 173

Hizbullah, 57, 152, 155, 249; formation of, 258n55; martyrs of, 169; Sunni/Druze groups in conflict with, 247; war with Israel (2006), 246

Hobsbawm, Eric, 57, 58

"inverse taqqiya," 16

Iqra' (satellite channel), 86, 98n11

al-Iquna [The Icon] (short film), 257n34

Iran, Islamic Republic of, xv, 26, 53, 169, 184; claims of territoriality and ethnicity, 10; Institute for the Intellectual Development of Children and Young Adults, 25, 54n2; "Islamic" identity in, 183; Islamic Revolution (1979), xvi, 32, 166; martyrs in terminology of, 164; Muqtada al-Sadr in, 151; propagandist imagery used by, 32; Revolutionary Guard, 155; Sadrist movement and, 152; Satirical Book of the Year competition, 25; Shi'i-Persian identity, 3, 5, 12, 15; "Year of the Noble Prophet" (2006), 22, 25. See also martyr murals, in Tehran

Iran-Iraq War (1980–1988), xvi, 3, 164; disabled veterans depicted in Tehran murals, 179–80, 181; Iranian martyrs (shahids) of, 16–17, 169; Saddam Hussein's cult of personality and, 145

Iraq, 58, 70, 112, 144–47; Coalition Provisional Authority (CPA), 150, 157; ethno-sectarian balance in, 145; evolution of communication sphere in, 147–49; flag of, 156, 158, 160, 162; Gulf War and, 65; Islamism in, xxii; Kata'ib Salah al-Din (Sunni guerillas), 57, 67; Saddam Hussein as Saladin reincarnated, 64–65, 66, 67, 74, 78n62, 78n65; Saladin as historical figure in, 59

Iraq war (2003), 25, 144, 145–46

Iraqi Islamic Party, 148

Ishraqat Al-Sadr [Splendor of Sadr] (newspaper), 147

Islam, 28, 172; anti-imperialism and, 56n45; archetypes from Islamic history, xvi; as "auditory" religion, 92; Crying Boy images and,
103, 104–105, 111–12; five pillars of, 14; identified with backwardness in Turkish reform period, 190–91, 205–207; ılımlı (moderate) Islam, 226–27; Islamizing strategies in Syrian television, 266–72; personified in Turkish cartoons, 188, 189–90; post-9/11 European views of, 24; public morality and, 90; Ramadan, 261, 264, 266, 268, 269, 271, 272; status of images and, xi, 4, 19; tears and childhood in Islamic imagination, 112, 114. See also Shi'i Islam; Sunni Islam; Wahhabiyya (Salafi Islam)

Islam, political, 103, 105, 117; aestheticization of suffering in, 117–18, 119, 120–23; cartoon images in Turkey and, 215; ethno-nationalism and, xvii; in Iraq, 144; Syrian television drama and, 272; as urban movement, 120–21, 125n54

al-Islam wal-Fann [Islam and Art] (al-Qaradawi), 94

al-Islam wal-Funun al-Jamila [Islam and the Beaux-Arts] ('Imara), 94

Islamic art, xvii–xix, xx, 19, 28; definition of, 11–12, 29n13; Neo-Traditional Iranian art, 13, 16; Qutb's manifesto on, 93

Islamic Front for the Iraqi Resistance, 67

Islamism, xvii, 254; criticized in Syrian television, 270; in Egypt, 84, 96, 97; in Iraq, xxii, 144, 145, 147, 149; "post-Islamism," 139; Saudi-Islamist discourses about television, 275–89; Syrian television drama and, 262, 273; in Turkey, xxii–xxiii, 127–39, 161, 215, 225; Western media reports on, 96. See also Wahhabiyya (Salafi Islam)

Israel, 57, 150, 175, 232; Arab/Palestinian resistance to, 233, 245; Lebanon war with Hizbullah

(2006), 246; October War (1973) and, 69; Sadrist zeal against, 152; Saladin figure and, 75n1, 75n12; Scud missiles fired at by Saddam Hussein, 65; Six Day War (1967) and, xxii, 237; Syria's conflict with, 67, 68, 72. *See also* Zionism

Istiqlal Party, 64

Al-'Itisam [The Guardian] (newspaper), 148

itjihad (independent interpretation), xxi

Jabar, Abdul, 67

Jafer ibn Ali Yahya, 55n18, 56n43

jahiliyya (pre-Islamic era), 284

al-Jazeera news network, 273, 280

Jesus, 117, 239

Jews, 41, 64, 68

Jordan, 237, 244

Joseph, Peter, 81n92

Jubb, Margaret, 59

Jyllands-Posten Danish cartoon controversy (2005–2006), xi, xv, 4, 19, 22, 26; analyses of, 30n41; anti-Muslim sentiments in Europe and, 23–25, 28; Syrian television drama treatment of, 270

Kaaba, in Mecca, 123, 175

Kahil, Mahmoud, 258n45

Kamil, Shaykh Salih, 86

Kanafi, Ghassan, 231–32, 238

Kaplan Grubu (Turkish Islamic organization), 120

Karagöz (journal), 190, 192–93, 206, 208n5, 209n18; censorship and, 192, 209n12, 209n16; Mustafa Kemal in cartoons of, 193, *194, 195*; Treaty of Sèvres cartoon, 210n19

Karagöz (shadow puppet character), 192–93, 195, 210n21

Karimi, Pamela, xv–xvi, 167, 178

Karimi-Hakkak, Ahmad, 38

Karkhanejat-i Montage [Montage Factories] (Tavaniyanfard), 51

al-Kata'ib, 249

Kata'ib Salah al-Din guerrillas (Iraq), 57, 67

Keane, Webb, 234

Keif al-Hal [How Is It Going?] (film, 2006), 290n11

Keikavus ibn Wushmgir, 36

Kelebek [Butterfly] (journal), 190, 199, *200, 206*, 208n4

Kemal, Namik, 77n33

Kemalism, 190, 192, 206; criticism of Kemalist elite, 218; Islamist challenge to, 220–21; politics of clothing/fashion and, 224; six arrows representing principles of, 218, *219*, 220. *See also* secularism, Turkish

Kennedy, Hugh, xi

Kerbaj, Mazen, 247

Keshmirshekan, Hamid, 13

Khaled, Amr, xiv

Khalid, 'Amr, 91–92, 95

Khalife, Marcel, 232

Khalili, Laleh, 249

Khamenei, Ayatollah, 3, 180; portraits of, in martyr murals, *171*, 172, 174, *176*; "Year of the Noble Prophet" declaration of, 25

Khandaniha (magazine), 38, 55n22

al-Khati'a wal-Takfir [Sin and Excommunication] (al-Ghaddhami), 279

Khoda va ekhteraat az didgah elm va qur'an [God's Creation and Manmade Inventions from the Point of View of Science and the Qur'an] (Shirazi), 32

al-Khoei, Grand Ayatullah Abu al-Qasim, 149–50

al-Khoei, Majid, 150

Khomeini, Ayatollah Ruhollah, xvi, 3, 51; chair of, 52, *53; fatwa* against Salman Rushdie, 169; on martyrdom, 168, 177, 180; portraits of, in martyr murals, *171*, 172, 174, *176*, 180–81, *181, 182; Tawzih al-Masa'il* and, 34; *velayat-e faqih* principle of, 166

Khoury, Elias, 246

and, xx, xxi; media and Arab experiences with, 277–80; as revival and reconquest of the past, 13, 29n22; Saudi debate over, 277–80, 282–87; Shi'i, 51; Turkish Republic and, 189, 201–202, 204, 205, 220; Western, 277

modernization, 60, 120, 139; childhood and family life transformed by, 129; secularism as, 199, *200*, 201–204, *203*

Möhring, Hannes, 59

Mojahedin-e khalq, 169

Molavi, Afshin, 37

Momen, Moojan, 37

Mongols/Mongol period, 10, 59

montage, 43, 51, 152, 156

Monument, The (Makiya), 145

monuments, national, xvi, 61, 69

Moses, prophet, 89, 117

"moving equilibrium" (Gramscian concept), xxiv, xxviin51

Mu'allim [The Teacher] (album and video), 95

Mubarak, Hosni, 255

Muhammad, Hind, 290n11

Muhammad, Prophet, 4, 18, 85, 89, 269; 'Ali's relation to, 15–16; bomb-turban digital image of, xv, 24–25; Crying Boy images and, 112; descent from, 156, 159; era of, 265; *hadith* literature and, 36, 54n7, 168; illustrated children's books on life of, 22, 25–26, *27*; images in transmission of teachings of, 91–92; martyrs and, 168, 169; political Islam and, 118; pop culture references to, 95; poster/postcard image of young Muhammad, 22, *23*; Saddam Hussein linked to, 64; *shahada* (proclamation of faith) and, 14–15; suffering of, 117, 120; tears shed by, 114; "Year of the Noble Prophet" (2006) in Iran, 22, 25

Muhammad, Prophet, mural painting of (Rahmati), xv, *2*, 3–5, 26, 28;

"classical" iconographic sources, 6, *7–9*, 10; custom made Persian/Islamic tradition and, 12–18; Danish cartoon controversy and, 22, 23–25, 26; history of representations of the Prophet and, 18–20, *21*, 22–26, *23*

Muhammad, Shaykh, 86

Mujir al-Din, 59

al-Munajjid, Muhammad Saleh, 281–83, 285–86, 287, 288, 290n35

musalsal (Syrian television drama series), xiv, 261, 262–63, 264, 271

music videos, xiv, 82, 96, 97n3; Egyptian debate over, 86–92; "family values," 95; Islamist critiques of, 84–85, 86, 98n6

Muslim Brotherhood, 85, 93, 148, 265, 280

Mustaqbal Movement, 249

Muştu (Turkish publishing company), 128, 131, 137

Nabard-i Millat (newspaper), 32, *33*

Nabulsi, Shakir, 240, 257n28

al-Nahar (newspaper), 244

nahda (revival, renaissance), xxi, 237–38, 252, 255

Najjar, Ramsay, 280–81

naqd (critique), 238

Naqd al-dhati ba'd al-hazima [Self-Critique after the Defeat] (al-Azm), 238

Naqd al-fikr al-dini [Critique of Religious Thought] (al-Azm), 238

Nasir, Jamal 'Abd al- (Gamal Abdel Nasser), 64, 69, 234–35, 238; media campaign against Saudi Arabia, 276; military defeats by Israel, 237

al-Nasir Salah al-Din (film, 1963), 64, 78n47

al-Nasir Salah al-Din al-Ayyubi (Syrian television series), 81n92

Nasrallah (Hizbullah leader), 57, 75n2

Nasser, Gamal Abdel. *See* Nasir, Jamal 'Abd al- (Gamal Abdel Nasser)

Poster, Mark, 289n5
poster arts, x, xxi
postmodern culture, xvi, xxvin24
post-Orientalism, 11
PostProduction (Bourriaud), 13
poststructuralism, xxvin13
prayer, 41, *52*, 268, 277
Progressive Socialist Party (Lebanon), 249
public spheres, xiv, xxi, 136, 216; Arab satellite television and, 246, 265–66; Handhala paraphernalia in, 249; ideological transformation of image use and, xvi; Iranian martyrs reburied in, 172; Islam removed from Turkish public sphere, 190, 201; Islamized, 261; liberalism and secularism in, xxi; representations of Muhammad impermissible in, 19; secular iconography in, 234
Purity and Danger (Douglas), 39

al-Qabbas (newspaper), 244
Qabl an Tuhasabu [Before You Are Judged] (TV talk show), 86, 87, 95
Qabusnama (Keikavus ibn Wushmgir), 36
Qadiyanlu, Mahdi, 178
Al-Qa'ida, 145, 148, 149; 'Askari Mosque bombing and, 151; "paradise" images associated with, 154, 157
Qajar period (Persian empire), 16, 20
al-Qaradawi, Yusuf, 94
Quarter Gate, The [Bab al-Hara] (al-Malla, television series), 270–71
Qubaisiyat piety movement (Syria), 269
al-Quds (newspaper), 244
Qur'an, 34, 35, 89; Arabic script and, 203; cleanliness rules in, 39; ethics literature and, 37; fundamentalism and, 265; *hadith* literature and, 36, 54n7; martyrdom discussed in, 168; on modesty and male-female interactions, 85; Qur'an verses in Al-Qa'ida videos,

157; *Shari'a* and, 36–37; on suffering of prophets, 117; *surahs* (chapters), 43, 44–45, *46*, 85, 168, 211n34; tape-recorded recitations of, 46; Turkish alphabet reform and, 211n34; on value of crying, 114
Qur'an va tabi'at [The Qur'an and Nature] (Shirazi), 32
Qutb, Muhammad, 93–94
Qutb, Sayyid, 93

radio, 93, 147, 148, 152
Rafidayn Satellite Channel, 148
al-Rahbani, Ziad, 232, 249
Rahmati, Faezeh, 5, 6, 15, 17–18, 22
Rahnamun, Mohammad-Ali, 164
al-Ra'is [Big Brother] (Saudi television show), 280
Ramazan Sevinci (Ertekin), *133*
Ramli, Hana, 257n34
al-Rasheed, Madawi, 277, 287
al-Rashid, Harun, 79n77
realism, in Tehran martyr murals, 164, 165, 168, 169, 178
reality, illusion of, xiii
Reawakening Councils, 148
"Rebirth of the Black Fluids" (al-Ali), 239–40, *241*
recitation, qur'anic, xi, 46
Refah (Welfare) Party, 121, 125n55, 135
Reinhart, Kevin, 41
Renegades [al-Mariqun] (Anzour, television series), 266–67
Republican Peoples Party (CHP), six arrows representing principles of, 218, *219*, 220
Reynaud de Chatillon, 59, 70, *71*, 76n20
"Rhetoric of the Image" (Barthes), xxiv
Richard, Jean, 59
Ricoeur, Paul, 216
Rida, Rashid, 64, 92–93, 98n8
Riders to the Sea (Synge), 93
al-Risala [The Message] (film, 1976), 30n34
al-Riyashi, Rim Salah, 5–6, 29n7

sounds, in Muslim-majority societies, xi

space: urban, xvi, xxi; virtual, xxiii, 4

Spotlight [*Buq'at Daw'*] (Hajjo, television series), 271

Star Academy (Saudi TV show), xiv–xv, 275, 278, 286, 289; clerics' sermons against, 281–82, 287, 290nn35–36; as cultural hybrid, 284–85; gender and, 283–84, 288, 291n46; Saudi debate over modernity and, 283–84; Wahhabbi governance undermined by, 287–88

Stein, Rebecca L., 256

subjectivities, Muslim/Islamic, xviii, xx, 28, 84, 96, 127, 235

Sufism, 20, 80n86

suicide bombers, 5–6, 180, 266

Süleyman Paşa, 210n29

Sultan, Huda, 94

Sunna' al-haya [Lifemakers] (satellite television show), 91–92

Sunni Islam, xxii, 144, 152; 'Abbasid caliphate and, 59; *hadith* literature and, 54n7; Iraqi Islamism, 145, 147, 148; *Kata'ib Salah al-Din* guerrillas in Iraq, 57, 67; in Lebanon, 247, 249; *shahada* (proclamation of faith) and, 14

Supreme Islamic Iraqi Council (SIIC), 144, 146, 148, 150, 158, 163n1

Süyür, Murat, 214, 225

Swedenburg, Ted, 256

Synge, John, 93

Syria, 58, 74; architectural modernity in, 60; banknote images of Saladin, 68, 69, 72, 73, 80n89; Crusader rule in, 59; Egypt united with (1959), 64; French Mandate in, 62, 63; monuments in, 60, 76n27, 80n84; October War (1973) and, 69, 79n82; Saladin as historical figure in, 59, 61. *See also* Damascus, city of

Syria, television in, 236, 261, 273; "drama outpouring" (*al-fawra al-dramiyya*), 261; Islamizing strategies and, 266–72; *musalsal* (drama series), xiv, 261, 262–63, 264, 271; politics of production, 263–65; Ramadan broadcasts, 261, 264, 269, 271, 272; Saladin as presence in, 72, 73, 81n92; subnational identity in Syria, 264

Tahrir al-Valsilah, 34

takfir (denunciation of heretics), 261, 270, 273n1

Takim, Liyakat, 16

Takrir-i Sükun Kanunu (Law on Maintenance of Order), 191, 209n12, 209n16

Taliban, 96, 169

Talisman, The (Scott), 60

talk shows, television, xiv, xxviin27, 86, 87, 95

Tanzimat period (Ottoman Empire), 60

taqlid (blind imitation), xxi

Tartoussieh, Karim, 94

tathqif agenda, 236

Tavaniyanfard, Hasan, 51

Tawzih al-Masa'il [Guide to Problems] (Ansari), 54n18

Tawzih al-Masa'il [Guide to Problems] (Shirazi). See *Imam Khomeini's New Risaleh*

al-Tayyib, 'Atif, 245

"Tears" (Gülen), 124n34

technology, x, xxi, 201, 276

television, ix, x, xxii, 89, 99n23; collective memory figures and, 58; in Iraq, 147; national identity and, 58; projection of reality and, xiii, xv; "reality TV," xiv, xxviin27, 275, 278, 284, 286–87, 289; Sadrist movement and, 152; Saudi-Islamist discourses about, 275–89; televisual discourses, xiv. *See also* satellite television; Syria, television in

terrorism, 96, 261, 267, 268–69

textuality, 18

theater, 85, 92–93, 99n23, 262

TİMAŞ (Turkish publishing company), 128, 130, 131
Timurid period (Persian empire), 10, 20
Tishrin War, 72
"To Stop This Pain, Child" (Gülen), 109–10
Transparent Society, The (Vattimo), 275
Trench, Battle of the (627 CE), 168
Tuğal, Cihan, 134, 135–36
Tuğcu, Kemalettin, 106, 123n13
Turkey (Turkish Republic), 103, 216; alphabet reform in, 190, 196–97, *198*, 199, *203*, 211n30; censorship in early Republic, 191–92, 209n12; Directorate of Religious Affairs, 130, 140n23; flag of, 221–22, *223*; Gülen movement, 108–11, 112, 122, 124n24; "Hat Law" (1925), 222, 224; Higher Education Commission (YÖK), 224; Islamism in, xxii–xxiii, 127–39; political parties, 121, 135, 218; reform period, 190, 208n8; religious schools (*medreses*) closed in, 190, 201; War of Independence (1922), 191, 193, 196, 204, 221. *See also* cartoons, Turkish; children's picture books, in Turkey; Crying Boy images
Turkish language, 77n33, 196, 210n29, 212n37
Turkmens, in Iraq, 147
Tusi, Nasir al-Din, 36

Uighur script, 10
Umm Kulthum, 86, 238
umma (Muslim community), 85, 86, 87, 91, 92, 175
Unable to Cry ['*Asiy al-Dam'a*] (Ali, television series), 269–70
United Arab Emirates, 271
United States, 32, 112, 145, 244, 268; Gulf War and, 65, 78n58; invasion and occupation of Iraq (from 2003), 146, 150, 154; Iran-Iraq War and, 169; Muslim World

Outreach program, 96; Sadrist zeal against, 152; Turkish AKP portrayed in association with, 217, 218, 227, *228*; U.S. natural monument image used for Sadrist visual narrative, 155, 157, 162; U.S. symbols depicted in Tehran martyr murals, 167
al-Uns al-Jalil bi-tarikh al-Quds wal-Khalil [The Exalted Friendliness in the History of Jerusalem and Hebron] (Mujir al-Din), 59

VanderLippe, John, xxiv, 254
Vatan [Motherland] (journal), 209n12
Vattimo, Gianni, 275
"Venus" (al-Ali), 240, *243*
video compact discs (VCDs), 152
videocassette recorders, 262
visual culture, xii–xiii, xv, xxiii, 122, 234; art history and, xvii–xix; critics of, xxvn3; expanded borders of, ix–xii, xxvn2, 289; as field of contention, 287–89; "Islamic" as flexible term, 11; of post-revolutionary Iran, 166, 167, 183; Saudi approaches to, 280–82
visuality, ix–xi, xxiii, 289
voyeurism, xi
Vozza, Annaliza, 177

Wahbi, Basma, 86–90, 99n13
Wahbi, Hayfa, 82
Al-Wahda [Unity] (newspaper), 148
Wahhabiyya (Salafi Islam), xiv–xv, 266, 275, 276, 278, 280; attack on reality television, 281–82, 290n35; fear and rejection of outside world by, 285; undermined governance of, 288. *See also* Islamism
Waiting [*al-Intizar*] (Hajjo, television series), 271–72
Wali Diya Pasha, 60
al-Walid, Khalid bin, 272
al-Walid bin Talal, Prince, 82, 290n11
Wannous, Sadallah, 237

al-Washasha, Abu'l -Tayyib
    Muhammad, 36
"way of God" (*fi sabil Allah*), 4, 5
Weber, Max, 117
websites, 148
Wendell, Charles, 100n27
West, the, 57, 84, 131, 141n31; Arab/
    Palestinian resistance to, 233;
    "moderate Islam" supported by,
    226–27; modernity and, 278; pop
    culture, 42; Saladin romanticized
    in, 59–60, 73, 81n96; secular tradi-
    tions, 232; secularism in Turkish
    Republic and, 201, 204; subservi-
    ence to, 239; Turkish emigrants
    in Western Europe, 120
Westergaard, Kurt, 24
Westernization, xxi, 12, 50, 121, 266
Wild Rue, The (Donaldson), 55nn22–23
Wilhelm II, Kaiser, 61, 74, 77n37
Williams, Raymond, 266
Winegar, Jessica, 96–97
Without Boundary (Museum of Modern
    Art show), xix
women: in al-Ali cartoons, 239–40, *241*,
    247, *248*, 257n28; broadcasters on
    television, 94; entertainers on
    satellite music videos, 82, 85,
    87–88, 98n6, 99nn13–14; ethics
    literature and, 36; illustrated
    guide for modern Muslim house-
    wives, 41–49, *42, 46, 48*; Islamic
    dress codes for, 127, 136; Islamist
    intellectuals, 127; Qubaisiyat
    piety movement (Syria), 269;
    restrictions on women in Saudi
    Arabia, 267–68; Saudi censorship
    of television and, 276; Saudi
    debate over modernity and, 282,
    283–84; scrapbooks from the

shah's era, 49, *50–51;* as symbols
    of vulnerability, *219,* 220; in the-
    ater, 92–93; Turkish children's
    picture book depictions, *134,* 136–
    37, *138;* veiled, 240, *242,* 257n28;
    women's magazines, 42, 43, *44, 47.*
    See also gender; headscarf,
    Islamic; sexuality
Word into Art (British Museum show),
    xix
World Islamic Media Committee, 280
World War I, 63, 191, 193

Yağmur magazine, 114, 124n24
Yalçınkaya, Aburrahman, 226
Yasin, Sheikh Ahmad, 175, *176*
Yavuz, M. Hakan, 108, 118
Yemen, 70
"Young Arab Boy" or "Muhammad"
    (photograph, Lehnert and
    Landrock), 22, *23*
Yusuf, Hassan Sami, 271
Yusuf, Sami, 95
Yusuf va Zulaykha [Joseph and
    Potiphar's Wife] (Jami), *21*
Yüzyıl (newspaper), 222

al-Zalame [fellow/guy] (poor refugee),
    238, 239, 255
Zaman (newspaper), 108, 124n24
Zan-i Ruz [Woman of Today] (maga-
    zine), 42, 43, *44, 47*
Zardosht, Jamshid-e, 174, *175*
Ziadeh, May, 269
Zionism, 63, 72, 74. *See also* Israel
Žižek, Slavoj, 235, 245
Zoroastrians, 41
Zurayq, Constantine, 237
Zyarid dynasty (Persian empire), 36

CHRISTIANE GRUBER is Associate Professor of Islamic Art, Department of Art History, University of Michigan. She is the author of *The Timurid Book of Ascension (Mi'rajnama): A Study of Text and Image in a Pan-Asian Context* (2008) and *The Ilkhanid Book of Ascension: A Persian-Sunni Devotional Tale* (2010). She also has edited several volumes, including *The Islamic Manuscript Tradition: Ten Centuries of Islamic Book Arts in Indiana University Collections* (2009); with Frederick Colby, *The Prophet's Ascension: Cross-Cultural Encounters with the Islamic Mi'raj Tales* (2009); and with Edward Linenthal and Jonathan Hyman, *The Landscapes of 9/11: A Photographer's Journey* (2013).

SUNE HAUGBOLLE is Associate Professor in Global Studies and Sociology at the Department for Society and Globalization at Roskilde University. His work deals with social memory, cultural production, and ideology in the modern Middle East. He is the author of *War and Memory in Lebanon* (2010) and he co-edited the volume *The Politics of Violence, Truth and Reconciliation in the Arab Middle East* (2009). His articles have appeared in a variety of journals, including *Arab Studies Journal, Journal of Middle Eastern Women's Studies, Contemporary Studies of South Asia, Africa and the Middle East,* and *Arab Media and Society,* for which he is a contributing editor. He is currently leading a research project about secularism and ideology in the Middle East.